side of private secretaries, are trying in
tip ... But one hardly sees where
one's grip of the complicated subject, & how
I shall manage to run a practice enquiry
side by side of one ran — at a different subject — for
it a different period — I hardly can be there.
What I shall aim at is to concentrate my
attention on ~~~~~~~~, of it R.L. ~~~~~~~
— leaving to ~ remainder to the other Co. At present.
these departments seem to be (1) the intersection
of Poor-Law-relief & to ~ staves ~ industries (2) the
exact working constitution of Br. of ~~~~~
~~~~~~~~~~~ I shall include ~~~~~ the
it sick, & children, & aged — subject
about the ... as known. these are in
these that matter succeeds from again as ~ the
find the aim at ~ the setting of treat
on large technical. Diet — ~~~~~ I ~~~~
~~~~~~ ~~~~~~ a ~ light expense
& consumption, I shall try & to my power.

The Diary
of
BEATRICE WEBB

Volume Three
1905–1924
"The Power to Alter Things"

The Diary
of
BEATRICE WEBB

Volume Three

1905–1924

"The Power to Alter Things"

Edited by
Norman and Jeanne MacKenzie

THE BELKNAP PRESS OF
HARVARD UNIVERSITY PRESS
CAMBRIDGE, MASSACHUSETTS
1984

Library of Congress Cataloging in Publication Data

Webb, Beatrice Potter, 1858–1943
  "The power to alter things," 1905–1924

  (The Diary of Beatrice Webb; v.3)
  Bibliography: p.
  Includes index.
  1. Webb, Beatrice Potter, 1858–1943. 2. Socialists—Great Britain—
Biography. I. MacKenzie, Norman Ian. II. MacKenzie, Jeanne. III. Title.
IV. Series: Webb, Beatrice Potter, 1858–1943. Diary of Beatrice Webb;
v.3.
HX244.7.W42A33   1982 vol. 3   335'.14'0924s   84–391
ISBN 0–674–20289–9   [335'.14'0924] [B]

Contents

Illustrations

(Acknowledgements and thanks are due to the individuals and institutions listed in brackets below)

Cover

Beatrice Webb c. 1920 (Passfield Papers, London School of
    Economics and Political Science)
Winston Churchill 1903 (Mansell Collection)
David Lloyd George 1914 (Mansell Collection)
Amber Pember Reeves date unknown (Thomas Blanco White)
H.G. Wells 1920 (Radio Times Hulton Picture Library)

Between Pages 238 and 239

Whittinghame House (Royal Commission on Ancient Monuments,
    Scotland)
The Rt Hon. Lord George Hamilton M.P. date unknown (Radio
    Times Hulton Picture Library)
Countess of Wemyss date unknown (Radio Times Hulton Picture
    Library)
Mrs Patrick Campbell 1914 (Mansell Collection)
Georgie Meinertzhagen 1910 (Passfield Papers)
Arthur Hobhouse with Barbara Meinertzhagen date unknown
    (Billie Love Collection)
View of Hadspen c. 1910 (Billie Love Collection)
Hobhouse family group at Hadspen c. 1911 (Billie Love Collection)
Maud Pember Reeves 1914 (Thomas Blanco White)
William Pember Reeves date unknown (Thomas Blanco White)
Rivers Blanco White date unknown (Thomas Blanco White)

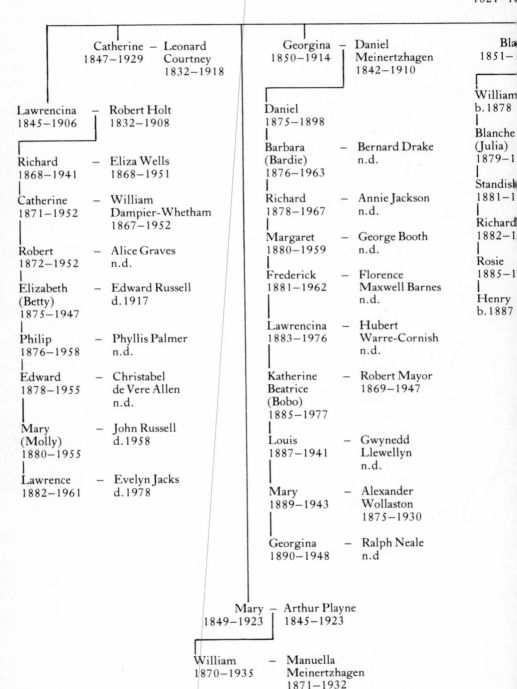

Lawrencina Heywo[...]
1821–1[...]

Catherine — Leonard
1847–1929   Courtney
           1832–1918

Georgina — Daniel
1850–1914   Meinertzhagen
          1842–1910

Bla[...]
1851–[...]

William
b.1878

Lawrencina — Robert Holt
1845–1906   1832–1908

Daniel
1875–1898

Blanche
(Julia)
1879–1[...]

Richard — Eliza Wells
1868–1941   1868–1951

Barbara — Bernard Drake
(Bardie)   n.d.
1876–1963

Standish
1881–1[...]

Catherine — William
1871–1952   Dampier-Whetham
          1867–1952

Richard — Annie Jackson
1878–1967   n.d.

Richard
1882–1[...]

Robert — Alice Graves
1872–1952   n.d.

Margaret — George Booth
1880–1959   n.d.

Rosie
1885–1[...]

Elizabeth — Edward Russell
(Betty)   d.1917
1875–1947

Frederick — Florence
1881–1962   Maxwell Barnes
          n.d.

Henry
b.1887

Philip — Phyllis Palmer
1876–1958   n.d.

Lawrencina — Hubert
1883–1976   Warre-Cornish
          n.d.

Edward — Christabel
1878–1955   de Vere Allen
          n.d.

Katherine — Robert Mayor
Beatrice   1869–1947
(Bobo)
1885–1977

Mary — John Russell
(Molly)   d.1958
1880–1955

Louis — Gwynedd
1887–1941   Llewellyn
          n.d.

Lawrence — Evelyn Jacks
1882–1961   d.1978

Mary — Alexander
1889–1943   Wollaston
          1875–1930

Georgina — Ralph Neale
1890–1948   n.d

Mary — Arthur Playne
1849–1923   1845–1923

William — Manuella
1870–1935   Meinertzhagen
          1871–1932

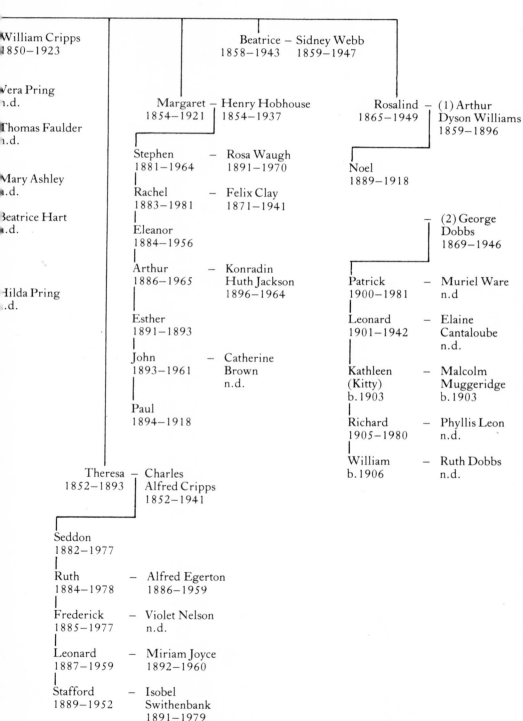

Richard Potter
1817–1892

William Cripps
1850–1923

Vera Pring
n.d.

Thomas Faulder
n.d.

Mary Ashley
n.d.

Beatrice Hart
n.d.

Hilda Pring
n.d.

Beatrice – Sidney Webb
1858–1943   1859–1947

Margaret – Henry Hobhouse
1854–1921   1854–1937

Stephen – Rosa Waugh
1881–1964   1891–1970

Rachel – Felix Clay
1883–1981   1871–1941

Eleanor
1884–1956

Arthur – Konradin
1886–1965   Huth Jackson
1896–1964

Esther
1891–1893

John – Catherine
1893–1961   Brown
n.d.

Paul
1894–1918

Rosalind – (1) Arthur
1865–1949   Dyson Williams
1859–1896

Noel
1889–1918

– (2) George
Dobbs
1869–1946

Patrick – Muriel Ware
1900–1981   n.d

Leonard – Elaine
1901–1942   Cantaloube
n.d.

Kathleen – Malcolm
(Kitty)   Muggeridge
b.1903   b.1903

Richard – Phyllis Leon
1905–1980   n.d.

William – Ruth Dobbs
b.1906   n.d.

Theresa – Charles
1852–1893   Alfred Cripps
1852–1941

Seddon
1882–1977

Ruth – Alfred Egerton
1884–1978   1886–1959

Frederick – Violet Nelson
1885–1977   n.d.

Leonard – Miriam Joyce
1887–1959   1892–1960

Stafford – Isobel
1889–1952   Swithenbank
1891–1979

Introduction

A Change in the Partnership

In 1905 Beatrice Webb and her husband Sidney were the best-known couple in public life. They had been married since 1892, and for all Beatrice's misgivings about their oddly matched partnership their marriage had proved to be happy and successful.

Beatrice was the eighth of the nine daughters of Richard Potter, a wealthy timber merchant and railway promoter, and Lawrencina Potter, the intellectual daughter of a Liberal businessman who became M.P. for Derby. She was born in 1858 at the family house at Standish in Gloucestershire, and brought up in the comfortable style of the Victorian upper middle class. For all its comforts, she had a troubled childhood that left its marks in persistent anxiety and periods of vague ill health. As a young woman she spent years searching for a creed that would satisfy her religious aspirations and a craft that would give her a useful occupation. Encouraged by the social philosopher Herbert Spencer, a family friend, she started to take an interest in the science of society and to train herself as a professional investigator. She began with charitable work, as a rent collector in a model housing scheme near the Tower of London, and went on to collaborate with Charles Booth — married to her cousin Mary Macaulay — in his pioneering study of the London poor; these researches (described in Volume I of her diary) took her into London's docklands and the East End sweatshops of the tailoring trade. By the time she was thirty she had started to write a history of the Co-operative movement, and as she finished this book she was planning a succeeding study of trade unionism. Seeking help in these tasks she was referred to Sidney Webb, and met him in January 1890.

He was born in London in 1859, in much more humble circumstances than Beatrice. His mother ran a hairdressing and millinery business just off Charing Cross Road, while his father combined rent and debt collecting for other tradesmen with a keen interest in municipal politics. Hoping to make Sidney a commercial clerk, his parents gave him a sound educational start in life, and his great abilities and diligent ambition carried him through a series of scholarships to a good post in the Colonial Office, to freelance journalism and to Fabian policy-making. He fell in love with Beatrice at their first meeting, but she bargained for sympathetic friendship only. She was still recovering from an intense and emotionally crippling infatuation for the Radical politician Joseph Chamberlain, whom she had met in 1883 when he was on the lookout for a third wife – an uneasy relationship which made her life miserable until he finally married an American woman in 1888, and continued to upset her at intervals after she had yielded to Sidney's insistence that marriage to him would let them both find fulfilment in a working partnership.

From the beginning the Webbs devoted themselves to social and political activity. Beatrice had a sufficient private income for Sidney to give up his civil service job, and shortly before they married in 1892 he was elected from Deptford as a Progressive member of the recently created London County Council. Soon afterwards he became the chairman of its Technical Education Board and turned it into a means of reforming secondary and higher education in London. They first set up in a flat in Netherhall Gardens, Hampstead, but soon moved to 41 Grosvenor Road, on the Embankment near the Houses of Parliament. This convenient address was to be their home for most of their married life.

They had complementary talents; and in fourteen years of marriage, in which Sidney played the more public and Beatrice the more private role, their partnership had brought great rewards. They had written the standard work on trade union history. They had founded the London School of Economics, played a considerable part in the reorganization of the University of London, helped to reshape the school system throughout England – Sidney had been much involved in the planning and passage of the Education Acts of 1902 and 1903 – and made friends with the great and the good of all parties. They shared the leadership of the Fabian Society with Bernard Shaw and H.G. Wells at a time when it was at the peak of its reputation, and were the epitome of its noted political tactic of permeation. In the first years of the century, indeed, the Webbs were on the threshold of fame and lasting influence, for the tide of public opinion seemed at last to be flowing towards the collectivism which they had been preaching for the past decade.

At the election of January 1906 the Liberal Party won the largest parliamentary majority to date, and every kind of reform seemed possible as the country moved from the Victorian age into the twentieth century. But the Webbs did not share in that Liberal triumph. Their friendship with Arthur Balfour, the outgoing Conservative Prime Minister, had enabled the Webbs to influence Tory educational policy; but, combined with their equivocal position on the Boer War and their estrangement from the anti-imperialist and Nonconformist factions in the Liberal Party, it had more or less alienated them from the new government. And Balfour's last act of office was to intensify those differences. In setting up a Royal Commission to review the ramshackle and unpopular Poor Law he nominated Beatrice as one of the commissioners, and set her on a path which was not only to lead her into active public life for the first time but also to bring her and Sidney into conflict with Liberal attempts to deal with chronic poverty. Beatrice fought tenaciously for the distinctive policies which she and Sidney set out at length in the celebrated Minority Report of that Royal Commission, and together they launched a personal and astonishingly vigorous campaign to rally support for their conviction that destitution should be abolished rather than merely alleviated. It was a wearing 'plunge into propaganda', Beatrice said. The campaign had a hardening as well as an exhausting effect on her personality. Under the rigours of public controversy she found herself developing traits she knew were disagreeable, even counter-productive, and yet she could not control them when she was under stress. A note of petulant self-importance creeps into the diary from the time that she exposes herself to public life, in striking contrast to the sensitive introspection of her adolescence and the lively optimism of the first years of marriage.

By the time the Webbs abandoned their campaign and set out on a tour round the world in 1911, Beatrice knew that they would have to make a fresh start on their return. Their journey through Canada, Japan, China and India is summarized in this volume. Coming after the excitements of the Poor Law campaign it seems to have had a radicalizing effect – on Beatrice at least – and she came back to a country which was also in a more radical frame of mind. They had sailed away at the beginning of the great constitutional crisis in which the Liberal government challenged the entrenched and permanent Tory majority in the House of Lords; and while they were gone there was a series of violent strikes which began in the fiercely hot summer of 1911 and ran on into 1912. The mood of confrontation, moreover, marked the militant turn of the women's suffrage movement, the drift towards civil war in Ireland, and the growing tension in foreign affairs which was dramatized by the Agadir incident in the summer of 1911, when Britain and France combined to object to the despatch of a German warship to Morocco.

Now lacking allies in the Tory and Liberal parties, the Webbs turned to their old supporters from the Poor Law campaign and their ever loyal friends, the Fabian Society, and set out to mobilize both groups. It was Beatrice's idea to found the weekly *New Statesman* as a spokesman for the reformist middle classes, and it was Beatrice again who took the initiative in organizing the Fabian Research Bureau. She saw the new magazine, and the new policies the young Fabian intellectuals would draft for it under her guidance, as the last contributions of the Webb partnership before she and Sidney retired to the country to spend their last years on their own research into English local government. But that dream of pleasant retirement was to elude Beatrice until she was well past middle age. The new ventures were no sooner launched than they were overtaken by the Great War.

Beatrice and Sidney found their normal activities disrupted without being offered any significant war work to take their place and, in the absence of such a stimulus to offset the relentless misery of the battlefields, Beatrice became prey to neurasthenic illness and a conviction that she was dying. In the period covered by this volume, she lost many of her relatives. Two nephews were killed in the war – Paul Hobhouse and Noel Williams. Her eldest sister, Lallie, died in 1906, and Georgina in 1914. In 1921 her favourite sister, Maggie Hobhouse, died, and yet another, Mary Playne, two years later. She also lost three brothers-in-law – Daniel Meinertzhagen, Leonard Courtney and Arthur Playne. Beatrice had never been close to her sisters in her younger days but as the years passed she increasingly valued family ties and the loss of these relatives aggravated her sad and pessimistic state of mind. She chose to relieve her distress by looking back over her own life, reading through earlier volumes of her diary and beginning the process of autobiographical reflection which led to the publication of *My Apprenticeship* in 1926. In the last year of the war Beatrice served on the Reconstruction Committee and on another body studying women's wages, but her heart was not in either of these tasks. She found public life increasingly irksome.

The Webbs began to work together again on the books that appeared in 1920 (*A Constitution for the Socialist Commonwealth of Great Britain* and *The Consumers' Co-operative Movement*), in 1922 (*English Prisons*) and 1923 (*The Decay of Capitalist Civilization*), but the old balance of the partnership could not be restored. Towards the end of the war Sidney was drawn into Labour Party politics, drafting a new constitution and a new policy for the party of which he had at last become an influential member. Once the war was over, and Labour's cause was marching on with 'the inevitability of gradualness' – as Sidney put it in his chairman's address to the Labour Party conference in 1923 – he began to consider again the parliamentary career which he had once contemplated and then forsworn when marriage to Beatrice had deflected him into London municipal politics.

When Sidney was elected in 1922 to the Durham mining seat of Seaham Harbour, Beatrice had to adjust to the responsibilities of an M.P.'s wife. She was reluctant to be drawn back into the political society of dinners and drawing-rooms that she had known first as a young woman and then in the early years of her marriage to Sidney. She had put salon politics behind her as she became more radical in temperament, more suspicious of the aristocratic embrace which Labour leaders were given by the smart world as they became first His Majesty's Opposition and then His Majesty's Government. She was willing to form the Half Circle Club to help their wives over the stiles of loneliness and embarrassment which they met as they moved from the provinces into their new milieu at Westminster, but even when Sidney became a member of the Cabinet she pleaded old age and ill health as excuses for keeping away from Court functions and the atmosphere of privilege that surrounded them. At the end of this volume she was once again looking forward to the day when she and Sidney could retire to the cottage they had bought at Passfield, near Liphook on the Surrey–Hampshire border.

All these changes in Beatrice's life are reflected in her diary. As she moved into public life with her appointment to the Poor Law Commission, the flow of diary entries is disrupted and their character altered. The entries are, for the most part, less intimate and less coherent. Beatrice made no systematic attempt to record the proceedings of the Commission; her observations are, as she later conceded, partial and often unfair to those who disagreed with her; and by and large they give a misleading impression of what happened in the Commission and her role in it. She used her diary to vent her feelings of frustration as she failed to get her way with the other commissioners; and her preoccupation with the Poor Law issue narrowed her vision. For ten years the diary became a spasmodic and subordinate enterprise as she coped with the stresses and strains of public life. There were weeks, sometimes months when she left her notebook unopened; and the long interruption of the world tour, when Sidney shared the task of keeping a routine travel diary, broke the habit of recounting her experiences and feelings. She tried to recover the habit after her return to London, but by then her energy was diverted into launching the *New Statesman* and the Fabian Research Bureau.

For all that, however, Beatrice still had an eye and an ear for gossip, as she shows so brilliantly in her reports on the domestic dramas of the Potter sisters or the philanderings of Wells and Shaw. She retained her capacity to be honest with herself – there are constant self-castigating complaints at her vanity and vainglory which reveal considerable self-knowledge – and although the entries during the war are patchy and limited, her comments are astute and she has many perceptive remarks about politicians and the warlike peace. As the post-war economic crisis unfolds, Beatrice reveals her understanding of the dilemmas of western democracy. At a personal level she is aware of the changing moral climate but she does not find it easy to accept the matrimonial eccentricities of her friends. In this volume Beatrice painfully makes the transition into our modern world.

As in the preceding volumes, the text of the diary entries is based upon the handwritten and typescript originals held among the Passfield Papers in the British Library of Political and Economic Science. From 1906 to 1911 they duplicate to a considerable extent those that Beatrice selected for the unfinished second volume of her autobiography, *Our Partnership* (edited and published after her death by her niece Barbara Drake and Margaret Cole). But there are significant differences. In her revisions for *Our Partnership* Beatrice broke up the sequence of the diary by clustering the entries into separate themes, such as London municipal politics, the history of local government, the foundation of the London School of Economics, the reorganization of London's educational system, the Poor Law Commission and the campaign that followed it. The result was confusing, and *Our Partnership* lacks the stylish vigour which characterized *My Apprenticeship*. All the entries have now been restored to their original chronological order. Almost all the personal material that Beatrice omitted from her draft has been restored (material that Margaret Cole also left out when she edited a volume of extracts from the diary for the years 1912–24), while the cuts have fallen mainly on the detailed entries relating to the Poor Law Commission and the ensuing Webb campaign for the Minority Report. Since her account can be read almost complete in *Our Partnership* (and in full in the microfiche edition of the diary published by Chadwyck-Healey, Cambridge, 1978), this volume has reduced the description of the Commission to those entries which carry the story forward or reveal some interesting aspect of Beatrice's personality.

Apart from these cuts the only substantial omissions have been occasional notes on books she read, character sketches of some minor public figures and acquaintances, and a few detailed descriptions of Labour conferences. Cuts of a few words are indicated by three dots and longer ellisions by four dots. The punctuation derived from Beatrice's scarcely legible writing follows that used by her in *Our Partnership* except where she made later alterations or where common practice suggests the insertion of commas or the substitution of semi-colons or brackets for dashes.

Many of those who were thanked in the first two volumes have again been most helpful and we particularly wish to reiterate our thanks to Joyce Bellamy, Lord Methuen, and Kitty and Malcolm Muggeridge. We very much appreciate the assistance given to this volume by the Baker Library at Dartmouth College, New Hampshire, the Croydon Public Library, Sussex University Library, the London Library and the British Library of Political and Economic Science. Quentin and Olivier Bell, William Dobbs, Michael Holroyd, Lord Fulton, Professor A.M. McBriar, Julia MacKenzie, Professor Lucy Mair, Philip Beveridge Mair, Lord Robbins, Dr and Mrs Southwell, Betty Vernon and the Salvation Army have patiently answered our queries and made helpful contributions. Finally we are extremely grateful to Professor Robert Webb and Faith Evans for reading the manuscript with such care and an eye to detail.

PART I

The Crime of Poverty
November 1905–April 1909

Introduction to Part I

ON 4 DECEMBER 1905 the long run of Conservative government was broken when Arthur Balfour (1848–1930) resigned. The next day Sir Henry Campbell-Bannerman (1836–1908), leader of the Liberal Party since 1898, took his place as Prime Minister and set about forming his government before dissolving Parliament and preparing for a general election. In the three weeks of polling which began on 12 January 1906 the Liberals won 377 seats, giving them an overall majority of 84 and a working majority that was even greater, since they were generally supported by 83 Irish nationalists, 24 'Lib-Lab' M.P.s (mostly mining and textile trade unionists elected under Liberal auspices) and 29 Labour members running independently with the support of the Labour Representation Committee. The Conservatives and their Liberal Unionist allies were reduced to 157 seats.

It had been clear for some time that the pendulum was swinging towards the Liberals. Balfour had been an uncertain leader of the Tories, trying to hold together a party acutely divided on the issue of Protection or free trade. But the sensational scale of the victory was unexpected and so was the sudden emergence of the Labour Party as a significant force. No doubt the Taff Vale case of July 1901, in which the courts had judged a railwayman's trade union financially liable for losses caused by a strike, had done much to rally the unions behind the new party; and more and more working-men were registering as voters. For all the disunity of the Liberals the Tory education policy had driven many middle-class Nonconformists back to their old Liberal loyalties, and confidence in the Tories was finally broken when thousands of indentured Chinese labourers were imported into the Transvaal to work on the Rand mines. This 'slave labour' was generally regarded as a moral outrage as well as an attack on the rights of labour.

3

The Liberal landslide reflected a decisive shift of social attitudes in Britain. 'Speaking broadly,' *The Times* declared on 24 January 1906, 'we should say that the result of the elections is a protest against dilettantism in politics, a vice common to both parties.' There were new, younger and more serious men seeking and gaining seats, a new generation of idealists going into the public service – clever young Fabians or graduates of the London School of Economics, or sociologically inclined dons from Oxford and Cambridge. They were less interested in philanthropy than in administrative efficiency, and they brought a utilitarian zeal to their work. Unlike the *laissez-faire* Liberals of the old school, who clung to the shibboleths of free trade and political reform, they had a collectivist bias and a belief that the state could and should act positively to ameliorate social conditions.

The Liberal Party had been superficially united in its fight against the Protective tariffs advocated by Joseph Chamberlain (1836–1914). He had split the Liberals over Irish Home Rule in the 80's and had now helped to bring his Conservative allies to disaster before he suffered the paralytic stroke in July 1906 that incapacitated him until his death in July 1914. All the same, Liberalism had begun to die at the moment of its greatest triumph. The party was moving away from its traditional stance of economic individualism, but it was no more able to manage the growing pressure for social reform than it was capable of solving the problem of Ireland. And when it set about getting its reformist programme through Parliament it soon ran into difficulties with the Conservative diehards who dominated the House of Lords. By 1908, when Campbell-Bannerman died and Herbert Asquith (1852–1928) became Prime Minister of a government more inclined to radical measures, the Liberals and the Lords were heading for a confrontation that became the greatest constitutional crisis since 1832.

The pressure for reform was already apparent when the Liberals came into office. In the last days of his government Arthur Balfour had set up a Royal Commission on the Poor Law, nominating Beatrice as one of the members, and both she and Sidney were instantly plunged into its work. Though they struggled to complete three volumes on English local government, though Sidney sat through a last routine term on the London County Council and kept a fatherly eye on the London School of Economics, they now became so committed to the break-up of the Poor Law system (and its replacement with their own remedies for destitution) that, as Beatrice remarked thirty years later in *Our Partnership*, her membership of the Royal Commission became an event of 'major significance' for them both, with Beatrice devoting herself to its public activities and Sidney acting as her adviser and amanuensis.

Beatrice was pleased by this chance to demonstrate her skills as a social investigator: it was a deserved recognition of the grinding work which had made her such a well-informed historian of the old Poor Law, which dated back to the end of Elizabeth's reign, and the new Poor Law which had replaced it in 1834. The time had clearly come for another great change, for which there was ample scope in the Commission's broad terms of reference. It was charged to enquire into the working of the Poor Law and into the means for relieving distress outside it; to consider whether there should be changes in the law or in the way it was administered; and, if it saw fit, to suggest 'fresh legislation dealing with distress'. All the clauses were so loosely worded that the Commission was to stagger from one set of problems and possibilities to another, without ever getting a firm grip on its business; and the last phrase so shifted its concern with pauperism to the much more general question of poverty that it was an open invitation to arraign the social system as a whole. The more closely the Commission enquired into the treatment of the aged, widows and orphans, the homeless and the chronic sick, the more it would be forced to consider the plight of millions whose condition was no better than those subsisting on outdoor relief or in the workhouses so hated by the poor.

The principles of the system established in 1834 were clear. A man must be destitute before he was offered relief, and the level of this relief should be lower than that of the poorest paid labourer – the principle of less eligibility. Secondly, there should be uniform application of this rule throughout the 600 Poor Law Unions which had replaced the 15,000 parishes which had cared for the poor for the past two centuries. Thirdly, a man must submit to the workhouse or 'stoneyard' test, in which he would have to earn his relief by degrading labour under near-penal conditions. These principles were designed to be a deterrent to the idle. The utilitarian majority on the Commission of 1832–34 agreed with Jeremy Bentham that the workhouse must 'grind rogues into honest men', believing that worklessness was due more to defects of character than defects of society.

All through the Victorian age there were complaints against the heartless severity of a system which deprived paupers of their liberty and political rights; the demoralization of general mixed workhouses which broke up families and herded the sick, the aged, the depraved, the orphaned and the workless together like cattle. And as the century wore on, other and often contradictory objections to the Poor Law emerged.

It was losing its deterrent effect, for an increasing proportion of those on indoor and outdoor relief were too ill, old or young to work even if they wished. It was no longer uniform in its application. Conditions varied so widely from a severe to a sympathetic board of the elected guardians responsible for each district that the haphazard contrasts made the officials long for central control over standards. Each year the Poor Law was costing much more, though an increasing number of poor people were being relieved by private charities or being treated by public health authorities outside its scope. This was another cause for grievance among the senior officials, who saw the role of the Poor Law being eroded by new agencies, and for annoyance among the influential members of the Charity Organization Society (the C.O.S., set up to co-ordinate philanthropy in London), who thought help should be given only after close enquiry by caseworkers and even then as part of a bargain struck to prevent 'demoralizing' alms-giving and to secure an improvement in attitudes and behaviour. The Poor Law, a C.O.S. statement claimed in 1904, had become 'an enormously rich, rate-aided charity open to all comers'. The election of guardians on a wider franchise after 1894, moreover, was thought to encourage corrupt practices, or at least to make them more amenable to pressure in places where many working-men had votes. Above all, as the enquiries of Charles Booth in East London and Seebohm Rowntree in York had recently demonstrated, the paupers, strictly defined, were only a fraction of the millions of people who lived in grinding poverty and disgraceful conditions of health, housing and education.

A succession of Royal Commissions and social investigations were making the middle and professional classes aware of what Beatrice repeatedly called 'the morass of poverty' and the need for 'draining' it before its squalor and disease engulfed them. By 1911, when Sidney and Beatrice summed up their case against the Poor Law in *The Prevention of Destitution*, they noted that two million

6

people had applied for help under the Poor Law in 1910, and added the other categories of distress known to them: one hundred thousand underfed children who were given free meals at school, the same number of persons afflicted by infectious diseases, and many more who were lacking the rudiments of medical care; the tens of thousands who applied for help by official Distress Committees, the hundreds of thousands eligible for the severely means-tested old age pensions that were now being introduced. Without even considering the social casualties assisted by private charities, they concluded that between three and four million people were 'demonstrably suffering in body and mind, in physique and in character, from a lack of the necessities of life'.

Where there were so many and such contradictory reasons for the decline of the Poor Law, any group of commissioners was bound to find it hard to settle on a diagnosis of what was wrong and what might be done to set it right. But the men and women selected by Balfour were at a disadvantage from the start. They were respected, able and in many ways suitably experienced; but like their predecessors who reported in 1834, they were a group much given to preconceptions and strong opinions. From the moment they met it seemed unlikely that they would find a common ground.

The chairman was Lord George Hamilton (1845–1927), an open-minded and charming Tory politician who had been First Lord of the Admiralty and chairman of the London School Board: he thought his colleagues would have been 'admirable witnesses', but found 'the task of keeping them together was very tiring and at times impossible'. The commissioners were F. Bentham, chairman of the Board of Guardians in Bradford; Beatrice's old friend and colleague Charles Booth (1840–1914); Helen Bosanquet (1860–1925), who with her husband Professor Bernard Bosanquet (1848–1923) was a leading member of the Charity Organization Society; Dr Arthur Downes (1851–1937), the senior Medical Officer of the Poor Law division of the Local Government Board (responsible for the Poor Law and the general supervision of local authorities), the Reverend Thory Gage Gardiner (1857–1941), a churchman interested in Co-operation, the C.O.S. and several boards of guardians; the veteran housing reformer Octavia Hill (1838–1912); George Lansbury (1859–1940), socialist leader in Poplar, strongly opposed to the rigours of the Poor Law, who was a pacifist, suffragist and later leader of the Labour Party; Charles

Stewart Loch (1849–1923), the doctrinally vigorous secretary of the C.O.S.; Sir James Patten-MacDougall (1849–1919), the vice-president of the Scottish Local Government Board (L.G.B.); Thomas Hancock Nunn (1859–1937), of the Hampstead Board of Guardians, who was another leading member of the C.O.S.; Charles Owen O'Conor (1838–1906), an Irish Liberal politician, who died and was replaced by Dr Dennis Kelly (1852–1924), the Bishop of Ross; the Reverend Lancelot Ridley Phelps (1853–1936), economist and fellow of Oriel College, Oxford, who was also active in the C.O.S.; Sir Samuel Butler Provis (1857–1927), permanent secretary of the L.G.B. from 1898; Sir Henry Robinson (1857–1937), vice-president of the Irish L.G.B.; Professor William Smart (1853–1915), professor of political economy at the University of Glasgow; the Reverend Henry Russell Wakefield (1854–1933), who had been a member of the London School Board, and became Bishop of Birmingham in 1911; and Beatrice Webb. Francis W. Chandler (1849–1938), secretary of the Amalgamated Society of Carpenters, was later added to represent a trade union view. The Commission thus included the three senior civil servants responsible for its administration in England, Scotland and Ireland, the senior medical officer concerned, and the permanent head of the government department concerned. The influence of the Charity Organization Society was strong, for six of the Commission members were active in the C.O.S. and had close associations with the senior officials of the L.G.B. Charles Booth and Octavia Hill, both past their best, were clearly appointed as eminent social theorists, as Beatrice, Russell Wakefield, Lansbury and Chandler were chosen to represent more advanced social ideas. Beside these main divisions within the Commission there were cross-currents of interest which can be seen eddying through Beatrice's account of its proceedings. The secretary of the Commission was Robert Duff (1871–1946), a member of the L.G.B. staff, assisted by John Jeffrey (1871–1947), who rose to high civil service posts in Scotland.

Beatrice said in *Our Partnership* that she and Sidney began with a 'destructive' view of the Poor Law, as well as a deep suspicion that the officials and the C.O.S. members were seeking to restore its deterrent effect; and as the months pass, one can see her feeling her way towards a set of ideas which would break up the old system and put something quite different in its place. These ideas were set out in the Minority Report which she and Sidney wrote for the dissenting members of the Committee. But one can also see her losing one opportunity after another to win friends and design a report that more of the commissioners might have signed – exaggerating the differences, indeed, as if she were afraid that she might be left no room for her more distinctive dissent. 'From first to last she has declined whilst in the Commission to merge her individuality in it, but claims the right of unrestricted free action outside in connection with matters under the consideration of the Commission,' Lord George Hamilton complained to Phelps on 22 August 1909. 'She is . . . hopeless.' She certainly annoyed her colleagues, and also confused them: for all her hostility to the C.O.S., for instance, she continued to share its view that cash payments should not be made without exacting some improvement in attitude or effort. That was the fundamental reason why she disliked the unconditional doles which were to be provided by the new 'National Insurance' schemes which Winston Churchill (1874–1965) and Lloyd George (1863–1945) were respectively devising as the Liberal Party's palliatives for short-term unemployment and sickness. Thirty years later, still convinced that doles encouraged malingerers, Beatrice was sharply critical of the famous 1942 Report in which William Beveridge (1879–1963) proposed the post-war extension of the social services.

Because Beatrice could not reconcile her old individualist impulses with her educated and collectivist view of social problems she muddled on, making it difficult for people to understand why the Webbs differed so contumaciously from the majority of the commissioners and why they needed two weighty volumes of argument to say so. Yet the main point of difference was relatively simple, even if it was never explicitly stated in either the Minority or Majority reports, or in these diary entries. A clever young lawyer named Harold Baker (b. 1877), asked by Asquith to summarize the two documents, rightly reported that the 'underlying question' was 'whether relief should be made available for the poor generally instead of the destitute and necessitous only'.

The Webbs were collectivists and administrative reformers. They were opposed to the 'pauper-only' policies of the Poor Law and the harshness of many of its officials. J.S. Davy (1848–1915), for example, the secretary of the Local Government Board, told the Commission bluntly that 'a man must stand by his accidents: he must suffer for the general good of the body politic.' They were equally hostile to the Liberal insurance schemes, seeing them as a combination of catchpenny ideas and electorally attractive slogans such as Lloyd George's 'Ninepence for Fourpence'. Bernard Shaw had recently written in *Major Barbara* that poverty was 'the worst of crimes'. For the Webbs it was the worst of social diseases, and they believed that society should attack its causes rather than alleviate its symptoms. Two decades earlier the first Fabian pamphlet had asked '*Why Are the Many Poor*'? In the Minority Report the Webbs tried to provide a comprehensive answer. It was not politically practicable: even Churchill and Lloyd George had to wait until the Peers were beaten before their schemes were applied. But it was politically appealing to a significant part of the middle classes. There was a new boom in Fabian membership and activity. There was even more support for the Webbs as they began to stump the country in a national campaign against the evils of destitution. They may not have had much effect on the elections of 1910 and 1911 but they were making converts for collectivism; and thereby helping to convert the emergent Labour Party from a trade union lobby into the movement which made the welfare state its stock-in-trade.

Auberon (Bron) Herbert (1876–1916), who became Lord Lucas on the death of his uncle in 1905, held office in the Liberal government 1908–15, and was killed in the Royal Flying Corps in 1916. His father, also Auberon Herbert (1838–1906) was an old friend of Beatrice's. Bron Herbert's cousin, Ethel (Ettie) Grenfell (1867–1952), became Lady Desborough in 1905 when her husband William Grenfell (1855–1945), a Tory M.P. and notable athlete, was given a peerage. Mrs Lindsay was the wife of David Lindsay (1871–1940), a Tory M.P. who succeeded his father as Earl of Crawford in 1913. Edward Bulwer-Lytton, first Lord Lytton (1803–1873) was an eminent Victorian novelist. Lord Rosebery (1847–1929) Prime Minister 1894–95, resigned as Liberal leader in 1896 but led the Liberal Imperialist group. In 1906 the Webbs published the first of their eleven volumes on English local government – *The Parish and the County*. *The Manor and the Borough* was published as volumes II and III in 1908. Work on the series continued until the last volume was published in 1929. The Webbs' numbering of the volumes does not correspond with the order of their appearance.

VOLUME 25
∽ 1905 ∾

23 November. [41 Grosvenor Road]
Appointed to the Royal Commission on the Poor Law. Awaiting anxiously the names of my colleagues, Charles Booth being the only one I know of. Yesterday evening we dined with Lord Lucas (Bron Herbert that was) in his great mansion in St James's Square; Mrs Willie Grenfell and Mrs Lindsay, flippant but clever little lady, and a pleasant young Tory lawyer made up the party. Our host interests me as the son of my dear old friend Auberon Herbert – as a boy, I remember, he eyed me with hostility when I came to stay with his father twenty years ago; perhaps he thought I was going to become his stepmother! But since he has come into the political world, first as a young Liberal candidate, now as a peer, he has cultivated our friendship. He is an attractive creature, dreamy and vague, with a charming veracity and gentleness of nature, with (for a *grand seigneur*) simple tastes and ways, and public-spirited and philanthropic impulses, the sort of ideal young aristocrat pictured in Bulwer-Lytton's novels. But from our point of view he is no good. He is steeped in his father's individualist philosophy (he is a mere child in knowledge and thought on social and economic questions), and the only direction in which he has broken away from his father's influence is in the desire for an Empire, dragged

11

thither by the Rosebery and millionaire associates among whom he lives. Moreover, he has no notion of work; he has great possessions and a most attractive personality. I fear that he must be 'written off' as useless though not dangerous. His cousin, Mrs Willie Grenfell, struck me last night as something more than the fashionable and pretty woman I took her to be. But when I sat with her and the other smart little woman in that palatial room I felt a wee bit ashamed of myself. Why was I dissipating my energy in this smart but futile world in late hours and small talk? Exactly at the moment this feeling was disconcerting me, the door opened and Mr Balfour was announced. I confess that the appearance of the P.M. dissipated my regrets. It is always worth while, I thought, to meet those who really have power to alter things – should I be on the Poor Law Commission, the tempter said, if it were not for my friendship with this great one? And I collapsed into complacency. He was looking excited and fagged, on the eve of resignation. We chatted over the fire – Mrs Grenfell, he and I – in a disjointed fashion until twelve o'clock, when Sidney and I left the tiny party to talk, perhaps more intimately.

Meanwhile the thought of the work on the Royal Commission, added to the pressure of finishing the book, is not altogether a happy outlook. Our enquiry for Book III is not yet complete – there are many gaps in our knowledge which I, aided by three private secretaries, am trying to fill up. But one hardly dare relax one's grip of the complicated subject, and how I shall manage to run a public enquiry side by side of our own, on a different subject for a different period, I hardly care to think. . . .

Beatrice took Balfour to the first performance of *Major Barbara,* a matinée at the Court theatre on 28 November. This morality play on poverty by the Fabian playwright George Bernard Shaw (1856–1950) shocked some critics. Shaw said that the audiences were 'pained, puzzled, bored in the last act to madness; but they sit there to the bitter end and come again and again'. This success, following the popularity of *John Bull's Other Island* in November 1904, established him as the oustanding modern playwright. Sir Oliver Lodge (1851–1940) was principal of Birmingham University and much interested in psychical research. Arthur Rücker (1848–1915) was a scientist and principal of London University. Herbert Spencer (1820–1903), the social philosopher, was an old friend of Beatrice's family.

29 November. [41 Grosvenor Road]
Yesterday A.J.B. lunched with us and went afterwards to GBS's

new play *Major Barbara*. The vanishing Prime Minister was looking particularly calm and happy, compared to six months or even six days ago; seemed like one with a load lifted off his mind. Quite unexpectedly the conversation drifted on to the whole underlying argument of the tariff question, the possibility of continuous exports, should a prohibitive tariff – say 100 per cent – be raised against us by the whole world. Though apparently dead against ordinary protection as unsound, he seems haunted by a somewhat theoretical fear of *universal hostile* discrimination against us. I think he accepts the rate of exchange reaction as a solution of the ordinary tariff war when each country blindly raises walls against all other countries, while insisting on importing from other countries. But in that extreme case he had the support of even Sidney. He cross-examined Sidney as to the rise in the price of commodities brought about by a tariff, and discussed the whole matter with perfect frankness and ease. Sir Oliver Lodge and Sir Arthur Rücker and a nice young Conservative lawyer – L.C.C. – were the party: after lunch he asked somewhat anxiously *who* the young man was, and looked reassured when I told him he was of the right colour. On the way to the play, in Herbert Spencer's victoria, he told me 'as a friend' all his difficulties with the Royal Commission, his refusal to have any politicians and difficulty in finding a chairman. 'George Hamilton is not the fool he looks,' he apologetically explained.

GBS's play turned out to be a dance of devils – amazingly clever, grimly powerful in the second act, but ending, as all his plays end (or at any rate most of them) in an intellectual and moral morass. A.J.B. was taken aback by the force, the horrible force of the Salvation Army scene, the unrelieved tragedy of degradation, the disillusionment of the Greek professor and of Barbara – the triumph of the unmoral purpose, the anti-climax of evangelizing the Garden City! I doubt the popular success of the play. It is hell tossed on the stage, with no hope of heaven. GBS is gambling with ideas and emotions in a way that distresses slow-minded prigs like Sidney and I, and hurts those with any fastidiousness. But the stupid public will stand a good deal from one who is acclaimed as an unrivalled wit by the great ones of the world.

The Shaws were living in a flat at 10 Adelphi Terrace. Louis Calvert (1859–1923), an outstanding actor, manager and producer, played leading parts in the Shaw season at the Court theatre. There had been revolutionary outbreaks in Russia after the Japanese victory in the war which had ended in August 1905. Gracedieu was the Booths' country house in Leicestershire.

2 December. [41 Grosvenor Road]
At work on the records of the Westminster Court of Burgesses with two secretaries. Today I called at the Shaws' and found GBS alone in his study. He was perturbed, indeed upset, by the bad acting, as he thought, of Undershaft and generally of all in the last scene, and by a virulent attack on the play in the *Morning Post.* Calvert, he said, had completely lost his nerve over Undershaft, could not understand or remember his part and was aghast at what he considered its blank immorality.

I spoke quite frankly my opinion of the general effect of his play – the triumph of the unmoral purpose. He argued earnestly and cleverly, even persuasively, in favour of what he imagines to be his central theme – *the need for preliminary good physical environment before anything could be done to raise the intelligence and morality of the average sensual man.* 'We middle-class people, having always had physical comfort and good order, do not realize the *disaster to character* in being without. We have, therefore, cast a halo round poverty instead of treating it as the worst of crimes, the one unforgivable crime that must be wiped off before any virtue can grow.' He defended Undershaft's general attitude towards life on the ground that until we divested ourselves of feeling (he said 'malice'), we were not fit to go to the lengths needed for social salvation. 'What we want is for the people to turn round and burn, not the West End, but their own slums. The Salvation Army with its fervour and its love might lead them to do this and then we really should be at the beginning of the end of the crime of poverty.'

I found it difficult to answer him, but he did not convince me. There is something lacking in his presentment of the crime of poverty. But I could honestly sympathize with his irritation at the suggested intervention of the censor, not on account of the upshot of the play, but because Barbara in her despair at the end of the second act utters the cry: 'My God, my God, why hast thou forsaken me?' A wonderful and quite rational climax to the true tragedy of the scene of the Salvation Army shelter.

Meanwhile, governments are changing in England and government of any sort is coming to an end in Russia.

A pleasant visit to Gracedieu colloguing in the old way with Charles Booth as to the proper course of the Poor Law Enquiry. I had extracted from Davy, the assistant secretary of the Local Government Board, in a little interview I had had with him, the intention of the L.G.B. officials as to the purpose and procedure they intended to be followed by the Commission. They were going to use us to get certain radical reforms of structure: the boards of guardians were to be swept away, judicial officers appointed and possibly the institutions transferred to the county authorities. With all of which I am inclined to agree. But we were also to recommend reversion to the principles of 1834 as regards policy: to stem the tide of philanthropic impulse that was sweeping away the old embankment of deterrent tests to the receipt of relief. Though I think the exact form in which this impulse has clothed itself is radically wrong and mischievous, yet I believe in the impulse if it takes the right forms. It is just this vital question of what and which forms are right that I want to discover and this Commission to investigate. Having settled the conclusions to which we are to be led, the L.G.B. officials (on and off the Commission) have pre-determined the procedure. We were to be 'spoon-fed' by evidence carefully selected and prepared; they were to draft the circular to the boards of guardians, they were to select the inspectors who were to give evidence, they were virtually to select the guardians to be called in support of this evidence. Assistant commissioners were to be appointed who were to collect evidence illustrative of these theories. And above all, we were to be given *opinions* and not *facts*. Charles Booth and I consulted what line we should take. Today at lunch I put Lansbury, the working-man on the Commission, on his guard against this policy.

At the first meeting this afternoon Lord George laid the scheme before us: the circular had been drafted, the witnesses had been selected, the assistant commissioner had almost been appointed; it remained for us to ratify. Fortunately, the scheme did not meet with approval and was virtually defeated; the only point settled on is the calling of the experts of the Local Government Board, for which we are all quite prepared. I suggested *all* the inspectors should be called, a suggestion to which Lord George made no answer. And no other commissioner supported me at the time, but the seed had fallen on some prepared ground. It will need all my self-command to keep myself from developing a foolish hostility

and becoming self-conscious in my desire to get sound investigation. Certainly the work of the Commission will be an education
in manners as well as in Poor Law. I was not over-pleased with my
tone this afternoon and must try to do better. Beware of 'showing
off' superior knowledge of irrelevant detail. To be single-minded
in pursuit of truth, courteous in manner and kind in feeling, and
yet not to betray one's trust for the sake of popularity and be
modestly persistent in my aim must be my prayer. Meanwhile, we
must get on with the book and not sacrifice our own work to what,
at best, can only be co-operation in a joint task with seventeen
persons with almost as many aims, and therefore certain to be a
partial failure.

But how interesting will be this conflict of wills. I will certainly
describe it as it goes along. For instance, there are four big officials
on the Commission, two from England, one each from Ireland and
Scotland respectively. The English officials think they are going to
direct and limit the enquiry, the Scottish and Irish officials told us
pretty plainly that they did not want any enquiry, and they had
already investigated the whole subject by departmental committees!
And as there were no Irish and Scottish representatives of the anti-
official view, the enquiry into Irish and Scottish Poor Law has been
indefinitely postponed and will probably hardly take place.

On the other hand, Charles Booth and I want a real investigation
of English administration as well as an examination into pauperism, though Charles Booth is more concerned with the question of
right treatment than of prevention by a better regulated life.
Lansbury, on the other hand, is willing and anxious to enquire into
the initial causes of pauperism, not so keen to investigate the effect
of indifferent methods of relief. C.S. Loch wants to drag in the
whole question of endowed charity, in which he has the support of
Mrs Bernard Bosanquet. She and I, and possibly Miss Octavia
Hill, may combine on the question of a rate-in-aid of wages to
women workers, the need for discovering how far it actually
obtains, and there will be a good deal of common ground, as far as
the enquiry goes, between Loch and myself. Certain other commissioners, such as Smart and Phelps, are going to look on, I
think, and intervene as the spirit moves them.

There had been difficulties over the formation of the Liberal government
arising from the long-standing split in the party. In September 1905, at a

meeting at Relugas, where Sir Edward Grey (1862–1933) was fishing in Scotland, Grey, Asquith and R.B. Haldane (1856–1928) had reached an agreement that none of them would serve under Campbell-Bannerman unless he took a peerage and left Asquith to lead the Commons. When the moment came to take office, despite some prevarication, all three Liberal Imperialists ('Limps') decided to serve. Asquith became Chancellor of the Exchequer and heir apparent to the premiership; Grey was to be Foreign Secretary, and Haldane was appointed Secretary of State for War. The Liberal Imperialists had thus secured the three most important posts in the Cabinet. John Morley (1838–1916) and James Bryce (1838–1922) were both Gladstonian Liberals. David Lloyd George, a Liberal M.P. since 1890, was appointed president of the Board of Trade and was the youngest member of the new Cabinet. Winston Churchill had joined the Liberals after disagreement with the Tories over tariff reform in 1902. He was appointed under-secretary at the Colonial Office. John Burns (1858–1943) had been arrested and imprisoned in unemployed demonstrations before he made his name as a labour leader in the 1889 dock strike. He was appointed president of the Local Government Board. Augustine Birrell (1850–1933) was a lawyer and essayist appointed as president of the Board of Education. H.O. Arnold-Forster (1855–1909) was the outgoing Conservative Secretary of State for War. Herbert Samuel (1870–1963) had been a friend of the Webbs' early in their marriage. C.P. Trevelyan (1870–1958), eldest son of Sir George Trevelyan, was an old friend of the Webbs' and became Parliamentary Secretary at the Board of Education in 1908. Thomas Lough (1850–1922), was a prosperous tea merchant appointed Parliamentary Secretary to the Board of Education. Reginald McKenna (1863–1933), a barrister protégé of Sir Charles Dilke and a friend of Asquith's was appointed Financial Secretary to the Treasury. Walter Runciman (1870–1949), a wealthy shipowner, was given a minor post under John Burns.

15 December. [41 Grosvenor Road]
Certainly the procedure imposed upon us by Lord George [Hamilton] was amazing. There was no agenda. A cut-and-dried scheme was laid before us, and we were not asked to vote on it, only to express our opinion on half-a-dozen points ranging from the hour of luncheon to the appointment of assistant commissioners [researchers helping the Commission]. The only subject really discussed was the issue of the preliminary circular to the boards of guardians. On this point there was almost unanimity against the course proposed. Whereupon Lord George called up out of the Commission [those members who were] guardians of the poor, and we left these five persons under the chairman's eye, sitting discussing the matter. Yesterday I got a formal announcement that unless the commissioners dissented by post the circulars would be sent out.

This was rather intolerable. I wrote a courteous but firm dissent and enigmatically suggested that I wished for some procedure that would enable those who objected to any course to record that objection. I did not stop there. I went and unburdened my soul to the secretary. Mr Duff is an attractive and sensible young civil servant, who gave me to understand that he had been against Lord George's high-handed action. So I elaborately complained to him of the absence of agenda, of concrete resolutions, of any formal appointment and authorization of the committee, and I claimed to have a formal procedure in future, with the circulation of all proposals, of the names of witnesses, of the précis of their evidence.

Apparently our chairman has decided against all those suggestions on the ground that 'we should know too much'! 'I don't want to make myself disagreeable,' I ventured to add. 'It is extraordinarily unpleasant for a woman to do so on a commission of men. But I don't, on the other hand, intend to hide my intentions. If a procedure and methods of investigation are adopted, or slipped into by the Commission which I think incompetent to elicit the truth, it will be my obvious duty to report such procedure and to describe and analyse such methods one by one. To enable me to do this without incurring a charge of bad comradeship, I must express, clearly and emphatically, my dissent. That is why I ask for a formal procedure for the business of the Commission.' I begged Mr Duff to report the gist of the conversation to Lord George. I await the result with some amusement, and a little anxiety. It is a new experience to me to *have* to make myself disagreeable in order to reach my ends. In private life one can only get one's way by being unusually pleasant. In official life, at least as the most insignificant member of a commission overwhelmingly against me in opinion, I shall only get my share of control by quietly and persistently standing on my rights as an individual commissioner and refusing altogether to be overawed by great personages who would like to pooh-pooh a woman who attempts to share in the control of affairs.

Whilst I am busy with my little teacup of a royal commission a new ministry has been formed. It is a strong government and felt to be so. All the possible actors have been included and the parts have been skilfully allotted. Our friends the 'Limps' have romped in to the leading posts under Campbell-Bannerman, Morley and Bryce being marooned on India and Ireland respectively. To put Asquith and Lloyd George and Winston Churchill dead in front of 'Joe'

[Chamberlain] on the tariff and the colonies, to place John Burns to look to the unemployed, to give Birrell the Education Office, are all apt placements. But the great *coup* is to get Haldane to take the War Office – the courtly lawyer with a great capacity for dealing with men and affairs and a real understanding of the function of an expert, and skill in using him.

Two of the new Cabinet have already come in to talk over their new life. The very day of his introduction to the Cabinet John Burns arrived, childishly delighted with his own post. For one solid hour he paced the room expanding his soul before me, how he had called in the permanent officials, asked them questions. 'That is my decision, gentlemen,' he proudly rehearsed to me once or twice. 'Don't be too doctrinaire about the unemployed, Mr Burns,' I mildly suggested. 'Economize your great force of honesty, Mrs Webb,' he rejoined solemnly. 'I am a different man from what I was a week ago; you read what I say tomorrow when I stand by Campbell-Bannerman at the deputation. You will see I shan't give myself away.' What he and the big officials will do with each other remains to be seen. To listen to him talking one would think he was hopelessly confused and blurred in his views and intentions. His best chance will be to refuse to be overwhelmed with routine administration, to devote himself to one or two points, and strike dramatic effects in one or two unconventional decisions. A sort of working-class [Theodore] Roosevelt is his role. The story goes that when C.B. offered him the Local Government Board with a seat in the Cabinet he clasped the Premier by the hand. 'I congratulate you, Sir Henry; it will be the most popular appointment that you have made'!

Yesterday afternoon Haldane came in. *He* also was in a state of exuberant delight over his new task. 'I chose the War Office out of three offices. Asquith, Grey and I stood together; they were forced to take us on our own terms. We were really very indifferent,' he added sublimely. 'Asquith gave up a brief of £10,000 to defend the Khedive's property that very week; I was throwing away an income of fifteen to twenty thousand a year; and Grey had no ambition and was sacrificing his fishing. But it was a horrid week, one perpetual wrangle. The King signified that he would like me to take the War Office; it is exactly what I myself longed for. I have never been so happy in my life,' and he beamed all over. And then he poured into my sympathetic ear all his plans.

'I shall spend three years observing and thinking. I shall succeed. I have always succeeded in everything I have undertaken.' I confess I was a little surprised at the naïvety of that last remark: alas! what hideous failures the wisest of us makes. But, of course, it was merely the foam of his excited self-complacency in the first novelty of power. He came straight from a whole day talking over matters with Arnold-Forster, a thoroughly English proceeding, showing the essential solidarity of the governing class.

The lower ranks of the government are filled with young men we know or have known. Herbert Samuel, an old friend but a young person to whom I have taken almost a dislike, has made a surprising advance in obtaining the under-secretaryship of the Home Office, leaving poor C.P. Trevelyan behind. Lough, McKenna, Runciman, all friendly acquaintances. . . .

A satisfactory interview with the chairman of our Commission, arranged by the secretary, whom I had apparently alarmed by my rebellious attitude. For a whole hour I listened to his somewhat weak proposals, quietly insisting on a regular procedure, the appointment of a committee to consider and report on methods of investigation, and the concentration of our efforts on ascertaining the facts about the relief of destitution, and not merely collecting casual opinions as to defects in law and practice. I felt strengthened by the fact that Sidney had helped me to draft a series of concrete proposals which I succeeded in making him ask me for. What upset his aristocratic mind was the notion that the Commission should appoint its own committees and regulate its own procedure. 'I saw the democratic method worked out on the London School Board when I was chairman,' he naïvely remarked, 'and I was not impressed with its results.' I tried to convince him that consent was a preliminary requirement to efficiency. 'Moreover,' I urged, 'you will find that you practically appoint the committees even if you submit the names formally to the Commission. It may be that one or two others will be added, but when the first flush of energy has exhausted itself we shall suffer not from too large but too small a membership of the working committee.' So we chatted on, getting more and more friendly. 'You must remember, Lord George, that we are all rather awed by our *grand seigneur* chairman,' was my parting shot, 'and with a nondescript body like the Commission, awe sometimes gets transformed into suspicion of being bossed. With a pertinacious spirit like C. S. Loch, for instance, this feeling might have inconvenient results.'

Meanwhile, I have sent my suggestions to one or two of the commissioners and have had a most friendly chat with Loch who, so far as investigation goes, will, I think, be a sturdy ally. Charles Booth, I fear, is too well-bred and too feeble in health to be much good. But we shall see.

∽ 1906 ∾

A.D. Adrian (1845–1922) had been assistant secretary to the Local Government Board and was now its legal adviser. In this, as in other entries, Beatrice runs to and fro over several days.

9 January. [41 Grosvenor Road]
Second meeting of the Commission went off well. The chairman introduced the motion for a committee on procedure and methods of investigation: Charles Booth (to whom I had sent my suggestions) backed it up: Loch somewhat demurred: Mrs Bernard Bosanquet objected, seeing, I think, an insidious proposal of mine which would give the London members and the experts in investigation complete control over the Commission. But the Commission on the whole was favourable. At any rate I have made friends with the chairman, and shall now be careful not to excite the jealousy of those who feel themselves opposed to me in doctrine. The C.O.S. are far more suspicious of me than I am of them. I believe that they *do* want investigation and should be glad if we could co-operate against those who do not. But I see that, at first at any rate, they will hold both C.B. and me at arm's length.

C.B. made a useful suggestion that no one need cross-examine Adrian until we have the proof of his evidence. The wisdom of this was quickly apparent. Adrian, a heavy, dull but conscientious official, began, in monotonous tone, to read a verbose disquisition on the law from the very beginning of poor relief to the end. The room was cold, and we all, I think, failed to take any intelligent interest in what he said. I stayed for lunch and chatted pleasantly with Lord George, and then escaped and went for a walk and service at Westminster Abbey. Thory Gardiner came to tea and I impregnated him with our views of investigation. I stay away today, and see clearly that my most important work will be done outside the Commission room at the Foreign Office. I will give my best *thought* but scamp attendance.

Third meeting of Commission. I did not attend, as Adrian's evidence-in-chief consisted in his reading from copious notes or long legal disquisitions — which, as it was all taken down in shorthand and served to us in printed form in two days' time and before his cross-examination began, it was sheer waste of time to sit there listening to it. On Monday (fourth meeting) the cross-examination began, and on that afternoon and the following morning I tried to make him admit that we must see and study the general and special orders, circulars etc. for ourselves, before we could understand the body of law and regulation under which the guardians acted. In this endeavour I was stopped by the chairman and Sir Samuel Provis, and I had a little tiff across the table as to whether he or we should judge whether documents were important or not. But I got a specific promise from the chairman that all the documents that we needed should be at the disposal of the Commission.

However, as the Commission seemed still in a rudderless condition, at the mercy of the little clique of officials, Sidney and I prepared a memorandum on 'Methods of Enquiry' which I have asked to be circulated to the whole Commission. That done, I feel that I have striven to get the enquiry on the right lines and can now rest a bit. To reform the procedure of royal commissions would be worth delaying the completion of our book. But up to now I find attendance at the Commission a most disagreeable business — it is extraordinarily unpleasant when one has to force people's hands and make them attend to one by sheer ugly persistency, at the cost, of course, of getting back a certain insolence of attitude on the part of hostile men. (A week after: *This is exaggeration!*)

Thought it wise to let the two secretaries see both our proof of *The Parish*, and also our first draft of the History of the Poor Law, 1689–1835. The publication of the work before the Report of the Commission is one of the trump cards in our hand, and as our object is to make them throw up the game of obstruction to investigation it is well to put the card on the table.

W.A.S. Hewins (1865–1931) was the first Director of the London School of Economics and he had resigned in 1903 to become secretary of the Tariff Reform Commission.

28 January. [41 Grosvenor Road]
Hewins and his wife came to lunch here after many months'
interval, owing to preoccupation on all sides. Both were very
depressed: he was somewhat bitter against all the Unionist leaders,
even including Joe; she was merely 'down on her luck' – dreary –
poor little soul! The result of the election has evidently been a
terrible disillusionment for Hewins: it never occurred to him that
the reaction might be so complete as to keep the Tories out for six
years. From a private point of view it is a catastrophe: he thought, I
am convinced, that in a few years, if not immediately, he would be
arranging tariffs, and tariff wars, and tariff treaties, at the Board of
Trade – hurrying from continent to continent, in close and confidential intercourse with Ministers and great financial personages –
one long delightful intrigue with the World Empire as the
result. . . .

Of course he is contemptuous of Balfour and those who surround
him. But he is also irritated against Joe – for reasons I do not
understand, except when there has been a gigantic fiasco, all
concerned condemn 'the others'. Poor Hewins, with his grand
castles in the air that he has been, for the last three years, inhabiting
– now lying in ruins about him! I suppose he will become a paid
organizer of the Protectionist cause – an occasional leader-writer in
Protectionist papers. . . .

A copy of Beatrice's memorandum was sent to George Lansbury on 6
January. (It appears in *The Letters of Sidney and Beatrice Webb*, Vol. II, 1978.) It
made a number of suggestions for improving the procedure of the Commission,
launching enquiries and handling witnesses. But she got little response. No one
wanted to 'enquire', she told her sister Mary Playne (1849–1923) on 21
January: 'They are all trying to lead up to some specific proposals and the
L.G.B. officials are dead set on thwarting all investigation that does not directly
point to these conclusions.' The reference to 'English unions' is to the local Poor
Law authorities, not to trade unions.

5 February. Royal Commission
The memo I sent in on 'Methods of Enquiry' led the chairman to
ask all the other commissioners for memoranda. And some six or
seven responded. Whereupon all have been referred to a committee
consisting of Lord George, Provis, Booth, Bentham, Smart, Loch,
Phelps, Mrs Bosanquet and myself, and we met on Monday 12th
to consider them. This morning I spent taking out all the questions

which the L.G.B. witnesses had told us we ought to enquire into, with a view of trying to persuade the committee to start on a systematic survey of all the unions with a view to more detailed investigation of some. Yesterday, Bentham – the ablest person (except perhaps Provis) on the Commission – came here and we talked Poor Law from 5.30 to 11 o'clock. Result, bad headache this afternoon!

Dear Charles Booth is as delightful as ever, but he is losing his intellectual grip and persistency of purpose – is not much use on the Commission. Happily, he is unaware of it. Alas! for the pathetic strivings of age – more pitiful to the onlooker than those of youth, because without hope of amendment. Want to get Commission, sooner or later, to undertake

(1) Survey of all English unions with regard to diversity of constitution and methods of administration of union.
(2) Analysis of the 'whence and whither pauperism' in some among them.
(3) Clear vision of course of legislation.
(4) Analysis of developments of policy of central authority.

It would be natural to begin with number (3) or (4): but owing to the fact that we shall be fully occupied until next autumn in completing our book, I shall suggest beginning at the other end. We want, if possible, to superintend, or at any rate supplement, (3) and (4).

William Pember Reeves (1857–1932) was a Fabian socialist from New Zealand. He came to England in 1896 as Agent General.

9 February. [41 Grosvenor Road]
About 9 o'clock yesterday evening, in walked John Burns. He had an indefinable air of greater dignity – a new and perfectly fitting jacket suit, a quieter manner, and less boisterous vanity in his talk. The man is filling in with good stuff. He described the three committees of the Cabinet upon which he had that day sat – one on the Trade Disputes Bill, the other on the unemployed, and the third on the Workmen's Compensation Extension Bill. He was naïvely delighted with his share in the proceedings, especially his insistence that workmen's compensation should include provision for illness or death from unhealthy occupations. He had filled in his

time with seeing all and sundry – philanthropists, labour representatives, great employers, and asking their advice. 'They are all so
kind to me,' he said in glowing appreciation, 'especially the great
employers, just the men who might have objected to my appointment.' Oh! the wisdom of England's governing class!

He pulled out a set of cards, upon which he had written the
measures which he had decided to bring forward in the first two
years – mostly measures that the L.G.B. had long ago pigeon-holed
– the abolition of overseers, further equalization of rates in London,
amendment of the Alkali Act; and finally (as a concession to the
Labour Party) an amendment of the Unemployed Act of last
session in the direction of greater contributions from the rates. 'I
want to be efficient,' he said with youthful fervour. 'If you and
Sidney can give me a tip I am always ready to listen. I am ready to
take tips from anyone so long as they mean business in my
direction.' If good intentions, and a strong vigorous and audacious
character, can make up for lack of administrative experience and
technical knowledge, John Burns may yet be a success as president
of the Local Government Board.

Altogether, Sidney and I are in better spirits as to the course of
political affairs than we have been for many years. We do not
deceive ourselves by the notion that this wave of Liberalism is
wholly progressive in character – much of its bulk is made up of
sheer conservatism aroused by the revolutionary tariff policy of
Chamberlain. But it looms as progressive in its direction and all the
active factors are collectivist. Moreover, it is clear that 'Joe' is
going to try to outbid the Liberals by constructive social reforms. It
is an interesting little fact that a fortnight ago he wrote in his own
hand to W.P. Reeves to beg him to send all the Acts, and literature
about the Acts, relating to old age pensions and compulsory
arbitration [in New Zealand] – as if he desired to convince himself
of their feasibility as an adjunct to his tariff policy. Whether or not
this socialistic addition will make for the popularity of Protection,
it will come at any rate as pressure on the Liberals to do something
for raising the standard of life of the very poor – it will bar the way
to a policy of the *status quo*.

B. Seebohm Rowntree (1871–1954) was chairman of the York confectionery
firm; his pioneering study *Poverty: A Study of Town Life* made a great
impression when it was published in 1901. It demonstrated that Booth's estimate

of one third of London's population living at or below subsistence level held broadly true in a provincial town. Samuel Barnett (1844–1913) was vicar of St Jude's, Whitechapel, and Warden of Toynbee Hall 1884–1906. He and Henrietta (1851–1926), heiress to the Rowlands macassar oil fortune, were old friends of Beatrice's. Sydney Buxton (1853–1934) was Postmaster General. Henry Hobhouse (1854–1937) was a Liberal Unionist M.P. married to Beatrice's sister Margaret. A compact in favour of Chamberlain's policy was reached with Balfour and confirmed at a party meeting on 15 February.

12 February. [41 Grosvenor Road]
I sent another memo to the chairman sketching out the work of three committees – on statistics, local administration, and central policy respectively. . . . The committee on statistics was agreed to, so was the committee on blue-books etc., to which the documents of the L.G.B. might be added; and, in the course of the discussion, it became clear that a committee on local administration would, in the end, be required. But most of the members were against taking any steps towards a positive scheme until after the inspectors' evidence. Charles Booth wants one committee only; Mrs Bosanquet objects to any but temporary committees; no member wants a systematic investigation but myself. I throw out the notion of a statistical officer and an assistant commissioner to undertake the investigation into local administration, but, as yet, it is not responded to. Meanwhile Sir Samuel Provis will not agree to anyone looking through the L.G.B. documents, insists that we must call for those we want to see and not have the run of the whole. In an interview we had at the L.G.B. he lost his temper and asserted that he 'would not have a poking enquiry into L.G.B. policy'. I kept my temper and we parted on friendly terms. Charles Booth blames me for having raised the hostility of the L.G.B. He may be right – the other policy would have been to 'wheedle' my way into the place. On the other hand, if one begins by being disagreeable, one may come in the end to a better bargain. It is, however, clear that I shall not have the support of the Commission in my desire for scientific research into the past seventy years.

There is one very pleasant feature about the Commission. We are all of us after public objects, however much we may disagree as to what these objects are and how to arrive at them. There is hardly any personal vanity, or personal ambition, and no personal 'interest' at work in the commissioners. A little jealousy of those who take the lead – but very little of that. And we are all getting fond of our

26

chairman – who, like many a *grand seigneur*, can afford to be modest and unassuming.

He and his wife dined with us yesterday, meeting Rowntree (author of *Poverty*) the Barnetts, the clerk of the Westminster Board of Guardians, Mrs Sydney Buxton and Henry Hobhouse – a most pleasant and useful party. Rowntree, who stayed the night here, is to help me to get an analysis of 1,000 applications – the whence and the whither of pauperism. I am beginning to enjoy the Commission work: but the grind of combining it with our own enquiry keeps one at a low level of strength and good spirits. . . .

Meanwhile, Balfour has succumbed to Chamberlain, and the Conservative Party has become definitely Protectionist – for the time – so long as Chamberlain lives. In so far as it commits the most *laissez-faire* party to the policy of state control and increase of taxation, we rejoice in it. Sidney still thinks that import duties are a wasteful device, though agreeing to the expediency of deepening the channels of trade between Anglo-Saxon communities. Personally, I don't believe much in the injuriousness of tariffs to a prosperous wealth-producing country like England. And, if a tariff were part and parcel of a deliberately conceived scheme of raising the standard of life by collective regulation and public expenditure, I should be willing to pay for this scheme in a slight rise in the price of commodities. And, other things being equal, I would rather pay more for commodities produced by our colonists under fair conditions of employment than fractionally less for commodities produced under unknown conditions by an oppressed people. This, as a matter of sentiment and as an argument for bettering conditions here. However, for the next six years we have to look to the Liberal Party for any reforms. It is well that Sidney is a 'free importer'. As for my private predilections, mum's the word.

Robert Morant (1862–1920) was an influential civil servant who worked with Sidney Webb on the 1902 Education Act. He was permanent secretary at the Board of Education from 1903. Beatrice greatly admired him, and at his early death described him as the greatest public servant of his day.

19 February. [41 Grosvenor Road]
Dined last night with Tommy Lough (now promoted to the secretaryship of the Education Department) and met three other minor members of the Ministry – the Lord Chancellor of Ireland,

Lord Advocate for Scotland, and Solicitor-General for Ireland, as well as two or three ministerial M.P.s. The minor Ministers were all on their best behaviour, with that peculiar combination of new-born discretion and modesty with obvious self-complacency at being within the mystic circle of the government. Tommy Lough was great on the reforms he intended to introduce in the financial transactions of the Education Department – horror-struck at the notion of 80,000 separate cheques a year on behalf of separate institutions. 'We might as well have a separate cheque for each packet of tea sold by the Tower Company.' The mysteries of education are still above and beyond him. 'As for the government's intention', he whispered to me, 'about education or any other matter, I know less than I did as a private member. You see I may not gossip and no one gossips with me,' he added sadly. 'We under-secretaries are just set down to do some departmental job and, as we know nothing of the subject, we have got to stick to it, instead of amusing ourselves in the lobby, picking up news. But it is interesting', he continued with glowing enthusiasm, 'to feel your-self right inside the machine. Morant is a fine fellow and we get on splendidly – but the office from a mere business point of view *does* want reforming.'

A boisterous tea dealer, whose business career has been divided between advertising packets of tea and starting doubtful companies, whose public interests are wholly Irish or working-class, who has neither literary culture nor scientific knowledge, as one of the heads of our Education Department! A rum thing is English government.

For all that, I like Tommy Lough; he has energy, he is no respecter of persons, he wants, in a philistine way, to make society more prosperous and happier, and he never says what he does not think. He is a rough, ugly instrument, but so far as he cuts at all, he cuts in the right direction.

C.F.G. Masterman (1874–1927) was a Radical politician and journalist. H.W. Massingham (1860–1924) was a Liberal M.P., journalist and Fabian, and editor of the *Nation* 1907–23. Sydney Olivier (1859–1943) was a civil servant in the Colonial Office and one of the first Fabians. John Simon (1873–1954) was a lawyer and Liberal politician who had a distinguished career as Solicitor-General, Foreign Secretary and Lord Chancellor. His wife, Ethel Venables, died in 1902 after three years of marriage. Rufus Isaacs, later Marquess of Reading (1860–1935) was a barrister who became Attorney-

General in 1910. Betty Holt (1875–1947) was the daughter of Beatrice's sister, Lallie. Ruth Cripps (1884–1978) was the daughter of another sister, Theresa. Alys Russell (1867–1951) was the wife of Bertrand Russell (1872–1970), both old friends of the Webbs'. C.R. Ashbee (1862–1942) was an architect-designer who founded the Guild of Handicraft, which he moved from Whitechapel to Chipping Camden in 1902. He and his wife, Janet, had met the Webbs through a mutual friend, Mandell Creighton, the Bishop of London (1843–1901), and when the Webbs were on holiday in the Cotswolds. 'I like her company more than I like her,' Ashbee wrote of Beatrice. Sir William Collins (1859–1946) was a surgeon and London county councillor. A.J. Shepheard was a Progressive on the L.C.C.

22 February. [41 Grosvenor Road]
Had a party of young Liberals dining here last night: Herbert Samuel and Reginald McKenna, Masterman and John Simon, Massingham and Sydney Olivier. Of these Simon, the young lawyer, is by far the most brilliant, making a big income as the rising junior at the Bar. He has a conventional mind but excellent working intellect, a charming person, agreeable voice and manner. But his spirit has been broken and his whole life made arid by the loss, some three years ago, of his young wife. He declares himself already 'bored' by Parliament after three days of it. 'Rufus Isaacs has shown me a quiet corner to which I retire and work at my briefs.' He is an individual Liberal of the Morley type, without Morley's idealism.

I sat between the two new under-secretaries, both full of the work and dignity of office – neither of them exciting personalities, but McKenna a genuine reformer of the ordinary kind, and both as respectable and hard working as Cabinet Ministers could desire in subordinates. Massingham exuberant in his half-cynical, half-sentimental talk; Sydney Olivier full of the possibility of going out to South Africa in an important post, all of them full of themselves and rather impatient of each other's obsessions. Betty Holt, Ruth Cripps, Alys Russell and the Ashbees made up the party. It was not fertile in thought, but cheerful.

This morning I took 'off' – the first holiday for a fortnight or more. I walked along the Embankment to St Paul's for the 10 o'clock service. The beauty of the music and the old-world charm of the words, the pious space of the dome, are always the best recreation when I am weary with straining my poor little mind. I prayed for strength to order my effort rightly and keep my motives pure, to preserve the patience and persistency of purpose needed to carry through our intentions. These next three years are going to try my strength of body, intellect and character: I sometimes wonder whether I shall keep going on or whether some day I may not find that I have stopped for repair. And yet it is little that I really accomplish, with all my abstinence and cutting down of all but business intercourse. Sidney can do about four times as much as I, whether measured in time or in matter.

Sidney thoroughly satisfied with the secondary education side of L.C.C. work: he gets through all his grants without opposition: he is building up a system of provided and non-provided schools side by side. He is happy in his work, as all antagonism to him personally has subsided. The little jealousies between the leading Progressives are now transferred from Spring Gardens [the L.C.C.] to Westminster – and Sidney does not appear in this higher sphere. Spring Gardens has become a mere backwater in which the remaining big fish of the Old Gang can swim without fear of creating disturbance. Thirty-two of the Progressives, including all the leaders, now in the House of Commons! There is actually some talk of making Sidney vice-chairman of the Education Committee! Collins even pressed him to accept that great position: Sidney modestly put himself at the 'disposition of his party' and acquiesced in the suggestion that he should work under Shepheard (who is to be promoted to the chairmanship) if the majority of the party actually desired it. (Later: they did not wish it, so he remains chairman of the Higher Education Committee – a post he prefers.) It is a great luxury to feel that he is beyond all question of dignity and personal position. If you are content to accept any position that is forced on you and never to compete, there is a good deal of excellent and happy work to be done in the world.

After ten years of outstanding success as a novelist, H.G. Wells (1866–1946) was becoming increasingly interested in politics and social problems. What he called his 'storm in a Fabian teacup' began in 1906, when he made a bid to take over the Fabian Society. Allying himself with the younger and more radical members against the 'Old Gang', he demanded a more vigorous policy than the 'municipal gas-and-water' socialism with which the Society had made its name. He gibed at the Webbs in a brilliant tract called *This Misery of Boots*, delivered as a lecture on 12 January, and again in *The Faults of the Fabian* on 9 February. He persuaded the Fabians to set up a committee, chaired by Sydney Olivier, to review the Society's organization and activities. Wells left for America on 27

March and the matter simmered until his return on 27 May. In the novel *Kipps* (1905), Wells told the story of a draper's apprentice, such as he had been, who inherits a fortune and aspires to be a gentleman. Hubert Bland (1856–1914) was a journalist married to the writer Edith Nesbit (1858–1924) and one of the first Fabians. R.B. Haldane introduced his first army estimates on 8 March and was working on his scheme for the radical reform of the army. H.J. Mackinder (1861–1947), was a professor of geography and Director of the London School of Economics 1903–08. Sir John French (1852–1925) was a cavalry commander who had made his reputation in the Boer War; he became commander-in-chief of the British Expeditionary Force in France in 1914.

1 March. [41 Grosvenor Road]

H.G. Wells has broken out in a quite unexpectedly unpleasant manner. The occasion has been a movement to reform the Fabian Society. The details are unimportant, for I doubt whether he has the skill and the persistence and the real desire to carry a new departure. But what is interesting is that he has shown in his dealings with the Executive, and with his close personal friends on it – Shaw, Bland, and Webb – an odd mixture of underhand manoeuvres and insolent bluster, when his manoeuvres were not successful. The explanation is, I think, that this is absolutely the first time he has tried to co-operate with his fellow men – and he has neither tradition nor training to fit him to do it. It is a case of 'Kipps' in matters more important than table manners. It is strange for so frank a man that his dealings have been far from straight – a series of naïve little lies which were bound to be found out. When at last he forced the Executive to oppose him he became a bully, and remained so until he found they were big enough to knock him down. I tell Sidney not to be too hard upon him, and to remember there was a time when 'the Webbs' were thought not too straight and not too courteous in their dealings (and that after a dozen years of mixing with men and affairs). But we have shown our displeasure by slight coolness; GBS has expressed himself with his usual scathing frankness, and it is more than likely that H.G.W., with his intelligent sensitiveness, will feel he has taken false steps into semi-public affairs and retire into his own world of the artist. It is more for 'copy' than for reform that he has stepped out of his study; when he has got his 'copy' he will step back again.

Meanwhile, my Royal Commission grinds slowly on. The three committees that I pressed for on the Procedure Committee have been appointed and have set to work: statistics, documents (on central policy), evidence (on local administration). I am trying to guide the Committee on Documents into making an analysis of all the documents of the central authority – statutes, orders, reports – with a view of writing a memorandum on the attitude of the state towards each class of pauper. Lord George gives me unhesitating support; my difficulty is with Sir Samuel Provis. But I had the most friendly chat with him this afternoon, and he comes to dine to meet a carefully selected party on Wednesday. Charles Booth has the Statistical Committee well in hand; Bentham has elaborated and improved my question as to the working constitution of the boards of guardians; I hope that investigations will be presently set on foot as to the life history of paupers in different unions [groups of parishes]. And I no longer find the association with my fellow commissioners disagreeable. But it is a somewhat disastrous interruption of work on the book, which drags on painfully.

We are trying to avoid dining out except when it seems absolutely desirable that we should be present (e.g. Liberal Ministers). We wish to be on friendly terms with the administrators and to make ourselves as useful as possible. Mr Haldane came in this morning – first to discuss with Sidney and Mackinder the organization of London University and, when Mackinder had left, to consult us about his scheme of army reform. So far as we could understand it, this scheme provides for a small and highly expert professional army with the militia in attendance for foreign service (a reduction of 50,000 men). Then, in the background, as material for reinforcements in time of war, a mass of half-trained material under a semi-civil authority – probably a county authority bearing some sort of likeness to the joint committee for police – with 'grants in aid' to promote extension and efficiency. . . .

A brilliant dinner for the Students' Union – A.J.B. and Sir John French as guests. One of those academic discourses from the ex-Premier in which he delights his hearers. In our talk together I gathered that he is set on continued leadership; would not hear the suggestion that he should take a holiday. 'It is exactly now that they are beaten and demoralized that they need me: I shall be with them as continuously as if I were Prime Minister.' Like all great personages there creeps out, now and again, a little touch of egotism – a sensitiveness, more than with the ruck of men, to any depreciation of his past work and present position. He pressed me to come, both of us, to stay at Whittingehame – perhaps we may go. I should like to talk out some matters of government with him and some aspects of the philosophy of public conduct. Is he an ingrained individualist incapable of change? Tariff reform has, at any rate, shaken the *laissez-faire* side of his philosophy. . . .

The Poplar Board of Guardians, in which George Lansbury played a leading role, had a record of hostility to the constraints of the Poor Law, and 'Poplarism' – defiance of regulations – remained a characteristic of the district. But early in 1906 a series of enquiries was started into the 'East End scandals', in which the guardians in Poplar and four other London boroughs were investigated for extravagance, negligence and corruption. J.S. Davy opened the Poplar enquiry in March. His findings were reported to Parliament in July and the full report appeared in October. He particularly criticized the conduct of the labour colony which the borough had set up at Laindon, in Essex. The report was politically damaging to Lansbury, and Will Crooks (1852–1921), who was the chairman of the Poplar guardians, resigned after it was published.

19 March. [41 Grosvenor Road]
Attended a meeting of the Poplar Board of Guardians held at 6.30. About thirty were present, a rather low lot of doubtful 'representatives' of labour, with a sprinkling of builders, publicans, insurance and other 'agents'. The meeting was exclusively engaged in allotting the contracts for the year, which meant up to something between £50,000 and £100,000. I did not ascertain the exact amount. The procedure was utterly reckless. The tenders were opened at the meeting, the names and prices read out; and then, without any kind of report of a committee or by officials, straight away voted on. Usually the same person as heretofore was taken, nearly always a local man – it was not always the lowest tender, and the prices were, in all cases, full, in some cases obviously excessive. Butter at 1*s* 2*d* a lb, when the contracts ran into thousands of pounds' worth, was obviously ridiculous! Milk at 9*d* a gallon, the best and most expensive meat, tea at 2*s* 8*d*. 'Give Bow a chance' was one of the relevant considerations urged successfully in favour of a change in the contractor. Will Crooks sat in the chair and did nothing to check the recklessness. Considering that he has had twelve years' experience of the businesslike and careful procedure of the L.C.C. in matters of contracts, it is gravely to his discredit that the Poplar guardians are as they are. If there is no corruption in that Board, English human nature must be more naïvely stupid than any other race would credit. Is Will Crooks (as John Burns asserts) a corrupt politician?

Or merely a demagogic sentimentalist? Even Lansbury, by constitution a thoroughgoing sentimentalist, and with no other experience of public affairs, protested, and was clearly ashamed of the procedure.

Count Benckendorff (1849–1917) was the Russian Ambassador in London for many years. George Goschen (1831–1907) was a Liberal Unionist who was Chancellor of the Exchequer 1886–92, and First Lord of the Admiralty in 1900. He was a strong supporter of higher education. Mary Lowther (d. 1944) was the wife of James Lowther, later Lord Ullswater (1855–1949), who was Speaker of the House of Commons 1906–21. Hugh Cecil (1869–1956) was a Conservative M.P., a friend and cousin of Balfour. Raymond Asquith (1878–1916) was Herbert Asquith's brilliant eldest son. He was killed in action in France. His sister Violet, who married Maurice Bonham Carter (1880–1960), became a prominent Liberal politician. Margot Asquith (1864–1945) was the second wife of Herbert Asquith. Anne Dickson-Poynder was the wife of Sir John Dickson-Poynder (1866–1936), a Conservative M.P. who turned Liberal in 1905. Sir Neville Lyttelton (1845–1931) was Chief of the General Staff 1904–08. Arthur Russell was the brother of the Duke of Bedford. His wife was Laura de Peyroutet (d. 1910). Sir Herbert Jekyll (1846–1932), assistant secretary to the Board of Trade 1901–11, was married to Agnes Graham, whose niece married Raymond Asquith in 1907. Sir Francis Mowatt (1837–1919) was permanent head of the Treasury, an Alderman of the L.C.C., and an influential figure in the Senate of the University of London.

20 March. [41 Grosvenor Road]
Two dinners that well illustrated a subtle distinction of atmosphere – one at the Asquiths', the other at the George Hamiltons'. The former consisted of the Russian Ambassador, the Desboroughs, Lord Goschen, the Dickson-Poynders, Mrs Lowther (the Speaker's wife), Lord Hugh Cecil, Mrs Lester (Mrs Cornwallis West's sister), one or two aristocratic young men, the Asquiths' daughter and Raymond. The large garish rooms, the flunkeys and the superlatively good dinner gave a sort of 'second Empire' setting to the entertainment. Lady Desborough, Margot, Mrs Lester and Lady Dickson-Poynder were all very *décolletée* and highly adorned with jewels. The conversation aimed at brilliancy – Margot sparkling her little disjointed sayings, kindly and indiscreet, Lady Desborough's somewhat artificial grace, Lady Dickson-Poynder's pretty folly, Mrs Lester's *outré* frankness, lending a sort of 'stagyness' to the talk. We might have all been characters brought on to illustrate the ways of modern society — a twentieth-century Sheridan play. They were all gushing over GBS and I had to

APRIL 1906

entertain the ladies after dinner with a discourse on his philosophy and personality – mostly the latter. We came away feeling half-flattered that we had been asked, half-contemptuous of ourselves for having gone. And not pleased with the entourage of a democratic Minister.

Very different, the George Hamiltons'. Here the party consisted of the Neville Lytteltons, Lady Arthur Russell, the Herbert Jekylls, Sir Francis Mowatt – persons belonging to much the same set as the Asquith party, though of a dowdier hue. But the reception in the cosy library was homely and the dinner without pretentiousness – the George Hamiltons treating us as if we were part of a family party – no attempt to shine, just talking about the things that interested each of us in a quiet simple way. It would have been almost impossible to 'show off', so absolutely sincere and quiet was the tone. And yet the conversation was full of interest and lingered willingly on each subject. After we ladies had left, Sidney said that he listened with eager interest to a long interchange of official experience between Lord George, Mowatt and Lyttelton as to the administration of the War Office and the relations between Cabinet, War Minister and permanent staff – Jekyll and Sidney listening and occasionally intervening. And, as we drove away, we felt that we had had a restful evening, learnt something and gained stimulus from the refinement and public spirit manifest in our hosts and their guests. The Tory aristocrat [Hamilton] and his wife were, in relation to their class, living the 'simple life'; and the Yorkshire manufacturer's son [Asquith] was obviously 'swelling it', to use the vulgar expression for a vulgar thing. . . .

Beatrice's sister Mary was married to Arthur Playne (1845–1923) and their home was Longfords, near Box, Gloucestershire.

The Webbs were interested in Haldane's scheme of 'voluntary conscription' that eventually became the Territorial Army, seeing in it a step towards the 'half-time' movement – a plan to absorb half the working hours and all the leisure of boys up to eighteen in some sort of training. They were much less favourably disposed towards the Education Bill introduced by the Liberals to placate the dissatisfied Nonconformists, who were still agitating against the concessions to Anglicans and Roman Catholics in the Tory Education Acts.

16 April. [41 Grosvenor Road]
A happy time at Longfords – and some progress with our chapter on the City of London. . . .

35

Mary Playne growing every year more benign: lost all her old cynicism and worldliness – not all her old restlessness. The spirit of religion becomes every day a more potent influence in her life – presently she will be a veritable saint. Will she end in the Catholic Church? There are signs that her inward eyes are turning that way. She prophesies great accessions to the Church universal through the virtual disestablishment of the English Church by the Education Bill if it passes into law. . . .

Sidney thinks the Education Bill a harsh measure, but takes no part in the agitation against it; does not care to discuss it, since it is clear he cannot influence the result. We have no kind of influence, either on Birrell or those behind him, or on any of the parliamentary groups that are likely to carry amendments in committee. And as we belong neither to the Church nor to the Catholics, we have no place in either of the movements in the country against it. If it is defeated, it will be through using the indifference of the bulk of parents and rate-payers to the whole question of religious education, combined with their objection to the cost of buying out the denominational schools. . . . The Catholics are fervent, logical and unanimous: their plea unanswerable, since to them undenominational teaching is the very devil.

Mary Longman was a Fabian social worker with a special interest in women's problems, whom Beatrice employed as a research assistant in the first months of the Royal Commission's work.

15 May. [41 Grosvenor Road]
A baffling time, divided between superintending two secretaries at work on the City of London records, and drafting a memo on the policy of the central authority of the Poor Law 1834–47 from Miss Longman's notes. The R.C. lumbers along: chaotic and extravagant in its use of time and money, each committee doing as it seems fit in its own sight. There is a lack of method and discipline with which some of us get impatient, and I fear I sometimes offend by my easygoing ways – intervening when I ought to hold my peace. 'You did not behave nicely yesterday,' said Lord George in kindly reproof. 'You should not have referred to current politics.' So I thanked him warmly for the hint, and I promised to be 'seen and not heard' in future. I find it so difficult to be 'official' in manner. However, I really will try. Dignified silence I will set before me,

except when the public good requires me to come forward. Ah! how hard it is for a quick-witted and somewhat vain woman to be discreet and accurate. One can manage to be both in the written word – but the 'clash of tongues' drives both discretion and accuracy away.

C.S. Loch was emerging as the chief spokesman for stiffening rather than relaxing the Poor Law. Henry Lockwood was a Poor Law inspector in London. Lady Elcho (1864–1937) was a prominent society hostess. Her home was at Stanway in Gloucestershire, where she often entertained her close friend Arthur Balfour. She became Lady Wemyss when her husband succeeded to his father's title in 1914. Their London home was in Cadogan Square.

22 May. [41 Grosvenor Road]
C. S. Loch completely lost his temper yesterday at my cross-examination of Lockwood. . . . What makes him angry is that the enquiry is drifting straight into the *causes of destitution* instead of being restricted to the narrower question of: *granted destitution is inevitable, how can we best prevent pauperism?* And the answer that is being extracted by our enquiry into the causes of destitution takes the form of *more regulation and more public provision without the stigma of pauperism* – probably compulsory provision which *must* be given and *cannot* be refused. . . .

Lady Elcho – a kindly, sympathetic, interested but somewhat weary woman: her friendship with 'Mr Arthur' [Balfour], as he is called in that set, the romance of her life (?), but a romance which has become somewhat faded. Now, at any rate, no sign of anything beyond old friendliness between them, 'Mr Arthur' having had a good many fantasies, I imagine. We met him at dinner at her house the other night, and I was allotted to him. If it were not for the glamour that envelops a man of charm who has been Prime Minister and the leader of the great party – should I like him? One thing, I know: I should dislike the set.

Theresa (1852–93) had been married to Alfred Cripps (1852–1941), lawyer and Liberal M.P. Blanche (1851–1905), had been married to William Harrison Cripps (1850–1923), a fashionable surgeon.

Lawrencina Holt (1845–1906), known as Lallie, had been very depressed by family difficulties and had taken to cocaine. Beatrice described Lallie's troubles with her son and her husband – Robert Holt (1832–1908), a wealthy Liverpool merchant. She had erred in doing too much for the children, Beatrice thought, and had ambitiously raised her husband 'from an honest little tradesman of narrow conventions, into a vainglorious egotist gloating on an unearned social esteem'. Turning to the Royal Commission, Beatrice noted that all her fellow commissioners were chasing their own hares, and concluded that 'quite clearly there is no one directing purpose shaping the enquiry to a predetermined end'; she wondered 'which of the many conflicting or diverging purposes will prevail'. Sidney was coming up to his last term on the L.C.C., and his main interest was in fostering the educational changes he had launched while devoting most of his time to helping Beatrice as her adviser and amanuensis. Bramdean is a village in Hampshire close to Brockwood Park, the home of Beatrice's sister, Georgina Meinertzhagen (1850–1914).

29 May. [Bramdean]
Another sister [Lallie], our eldest, passed away. . . . When I think of our three dear dead ones – Theresa, Blanche and Lallie – the one quality that seems to bind them together in one's memory is impulsive generosity. In Theresa this was combined with charm, graciousness, refinement, artistic talent and a saint-like asceticism; in Blanche it was marred by deficient intellect and wild melancholy, though she was possessed of mad talent and beauty of form and expression; in Lallie there was executive ability of uncommon degree, a vivid force and picturesqueness of speech, but ugliness of body and uncouthness of manner. But in each one, real genuine generosity towards individuals and towards causes shone out as the dominant note in feeling and conduct. They each and all *spent themselves* for others – children, husband, dependants and the community at large. Let those of us who have still the day in which to work keep up this family tradition, and find our place with them, in the world's all-embracing memory of what is good in humanity, in adding our mite to the world's generosity of feeling, of thought, of action.

Georgina Meinertzhagen was married to Daniel (Dee) Meinertzhagen (1842–1910), a banker. They had moved to Brockwood from Mottisfont Abbey after the death of their eldest son in 1898. A wrangler was a person awarded a first-class degree in mathematics at Cambridge.

15 June. [Bramdean]
The last days of the Whitsun recess spent in this little country hamlet, close to Brockwood Park – whither we came for rest and work and a sight of Georgie and her children. A happy peaceful time: good work done, though less of it than we hoped – the 'City of London', with our wealth of material, proving a longer job than

we expected. . . . Still, it is important to get on – we are becoming elderly and our days of work are obviously limited. *Poverty and Crime* must be out before the Report of the Royal Commission. . . .

All this while Sidney is giving at least half his time and thought – perhaps more – to the organization of secondary and higher education in London. This year, four wranglers (Camb.) from the L.C.C. scholars selected nine years ago! He is very happy in the success of his unseen work – all his little schemes, or at any rate the most dearly cherished of them, have come off – the scholarship ladder, the innumerable educational institutions, secondary to university, which he has kept alive and under a semi-voluntary management; and, lastly, the London School of Economics has grown in size, significance and 'grace'. These successes are a constant source of half-conscious satisfaction and make up a good part of his happiness. . . .

The Meinertzhagen *ménage* at Brockwood is happier than when we were here two years ago. The arrangement by which Dee lives at The Albany, quite apart from Georgie, with occasional visits from his daughters, and week-ends for himself at Brockwood, works most peacefully. Georgie has made Brockwood into a charming home, Dee having relinquished the whole management of it to her. . . . But the atmosphere of Brockwood is still purely materialist – no religion and no public spirit – very little philanthropy. As to religion, the situation is positively comic. Dee, who never goes to Church in London, goes regularly here for 'example's sake' to the Bramdean Church – neither his parish church nor the one nearest Brockwood – because the walk to it lies through his own land, which he likes to inspect. But, as Georgie says, someone has to go with him, because, as he does not attempt to listen to the service, and becomes wholly absorbed in business calculation, he forgets to stand up or sit down in the proper place. . . . Georgie herself, who has a sort of vague mystical faith in prayer and aspiration, stays at home, because she is not strong enough to sit through a long country service and sermon. . . . The Meinertzhagen household is, I think, typical of the state of mind of many of the wealthy middle classes with reference to religion: it is the 'country house' attitude – complete indifference tempered by social convention. . . .

After a 12.30 lunch I cycled off in a grey windy afternoon, up the Winchester hill along the ridge of the highland towards West

Meon, through fields of red clover and hay grass, under avenues of beach and fir – delighting in the sense of a holiday and in the physical vigour springing from the morning's rest. This country-side is like a beautiful but pale and somewhat stately lady – the white undertone yielded by the chalk, and the long unbroken lines of undulating down and wide stretches of valley, lack warmth and interest unless the landscape is flushed with sun or made glorious by thunder clouds. Still there is a sort of gentle unassuming sympathy – restful and meditative – in the rolling hill and dale. . . .

G.P. Gooch (1873–1968) was a Liberal politician and historian. H.W.C. Carr-Gomm (1877–1939) was a Liberal M.P. 1906–18, and private secretary to Campbell-Bannerman. Beatrice Creighton, born 1874, was the daughter of the Webbs' close friend Mandell Creighton, then Bishop of London. Sir Julius Wernher (1850–1922) was a South African millionaire and philanthropist. He gave money to found the Imperial Technical Institute, based on the Technical High School at Charlottenburg, near Berlin.

2 July. [41 Grosvenor Road]
A freakish dinner – arranged before Lallie's death, and one I did not like to put off. Balfour and Lady Elcho to meet four young Liberal M.P.s – Masterman, Simon, Gooch and Carr-Gomm, with Sir Oliver Lodge and Beatrice Creighton thrown in. I am wondering whether Balfour will recover his position as a leader; at present there is a note of contempt in most persons' opinion of him, his charm and reputation for charm increasing the irritation at his intellectual indecision. I asked him after the dinner, when we sat on the balcony, whether there had ever been a cause (apart from general good government) about which he had been really concerned: 'Have you ever wished to bring about another state of affairs to what at present exists?' I insisted, perhaps somewhat rudely. 'I am a conservative,' he rejoined quietly. 'I wish to maintain existing institutions.' Then presently he added: 'There are some things about which I have been keen: take for instance the clause in the Scotch Free Church Bill enabling the established Church of Scotland to change its formulas – freeing it from the dead hand – I worked very hard to secure that.' I sympathized and we dropped the subject. Afterwards, I wondered whether it is not exactly this basis of pure conservatism combined with extraordinary ingenuity and resourcefulness in evading demands for advance – whether it is not this combination that leads to an appearance of shiftiness. It is

characteristic that the liberty for an association to change its opinion seemed among the most important reforms to be secured. I imagined he might have added a Catholic university for Ireland – another reform affecting the opinion or the creeds of men – all in the direction of tolerance for varieties of opinion. Perhaps faith in this sort of freedom of mental development is the most positive side of Balfour's political opinions. Mixed up with his conservatism and with his over-subtle opportunism there is a solid layer of Whig doctrine. By birth and tradition he is a conservative, by conviction he is a Whig, whilst by temperament he is a manipulator, delighting in finesse. An unpopular combination just at present.

Altogether I have had this week thirty persons to lunch or dinner, as well as half a dozen in the afternoon – nearly all of the lot being on business of some sort. Assistant commissioners coming to be instructed in the art of investigation and the scope of their enquiry, the secretary of the Poor Law Commission to talk over the former, a German lady needing information on education, a clever woman requiring advice as to her career; also, nephews, nieces. For the next six weeks my days will be taken up in much the same way, tiring and leading to little result that is apparent to oneself. But I never like to refuse to see those who think I can help them when they are in any way connected with my side of things. It all distracts one from our main work.

Dined at the house of a millionaire – Sir Julius Wernher, Bath House [Piccadilly]. We went there partly because of Sidney's connection with him over the 'Charlottenburg' scheme, partly from curiosity to see inside such an establishment, partly because we both respect and like the man. He is a German giant, not unduly self-indulgent and a real drudger at his business. But he is better than that. He is noted for generosity inside his own circle, regarding the South African commercial world as something for which he is responsible, perpetually carrying the weaker men on his back. He is good, that is to say, to his own community. He is also public-spirited in his desire for the efficiency of all industry, and the advancement of its technique. Moreover, he is obviously unconcerned with social ambition or desire to push himself by his wealth. 'I have no time, even to know that I am wealthy: the only result of my millions is to make me dread being introduced to a new person lest they should begin to beg from me. The really happy person is the man with £10,000 a year, reputed to have £2,000.'

41

But though our host was superior to his wealth, our hostess and her guests were dominated by it. She was not a bad sort, an able woman with a clever tongue, direct and good-natured by disposition. But she had become a mere slave to the consciousness of her wealth; her possessions and the petty power that these gave her were always with her, making her restless, rushing about from place to place, hard-headed, thinking only of material things. Her thoughts are centred in the admiration of others for her millions. Consequently, both in person and manners and speech she was essentially ugly: her dress crude in colour and *outré* in form, covered with extravagant and ill-assorted jewels, her talk of nothing else but herself and her possessions, and her expression a curious mingling of boldness and uneasiness. The company was composed either of financial magnates or of the able 'hangers-on' of a magnate. The setting, in the way of rooms and flowers and fruit and food and wine and music, and pictures and works of art, was hugely overdone – wealth! wealth! wealth! was screamed aloud wherever one turned. And all the company were living up to it, or bowing down before it. There might just as well have been a Goddess of Gold erected for overt worship – the impression of worship in thought, feeling and action could hardly have been stronger. Always excepting Wernher himself. He looked wistful as I suggested that the fallacy of wealth was becoming apparent. 'My husband and I have all the wealth we could possibly make use of without diminishing our delightful happiness. Four private secretaries on £1,000 a year: a fifth would break me down. What you enjoy', I ventured to add, 'is not your wealth but the power it gives you to organize the affairs of the world.' 'Yes, perhaps that is so,' he answered wearily. . . .

During the summer Wells had been writing *The Future in America* and seeking allies against the Old Gang. The reception of his novel *In the Days of the Comet*, which foresaw great changes in society brought about by a magical gas, was disappointing; reviewers commented on his advocacy of common property and common wives. On 12 October, in a lecture on 'Socialism and the Middle Classes', he advocated endowed motherhood and sexual freedom. He attacked the 'unimaginative' Webbs as 'district visitors' whose socialism lacked 'any warmth to qualify their arrogant manners'. Franklin Henry Giddings (1855–1931) was professor of sociology at Columbia University. This period of 'muck-raking' in America saw the appearance of *Frenzied Finance* by T.W. Lawson (1857–1921), an attack on the Amalgamated Copper Company published in 1904, and *The Jungle* (1906), a sensational novel in which Upton Sinclair (1878–1968) exposed conditions in the Chicago meat industry. Edward

Pease (1857–1955) was secretary of the Fabian Society and one of its founders. Charlotte Shaw (1857–1943), the wealthy wife of GBS, was a member of the Fabian Reform Committee.

15 July. [41 Grosvenor Road]
Spent Sunday with the H.G. Wellses at Sandgate. The friendship between them and us is undergoing the strain of a certain disillusionment. He is, we think, grown in self-confidence, if not conceit, as to his capacity to settle all social and economic questions in general, and to run the Fabian Society in particular, with a corresponding contempt for us poor drudgers, who go on plodding painfully at administration on the one hand and investigation on the other, without, as he thinks, producing any betterment. He dreams of a great movement of opinion which would render all this detailed work unnecessary, which would jump all obstacles, whether brought about by man's selfishness or by his ignorance. He distrusts the devious and narrow ways whereby we reach one position after another – minute steps in advance – when, as he thinks, the position could be rushed at one sweep. Hence he is delighted with America and Americans. Two months rushing about from New York to Washington, Philadelphia to Chicago, has convinced him that America is much nearer the promised land of economic equality than we in England are: that ideas are understood by a great number of people and that all else is unimportant. The new sociologists like Giddings and the 'literature of exposure' like *Frenzied Finance* and *The Jungle* are far more likely to force on a complete and right change than our laboured investigations and Sidney's perpetual presence in committee rooms of L.C.C. and Senate, or Edward Pease's continuous guidance of Fabian representatives on boards of guardians and town councils. All this is so contrary to our view of the relative state of America and England and of the relative hopefulness of various places that there is little room for friendly and hopeful discussion. And the difference of opinion is heightened by his desire to discredit the old methods of the Fabian and supersede them by methods of his own. About these methods he will say, at present, nothing: all we can extract from him is an animus against Pease and a desire to oust him from the secretaryship. He seems confident that Sidney and GBS will also have to retire if they do not fall in with his scheme, and is constantly apologizing to us in advance for this sad necessity. To all

of which we return a puzzled attitude: Sidney and GBS would gladly give up the leadership of the Fabian to younger hands – they are so full of work that they would be relieved if someone else would take it over and push ahead on other lines. But they cannot yet see what lines Wells is going on – he proposes no new departures that he himself is willing to carry out. Moreover, by his curious combination of secretiveness and insolence, he has roused furious hostility among some of the members who do not happen to be his personal friends (as GBS, Charlotte and we are), or who attach more importance than we do to holding a prominent position in the Fabian Society. What exactly will come of the movement seems, at present, doubtful. I incline to the prophecy that five years will see H.G. Wells out of the Society. He has neither the patience nor the good manners needed for co-operative effort – and just at present his conceit is positively disabling. A little failure – and failure, I think, will be his fate – in the course of the next ten years may sober him as it has sobered Hewins, or it may embitter him. It will be interesting to watch. He is in a state of unstable equilibrium – that is clear.

It would be interesting to know what exactly constitutes Wells's disillusionment with regard to 'the Webbs'. But generally, I think he would say that I was not so good and Sidney was not so able as he had previously thought. He suspects me of a kind of worldliness – a suspicion aroused by my association with such reactionaries as A.J.B., smart ladies, bishops. I think he believes I am playing a long deep game of personal advancement into the High Places of the World. He has no such suspicion of Sidney's motives: but he thinks that Sidney is not a strong enough character and intellect to withstand my sophistical and Jesuitical methods of reasoning. Compared to his former estimate of us, Sidney is weak, and I am bad, and we are partially deceiving the world and ourselves as to our motives and methods. All of which attitude on his part interests me. It would require a good deal of self-assurance to feel confident that his suspicion was entirely groundless, though one must forge ahead without bothering too much about the state of one's soul. As for Sidney's will-power and capacity – that, I think, can take care of itself. . . . I am much more his instrument than he is mine.

On 29 July Beatrice wrote to Mary Playne complaining of the 'amazingly incompetent' way in which the Royal Commission 'rumbled along', wasting time, energy and money through 'having no fixed procedure and no trained person in any position of responsibility'. She estimated that it was spending about £12,000 a year, and that she could get 'more information and better verified information' for a tenth of that sum. Amy Spencer was looking into the administrative practices of boards of guardians and Mildred Bulkeley, a research secretary who worked for Beatrice until 1912, was reading through sets of their minutes. Dr Louisa Woodcock was considering medical relief, and Marion Phillips (1881–1932) – who eventually became Chief Woman Officer of the Labour Party – worked on public health problems. Beatrice also started an enquiry into the 200,000 children on outdoor relief. The Commission appointed Dr Ethel Williams (1863–1948), who later became president of the British Federation of Medical Women, to supervise this enquiry. Eventually the Commission paid the salaries of the women Beatrice had originally engaged. It also employed two assistant commissioners on its own study of the destitution caused by unemployment. Cyril Jackson (1863–1924) was chief inspector of the Board of Education 1903–06, and a member of the L.C.C. 1907–13; John Pringle (1872–1938), who later became secretary of the C.O.S., was at this time a curate in the East End.

17 July. [41 Grosvenor Road]
Yesterday we had a field day at the R.C. discussing our future procedure. . . . At the afternoon sitting we roamed over the whole field – spreading out our enquiry into the furthermost points that any individual commissioner desired to reach, Lord George always giving way with a weak protest against doing any one investigation 'too thoroughly'. I confined my effort to keeping open for further consideration questions which he, or the Commission as a whole, wished to close: old age pensions, the condition of the 200,000 children now receiving outdoor relief, the administration of relief by boards of guardians, and more important than all, the relation of Poor Law medical treatment to public health.

This is a new hare that I have recently started. In listening to the evidence brought by the C.O.S. members in favour of restricting medical relief to the technically destitute, it suddenly flashed across my mind that what we had to do was to adopt the exactly contrary attitude, and make medical inspection and medical treatment compulsory on all sick persons – to treat illness, in fact, as a public nuisance to be suppressed in the interests of the community. . . . I am elaborating an enquiry of my own – with funds supplied by Charlotte Shaw – so I merely said that I should, in the course of the next six months, present the Commission with a further memorandum. 'You might elaborate with a few more details the one you have already promoted,' said Lord George in a frightened way. And so it was left. At present I am engaged in finding a medical woman to undertake the enquiry, and on rousing the interest of the M.O.H.s throughout the country.

Meanwhile, despairing of any action on the part of the Commission, I have undertaken (unknown to them) an investigation into the administration of boards of guardians. . . . I therefore look forward to at least three memos handed in by me: (1) Central policy; (2) The relation of poor law medical relief to public health; (3) Administration of relief by boards of guardians, as well as the report of the assistant commissioners on the relation of bad conditions of employment to pauperism. On these documents I shall base my report.

My relations to my fellow commissioners are now quite pleasant. I am completely detached from them and yet on most agreeable terms. I just take my own line, attending for just as long as it suits me, cross-examining witnesses to bring out my points and conducting the enquiries that I think important, independent of the Commission's work. The lines of reform both in constitution and policy are gradually unfolding themselves to me. Whether I shall embody them in a report of my own, or give up part of my way in order to bring the whole Commission along, will be a question of expediency and delicate negotiation — about which nothing can at present be foreseen.

William Jennings Bryan (1860–1925) was an American Democrat, twice beaten for the Presidency. The Webbs had met him in 1903. Horace Plunkett (1854–1932) was an Irish M.P. until 1900 and a wealthy enthusiast for the Irish Co-operative Movement.

31 July. [41 Grosvenor Road]
. . . On Saturday a luncheon party to meet Mr W.J. Bryan, Sydney Buxton, Horace Plunkett. Exactly the same impression as before of the wide-mouthed Democrat — upright and kindly but infantile in his administrative notions. Thought he could solve the question of administration by allotting all offices after each election to the political parties according to their voting strength. Was going to parcel out all the railways among the states. Proposed to deal with trusts by making it penal to do more than 50 per cent of the trade in one article. Sydney Buxton appeared quite a statesman comparatively. Mrs Bryan a plain

middle-aged woman of the assertive American type, full of the political shibboleths and self-deceptions of the ordinary American. Bryan took very much the same view as H.G. Wells of the prospects of great social reforms in America – with this difference, that he is not a collectivist. All good is to come by ultra-democratic machinery – election, election, election, the cure for all evils.

VOLUME 26

The Webbs spent August at the house the Bertrand Russells had built near Oxford in 1905. They were working on the second volume of *English Local Government*. Harley Granville-Barker (1877–1946), an actor and playwright who appeared in and promoted Shaw's plays when he managed the Court theatre in 1903 and after, had married the actress Lillah McCarthy (1875–1960) in March 1906 (they divorced in 1918). Alfred Milner (1854–1925) was a civil servant who became High Commissioner for South Africa in 1897. His imperialist policy prepared the way for the Boer War. Leonard Courtney (1832–1918) was a Liberal Unionist M.P. married to Beatrice's sister Kate (1847–1929).

4 September. [Lower Copse, Bagleywood]
Five weeks passed like one day – all the more like one day because even the sun, moon and starlit nights have been continuous – the darkness just sufficient for the five hours' sleep. A happy day, with no cares, no sorrows, no irritation, just the interest of our work, each other's companionship, pleasant converse with friends and dreamy restful hours in the garden and the wood, or walking or cycling through lanes and by sleepy villages, wandering by the river or gazing at church towers and empty Oxford colleges. The net result: Volume I through the press, the whole material for the two pivotal chapters of Volume II sorted, together with our ideas as to the substance and order of these chapters . . . the circular to the M.O.H.s sent out, some hundred replies received, the plan of the investigation of the relation of Poor Law medical relief and public health settled with Dr Woodcock; the article on the birth-rate written (I contributing only part of the final section of it), articles on factory legislation and trade unions finished by Sidney for Mackinder's encyclopaedia; three boards of guardians attended, five Poor Law institutions inspected by me – not a bad record for five weeks' holiday time. And we do not feel fagged. We are both

in excellent health and good spirits, having really 'lazed' considerably.

Among the friends who have visited us are the Granville-Barkers, he staying for ten days, she for Sunday. G.B. is a most attractive person, young and good-looking – good-looking in a charming refined fashion, with a subtle intellectual expression – faculties more analytic than artistic? I think with self-control, industry, freedom from vulgar desires and common fears – with varied interests, good memory; a sharp observer of human nature and above all [with] a delicate appreciation of music, poetry and art – a medley of talents of which I do not yet see a very definite whole. He has not yet emancipated himself from GBS's influence or found his own soul. I think what he lacks is warmth of feeling – he is cold, with little active pity or admiration, or faithful devotion. A better acquaintance than a friend, a better friend than a husband. At least that is his pose, and it is difficult in ten days' uneventful companionship – a companionship of talk not acts – to distinguish the pose from the reality.

She is a strikingly handsome lady, also hard-working and dutiful – a puritan, I think, by temperament; her acting is a craft, not an art. Otherwise, I fear she is not otherwise than commonplace, and he has all the appearance of being bored by her after two months' marriage. Her little actress ways – the gush, the over-emphasis, the odd effect of *hardness* which seems to follow from the perpetual publicity of an actress's life – are to me distressingly unattractive, not to be counterbalanced by the really fine form and colouring of her person.

We took G.B. to see Lord Milner. An old Tudor house, giving almost the impression of an inhabited ruin, a garden surrounded by a deserted backwater of the Thames, seemed a fit setting for that stern, rigid man, brooding over the South African victory – or disaster? At first he was constrained; but after lunch he unbent and, from democracy to the present government, from the present government to their policy in South Africa, from this to the war and its results, we drifted on until we reached intimate conversation. We tried to cheer him by suggesting that after all the friction and abuse after the war and its devastation, there still remained the two republics merged in the Empire. That was (if you believed in its rightness) a sufficient accomplishment for one man. This government would not last more than four years and they could undo little

48

of the past. But he would not be comforted. 'It is well for you to be optimistic,' he retorted. 'You say you are always in a minority, but events are moving your way; whilst my house of cards is tumbling down.' And then he explained that he had started all kinds of elaborate enterprises and experimental governmental organizations of agriculture and industry in South Africa, whereby the country might really become independent of gold production; all this good work would, under self-government, certainly be dismantled — salaries reduced, officials dismissed, plant disused.

He practically admitted the mistake of the introduction of Chinese labour (given the crass stupidity of the English electors and wicked lies of the radical agitators), but he defended its introduction as inherently right on the ground that you had to create material wealth before you could give the start to the higher things. 'Blood and money' (the philosophy that GBS tried to dramatize in Undershaft's character and career) had, in fact, been the underlying philosophy of Milner's government. Like Mackinder, he seems to me to enormously overestimate the value of the purely material forces; he is willing to rely on these forces though they be necessarily joined with at least a temporary demoralization of character. Milner, though a public-spirited, upright and disinterested man, does not believe in the supremacy or even in the relevance of the spiritual side of things — goodness is a luxury to be arrived at after a course of money-getting by whatever means, and of any blood-letting that may be necessary to the undertaking. As I listened to his feeble, forceful voice, watched his rigid face and wrinkled narrow brow, noted the emphasis on plentiful capital, cheap labour and mechanical ingenuity, I thought that perhaps, after all, there was some justification for Leonard Courtney's hard epithet, 'a lost mind'. A god and a wife would have made Milner, with his faithfulness, persistency, courage, capacity and charm, into a great man: without either he has been a tragic combination of success and failure. 'He would have been made by being loved,' summed up G.B. as we rode away. . . .

Alice Balfour (1850–1936) was the younger and unmarried sister of Arthur Balfour. Eleanor Sidgwick (1845–1936) was the older of the Balfour sisters, and the widow of the Cambridge philosopher Henry Sidgwick (1838–1900). She was principal of Newnham College, Cambridge, 1892–1910. Lady Elizabeth (Betty) Balfour (1867–1945), wife of Gerald Balfour, was a well-known Society hostess and a student of social problems. Lady Frances Balfour

(1858–1931) was the daughter of the Duke of Argyll and the wife of Eustace Balfour. H.J. Tennant (1865–1935) was a Liberal M.P. and brother of Margot Asquith. His wife, May, was the first woman factory inspector. Henry George Percy, Duke of Northumberland (1846–1918), was one of the greatest landowners in England, and Alnwick Castle in Northumberland was his family seat. His wife was Lady Edith Campbell, sister of Frances Balfour. The 'Little White People' are the Eloi, the charming but purposeless creatures in Wells's novel *The Time Machine*, who are preyed upon by the cannibalistic Morlocks – a parable on decadent intellectuals and a degenerate proletariat. The Balfour home, Whittingehame, was in East Lothian, not far from Edinburgh. The Webbs were touring to study local government archives. In 1901, Beatrice had been converted to the food reform diet of A.C.F. Rabagliati.

16 September. [Whittingehame]

An unattractive mansion with large formal rooms and passages, elaborate furniture and heavy luxury totally without charm, somewhat cold in the fireless September phase. The atmosphere of gracious simplicity, warm welcome, intellectual interest, is all the more strikingly personal to the family that inhabits it. The four women – sisters and sisters-in-law – are in themselves remarkable: Alice Balfour neither brilliant nor very capable, but singularly loving, direct and refined, with talents both artistic and scientific wholly sacrificed to the endless detail entailed by her brother's political career and patriarchal establishment. Mrs Sidgwick, weirdly silent but also the soul of veracity and moral refinement – open-minded, too, in a limited way. Lady Betty (Gerald's wife) a woman of quite unusual delightfulness, good to look at, sweet to listen to, original in purpose and extraordinarily gracious in disposition. Even Lady Frances, whom I expected to dislike, was attractive in her impulsive indiscretions and straightforward friendliness, with her vivid wit and large experience of political affairs. As kind as kind could be were these four women to me on the day of our arrival. In the afternoon 'Prince Arthur' arrived from North Berwick – a veritable prince of the establishment – the medieval and saintly knight (Gerald) and the bore (Eustace) completing the party. Some dozen children hovered around at intervals but did not join us.

What shall I say of our visit? Too self-consciously Arthur's 'latest friend' to be quite pleasant, the party each night becoming a watched tête-à-tête between us two, the rest of the company sitting round, as Sidney said, 'making conversation'. In fact, the great man is naturally enough too completely the centre of the gathering, without perhaps deserving that position of pre-eminence – all the family worshipping him and waiting on his fancies. 'A Prime Minister of the Little White People', I said sometimes to myself, 'without any guiding social purpose, floated to leadership without any strong desire to lead anywhere in particular.' Charm he has, almost too obviously, a genius for destructive criticism of the logic of other people's ideas, but not the remotest desire to verify his own by testing his order of thought by the order of things. It is always theories that he is building up or pulling down in his mind, when he is not merely playing the game of office-holding or office-getting. Does he ever think of the state of affairs and wish to alter it? He was contemplating a treatise on economics. I suggested that there were only two things to be done in economics: either a mere sweeping away of fallacies – comparatively easy and somewhat futile, but a task for which he was extraordinarily fitted; or a concrete study of phenomena – say, the course of trade and the effect of different kinds of taxation on it – a task that demanded the devotion of a lifetime, and therefore one which he could *not* undertake. But I pressed him to undertake a quite other work – a careful account of his own experience of political life and great administrative affairs, to be published after his retirement and, perhaps, even after his death. But I doubt whether he takes my suggestion either negatively or positively. I learnt little about him on this visit except that he is self-absorbed and lonely, seldom consulting anyone. 'Brother Arthur is independent of human companionship,' sighed Lady Betty, somewhat hurt, perhaps, that even Gerald was not admitted to his complete confidence.

Gerald is really a more attractive nature, though far less sub-stantial than Arthur – a dreamy poetic metaphysical soul, saintly in his motives and subtle in his thoughts, but with small capacity for transacting business and lacking broad sympathies. He is unspoilt, has none of the self-consciousness and egotism which lies beneath Arthur's perfect manner, has not developed the cunning of the leader, fearing deposition, or the sentimentality of the lifelong philanderer, never thoroughly in love. For philanderer, refined and consummate, is 'Prince Arthur', accustomed always to make others feel what he fails to feel himself. How many women has he inspired with a discontent for their life and life companion, haunted with the perpetual refrain, 'If only it had been so'. Not a good or wholesome record, and demoralizing to the man himself – and not a worthy substitute for some sort of social fervour. But this is a harsh judgement, one aspect only of the man. Deeper down there are other and better things, but they were hidden from me in these hours of philandering!

From the glamour and charm of Whittingehame we cycled with Lady Betty to Berwick – a happy ride chatting over 'Brother Arthur', Gerald and his literary and philosophical tastes, social questions – altogether the opening of a pleasant friendship? The dirty crowded railway station from which we saw her off to Whittingehame was a fit prelude to our five days at Berwick. . . .

A Sunday at Hutton Castle with the Jack Tennants, restful and unexciting, and then on to Alnwick, [where] we found useful material in the records and enjoyed the novelty of lunching with the ducal family [the Percys] – a courtesy we owed to Lady Frances Balfour. This glimpse of 'high life' interested us. Entombed in that magnificent pile exists a family of exceptional worthiness. The present chief is just a commonplace stupid Englishman – all the commoner and stupider because he feels himself to be a Duke. He is 'got up', as Sidney remarked, 'like a stage Englishman of early Victorian time' – red whiskers, clean-shaven upper lip and chin, well-fitting countrified clothes, self-righteous smug expression, formal manners – above all, stiff and silent. The Duchess is a humpy little person with delicate features, powdered and dressed like a stage Duchess in soft satins and laces, with the manners of a great lady but more kindly and far more distinguished than her lord. Poor little woman, she looks sad and mentally starved – her soul, which has its charm, pining away in its isolation – an outstanding contrast to her strong-minded vivid sister Lady Frances. The latter has lived by her wits; the other has cut her wits down to suit the temperament of her intolerable husband and still more intolerable position. Two or three badly mannered and dull girls represent the younger members of the family present on this occasion. An aristocratic old couple (friends of the family) [and] a heavy, bored-looking tutor or private secretary completed the party that sat down to an elaborate luncheon waited upon by six man-servants and served in a palatial banqueting chamber.

Of course, I got nothing to eat but peas and apricot tart – the six manservants, finding I did not take the regulation dishes, refused to hand me anything else – denied me the bread sauce and the plain pudding or another piece of bread. His Grace was far too much absorbed in his own dignity to note that I was unprovided with the necessaries of life. The poor man was in fact struggling to keep us at a distance, scared by the assumed attempt of these notable socialists to get access to the records of his manor courts. He had, owing to the pressure of Lady Frances, secured for us access to the records of the Alnwick Borough (now a private company of freemen), and he was determined that he would do no more. This determination made him, at first, almost discourteous to me – which I, discovering, turned round and talked to the daughters. At the other end of the table I heard Sidney discoursing most pleasantly with the Duchess. Indeed, if it had not been for ourselves it seems to me the party would have eaten its meal in heavy silence. When the Duke awoke to the fact that we were not otherwise than well-bred people, not likely to push our desires on an unwilling host, and that we were ready to talk pleasantly on other subjects, he relaxed a little and after lunch discussed county council business with Sidney – self-important and stupid but not otherwise objectionable. . .

All through September, the members of the Fabian Enquiry had been trying to prevent Wells turning it into what Charlotte Shaw on 4 September called 'a Committee of Public Safety to try the Executive'. On the previous day Sidney Webb had written Wells a reasonable letter, urging him not to ask for too much too quickly; and Shaw wrote to complain that the wrangle was lapsing from principle into personalities. But Wells remained on the rampage, campaigning for his views on sexual freedom and for the defeat of his Fabian critics. James Ramsay MacDonald (1866–1937) had been a dissident member of the Fabian Society and critical of the Webbs over the founding of the London School of Economics. He was now the effective leader of the emergent Labour Party. 'Trusty and well-beloved' is the conventional phrase used in appointing royal commissioners. 'The Souls' were a clique of country-house aristocrats – including Balfour, Lady Desborough and Lady Elcho – who had intellectual aspirations.

1 October. [41 Grosvenor Road]
First meeting of the Poor Law Commission after the recess – all very friendly – to discuss our future plans. Lord George brought forward some proposals . . . to be considered by two committees into which the whole Commission might be divided. . . .

As I wanted to keep my Monday morning free, and as I thought the time had not arrived for pushing my views, I quietly said that I did not feel sufficiently at one with the Commission to co-operate usefully in the discussion at this early stage, rather giving them to understand that I should have to have my own report. This is the line I am now taking, as I fancy they will be more anxious to meet me if I do so even if I eventually decide to throw in my lot with all the Commission or any section of it. Discussion now is premature and I think a waste of time. But it is pleasant to find that there is no tension between myself and any of the other commissioners. It is generally understood that I am undertaking a good slice of work on documents, exactly as Charles Booth is on statistics. The first part of my memo on central policy is to be circulated to the whole Commission.

The week before the Commission met we had a most pleasant two days with the George Hamiltons at Deal Castle. Certainly those two are the simplest-mannered, kindest and most public-spirited aristocrats I have ever come across – not intellectual but quite open-minded and anxious to understand the point of view of other classes of the community. I think we and they thoroughly like each other in private life – though the chairman of the Royal Commission finds the 'trusty and well-beloved Beatrice Webb, wife of Sidney Webb' somewhat of a handful. He talked much about his former colleagues in late Conservative governments: Dizzy [Disraeli] is his hero, Salisbury's memory he respects, Joe he has a sentiment for as a warm-hearted, impulsive and forceful enthusiast – somewhat of the 'vulgar boss' in his manners, but genuinely a patriot. Toward Arthur Balfour he is cool: thinks that his ingrained laziness encouraged by his contact with the 'brilliant but silly "Souls"' and his tendency to regard politics as only one part of a somewhat amusing game, has resulted in devious ways, disloyal to colleagues and upsetting to the party. Also, his sense of decorum in public affairs was offended by Balfour's 'cliquey' friendships. 'When Salisbury sat at the head of the table at 10 Downing Street we were all addressed by our official designations – the secretary for the Colonies, the president of the Board of Trade, and so on. When Balfour took his place, Cabinets degenerated into cliquey conversations between "Arthur" and "Alfred" and "Bob" and "George" – sometimes almost unintelligible, in their intimate allusions, to the outer circle of the Cabinet. I was one of the old gang of youthful friendships, but I always felt such an atmosphere to be objectionable in the conduct of great affairs by a group of men representing different interests and coming from different sections of the governing class, perhaps in some instances even hostile to one another – at any rate not on the terms of personal friendship'. . . .

On our way back from the Hamiltons' we called on H.G. Wells and his wife at Sandgate – deliberately, to relieve the strain caused by the Wells revolt in the Fabian Society. We found him in a depressed and rather angered state. His own affairs had not been going well. *In the Days of the Comet* had fallen flat: 'Another failure and I should have to go back to journalism for a maintenance.' His committee of the Fabian Society had cut about his report – cut out all the little clever malicious things he had put in about the Executive and watered down his grand schemes. He was angry with the Old Gang, partly because he thought they would carry the Society against him, partly because he thought they might retire from it and leave him all the bother – the unremunerative bother – of 'running it' without them. He did not know which eventuality he would dislike most. He wanted them to accept his ideas and carry them out. Nothing less would satisfy him.

We tried to smooth him down. 'We must not have another J.R. MacDonald either in or outside the Society,' I suggested to Sidney. 'We must remain good friends with H.G. Wells – properly managed, he will count for righteousness in his own way, and it is no good wasting his and our strength in friction.' So we steadily took the position that this little storm in the Fabian Society (as compared to the importance of his work outside the Society, and perhaps even compared to ours – this a mere deduction) was insignificant. We wanted to build up again his consciousness of helpfulness without backing up his iconoclastic fervour. Just at present, in the reaction from exaggerated self-complacency, he is anxious to 'gore' everything and everybody – the Executive of the Fabian Society, the family, the Anglican clergymen, the Nonconformist conscience, the anti-puritan and the believer in regulation. But in the place of these worn-out institutions and new-fangled frauds he has nothing to suggest but a nebulous utopia by H.G. Wells.

18 October. [41 Grosvenor Road]
H.G. Wells gave an address to the Fabian Society on 'Socialism and the Middle Classes', ending up with an attack on 'the family'. Some of the new members welcomed his denunciation, but the

meeting, which was crowded, was against him, for the simple reason that he had nothing constructive to suggest. Since then I have read *In the Days of the Comet*, which ends with a glowing anticipation of promiscuity in sexual relations. The argument is one that is familiar to most intellectuals: it has often cropped up in my own mind and has seemed to have some validity. Friendship between particular men and women has an enormous educational value to both (especially to the woman). Such a friendship is practically impossible (or, at any rate, impossible between persons who are attractive to each other, and therefore most remunerative as objects of study) without physical intimacy. You do not, as a matter of fact, get to know any man thoroughly except as his beloved and his lover — if you could have been the beloved of the dozen ablest men you have known, it would have greatly extended your knowledge of human nature and human affairs. This, I believe, is true of our present rather gross state of body and mind.

But there remains the question whether, with all the perturbation caused by such intimacies, you would have any brain left to think with? I know that I should not, and I fancy that other women would be even worse off in this particular. Moreover, it would mean a great increase in sexual emotion for its own sake and not for the sake of bearing children. And that way madness lies? This is omitting the whole social argument against promiscuity, which is the strongest. Regarding each individual as living in a vacuum with no other obligations than the formation of his or her own character, I still reject 'free love' as a method of development. I suggested to Sidney for consideration whether our philosophy was not tending to the restriction of all physical desires to the maintenance of health in the individual and the race — meaning by health, the longest continued and greatest intensity of mental activity — and to the continuance of the species at its highest level of quality?

H.G. Wells is, I believe, merely gambling with the idea of free love — throwing it out to see what sort of reception it gets, without responsibility for its effect on the character of hearers. It is this recklessness that makes Sidney dislike him. I think it important *not* to dislike him: he is going through an ugly time and we must stand by him for his own sake and for the good of the cause of collectivism. If he will let us, that is to say. I am not sure he is not getting to dislike us in our well-regulated prosperity. . . .

In 1889 Beatrice had signed an anti-suffrage manifesto drafted by the novelist Mrs Humphry Ward. 'I reacted against the narrow outlook and exasperated tone of some of the pioneers of women's suffrage,' Beatrice explained later in *Our Partnership*. 'Also, my dislike of the current parliamentary politics of the Tory and Whig "ins" and "outs" seemed a sort of argument against the immersion of women in this atmosphere. But the root of my anti-feminism lay in the fact that I had never myself suffered the disabilities assumed to arise from my sex.' Her present recantation was related to a new wave of militancy. Frustrated by the failure of the middle-class suffrage societies to make headway and by the refusal of the Liberal government to introduce votes for women, though a majority of M.P.s had pledged their support, Emmeline Pankhurst (1858–1928) broke with the constitutional suffragists led by Millicent Fawcett (1847–1929) and formed the militant Women's Social and Political Union. In October, large bodies of women lobbied M.P.s and several were arrested for riotous behaviour that began a trend towards 'direct action'. On 13 October Christabel Pankhurst (1881–1958) and Annie Kenney (1879–1953) heckled Sir Edward Grey and Winston Churchill at a meeting in Manchester. Beatrice copied her correspondence with Mrs Fawcett into the diary.

5 November. [41 Grosvenor Road]
Here is my formal recantation. For some time I have felt the old prejudice evaporating. And as the women suffragists were being battered about rather badly, and coarse-grained men were saying coarse-grained things, I thought I might as well give a friendly pull to get the thing out of the mud, even at the risk of getting a little spattered myself. What is, perhaps, more likely is that I shall be thought, by some, to be a pompous prig. The movement will stand some of that element now!

The Times, 5 November 1906

Sir – I have just received the enclosed letter from Mrs Sidney Webb. As she generously allows me to make any use of it I like, may I beg the favour of its insertion in *The Times*?

Those who have been working for many years for women's suffrage naturally regard with extreme satisfaction the adhesion to the movement of two of the ablest women who have hitherto opposed it, Mrs Creighton and Mrs Sidney Webb. Mrs Creighton's change of view was chronicled in your columns about a week ago.

Yours obediently,

Millicent Garrett Fawcett

41 Grosvenor Road, Westminster Embankment, 2 November [1906]

Dear Mrs Fawcett,

You once asked me to let you know if I ceased to object to the grant of the electoral franchise to women. The time has come when I feel obliged to do so.

My objection was based principally on my disbelief in the validity of any 'abstract rights', whether to votes or to property, or even to 'life, liberty and the pursuit of happiness'. I prefer to regard life as a series of obligations — obligations of the individual to the community and of the community to the individual. I could not see that women, as women, were under any particular obligation to take part in the conduct of government.

I have been told that the more spiritually-minded Eastern readily acquiesces in the material management of his native country by what he regards as the Anglo-Saxon 'man of affairs'. In the same way, I thought that women might well be content to leave the 'rough and tumble' of party politics to their mankind, with the object of concentrating all their own energies on what seemed to me their peculiar social obligations — the bearing of children, the advancement of learning, and the handing on from generation to generation of an appreciation of the spiritual life.

Such a division of labour between men and women is, however, only practicable if there is, among both sections alike, a continuous feeling of consent to what is being done by government as their common agent. This consciousness of consent can hardly avoid being upset if the work of government comes actively to overlap the particular obligations of an excluded class. If our Indian administrators were to interfere with the religious obligations of Hindus or Mohammedans, British rule in India would, I suppose, come to an end. It seems to me that something analogous to this is happening in the Europe of today with regard to the particular obligations of women. The rearing of children, the advancement of learning, and the promotion of the spiritual life — which I regard as the particular obligations of women — are, it is clear, more and more becoming the main preoccupations of the community as a whole. The legislatures of this century are, in one country after another, increasingly devoting themselves to these subjects. Whilst I rejoice in much of this new development of politics, I think it adequately accounts for the increasing restiveness of women. They are, in my opinion, rapidly losing their consciousness of consent in the work of government and are even feeling a positive obligation to take part in directing this new activity. This is, in my view, not a claim to rights or an abandonment of women's particular obligations, but a desire more effectually to fulfil their functions by sharing the control of state action in those directions.

The episodes of the last few weeks complete the demonstration that it is undesirable that this sense of obligation should manifest itself in unconstitutional forms. We may grant that persistent interruption of public business is lowering to the dignity of public life. But it is cruel to put a fellow citizen of strong convictions in the dilemma of political ineffectiveness or unmannerly breaches of the peace. If the consciousness of non-

58

consent is sufficiently strong, we can hardly blame the public-spirited women who by their exclusion from constitutional methods of asserting their views are driven to the latter alternative, at the cost of personal suffering and masculine ridicule. To call such behaviour vulgar is an undistinguished, and I may say an illiterate, use of language. The way out of this unpleasant dilemma, it seems to me, is to permit this growing consciousness among women – that their particular social obligations compel them to claim a share in the conduct of political affairs – to find a constitutional channel.

This reasoning involves, of course, the admission to the franchise of women as women, whether married or single, propertied or wage-earning.

It is, I feel, due to you that I should tell you of my change of attitude, and I thought you would perhaps be interested in my reasons.

Yours very truly,

Beatrice Webb

21 November. [41 Grosvenor Road]
Haldane came in for a quiet talk – during an enlarged dinner-hour. He is completely absorbed in his office, thinking out the problems of army administration and attempting to adapt the experience of Germany to the character and ways of the English officer. Among other developments there is that connected with the School of Economics – a permanent departmental committee of business magnates, distinguished soldiers, Sidney, and H.J. Mackinder. We are to have forty officers to instruct in business methods and, in return, to receive about £2,000 a year. It all goes to build up the School as the national institution for administrative science, which is perhaps an aspect of the scheme which appeals to us more than the honour of instructing the army. On general politics, Haldane gave us the impression that the P.M. offers no lead to his Cabinet – allows each Minister to go his own way and relies on his personal popularity, and perpetual concessions, when a Whip reports disaffection, to carry his huge majority in favour of the policy, or no policy, of each department. 'But I see little of the House of Commons,' beamingly remarked our War Minister. 'My own department takes up all my thought and time'. . . .

Meanwhile, it looks like a *débâcle* for the Progressive forces at the March L.C.C. election. We always thought that the first Liberal ministry would see us defeated. We are even getting anxious about the Deptford seat. But Sidney is really very unconcerned. 'I have done my level best for London these last fourteen years, and if London does not desire my services there are plenty of causes to which I could devote my energies.' He would like, for instance, to give more time both to our own research and also to the School of Economics. Nevertheless, he is putting a good deal of thought into the organization of the election, and means to make a hard fight for it. Administrative work in the afternoons exactly suits his temperament. And during the last year or so he has been singularly happy in the L.C.C. work. He feels without responsibility for the general Progressive policy, since they have turned him off the Party committee and never consult him. And yet he has got all his pet schemes through and feels that in the last three years he has placed both university and secondary education on a thoroughly sound public foundation. 'Most of my work they can't undo even if I am turned out,' he chuckles to himself. . . .

29 November. [41 Grosvenor Road]
Sidney making up his mind to retire from the L.C.C. in 1910, before we go abroad for our sabbatical year. 'I want to be rid of electioneering and all the devious ways of the elected person. Eighteen years is a fair term of service.' His desires turn more and more to investigation and constructive thinking, and to the organization of the social sciences. Administration he is willing to go on with, if those concerned are ready to have him as a co-opted colleague. 'But I am weary of doing harmless things for ulterior motives: it is, after a time, irksome to distribute prizes because an election is at hand.' He feels he has a right to be fastidious in his methods and single-minded in his aims. A luxury I think we elderly folk ought to be allowed.

30 November. [41 Grosvenor Road]
H.G. Wells, who was staying here for two nights, first justified the last chapters of *In the Days of the Comet* by asserting that it was a work of art and therefore could not be criticized from the standpoint of morality. 'When Michelangelo displayed groups of nude figures in stone or colour, it does not follow that he desired to see all his acquaintances sprawling about without clothes' – a specious retort to my criticism. However, he afterwards admitted that he thought 'free-er love' would be the future relation of the sexes, when we had got over the sordid stage of the masculine proprietorship of the woman. 'At present, any attempt to realize this free-er

love means a network of low intrigue – assumes, and therefore creates, an atmosphere of gross physical desire – but this is only an incident of a morality based on the notion of private property in women. No decent person has a chance of experimenting in free-er love today – the relations between men and women are so hemmed in by law and convention. To experiment, you must be base: hence to experiment starts with being damned.' There is, of course, truth in this argument: it has a negative value – detracts from the argument against free love based on the disastrous results of present-day experience. But I cling to the thought that man will only evolve upwards by the subordination of his physical desires and appetites to the intellectual and spiritual side of his nature. Unless this evolution be the purpose of the race, I despair – and wish only for the extinction of human consciousness. Without this hope, without this faith, I could not struggle on. It is this purpose, and this purpose only, that gives a meaning to the constantly recurring battles of good and evil within one's own nature – and to one's persistent endeavour to find the ways and means of combating the evil habits of the mass of men. Oh! for a Church that would weld into one living force all who hold this faith, with the discipline and the consolations fitted to sustain their endeavour.

As it is, I find myself once or twice a week in St Paul's, listening to the music of the psalms and repeating, with childlike fervour, the words of the old Elizabethan prayers. It is this recreation that sustains me in these days of murky feeling. Perhaps I am suffering from a sort of brain fag. I long for the rest of a long and complete change of thought and scene. But there is no holiday for us until 1910.

The report of the Fabian Reform Committee (largely the work of Wells) and a reply by the Fabian Executive (the ideas of Webb and Shaw) were circulated in advance of an open meeting of members at Essex Hall, just off the Strand, on 7 December. Wells put the case for turning the Society into something more like a socialist party with its own parliamentary candidates. The Executive statement welcomed the idea of rejuvenation but defended the traditional tactic of permeation. The question was whether Wells would be able to use a vote in his favour as a means to gain control of the Society. The meeting was inconclusive and adjourned to a larger and more excited gathering a week later. Even before Shaw delivered a brilliant counter-attack, it was clear that a majority would not follow Wells if it meant driving the Old Gang into the wilderness. When Wells sensed that he was beaten, he withdrew his motion without a vote. Wells perfunctorily maintained his membership until 16 September 1908.

61

15 December. [41 Grosvenor Road]
H.G. Wells made a bad failure of his effort to capture the Fabian Society by turning out 'with dishonour' the old Executive. The odd thing is that if he had pushed his own fervid policy, or rather, enthusiasm for vague and big ideas, without making a personal attack on the Old Gang, he would have succeeded. The Old Gang are anxious to retire – are aware that for propaganda of popular principles they are played out, their work lying in other directions. Wells has just now a great glamour for the young folk, with his idealism for the future and clever biting criticism of the present (including the Executive of the Fabian Society). But his accusations were so preposterous, his innuendoes so unsavoury and his little fibs so transparent, that even his own followers refused to support him, and the 80 per cent of undecided members swayed round to the old leaders. GBS, by a scathing analysis of his whole conduct, threw him finally to the ground and trampled on him, somewhat hardly. With a splutter the poor man withdrew his amendment and announced his intention of falling back into inactivity. An altogether horrid business. There are fine qualities in the man – of heart and intellect – but he has no manners in the broadest meaning of the word, is suspicious, insolent and untruthful when he gets on the war-path. What a lot of training it takes to make a man show good qualities when he is actually in the fight. And except for saints and scoundrels it *is* training and the habit of public affairs that enables a man or a woman to play fair when their passions are roused. Now we shall see whether he will forgive GBS and the Fabians, or become a second J.R. MacDonald in our little world, just at the time when J.R. MacDonald has emerged from that position into brilliant success on another and larger stage. However, his nine months' fight in the Fabian will be excellent 'copy' for Wells: that will console him, I think, in the end. . . .

∽ 1907 ∾

Rosy Dobbs (1865–1949) was Beatrice's youngest sister. Her second husband was George Dobbs (1869–1946), a travel courier. They were living at Cantelope Rd, Bexhill, Sussex, where their youngest child, William Ronald, was born on 29 November 1906.

18 January. [41 Grosvenor Road]

Three vacation weeks at Bexhill in order to be near Rosy Dobbs, who was having a baby with her husband away. Her state is extraordinarily satisfactory. Here she is with six healthy children, all of whom seem likely to be quite as well gifted by nature and quite as well brought up as the children of her sisters. She is wholly devoted to them, thinks of nothing else but their welfare. The home is almost intolerably uncomfortable for outsiders or servants, and not attractive to her husband, but the only effect on the children is to make them squall at home and be good abroad – all of them starting with a low standard of personal comfort. Apart from her real genius for making an uncomfortable and untidy interior, she is an excellent person, and barring occasional screaming fits, she has lost most of her strange manias. Her children, from Noel downwards, are devoted to her, and George apparently is still very fond of her, though suffering a good deal from the disorderly home. There stands the solid fact that the sum total of her life is good – and to think what she might have been, but for a strong family and means to tide her over a bad strain in her nature!

In those three weeks we got through the most difficult chapters of the second volume: as we are now starting on the short chapter on Municipal Disintegration, so far as Sidney's electioneering and my Poor Law Commission permits. Meanwhile the evidence is coming in nicely. My paper on Poor Law medical relief and public health has started a ball rolling and it promises, I think, to be a snowball. The idea of universal medical inspection and medical treatment was already afloat: all I have done is to make the Poor Law Commission into a landing stage. The reports of the assistant commissioners are all pointing away from bad administration as *the* cause of pauperism and towards bad conditions among large classes of the population as the overwhelmingly important fact – conditions which, if we are to check destitution, must be changed; and if we do not see that destitution is checked, it is, thanks to democracy, too late in the day to check pauperism. That is the little lesson the C.O.S. will have to learn from the Commission. But if I am to carry the majority along with me any part of the way, I shall have to be discreet. . . . I am clearly better out of this business: the less I say on abstract questions the better. It only irritates or frightens the bulk of my fellow commissioners. I lack discretion in the 'spoken word': to that extent I lack manners.

18 February. [Beachy Head, Eastbourne]

Alone in Beachy Head Hotel with a hurricane roaring around. Came here with Sidney, completely exhausted – so exhausted that he hardly liked to leave me and return to his electioneering, which is imperative. The exhaustion was brought on by two events: a most tiring five days with the Commission in Yorkshire and a tempestuous upset in the Evidence Committee with regard to my special enquiries. As for the first effort, to a 'short hour' worker like myself it was suicidal – running about from 9 a.m. to 5 p.m., then writing a report, then discussion from 9 to 11 p.m.; consequently no sleep. Moreover, my inveterate social instincts always mean that I lavish entertainment on my companions. I don't simply do my work. Following on that, and partly because I was deliberately or carelessly frank about the enquiries I had on hand, I received from the chairman a somewhat curt and crude request to give up investigating on my own account– a sort of badly delivered message from the Evidence Committee. I seized the opportunity to regularize the whole situation. Whilst gently complaining that my action had been discussed and condemned in my absence, I laid bare all my doings and ended up by saying politely but firmly that I intended to continue, basing myself on the practice of the royal commissions and select committees that I had known. 'Splendid,' said R.B. Haldane (to whom I submitted the correspondence). '*They* won't encounter you in a hurry again.' But all this took a good deal out of me. A Sunday at the Elchos', pleasant enough but late hours and talk, finished up my strength. I lasted out two days' Commission evidence, and a dinner to some medical officers, and then fled here and completely collapsed with sleeplessness and indigestion. If it were not for my reliance on Sidney's strength, I should almost retire from business. I tremble to think how utterly dependent I am on him – both on his love and on his unrivalled capacity for 'putting things through'. When he is late, I get into a panic of fear lest some mishap has befallen him. This fear of losing each other is always present – more with me, I think, than with him. 'I don't think about it,' he often says. Sometimes we try to cheer each other in advance, by remembering that we have had a happiness which death cannot take from us.

What has again been troubling me is the question of social engagements. I go out hardly at all; and except for business interviews at lunch and dinner, entertain even less. But such 'society' as we have, apart from professional society, is tending to become of an aristocratic and fastidious character. This is partly because I like brilliant little parties, and interesting folk versed in great affairs, and partly because my reputation of knowing them helps forward the various works we have on hand. But there are grave disadvantages to this 'dallying with fashion'. Least of them, perhaps, is the spiteful things that are said – partly by envious folk, partly by fanatics. More important is the drain on energy, both financial and personal, that any association with the great world involves. Better clothes, fares to country houses, and most of all the exhaustion of living up to a reputation, or even of 'letting myself go'. It seems ludicrous to bother about the question – the amount we do is very little – and any day we could give that little up without a pang. For all that, my conscience about it is not quite easy. What exactly will be gained by two days' motoring with A.J.B. at Stanway? The only reply is that I have asked him to dinner to meet the two most accomplished of my medical officers of health – the keenest for a new idea – and I have even bored him by sending him the pamphlet on Poor Law medical relief and public health. 'It is the sort of reform that the Conservatives might bring about,' say I – and go to Stanway.

Charles Bowerman (1851–1947), who became secretary to the Trades Union Congress in 1911, had won the Deptford parliamentary seat for Labour in 1906 and was to hold it until 1931. This was one of the first group of seats to be permanently lost by the Liberals to Labour. The Progressives and Moderates were broadly the municipal counterparts in London of the Liberals and Conservatives. Alfred Harmsworth (1865–1922) later Viscount Northcliffe and his brother Harold, later Viscount Rothermere (1868–1940) founded a newspaper empire which included the *Daily Mail*. Cyril Arthur Pearson (1866–1921) founded the *Daily Express* in 1900.

24 February. [41 Grosvenor Road]
A week today and we shall know the fate of the Progressive majority in general, and Sidney in particular. There has been a torrent of malicious denunciation of the Progressives by the yellow press, backed discreetly by the respectable Conservative papers. This time the Moderates are being 'run' by the yellow press – almost 'run' on commercial lines – the *Daily Mail* and the *Daily Express* taking command of the campaign. The aid of the Conservative Party has not been evoked; the L.C.C. Moderates themselves

are completely overlooked – almost snubbed. But the Harmsworth– Pearson gang are shovelling out money, using their daily and evening papers as great advertisement sheets for the Municipal Reformers and against the Progressives. It will be an amazing testimony to 'John Bull's' steady head if there is not a complete smash of the Progressives. How exactly Sidney stands compared to other Progressives it is difficult to say. On the figures of past elections he ought to be in, if there are forty Progressives left – perhaps even if there are thirty. But there is Nonconformist disaffection to his personality, a split between Liberals and Labour over the last parliamentary and borough council elections, leaving soreness; and also the fact that he is identified with high rates – the twenty shillings in the pound cry, which is being used as malignantly as the enemy knows how. On the other hand, he has the Church and the Catholics on his side; he is personally popular with all sections of the Progressive party at Deptford; he has a record of long service; and he is 'distinguished'.

In electioneering, I fear I am useless to him. I loathe the whole business; the mechanical office work tires me out of all proportion to the amount I do; finally, Sidney does not encourage me to sacrifice strength to it. The result is, I fear, a certain feeling of discouragement on the part of the women workers down at Deptford – very naturally, they feel, 'If the wife does not work, why should we?' The fact that I send down a private secretary does not quite make up for it.

If he is beaten I shall regret my apathy – feel that I have been an indifferent helpmate. And a beating I think we are going to get. He is singularly calm, almost indifferent. If the London elector decides against him, he is willing to turn to other work, accepting the check as part of the 'day's work'. Moreover, most public-spirited persons, including ourselves, think it would be better for the other side to come into office: it is clear that some Progressives have to lose seats. There would be a certain abstract justice in Sidney, who has been a bad 'party man', doing so. You can't both push unpopular opinions and remain popular. It is only his skill as a manipulator that has enabled him to do it so far. It would be pleasanter if this state of things would last just three years more. But it is unreasonable to expect it.

Though Sidney held his seat, there was a sharp swing against the Progressives all over London. Beatrice, who never greatly cared for Sidney's L.C.C. colleagues, was not displeased at the defeat of this 'mean lot'. R.C. Phillimore (1871–1919) had been a member of the L.C.C. for Deptford since 1898. He and his wife, Lucy – 'Lion' – were rich Fabian friends of the Webbs'. Frank Galton (1867–1952) was secretary to the Webbs until 1898 and was now with the London Reform Union. F.H. Spencer and his wife were research secretaries of the Webbs.

3 March. [41 Grosvenor Road]
Escaped with our bare lives in the general rout. But still here they are, Phillimore and Webb – L.C.C.s again! On Wednesday the seats were, I am convinced, lost. But we poured some 300 Fabians into the constituency on polling day, admirably marshalled under eleven captains in eleven committee rooms, and by their dogged work we won the constituency back again by 200 and 100 majority for Webb and Phillimore respectively. A narrow margin, but sufficient. From 8.30 to 8 p.m. I toiled, organizing the bringing up of the slum wards – and GBS, W.P. Reeves, E. Pease, Galton, the Spencers and one or two other friends did the same for the other wards. At the end I felt singularly indifferent as to the result. We had fought hard and really it was a toss-up which ending was the best for us personally. But now it is all over and we see that the Progressives have been completely smashed, I am proud that my man has survived in spite of his independent attitude. It is a tribute to my boy's personality. How will he find a council run by the Moderates? And by an overwhelming 'majority'. Not so satisfactory as government by a weak majority, the result we desired. . . .

The doctors invited to meet Balfour probably included Dr George McCleary (1867–1962), the Medical Officer of Health for Battersea, who was Sydney Olivier's brother-in-law and an active Fabian; Sir Arthur Newsholme (1857–1943), Medical Officer of Health for Brighton, who had just been appointed Medical Officer to the Local Government Board, and was to go on to a most distinguished career in public medicine; and Sir George Newman (1876–1948), who became Chief Medical Officer of the Board of Education and developed the school medical service. Beatrice was closely advised by all three men and was influenced by their support for public health authorities.

19 March. [41 Grosvenor Road]
A delightful Saturday and Sunday with the Elchos at Stanway, A.J.B. bringing down his motor. An answer to the last words of

my description of the visit to Whittingehame. In his courtly devotion to Lady Elcho, in the intimate and sincere talk about men and thought that seems to be natural to him in her presence, 'Prince Arthur' is at his best. It is clearly an old and persistent sentiment – good sound friendship, with just that touch of romantic regret that it could not have been more, that deepens sex feeling and makes such a relation akin to religious renunciation. One can believe that the relation between these two has always been at the same high level of affectionate friendship, without taint of intrigue. With this background, the intellectual camaraderie of the Conservative leader with 'the Webbs' dropped into its right place, as a slight new thing agreeably stimulating to all concerned. Round about the central figures of the party were a dozen or so accomplished men and maidens, and intermediate between these and the distinguished elders came the fascinating Lady Desborough. 'No intellect, but great organizing capacity; ought to be the head of a great institution,' was my suggestion as to her characteristics, to which her friends agreed. To outward appearance she is a smart, handsome, cleverish woman. Beneath it she has an iron will, excellent temper and methodic mind, but with neither wit nor reasoning power. She was an admirable foil to the beautiful-natured Mary Elcho – neglected wife, devoted and tenderly loved mother, and adored friend – a beautiful Soul in a delicately refined form. Brilliant and pleasant was the talk as we whirled through the countryside in A.J.B.'s motor, or lounged in the famous hall of Stanway. Amused and interested we undoubtedly were (but hardly rested). What was, I think, achieved, was a wholesome settling of our new friendships. The 'sensationalism' apparent at Whittingehame had wholly departed.

But shall we advance matters by our friendship with A.J.B.? A week ago I had him to meet the two most eminent of the M.O.H.'s and the two most distinguished of the Poor Law medical officers. The dinner delighted the medical men, who found themselves subject to A.J.B.'s deferential curiosity on all scientific questions. So far it was wholly to the good, because they were more likely to become Mrs Webb's whole-hearted allies after that most pleasant evening. But whether the talk made the slightest practical impression on the leader himself, I could not tell. What interested him, clearly, was not the side of the discussion which touched the public welfare (with this aspect he was slightly bored), but the merely pathological problems, such as the relative part played by bacteria and constitutional tendencies in contracting disease, the interchangeability of bovine and human tuberculosis, etc. Now and again, I fancy, I interested him on the human side; but then he seemed to drift away, eluding the issue – sceptical or indifferent. No virility, either of thought or 'feeling, in respect to the constitution of society as it affects human development. That makes one wonder whether, except 'for the honour and glory of it', there is any good purpose served by his friendship? (The very notion of there being a purpose in social intercourse other than amusement and recreation would repel him.) And so we may be playing an elaborate game of cross-purposes, out of which nothing can come but waste of energy – beyond gratified vanity and a little pleasure.

Fridtjof Nansen (1861–1930) was a Norwegian explorer who almost reached the North Pole in 1893. He was professor of oceanography at Oslo, and became renowned for his work on behalf of prisoners-of-war and stateless persons after the First World War. He was currently Norwegian envoy in London. Bertrand Russell was running for Parliament in Wimbledon in support of women's suffrage.

22 March. [41 Grosvenor Road]
A brilliant little luncheon typical of the 'Webb set'. Dr Nansen (new Norwegian Minister), Gerald and Lady Betty Balfour, the Bernard Shaws, Bertrand Russells, Masterman and Lady Desborough – typical in its mixture of opinions, classes, interests – all as jolly as jolly could be, a rapid rush of talk. The present diplomat and past explorer, a fascinating Viking of simple character and romantic strength, a hero out of a saga (perhaps even too much so), with the philosophy of the secularist of 1870 – holding that religion is no more than folklore and that there is nothing worth considering but the scientific method, the spirit of adventure and a bureaucratic government.

As the results of her enquiries came in, Beatrice thought of leaving the nominal structure of the Poor Law intact (preserving the boards of guardians rather than setting up any new authority). 'The majority will flounder about seeking a new bottle for the old wine,' she wrote. 'Why not leave the old thing standing, and take the stuff out drop by drop – the sick first, and place them under the sanitary authority; then the children, placed under the education authority; then the aged (pensions), perhaps the unemployed and the vagrants.' This line of thought was to lead directly to the proposals she and Sidney built in to the Minority Report. Within a few days, as Beatrice noted on 27 April, she had begun lobbying officials and Ministers to support her notion of distributing relief to the appropriate government departments: if this prevailed, she believed, it would be impossible to maintain a separate class of paupers; and without such a distinction the hated 'Principles of 1834' would become irrelevant. The recent decision of the government to introduce old age pensions for the poor seemed to her another proof that distress far beyond the formal limits of pauperism was being recognized. The Webbs now turned their thoughts to the able-bodied unemployed, of whom only a small proportion (an average of about 12,000 men) fell within the range of the Poor Law: most of the unemployed were assisted by their trade unions, or under the ineffective Unemployed Workmen's Act (which provided more money than could be disbursed under its narrow terms), or by various local and charitable distress committees.

10 April. [Bramdean]

Two weeks and three days' happy recess in these little lodgings. For two days (brilliant warm weather) we rested, spending the hours lying out of doors dreaming and reading pleasant literature, lunching and chatting with Georgie and her children at Brockwood, or toddling around the lanes on our cycles. As a recreation from the wear and tear of the Royal Commission and L.C.C. I plunged into mysticism . . . whilst Sidney read books of all degrees and kinds borrowed from Brockwood, with intervals of the fifty volumes of L.G.B. reports that we had brought down. . . .

What interests me as an observer of human nature is that I have become wholly indifferent to the Royal Commission. I merely work as hard as I know how in my own direction, without caring much what happens. I find myself perpetually watching my colleagues, dashing in when I see an opening. I sometimes push or squeeze through, sometimes the door is slammed in my face, and I accept either fate (with equal equanimity). At first, I was so horridly sensitive to their dislike. Now I watch the chairman's expression of puzzled displeasure, or listen to C. S. Loch's rude ejaculations (I heard him say 'what cheek' to one of my questions to a witness), and find myself calmly calculating on how much they will stand, or wondering whether Loch is really seriously ill, since he so often loses his temper. I sometimes ponder over whether this aloofness is quite a good quality. But then I recollect that, after all, I am in a minority and that it is my business to be hostile to the government; and if I can be comfortably and good-naturedly hostile, so much the better. With Sidney, this attitude of indifference to his colleagues on public bodies is habitual – perhaps I am merely becoming masculine, losing the 'personal note' which is the characteristic of the woman in human intercourse. What is rather disconcerting is that I catch myself 'playing the personal note' when it suits my purpose, playing it without feeling it. Is that a characteristic of the woman on public bodies? I do try to check myself in this mean little game; but it has the persistency of an inherited or acquired habit.

R.B. Haldane was the eldest child of his father's second marriage (there were six children of the first marriage). The other children were George, who was born in 1858 and died at the age of sixteen; John, born 1860, who was reader in physiology at Oxford; Elizabeth (1862–1937), who wrote a history of nursing and a life of George Eliot, was the first woman magistrate in Scotland, and her brother's hostess; and William, born in 1864, who was a lawyer, and looked after the family's business affairs. Haldane's Army Bill, the first since 1872, was soon to become law.

The failure of Campbell-Bannerman's government to follow a policy of social reform led to dissatisfaction among progressive Liberals and the increasingly vocal Labour Party. A desire for change among the enlightened middle classes, in particular, was reflected in the Fabian 'boom', and a little later in support for the Webb campaign for the break-up of the Poor Law. The novels of Wells and the plays of Shaw played an important part in shaping this climate of opinion. Winston Churchill and Lloyd George had begun to emerge as the champions of advanced opinion in the government, but they were looking for palliatives for the evils of poverty which were more politically acceptable and less drastic than the collectivist solutions propounded by the Webbs. McKenna had succeeded Birrell at the Board of Education in December 1906. Birrell was now Chief Secretary for Ireland.

3 May. [41 Grosvenor Road]
Dined alone with Haldane, his two brothers and sister to talk about the Poor Law report. He is completely absorbed in his own department – and singularly aloof in his attitude both towards Parliament and towards his colleagues. 'Not a good Parliament,' he remarked. 'No constructive ideas, merely objections to other people's ideas. I spend very little time there,' he continued (I thought he added, but I could not be quite sure, 'nor does the Cabinet interest me'). I suggested that he, at any rate, had got his reforms over the footlights, but that it was impossible to make a success of a government that was made up of men either with no settled opinions or with contrary opinions on the questions with which they had to deal. 'You are not even agreed as to whether you want public expenditure, assuming it to be right expenditure, or

object to it.' 'No,' he answered in a detached tone. 'We are not agreed on root questions.' The only person he volunteered kindly interest in was the leader of the Opposition! 'I see a good deal of Balfour,' he genially remarked. 'What do you think of Churchill?' he asked with a note of anxiety. I gathered that Mr Churchill is the only man who arouses R.B.H.'s anxious interest – a mixture of respect for capacity and suspicious dislike? He feels in him the man that may push him on one side.

The same aloofness from his colleagues and absorption in his own career I noted in McKenna. I gather also from Morant, who has seen a good deal of Birrell and McKenna and heard from them about the others, that the Cabinet is an incoherent body – intensely individualistic – each man for himself, C.B. presiding merely. There is not even a clique of intimate friends round the Premier, or a clique of enemies concerting against him, as in A.J.B.'s case. The separate individuals forming the government have neither repulsion nor attraction for each other, so I suppose the Cabinet will hold together so long as the outside pressure of a great House of Commons majority, Liberal public opinion in this country, and each Cabinet Minister's desire to keep in office, binds them together.

R.B.H. asserted that, as with the government, so with the public, there was no common opinion about anything. He was conscious merely of chaos and indifference leading to the amassing of electors now on this side, now on that. Moved more by impatience of what was than by any clear notion of what state of affairs they desired to bring about.

The little boom in the Fabian Society continues, and Sidney and I, GBS and H.G.W., sometimes ask ourselves and each other whether there is a bare possibility that it represents a larger wave than we think – are we, by our constructive thought, likely to attract considerable numbers of followers in the near future? If this pleasant suspicion grows, it will consolidate the Society and draw the leaders nearer together. There are no personal jealousies to keep us apart since none of us have political ambition, and our literary spheres are wholly distinct. Indeed, as a matter of fact, we stand to gain by each other's success, each one introducing the other two to new circles of admirers. With the Shaws our communion becomes ever closer and more thoroughly complementary and stimulating, and I hope and believe it will be so with H.G.W.

Meanwhile Sidney and I are living at the usual high pressure. We are seeing little or nothing of general society. But whilst he is working hard at my memorandum on the central policy, I am somewhat distracted with the two days of Commission meetings, seeing M.O.H.s and other medical experts, directing our secretaries, interviewing students and generally fussing around. When I see him settling down every morning to my work, I feel rather a fraud. Just now our usual positions are somewhat reversed: it is he who sits at home and thinks out the common literary work, it is I who am racing around dealing with men and affairs! And the book is completely shelved until these two memoranda are out of the way [on the policy of the central authority and Poor Law medical relief].

Beatrice's attempt to launch a draft report so soon was to prove a tactical error, for it both showed her hand and committed her to playing it. Before the other commissioners had time to digest her proposals she was already lobbying for support outside the Commission: she first turned to Balfour, in the hope of getting Conservative backing, and then began a series of approaches to possible witnesses, civil servants and Liberal politicians. From this point in the Commission's work there was an anxious breathlessness about all she said or did, as if she felt it more important to promulgate the new Webb policy than to get an agreed report. On 26 November she admitted in a diary entry that 'one reason for attempting to rush the Commission on the "break-up" of the Poor Law is to clear the decks for the more revolutionary scheme of dealing with unemployment. . . . It will be amusing to see how much "Webb" this Commission will stand.' These intrigues annoyed her fellow commissioners, irritated many Liberals and so upset John Burns, who was in a position to obstruct the Webbs, that their practical influence diminished inversely to their effort and ingenuity.

15 May. [41 Grosvenor Road]
Launched my scheme of Poor Law reform in strict confidence to the chairman, H. Nunn, Smart and Thory Gardiner, Charles Booth, Phelps and Sir Henry Robinson. Wakefield and Lansbury are practically agreed and Chandler will have to agree to everything we three decide on. The Bishop of Ross will probably be prepared to sign an advanced report. These eight commissioners represent the largest possible contingent that I might win over; the chairman would only come if he saw I was going to get a majority without him. But to get even eight would be almost inconceivable with the packed Commission; probably four only will sign my report, and of course I might be left with Wakefield and Lansbury only. What

73

I have to aim at is to draw up a rattling good report, vivid in statement of fact, and closely reasoned with a logical conclusion and immediately practicable proposals of a moderate character.

11 June. [Edinburgh]
Sidney and I spent Sunday with the Gerald Balfours, A.J.B. joining us on Sunday morning. Took my scheme down to lay before Gerald, as a past and possible future president of the Local Government Board. 'If anything like this issues from the Poor Law Commission it will be as great a reform as the 1834 Commission.' On the whole he was favourably impressed. . . . He agreed that curative treatment must be applied to all classes if we could find sufficient administrative capacity to do it; he was sympathetic to free medical assistance. From what he said, I should think he by no means expects to be out of office in any future Conservative government, and perhaps he expects to resume the L.G.B. Anyway, he seemed to spend more time in considering the results of the Poor Law Commission than would have been the case if he had made up his mind to retire from politics. I did not attempt to talk to A.J.B. about it: he regards himself too much as the general manager of the party, the party tactician, even to consider a purely departmental topic. Sunday evening the brothers Balfour, Lady Betty and we two talked of many things – all of us at our best – the central topic being political philosophy of one kind or another. Certainly, we and they are sufficiently sympathetic to be absolutely frank and free to range at large – Sidney is more at home with these men than with almost any others, except GBS. Full of charm and stimulus was this visit: on the whole I prefer Gerald, a finer and purer temperament than the 'greater brother'. But for sheer charm, for that delightful combination of intellect, public spirit, artistic sense and moral refinement, this family of Balfours has no equals. It is the oddest fact in English politics that they should be mixed up, predominantly mixed up, with democratic politics.

Edward Carpenter (1844–1929), anarchist, sage of the Simple Life and author, lived a reclusive life at Millthorpe in Derbyshire. The *Art of Creation* was one of several books which reflected his mystical view of life.

21 June. [Edinburgh]
Here a fortnight with the Commission at Edinburgh. Scottish poor law is in just as bad a mess as English poor law. The principle of

'less eligibility' more deeply rooted in the administration; that of 'curative treatment' less understood. The boarding-out of children the only bright spot in the system — twenty years behind us in institutional treatment. But on account of facts of structure, Scotland is almost more ripe for my scheme than England.

I am not impressed with Scottish local government: there is less capacity, public spirit and integrity in the unpaid representatives than in England, especially those of the greater towns — more 'graft', I think. On the other hand, the officials are good, perhaps better than in the ordinary English town. Hence, the officials occupy a more predominant position than in England. I suppose it is the deep-rooted individualism of the Scots. They don't believe in government; it is only when they are actually paid for performing its functions that they take it seriously — unpaid governmental work is left to the busybodies, the vain people and to corrupt self-interested folk.

I have been reading in the morning hours Edward Carpenter's *Art of Creation*. Here is another helpful book — not a great work, but adequately resuming the trend towards a sort of synthesis of the scientific with the mystical spirit, opening up vistas to human thought and feeling, the vision of which gives me hope and courage, assurance in a reality underlying one's own and every other life. . . . This little book has helped me much, has given me a lift up, has made bad feelings and silly thoughts more difficult to me, and good feelings and strenuous but peaceful thought more easy. It is strange how ideas change feelings, and feelings change outward expression and action of all sorts. Ideas seem to be almost as actual as physical food, or physical poison, running their course through the body. They produce not merely states of mind, but states of body? Edward Carpenter has consoled me with his ideas, made me feel not merely morally better but physically stronger, more ready to work and to pray.

Tonight I rush back to my boy just for two days and one night, and then begin again at Aberdeen for the inside of a week. It is hard to be away from him. Apart, we each of us live only half a life; together, we each of us have a double life. . . .

Cosmo Gordon Lang (1864–1945) was Bishop of Stepney 1901–08 and Archbishop of Canterbury 1928–42. He was interested in social problems. The Reverend Percy Dearmer (1867–1936) was a prominent member of the

Christian Social Union and an active Fabian who later became Canon of Westminster.

5 July. [41 Grosvenor Road]
Had the Bishop of Stepney to lunch, also Percy Dearmer, separately to start propaganda in the Church in favour of our scheme of Poor Law reform. I want to make an atmosphere favourable to it, partly to influence Lord George and partly to influence possible witnesses. The Bishop of Stepney, a wily ecclesiastic, was cautious but encouraging. He is inclined to trust us in social matters. I gave him both my memo on 'central policy' and that on 'medical relief' to take away and read, besides having sent him my scheme. Percy Dearmer is the Fabian in the Christian Social Union – an attractive enthusiastic propagandist, easily 'tuned' because in general harmony with us. . . .

The Shaws took a Victorian rectory at Ayot St Lawrence in Hertfordshire in the autumn of 1906, and it remained their home until their deaths.

19 July. [Ayot St Lawrence]
The Bernard Shaws have lent us their little week-end house for two-and-a-half months, they having migrated to a large mansion in Wales, close to the Fabian Summer School. Now we are going to set to work to finish up our volume on *The Manor and the Borough*, laid aside for six whole months in order to complete the report for the Poor Law Commission. This somewhat abstruse historical work is restful after the contriving of schemes and the drafting of analyses meant to affect action. And I am convinced that this intimate knowledge of what past generations of one's own race have actually done, of the motives upon which they have acted, of the potential machinery they have invented or cast on one side, gives larger scope to one's imagination as a reformer of the present state of things. Moreover, history teaches one the impermanence during one generation, even during one decade, of any kind of social structure, and it gives one leading ideas as to what is practicable. For example, the whole theory of the mutual obligation between the individual and the state, which I find myself working out in my Poor Law scheme, is taken straight out of the nobler aspect of the medieval manor. It will come as a new idea to the present generation, but it is really a very old one that has been thrust out of

76

sight in order to attain some measure of equality in political rights. There are some who wish to reach a socialist state by the assertion of economic equality – they desire to force the property-owners to yield to the non-property-owners. I prefer to have the forward movement based on the obligation of each individual to serve the state, in return getting maintenance; to serve the state not merely by making commodities and fulfilling services, but by being healthy, intelligent and loving. . . .

Mary Playne was suffering from cancer but an operation proved successful and she survived until 1923. William Beveridge, who was to have a notable public and academic career, first met the Webbs when he was sub-warden at Toynbee Hall in 1904. He left in 1905 to join the Central Body for Dealing with the Unemployed in London and to write on social problems for the *Morning Post*. He visited the Webbs at Ayot St Lawrence in August 1907, when he was asked by the Board of Trade to prepare and submit their evidence to the Poor Law Commission. He had already come to the conclusion that a national network of labour exchanges was essential for the efficient organization of the labour market, and the Webbs took up the idea. The Labour Exchanges Act was passed in September 1909 and the system inaugurated the following January. The Webbs were much less disposed to the principle of unemployment insurance which Beveridge also suggested to the Royal Commission, but it was his practical ideas, rather than the schematic proposals of the Webbs, which appealed to the Liberal politicians. Beveridge became an official in the Board of Trade in July 1908 on the Webbs' recommendation to Churchill, when he was its president. The problem of unemployment – the 'able-bodied poor' in relation to the Poor Law – dominated the Commission from July 1907 to December 1908. Sir Leslie MacKenzie (1862–1935) was the medical member of the Scottish Local Government Board 1904–19.

28 September. [Ayot St Lawrence]
We were working down here, well and happily, when a letter from Mary broke up our peace. For the next week or so, I lived haunted by terror for the life of this dearest sister. Now I have become accustomed to the fear of recurrence – I refuse to think of it – but the fear is there in the background, casting a gloom over my otherwise delightful existence. Now and again the fear for Mary seems to extend into fear for Sidney, or even, in my worst moments, for myself, unnerving me for a while. Meanwhile, Mary is full of hope and energy. Now the operation is over, she has returned to her everyday life and work – an example to us all. How hard it is, when one feels life throbbing through one – physical well-being, intellectual interest and love – how horribly hard it is

to face death calmly. As a child I had no fear of death: sometimes I longed for it. But with growing strength, with increasing consciousness of capacity, death seems a cruel wasteful destruction of what is good to feel and good to be.

Except for this sorrow, the time here has been enjoyable and unexpectedly fruitful. We have sent off the last word of *The Manor and the Borough* to the printer (we have written what equals 174 pages), we have corrected a good deal of the proof, I have organized with Mrs Spencer the 'Able-bodied' enquiry, and Sidney has fixed up many small jobs. We have had all three secretaries down here – the two assistant investigators (Miss Longman and Miss Phillips), Jeffrey of the Poor Law Commission, Beveridge, Pringle, Jackson (enquiries into able-bodied) the Barnetts, Leslie MacKenzie, the Granville-Barkers and numerous young Fabians. Altogether our society has been of the useful kind, doing business – chiefly Poor Law – always excepting the fascinating Granville-Barker.

I gathered from Jeffrey that there had been a row about my Central Policy report, that Lord George had actually thought of not circulating it. What he had done is to issue a ukase that we are none of us to show even our own productions to other people. This I do not mean to obey. He has no right to lay it down. At present my two reports are being read by a committee of the Cabinet . . . Lord George has, however, issued strict orders that we are not to have copies supplied to us. But you cannot treat commissioners like children, and I shall find some way of getting all the copies I require. . . .

8 October. [41 Grosvenor Road]
The first meeting of the Commission was a stormy one . . . an astonishing memo has been circulated from the chairman. This proposes the evisceration of the Poor Law by taking out the sick, the aged and the vagrant, but proposes to set up a new *ad hoc* elected Poor Law authority for each county and county borough. . . . The whole scheme is impracticable – but it is all in the right direction. . . . After the discussion today, it is clear that there is nothing between the *status quo* and my scheme – the county council and the county borough as the authority, and the withdrawal of some of the functions from the stigma of pauperism and the deterrent test. . . .

Meanwhile I am trying to create 'an atmosphere' in favour of the scheme. Mr Haldane, who came in this morning, is adumbrating it in the Cabinet, but he wants me to get hold of Burns. 'He is vain and ignorant and in the hands of his officials, and opposes everything and talks so much that we find it difficult to get to business; if you could get him to take up the scheme as his own, then I could follow, but he is at the head of the department concerned, and would resent a lead-off by another member of the Cabinet.' What I want to secure is that when old age pensions are discussed next year, the 'break-up' of the Poor Law should be quietly taken for granted by both Front Benches. That would be immensely impressive to Lord George and the less resolute members of the Commission – it would make it almost impracticable to set up a new authority with the stigma of pauperism and the test of destitution. . . .

Gerald Balfour, Beveridge, Mackinder and Dr Newman (now head of the medical department at the Board of Education) dined here on Tuesday to discuss the labour exchanges and other ways of dealing with unemployment. They stayed from 7.30 to 12 o'clock – which left me rather a rag the next day. Altogether, I can foresee that this year's work is going to be straining, and I shall have to economize my strength in all directions, but the Commission's work must take the front place. I have succeeded so well up to now in my enveloping movement that I must do the job completely and tumble down Humpty Dumpty so he will never get set on the wall again.

Beatrice aggravated her worsening relations with John Burns by her efforts to get Dr Newsholme and Robert Morant appointed to the key posts in the L.G.B. Newsholme was nominated, but Burns declined to take Morant, and thereafter Beatrice hoped for his replacement by Haldane, Churchill or some other more responsive Minister.

30 October. [41 Grosvenor Road]
John Burns has become a monstrosity. He is, of course, a respectable hard-working man, who wants, when he is not blinded by vanity and malice against those who have abused him, 'to see straight'. But this faculty of seeing facts as they are is being overgrown by a sort of fatty complacency with the world as it is: an enormous personal vanity, feeding on the deference and flattery yielded to patronage and power. He talks incessantly, and never listens to anyone except the officials to whom he *must* listen in order to accomplish the routine work of his office. Hence, he is com-

pletely in their hands, and is becoming the most hidebound of departmental chiefs, gulled by an obstructive fact or reactionary argument – taken in by the most naïve commonplaces of middle-class administrative routine. Almost unconsciously, one treats him as a non-responsible being – a creature too unintelligent to be argued with, too crazily vain to be appealed to as one self-respecting man appeals to another. What is the right conduct towards such a man? . . .

Beatrice had been asked to show the members of the Commission her correspondence with the medical officers of health – as she thought, to discredit her. She had held back those that were compromising to the author.

12 November. [Beachy Head]
The row about my investigations developed: the chairman coming on the track of my investigations into the Unemployed Workmen's Act. Unfortunately I was, at the moment, in a state of high fever and there ensued a somewhat angry correspondence between us – he censoring me and I asserting my right to get at facts for myself. All this has meant, on the top of a year's hard work, a bad nervous breakdown, and I am here for ten days' absolute quiet – a truce having been proclaimed in my absence on sick leave. Perhaps when I return it will all have blown over. . . .

But I am low and disheartened. I don't like all this intriguing. I should prefer to play with my cards on the table. It is partly remorse for my little lack of straight dealing with regard to the M.O.H. correspondence that has brought about my nervous collapse. Was I bound to hand over everything? Not legally certainly, but perhaps I ought simply to have refused to give up *any* private correspondence. I was surprised into acceding to an unwarrantable demand and then did not choose to fulfil it completely. Another time I will ask for 'notice of the question' and will accept or refuse deliberately and fully. . . .

26 November. [41 Grosvenor Road]
Reappeared at the Commission yesterday for the general palaver. Colleagues kindly but not specially oncoming. . . .

Meanwhile, a most unexpected development has taken place. The general palaver on all the memoranda revealed the fact that I was the only person with a compact following of four or five, and that various other members were veering round to me. Hence, at a certain point of the discussion, there was a call for my 'scheme' from many quarters. To this I gracefully responded. So I am now submitting a fully formed scheme of reform – the 'Break-up of the Poor Law' – in all its detail. I propose to submit myself to cross-examination, so as both to convert my colleagues, if possible, and also to learn the exactly weak points in my own armour. It is a bold move, on my part, but I think on the whole a wise one. The majority of the Commission are tired of wandering about the subject without a leader and, though I may not attract many more than I have already, the planking down of an attractive and logical scheme of reform will make the other members nervous of being contented with muddle-headed generalizations. . . .

The charge that the Webb scheme was 'undemocratic' as well as bureaucratically complex and expensive was to be made repeatedly once the Minority Report was published. It was also difficult to explain succinctly, by comparison with the Liberal government's measures for old age pensions and social insurance; and it was many years later, after the social machinery of government had been greatly extended, that the responsibility for the aged, sick, orphans and unemployed was finally allocated to different departments within an overall frame of welfare policy. Beatrice herself evidently found it hard to clarify her differences with her fellow commissioners, and this compounded the tensions generated by her abrasive manners. 'Mrs Webb comes here to drive a wedge between us,' Mrs Bonsanquet said angrily at the first meeting in the New Year.

9 December. [41 Grosvenor Road]
Lord George scored a great victory today, and I a great success. The scheme for the break-up of the Poor Law, which the Commission had hastily demanded, was, as is usual with my productions, received in stony silence, no reference being made to it in the course of the discussion. Lord George had circulated another memorandum denouncing my scheme as 'anti-democratic', but accepting a large part of it – transference of Poor Law to county and county borough councils, a veiled county stipendiary officer, the principle of curative and preventive treatment – everything, in fact, except the distribution of the services among the county council committees and the stipendiary officer for the administration of outdoor relief. In their hatred of me, all the C.O.S. members rallied to him, giving up the *ad hoc* Poor Law body, the principle of deterrence, the strict administration of outdoor relief –

a real stampede from the principles of 1834. I insisted on taking a vote on the crucial question of a Poor Law statutory committee of the county council versus a distribution between the education committee, the health committee, etc. Lansbury and Chandler voted with me, Smart and Phelps refused to vote, all the others present (not present Booth, Robinson, Wakefield, Nunn) voted for Lord George's scheme of a statutory committee. Thereupon, I gave them to understand that we considered the issue vital and should have our Minority Report. Short of getting a majority report written by ourselves, this large measure of conversion to our proposals on the part of the majority, with freedom for a great report of my own, is exactly the position which I prefer . . . a thoroughly Webbian document − in tone, statement of fact and proposals. Meanwhile, our chairman is overjoyed at the victory and received my hearty congratulations most graciously. He and I are excellent friends. With my other colleagues, there is a most distinct consolidation against me − amounting almost to boycott, at any rate to a discourteous coldness. Honestly, I think they are somewhat justified in their dislike of me. I have played with the Commission. I have been justified in doing so, because they began by ignoring me, but it is unpleasant to be played with, especially by a person whom you want to despise.

The activity of the majority will be on the Commission: my activity will be outside it − investigating, inventing, making an atmosphere favourable to my inventions and, where possible, getting the persons with right opinions into high places, and persons in high places in the right state of mind. The two reports on the able-bodied and the children must be finished by the summer, and we must be thoroughly equipped to turn off, on short notice, a first-rate minority report.

12 December. [41 Grosvenor Road]
The next day's meeting was like pleasant sunshine after a drifting storm. The chairman was enjoying an unaccustomed sense of personal power, the C.O.S. was chuckling over the defeat of my scheme, I was thoroughly complacent with having dragged the whole Commission so far in my direction whilst preserving my freedom for a minority report; others, like Nunn, Wakefield, Smart and Phelps, felt that they alone were free of any decision, since they had either been absent or not voted. Perhaps it was this

undeterminate party that was least comfortable. Among these and the office staff, there was a reaction in my favour — a feeling that I had been treated somewhat cavalierly in having my elaborate report peremptorily dismissed, without any kind of discussion. So we all parted for the month's recess the best of friends — and, so far as I am concerned, this attitude will persist. Whether the majority will fall out among themselves and split into factions, it is impossible to foretell. Now that the pressure brought about by fear of a 'Webb majority' has been removed, it is doubtful whether the chairman's party will hold together. All I have to do is to get on with my own work and leave them alone to settle their own report; merely use the Commission to get the information I need and they can give me, be pleasant with each and all of them personally, without troubling myself about the Commission as a whole. By persistent discourtesy, they have absolved me from obligations of good-fellowship.

The current remedies for unemployment included public works (disliked because they might drive down the wages or reduce the job opportunities of men already in employment); emigration, which was encouraged by the Salvation Army and groups which believed in settling the empty tracts of the Empire; and land colonization at home, which combined the reclamation of a failing agriculture with training and employment for the destitute. The movement for such labour colonies strengthened in the early years of the century, and the Poplar guardians — encouraged by George Lansbury — were among its most active supporters. In November 1903 Lansbury persuaded Joseph Fels (1854–1914), an American millionaire with radical ideas, to buy land for a colony at Laindon, in Essex, and in 1904 Fels bought a second tract at Hollesley Bay, near the mouth of the Thames. There was much argument about these schemes (which fell under the general strictures that T.S. Davy laid on the guardians of Poplar), and John Burns in particular was scathingly contemptuous of 'a costly piece of political bribery . . . a holiday for 250 men from London who deteriorate and get soft by a process of coddling that unfits them for emigration'. Beatrice was attracted by the principle of training centres that had a reformatory purpose — even by the idea of detaining what the 1904 Committee on Physical Deterioration had called 'the waste elements of society'; and despite the small scale and evident failure of these early colonies both the Majority and Minority reports favoured them. The more utopian schemes of co-operative land settlement, advocated by the back-to-the-land and Simple Life movements, never had the financial support or the labour skills and capacity for social organization to make them more than an oddity.

∽ 1908 ∾

13 January. [41 Grosvenor Road]
A weird Christmas recess at Hollesley Bay Colony, investigating the daily routine of the 300 men's lives, getting particulars about their former occupations and present views, having long talks with the superintendent, the works manager, the farmer and the gangers, with a view to ascertaining the possibilities of the working colony as an element in any scheme for dealing with unemployment. The atmosphere, the impression of the place was mournfully tragic. Half-educated, half-disciplined humans, who felt themselves to have been trampled on by their kind, were sore and angry, every man of them in favour of every kind of protection — protection against machinery, protection against female, boy and foreign labour, protection against Irish, Scottish and country men, protection against foreign commodities, protection against all or anything that had succeeded whilst they had failed. There was a growing assumption in their minds that they had the *right* to 30*s* a week — in London, the rate for borough council work — though this assumption was, as yet, tall talk to most of them. They were a faint-hearted nerveless set of men, their manner sometimes servile, sometimes sullen, never easy and independent. Both the organization of their work and the organization of their leisure was defective. . . .

30 January. [41 Grosvenor Road]
Charles Booth has resigned from the Commission, mainly on grounds of health — strengthened by the feeling that he has lost his foothold and that in the scramble during the next months he is not likely to regain it. A few days before Christmas he circulated another volume of his statistics and another edition of his scheme for a new *ad hoc* authority. Both statistics and scheme were wholly ignored by the chairman. When we all met to discuss the chairman's memorandum and Charlie presented himself for the first time for six months, no mention was made of his contributions. He sat melancholy by the fire and quietly remarked that he seemed 'in a minority of one'. It is clear that the feeling of isolation, of almost neglect, contributed to his resignation. . . .

84

We have remitted our unemployment scheme to the leading members of the Labour Party (barring MacDonald) and have met with quite unexpected response – almost a promise of active support. I have also sent this scheme with a long letter to A.J.B. and he has suggested coming to discuss it. And Haldane and Asquith have had the Poor Law scheme, and we are to meet them tonight at Haldane's house to discuss details of it. The Christian Social Union is circulating both schemes as tracts and we are putting them in circulation elsewhere – so that they will be cropping up in altogether unexpected quarters. Shall we advance matters by all this tireless investigation, invention, and propaganda? At times one gets disheartened: if it were not for the comradeship of our effort, I should be tempted to give up the struggle. It will be a real relief when the Commission is closed and we can go back to the peaceful life of research. The strange foreboding occasionally takes possession of me that my life will not be long, making me anxious to finish my big task before the night comes down – this is pure unreason arising perhaps from a chronically overwrought brain. Also the shock of Mary's disaster. Why not I also?

Since 1890, when William Booth published *In Darkest England* and directed the Salvation Army to redeem 'the submerged tenth', the Salvationists had made many attempts to provide work, food and spiritual uplift for men from the lowest depths. They had promoted emigration schemes and at Hadleigh, in 1891, they had set up a farm colony on three thousand acres of bleak Essex marshland. There was much controversy about their evangelizing fervour. Beveridge criticized them for blackmailing the hungry into repentance. Yet their selflessness, discipline and probity were so much admired that Rosebery suggested they be given a government contract to deal with the refuse of the industrial system. In her Minority Report, Beatrice proposed a partnership between public and voluntary agencies in dealing with the hard-core unemployed. Colonel David Lamb (1866–1951) was in charge at Hadleigh, and was assisted by Colonel William Iliffe (d. 1938) and Commander Adelaide Cox (1860–1945). Brigadier William Jackson (d. 1930) was probably the visitor Beatrice mentions. After the Japanese victory over Russia, H.G. Wells had taken up the idea of the Samurai as the disinterested governing élite in his social futurist novel *A Modern Utopia*.

2 February. [Hadleigh Farm Colony]
Here for a week-end watching the Salvation Army at work among the unemployed and unemployable. The most interesting fact is the Salvation Army itself. I have seen something of the officers in

London – Colonel Lamb, Colonel Iliffe, Commander Cox and others, all belonging to the social side of the army. On the colony are some half-dozen other officers engaged in philanthropic administration [and] two spiritual officers (women). Two 'specials' came down for Sunday – Brigadier Jackson and his wife. In respect to personal character, all these men and women constitute a Samurai caste: that is, they are selected for their power of subordinating themselves to their cause – most assuredly a remarkable type of ecclesiastic – remarkable because there is no inequality between man and woman, because home life and married life are combined with a complete dedication of the individual to spiritual service. A beautiful spirit of love and personal service, of content and joy, permeates the service; there is a persistent note of courtesy to others and open-mindedness to the world. . . .

How does Hadleigh differ from Hollesley? A more mixed lot of men – ex-convicts, ex-tramps, workhouse able-bodied and men picked up in shelters – far more human wreckage, but, on the other hand, less the ordinary ruck of casual labourers. Here they are, I think, more successful in getting the men to work. There is less foul talk, perhaps less discontent and jeering. The self-devotion of the officers counts for something in raising the tone of the colonists. On the other hand, there is tremendous religious pressure – far more than I had realized. The colonists must attend the Saturday evening 'social' and the Sunday evening religious service, whilst they are invited, almost implored, to come to prayer meetings all day on Sundays and on the other evenings. The Sunday evening service is a stirring and compelling ceremony, at which every art is used to attract the colonists to the penitent's form. Music, eloquence, the magnetic personality of the trained Salvationist preachers – a personality that combines the spiritual leader with that of the refined variety artist – all these talents are lavished on the work of conversion. And would it be very surprising if the ignorant and childishly suspicious men who make up the colonists should imagine that they would do better, even from the worldly point of view, if they accepted the creed of their governors? The Saturday entertainment, though permeated with religious feeling, even the Sunday morning and afternoon services, did not transgress the limits of reasonable influence. But the intensely compelling nature of the appeal to become 'converted' made tonight by Brigadier Jackson and his wife, I confess, somewhat frightened me off recommending that the Salvation Army should be state or rate-aided, in this work of proselytizing persons committed to their care for secular reasons! Is it right to submit men, weakened by suffering, to this religious pressure exercised by the very persons who command their labour?

The Salvation Army ritual is certainly a wonderful work of art. The men and women who conduct it are thoroughly trained performers with well-modulated voices, clever gestures, all the technique of an accomplished artist – something between melo-drama and the music-hall. But this technique is possessed by no mere 'performers'. The men and women are, for the most part, real living saints, who feel intensely all they are saying and acting. To those who do not hold their faith and who look at them critically, their passionate pleadings, their dramatic gestures, their perpetual impromptus – sometimes speaking, sometimes singing, sometimes playing on various instruments, calling to each other – all this wonderful revivalist business leaves on the outside observer a feeling of amazement that these wondrous beings should be ordinary English citizens brought up in ordinary English traditions. They seem possessed with some weird faith belonging to another civil-ization. And yet, once the meeting is over, the Salvationist is a particularly shrewd, kindly, courteous, open-minded individual, eminently easy and satisfactory to do business with.

One of the main reforms in the 1908 Budget was a system of non-contri-butory old age pensions, providing 5s a week for persons over seventy whose total income was less than 10s. Even this modest measure, which benefited about half a million of the aged poor, was bitterly criticized. Rosebery thought the plan was 'so prodigal of expenditure as likely to undermine the whole fabric of Empire', and more reactionary peers saw in it yet another reason to resist Liberal policies. In 1907, the conflict between the two houses of Parliament had reached a point where Campbell-Bannerman had set up a special Cabinet Committee to consider whether to 'fill the cup' with Bills for the Lords to veto, to make a head-on attack on the Lords, or to negotiate with Balfour and Lansdowne (the Tory leader in the Lords) to find a compromise. The L.S.E. had a special course for army officers. Alfred Lyttelton (1857–1913) had been Colonial Secretary 1903–05.

10 February. [41 Grosvenor Road]
A series of political dinner-parties. Haldane and A.J.B. to meet the Advisory Committee on Army Education, with the thirty young officers already at the School coming in after dinner; dinner with Haldane, at which I went in with Asquith and had some talk with

Winston Churchill — renewed our acquaintance; dining tonight with Sydney Buxton and on Monday with Asquith, and seeing such folk as Masterman, Lyttelton and other M.P.s. The net impression left on our mind is the scramble for new constructive ideas. We happen just now to have a good many to give away, hence the eagerness for our company. Every politician one meets wants to be 'coached'. It is really quite comic. It seems to be quite irrelevant whether they are Conservatives, Liberals, or Labour Party men — all alike have become mendicants for practicable proposals. . . . We are inclined to plunge heavily in all parties, give freely to any one who comes along — the more the merrier. Asquith actually asked me whether he should 'adumbrate' the break-up of the Poor Law, in the Budget speech, when he introduces [old age] pensions. What effect would that little bomb have on my Commission, I am wondering? Would it blow them forward or blow them back? Meanwhile, life is decidedly too exciting: it is hard to keep one's head cool and free for real downright grind. And yet it is the grind that tells far more than the gamble.

Four commissioners signed the Minority Report — George Lansbury, Francis Chandler, Russell Wakefield and Beatrice Webb.

17 February. [41 Grosvenor Road]
These two meetings of the Commission, the first of which is just over, settle the fate of the Majority Report. The majority have definitely decided to abolish the boards of guardians and set up the county council and county borough council as the supreme authority. But this authority is to be exercised by a Poor Law statutory committee of the council itself, as regards institutions, and by local committees, nominated by the council, as regards outdoor relief. Today, they decided to retain Poor Law medical relief in the Poor Law; tomorrow they will, I think, decide to throw back the unemployed into the Poor Law. Clearly, I cannot get them any further along my road. But there is every sign that they will 'stay put' in their present position. I shall have at most four signatories to my Minority Report, possibly only two besides myself (Lansbury and Chandler) — Phelps contemplates the possibility of signing both! Russell Wakefield will revert to the chairman (mean dog that he is!).

After tomorrow, I shall not bother to attend their palavers, and must grind at my own report, as they evidently *mean* to hurry the [Majority] report on to the finish before the autumn recess. They are, as a body, so light-headed and careless of form and substance that I think it conceivable that they will accomplish it. But what a document it will be! The unanimity of the Commission outside my clique is a personal triumph for the chairman. . . . I like the man so much that I am inclined to be pleased with his success – since it pleases him and doesn't hurt me! . . .

18 February. [41 Grosvenor Road]
Half a morning's discussion of the unemployed question. Unanimity in favour of a system of labour exchanges – really half-hearted on the part of the Charity Organization Society, regarded as a safe futility, not compulsory or nationally managed. Such relief as is given to be doled out by the public assistance authority. . . .

What, however, is clear is that the C.O.S. party are desperately anxious to slur over everything which distinguishes one destitute person from another destitute person. The category of the destitute is to be kept absolutely separate from the rest of the population. Yesterday it looked like a possible report by the end of this summer; today we were again in the morass of unsettled opinions, and were surrounded by big controversies. A majority report became again a nebulous affair, but with this extreme muddle-headedness on the part of the chairman and most of the members, there is no saying where the Commission may be dragged by the C.O.S. faction. Just at present they are in the ascendant. Having given way to the chairman as regards the constitution of the authority, they are forcing him to accept their policy with regard to each class of destitute person – i.e. rooted objection to the curative policy and determination to stand by the principle of merely *relieving destitution*, whether that destitution be due to childhood, age, illness, unemployment or vagrancy.

23 February. [Leeds]
Off on a tour round able-bodied workhouses and labour yards in Lancashire and Yorkshire – an unpleasant and costly business (Commission won't allow me even my travelling expenses), but necessary to my work. The Sheffield test house and test yard represents the most deterrent Poor Law practice. But it is interesting to note that neither the master of the workhouse nor the

89

superintendent of the yard feel satisfied that they are doing more than shift the problem for others to deal with. It is a horrid business: ah me! when will all this wicked misery cease – misery that leads to wickedness and wickedness that leads to misery? An abomination. Oh! ye politicians, what a work before you if you could only be forced, everyone of you, to realize the needlessness of this abomination.

Morton Sands was researching for the Webbs. 'Masterman is rather horrified at Mrs Webb's zeal for disciplining people and prayed that above all things he might never fall into her hands as an unemployed,' Beveridge wrote on 12 March.

11 March. [41 Grosvenor Road]
Winston Churchill dined with us last night, together with Masterman, Beveridge, Morton Sands: we talked exclusively 'shop'. He had swallowed whole Sidney's scheme for boy labour and unemployment, had even dished it up in an article in the *Nation* the week before. He is most anxious to be friendly and we were quite willing to be so. He and Masterman seem to be almost sentimental friends. Rhetoricians both are, but Winston has a hard temperament, with the American's capacity for the quick appreciation and rapid execution of new ideas whilst hardly comprehending the philosophy beneath them. But I rather liked the man. He is under no delusions about himself. And I am not sure that he is not beginning to realize the preposterousness of the present state of things – at any rate he is trying hard to do so, because he feels it necessary that he should do so, if he is to remain in the Liberal ranks. Will he remain in the Liberal ranks? . . .

24 March. [41 Grosvenor Road]
Gave A.J. Balfour my Poor Law scheme whilst we were staying at Stanway. Lord Elcho had read it and been captivated by it and begged me to hand it on, in A.J.B.'s presence. 'If he will really read it and remember to return it to me,' I graciously remarked. 'I promise on both counts, Mrs Webb.' So having reported to H.M. Government I report to H.M. Opposition. . . .

For my part I have returned to the 'anti-Poor Law Commission' state of mind. The meetings seem no longer to concern me and, if I look in after lunch, it is only to show that I bear no ill will. Moreover, the Commission has run dry, both in evidence and in capacity for palavers – on two successive Tuesdays we have not met at all, and Monday's meetings have been very perfunctory and ill attended. Sidney and I are hard at work on the 'Treatise on Able-bodied Destitution: its Prevention and Treatment', and we foresee that for the next six months or a year we shall be absorbed in preparing the various reports arising out of the Commission. Just at present, the bulk of the work is falling on him, as I feel dreadfully tired – habitually tired – not ill, merely physically and mentally weary. Owing to his blessed strength and capacity, I can lie back in these times, just giving him all the suggestions and help that I can, and waiting calmly for returning strength. . . .

Campbell-Bannerman, who died of a heart attack on 22 April, had relinquished the premiership to Asquith on 5 April. In the new government McKenna became first Lord of the Admiralty. With Lloyd George as Chancellor of the Exchequer and Winston Churchill as president of the Board of Trade, the Liberals launched a progressive social policy. Lewis Harcourt (1863–1922) was a Radical. His father, William Harcourt, had introduced death duties in 1894.

18/20 April. Kilteragh, Kingston, Co. Dublin
Horace Plunkett's comfortable bachelor abode – three days' complete rest before ten days' motoring in West of Ireland on the pretence of investigating the Irish Poor Law – but really for a much needed change of scene and idea. . . .

The last days watching the formation of the Asquith ministry have been exciting. We have not seen any of the principals, so all we have heard has been mere hearsay. But two facts seem certain. Asquith wanted McKenna as his second man and had actually decided to make him Chancellor! But the public opinion of colleagues, press and rank and file, forced him to accept Lloyd George. He and L.G. seem to be on bad terms, according to Morant; the new Cabinet starts with two parties: Asquith and McKenna v. Lloyd George and Harcourt. . . .

On the whole, I incline to think that this government will *not* be able to do either Poor Law or Unemployment. In some ways it would be better that they should not, if we can get Morant settled at the Local Government Board or both Front Benches impregnated with the idea of the break-up. But, as Sidney says, 'A Bill in the hand is better than a Bill in the bush.' So we are content to leave the matter in the lap of the gods and go quietly on at our work. . . . It is odd how all these commissioners and the Commission as a whole seem [to be] receding from my sight. The expediency and the feasibility of our two schemes are the big facts before us; after that, Ministers and potential Ministers, civil servants, for or against – these are the means we are mostly thinking of. In the background, public opinion in the country, to be converted so as to give the right atmosphere. The R.C. is little more than an obstruction – difficult to kick out of the way.

29 April. [Rian Hotel, Co. Galway]
A pleasant and useful time with eight or nine colleagues at Dublin – chairman, Phelps, Bentham, Downes, Robinson, Bishop of Ross, Smart, H. Nunn, MacDougall – all most friendly. The chairman is quite satisfied that the Commission, as a whole, has accepted the resolutions agreed to as a final basis for the report, and is now beginning to write it, with the help of his three secretaries. He believes he can get the whole draft ready for discussion by the end of July – and that he will get it passed by the middle of August. . . . But my impression is that the end of August will see us in a morass of conflicting ideas. . . .

3 May. [Mallaranny]
. . . Feeling the impossibility of getting any kind of knowledge – even the most casual – from my trip, I have merely taken it as a holiday jaunt at the Treasury expense, with just the excuse of investigation to give a flavour to our touring. These days of motoring and steaming along coasts and between islands have been a most delightful rest to me. The beauty of the scenery, the freshness and pathos of Irish life, the complete break in the continual routine grind of the last two years, have done me a world of good. But this very enjoyment shows how hopelessly irresponsible I feel with regard to Irish affairs – no more responsible than if I were travelling in Norway or Sicily. For the misery is genuine – the men, women and children who crouch in those filthy huts and toil hour by hour on those boglands in a listless fashion, are in this their beloved country hopeless and helpless with regard to this world's affairs. There is heaven and there is America – and, according to whether they are the children of this world or of the next, they desire to escape to one or the other. Until this escape opens to them, they are drearily indifferent to varying degrees of

squalor and want — mechanically day after day they toil, but they do not struggle to survive the ordeal. In the West of Ireland, one realizes for the first time the grim fact of the existence of a whole community on the margin of cultivation. . . .

T. McKinnon Wood (1855–1927) was parliamentary secretary to the Board of Education. Walter Long (1854–1924) had been president of the Local Government Board 1900–05 and was opposed to municipal enterprise. Austen Chamberlain (1863–1937) was Chancellor of the Exchequer 1903–05.

15 May. [41 Grosvenor Road]
Yesterday we met for the last time before adjourning for the chairman to write the report. This, he believes, he and the secretaries, with Mrs Bosanquet's and Professor Smart's help, will accomplish by the first week in July. He then proposes to sit every day until the report is passed, even in August; it will then be handed over to someone to smooth out inconsistencies and we shall meet to sign it in October. Meanwhile, the minority and the partial dissentients will be expected to produce their documents equally ready for signature in October. This forecast is either ludicrously optimistic or this Commission is the most amazingly acquiescent body ever thrown together. But no one protested, no one except I, speaking for myself, Lansbury and Chandler, objected to the majority proposals. So the chairman will have some right to be angry if, when the report appears, there is a chorus of dis-approval. . . .

Meanwhile, Morant has provided me with some 100 copies of my scheme for breaking up the Poor Law, which he has had printed for his own consideration. I have sent or given it in confidence to Asquith, Lloyd George, Haldane, W. Churchill, McKenna, Sydney Buxton, Runciman, Harcourt, H. Samuel, John Burns, McKinnon Wood of the present government, and Balfour, Long, Austen Chamberlain, Lyttelton, Gerald Balfour, of the late government, and to a select few important civil servants, journalists and local administrators. I have a notion that when we have got our 'Unemployment Scheme' drafted in its final form, we will get Winston Churchill to print it at the Board of Trade and do ditto with that. Such big schemes require careful consideration by many brains; they have to sink in to the minds of those likely to carry them out if they are to become practical politics within a generation. And to my schemes of reform there are, at present, no rivals; they have the field to themselves. The sort of conglomeration of disjointed changes, which the majority are likely to agree on, will seem mere scraps and scrapings by the time they appear. Personally, I am inclined to hope that the report will be delayed for another year, so that my scheme may be digested. If I thought this government were capable of carrying out any scheme I would risk rushing it. But John Burns is no good, and they can't be rid of him. Of course, my colleagues have a sort of idea that I am at work propaganding – and that will hurry them to produce and publish something. But men in a hurry, with many obstacles before them, sometimes break their necks! We shall see.

Beatrice made another inconclusive but not unfriendly visit to Burns before going on to meet Haldane. She and Sidney were concerned to find a satisfactory successor to Mackinder at L.S.E., and their short-list of candidates included H.A.L. Fisher (1865–1940), the Oxford historian who became Minister of Education in Lloyd George's wartime coalition; W.P. Ashley (1876–1945), who had been teaching at the L.S.E. until he joined the Board of Trade in 1906; George Trevelyan (1876–1962), the historian; and their Fabian friend W.P. Reeves.

19 May. [41 Grosvenor Road]
. . . From John Burns we went to lunch alone with R.B. Haldane and found him as friendly as ever. Clearly his *bête noire* is Lloyd George, and after him Winston Churchill – the young generation knocking at the door. He is full of confidence in his Territorial Army and in all the reforms he has brought about at the War Office. . . .

What interested me, somewhat sadly, in both these men, was the manner in which their own personalities and their own careers loomed large before them; with Burns, blocking out everything else; with Haldane, detracting from the charm of his public-spirited intelligence. This was shown in both cases by an extra-ordinary anxiety to prove to us that they were the important factors in the government, and to run down other members of the Cabinet. Probably every poor mortal suffers from this obsession of self: but actors and actresses, and politicians, seem really plagued by it. Fine-natured men like Haldane, fastidious-natured men like A.J.B., neither of whom, as *littérateurs* or as lawyers or as doctors would be self-conscious, are, in their character as politicians, teased by the spirit of competitive fame.

H.J. Mackinder came to lunch today to discuss who should be his successor as Director of the School. For the last months we have known that his resignation was imminent, he intending to devote himself to the affairs of the Empire, in preparation for Parliament and office in the next Conservative ministry. He has been the best of colleagues during these four years, and has improved both the internal organization and the external position of the School. Indeed so competent a Director has he been, that he has virtually run the whole business, Sidney trusting his initiative and executive capacity. We part company with the highest regard for him, and I think he for us, but with no particular friendship. It is an instance of the absence of a common creed: our views are not mutually antagonistic, but they never meet and would never meet if we went on working for all eternity. . . .

27 May. [41 Grosvenor Road]
. . . W.P. Reeves accepted the position [Director of the L.S.E.] at £700, resigning his High Commissionership but retaining a salary of £400 as financial adviser, and another £200 or so as a director of the Bank of New Zealand. We are quite content and he begins with enthusiasm.

Sir Julius Wernher's country house was Luton Hoo, near the Bedfordshire industrial town of Luton.

27 July. [41 Grosvenor Road]
. . . Our stay in the cottage of the millionaire whilst we were composing this great collectivist document was really rather comic. Sir Julius Wernher wrote in May to offer us 'The Hermitage', a pleasant little house in its own grounds but in his park, for as long as we cared to accept it. From the extreme corner of the millionaire's park, we surveyed a machine for the futile expenditure of wealth. Wernher himself is a big man – big in body and big in mind and even big in his aims. To make wealth was his first aim; to carry on great enterprises because he delighted in industrial construction was his second aim, and now to advance technology and applied science has been his latest aim. It was over the establishment of the London 'Charlottenberg' scheme that Sidney came across him, and found him the best of fellows according to his own lights. Hence, we felt free to accept his hospitality. Part of the minor convention of his life has been the acquisition of a great country mansion, with an

historic name, a counterpart to Bath House, Piccadilly. This was no doubt to please his society-loving wife. . . . The family spend some Sundays at Luton Hoo and a few months in the autumn, but all the rest of the 365 days the big machine goes grinding on, with its 54 gardeners, 10 electricians, 20 or 30 house servants and endless labourers for no one's benefit, except that it furnishes dishonest pickings to all concerned.

The great mansion stood closed and silent in the closed and silent park – no one coming or going except the retinue of servants, the only noises the perpetual whirring and calling of the thousands of pheasants, ducks and other game that was fattening ready for the autumn slaughter. At the gates of the park, a bare half-mile distant, lay the crowded town of Luton – drunken, sensual, disorderly – crowded in mean streets, with a terrific infant mortality. The contrast was oppressingly unpleasant, and haunted our thoughts as we sat under the glorious trees and roamed through wood and garden, used their carriages, enjoyed the fruit, flowers and vegetables, and lived for a brief interval in close contact with an expenditure of thirty thousand a year on a country house alone.

The Webbs went to stay at a cottage near Leominster before going on to the Fabian summer school at Llanbedr; Pen-yr-allt was a large residence on the North Wales coast, three miles from Harlech. The secretary had taken a lease on the house and the Society held its summer school there for the next three years. Leo Amery (1873–1955), at this time a Fabian Socialist, worked for *The Times* 1899–1909. Frederick Lawson Dodd (1868–1962) was a dentist and an active Fabian; he had first suggested the idea of a summer school to the Society. Frederick Keeling (1886–1916), known as 'Ben', was a founder of the Cambridge Fabian Society in 1905. He became manager of the Leeds labour exchange, then assistant editor of the *New Statesman*. He was killed in France. Hugh Dalton (1887–1962), one of the Cambridge Fabians, became an academic economist, a Labour M.P. and Chancellor of the Exchequer in the 1945 Labour government. David Schloss, a Fabian civil servant, was a specialist in industrial relations. James Strachey (1887–1967), brother of the critic Lytton Strachey, joined the Fabians in 1908. He later translated the works of Freud. Rupert Brooke (1887–1915) was a poet and Cambridge Fabian who died on active service in Greece. Gerald Shove (1887–1947) was a left-wing economist who became a fellow of King's College, Cambridge. Dudley Ward (1885–1957) became a banker, worked at the Treasury during World War I and was a member of the British delegation to the Versailles Peace conference. Amber Reeves (1887–1981), the daughter of W.P. and Maude Reeves, was a student at Newnham College, Cambridge, and leading member of the Fabian 'Nursery' which an informal group of young Fabians set up in April 1906.

Catherine Wells, known as Jane, was the second wife of H.G. Wells with whom he had eloped in 1894.

15 September. [41 Grosvenor Road]
After another six weeks at a little house in Herefordshire and four days at the Fabian summer school, we are again back in London. Not yet finished the 'non-able-bodied' report, though nearly through with it. Meanwhile, I am again in disgrace with the Commission – this time somewhat seriously. As part of the newspaper campaign for the break-up of the Poor Law, we gave our Poor Law scheme to [Leo] Amery of *The Times*, telling him he could use the idea, but was *not* to mention either our names or the Royal Commission. About the middle of August there appeared special articles on the breaking-up of the Poor Law, giving the whole of the scheme – the last part verbatim. This really indiscreet use of our composition roused Lord George Hamilton to fury, and he fired off angry letters denouncing a breach of confidence. The last of these letters is not only amazingly indiscreet but contains a malicious fib. There are no two separate series of propositions before the Commission, there is only his draft report. He stuck in this statement in order to make it appear that there had been a breach of confidence, and of course to anyone who knows the make-up of the Commission the evil one must be 'the Webbs', in their combined capacity of commissioner and publicist.

To this attack there was no public rejoinder possible. I circulated a letter to the Commission saying that neither Sidney nor I had contributed the articles, but that we had circulated freely our scheme of reform and that the writer had evidently had a copy of it beside him. I was worried about the business, but Sidney remained imperturbable. Of course, the publication in *The Times*, together with Lord George's indiscreet letter, have boomed the scheme enormously, the *Morning Post, Standard* and many provincial papers accepting it as the obvious reform. The net result of our indiscreet, or, as some would say, unscrupulous activity, has been to damage the Webbs but to promote their ideas. We seem destined to use ourselves up in this breaking-up of the Poor Law – the fate of capacity and good intentions combined with bad manners! And the worst of my temperament is that I have far more audacity than I have passive courage. I do this thing with splendid dash and then tremble with fear afterwards. All of which means nervous strain.

97

Fortunately, there is always Sidney to fall back on, with his genuine indifference to what the world says. . . .

The Fabian summer school has become an odd and interesting institution. Two or three houses on the mountainous coast of North Wales are filled to overflowing for seven weeks with some hundred Fabians and sympathizers – a dozen or so young university graduates and undergraduates, another stratum of lower middle-class professionals, a stray member of Parliament or professor, a bevy of fair girls, and the remainder – a too large remainder – elderly and old nondescript females who find the place lively and fairly cheap. The young folk live the most unconventional life, giving the Quaker-like Lawson Dodd, who rules the roost, many an unpleasant quarter of an hour – stealing out on moor or sand, in stable or under hayricks, without always the requisite chaperone to make it look as wholly innocent as it really is. Then the 'gym' costume which they all affect is startling the Methodist Wales, and the conversation is most surprisingly open. 'Is dancing sexual?', I found three pretty Cambridge girl graduates discussing with half a dozen men. But mostly they talk economics and political science, in the intervals of breaking off the engagements to marry each other they formed a year ago. Meanwhile, there is some really useful intellectual intercourse going on between the elders, and between them and the younger ones. The Cambridge men are a remarkable set, quite the most remarkable the Fabian Society has hitherto attracted – fervent and brilliant.

I had seven of the Cambridge Fabians to stay with me on their way to Wales. Two are remarkable men – Keeling and Dalton – the one a fervent rebel (who reminds me of sister Holt [Lallie] in his generous vitality and incontinent intelligence), and the other an accomplished ecclesiastical sort of person, a subtle wily man with a certain peculiar charm for those who are not put off by his mannerism. The other five were, I think, commonplace – Schloss, Strachey, Brooke (a poetic beauty) and Shove; perhaps Dudley Ward was a little over the line of medium capacity and character. I also had the brilliant Amber Reeves, the double first Moral Science Tripos, an amazingly vital person and I suppose very clever, but a terrible little pagan – vain, egotistical, and careless of other people's happiness. This may be a phase, for she is a mere precocious child, but the phase is unpleasant and not promising for really sound work. However, the little person can work, and can work easily and play at the same time. A somewhat dangerous friendship is springing up between her and H.G. Wells. I think they are both too soundly self-interested to do more than cause poor Jane Wells some fearful feelings, but if Amber were my child I should be anxious.

2 October. [41 Grosvenor Road]
Sidney and I are living at the highest pressure of brainwork. We are working against time on the report, fearing lest the majority should agree to their report before Christmas. . . . To enable me to fill my part of the work I am living on the most rigorous hygienic basis – up at 6.30, cold bath and quick walk or ride, work from 7.30 to 1 o'clock, bread and cheese lunch, short rest, another walk, then tea and work until 6 or 6.30 – sometimes as much as seven hours' work in the day. I feel it is too much, and am sleeping badly from brain excitement. But short of breaking down, I must continue at it until Christmas. After the report is done with we *must* and *will* have a complete rest – Egypt or Italy – somewhere where we shall rid our minds of the whole business. The majority have no standard of excellence: their report is an amazingly useless document – except as a system of the break-up of the old idea of a deterrent Poor Law. But will the C.O.S. stand it?

5 October. [41 Grosvenor Road]
First meeting of the R.C. after the recess. . . . The chairman somewhat haltingly described the difficulties in drafting the Majority Report and desired a general discussion on its reception by the Commission. . . . No member objected to the doctrines contained in it, but everyone held themselves free to alter it. Settled that we are to meet twice a week, and that we are to try and get finished by Christmas, so far as discussion is concerned, leaving one month to get the report revised and out before the [parliamentary] session begins. There was coldness towards me, and Lansbury says they are very angry both at *The Times* episode and at the length of my report. . . .

In September Winston Churchill had married Clementine Hozier (1885–1977). William Blain was currently assistant secretary to the Treasury. Harold Cox (1859–1936) was a Fabian and a Liberal M.P., and the brother-in-law of Sydney Olivier. An economist and journalist who had collaborated with Sidney

Webb on a book on the Eight-Hour Day, he later became strongly anti-socialist. The meeting with Lloyd George was really the last chance for the Webbs to collaborate in drafting the social insurance measures which Lloyd George and Churchill were now preparing; but Beatrice's effort to see some moral or practical improvement in return for doles from the state, and her effort to get her own scheme ready before (as she wrote on 29 October) 'this mad dog of a Commission rushes at the public with its report', made her unsympathetic. The role that the Webbs might have played in shaping these reforms then passed to William Beveridge and Hubert Llewellyn Smith (1869–1945), permanent secretary to the Board of Trade 1907–19.

16 October. [41 Grosvenor Road]
. . . On Sunday we lunched with Winston Churchill and his bride – a charming lady, well-bred and pretty, and earnest withal, but not rich, by no means a 'good match', which is to Winston's credit. Winston had made a really eloquent speech on the unemployed the night before and he has mastered the Webb scheme, though not going the whole length of compulsory labour exchanges. He is brilliantly able – more than a phrase-monger, I think – and is definitely casting in his lot with the [cause of] constructive state action. No doubt he puts that side forward to me, but still he could not do it so well if he did not agree somewhat with it. After lunch Lloyd George came in and asked us to breakfast to discuss his insurance scheme.

On Friday we fulfilled the engagement at 11 Downing Street, meeting Haldane, Blain of the Treasury, two secretaries, Harold Cox and, after breakfast, Winston. We had a heated discussion with the Chancellor about the practicality of insurance against invalidity; tried to make him see that the state could not enter into competition with the friendly societies and insurance companies, that it could hardly subsidize a voluntary scheme without becoming responsible for the management, and that any insurance scheme would leave over all the real problems of public assistance. I tried to impress on them that any grant from the community to the individual, beyond what it does for all, ought to be conditional on better conduct; and that any insurance scheme had the fatal defect that the state got nothing for its money – that the persons felt they had a right to the allowance, whatever their conduct. Also, if you did all that was requisite for those who were uninsured, there was not much to be gained by being insured, except more freedom. Now insurance against unemployment had the great advantage that you could offer more freedom to the person who insured, compared with the person whom you maintained and forced to accept training. Hence, insurance against unemployment *might* be subsidized by the state as a sort of 'set-off' to the trade unionists to get them to accept 'maintenance with training' for all the others.

He [Lloyd George] is a clever fellow, but has less intellect than Winston, and not such an attractive personality – more of the preacher, less of the statesman. Haldane intervened, as the peacemaker, and suggested that insurance had to be part of a big scheme with conditional relief for those at the bottom, and insurance for those struggling up. . . .

29 October. [41 Grosvenor Road]
. . . I was sorry to hear from Kate that the Booth family feel aggrieved – say that somehow or other I 'drove Charles Booth off the Commission'. This is the most annoying story. C.B. from the first gave me the cold shoulder, and even upbraided me for insisting on getting at the documents of the central authority. I took both his rebuke and his coldness with good-natured equanimity – feeling that he had a perfect right to keep clear of me, if he thought I should injure his influence on the Commission. Now it appears that he thinks that I intrigued against him or his scheme, in his absence, and that it was my malign influence which made the Commission so unappreciative when he returned. As a matter of fact, I was surprised at the Commission's rudeness; that was only another instance of the chairman's incapacity to handle the members, and his strange combination of light-headedness and obstinacy. Now Charles Booth, who feels strong enough to join in the Commission's work, is angry with himself for resigning, and puts the blame on me; which chimes in with the anger of the rest of my colleagues. By the time that Commission ends, I shall be a well-hated person. Even the docile Robinson has turned against me! Every reference in the press, every unfavourable speech, every straw that points my way is the result of a Webb intrigue! The present mad hurry-scurry to get out their report is due, I think, to feeling that I am secretly at work preparing for their discomfiture – they imagine that the longer they wait the worse it will be. But once the great report is out, with all its weighty signatures, then the Webbs will sink again into oblivion! Bless them!

The Labour M.P.s, with the exception of a few more socialistic I.L.P. members, were little more than parliamentary spokesmen for the trade unions, and generally supported the Liberal government in return for political favours. They were regularly though casually consulted about social policy. David Shackleton (1858–1940) was a trade unionist and Labour M.P. who became labour adviser to the Home Office and then permanent secretary to the Ministry of Labour. George Barnes (1859–1940) was general secretary of the Amalgamated Society of Engineers 1896–1908: he became an M.P. in 1906, and Minister of Pensions in the wartime coalition. Peter Curran (1866–1910) was one of the socialist leaders thrown up by the 'New' unionism after the 1889 dock strike, and he became an M.P. in 1906. Arthur Henderson (1863–1935) was an ironmoulder who entered Parliament in 1903. First treasurer and then secretary of the Labour Party, he played a vital role in its organization, and after serving in the wartime coalition he resigned to collaborate with Webb and MacDonald in preparing its post-war constitution and policy. He was to serve as Home Secretary and Foreign Secretary in the first two Labour governments. W.A. Appleton (1859–1940) was secretary of the Lacemakers' Union 1896–1907 and was currently secretary of the General Federation of Trade Unions. He strongly supported Lloyd George's insurance schemes.

15 November. [41 Grosvenor Road]
The Prime Minister wrote about a fortnight ago to Lord George Hamilton to ask for the evidence taken before the Commission. Without any notice, Lord George brought the matter before the Commission and persuaded those who were present to refuse to supply the evidence, but to offer the draft report after it had passed the drafting committee. . . .

On Saturday, Haldane came round in his motor. 'I have come to ask you whether you would object to our seeing your report.' 'Certainly not,' I replied. 'I feel quite at liberty to give you all I have, as I understand that the majority are sending you their draft. But get the evidence and the investigators' reports,' I added. 'Asquith has written again for it, and he quite hopes to get it.' 'Well, if they *don't* give it you, I shall feel free to do so, as I know John Burns has had some of it – I saw it on his table a year ago.'

This morning Haldane again appeared. 'I want another copy of your report; I have given mine to a young man to master, and I want one for myself. Also *could* you possibly give the Cabinet a loan of the evidence?' 'I will get you Lansbury's if possible.' Poor dear ninnies of a Commission: a futile refusal producing the worst impression. And not to realize that the government had only to ask me for it!

Haldane explained that he had been deputed by the P.M. to get up the whole subject, with a view to drawing up a comprehensive scheme of reform. . . . He was rather woolly about it. But we chaffingly told him that if the Liberals did not 'Break up the Poor Law', we would give the whole business to the tariff reformers; they were in want of a good social reform cry wherewith to go to the country. My own idea is that the Liberals will adumbrate the scheme, but the Tories will carry it out. Which I should prefer in many ways – there would be no nonsense about democracy!

About a fortnight ago, we were invited to breakfast at the Board of Trade. We found assembled some half-dozen of the Labour M.P.s – Shackleton, Barnes, Curran, Henderson, Appleton, the principal officials of the Board of Trade, Winston and Lloyd George and Masterman. After breakfast we sat round a table and discussed this agenda for a couple of hours – Winston using us to explain the theory of labour exchanges to the Labour men. . . . In despair, when they realize the danger of displacement of the ordinary workers by unemployed labour, they sometimes suggest unemployed benefit paid by the state *with no conditions*. That is, of course, under the present conditions of human will, sheer madness – whatever it may be in good times to come.

The difficulty of solving the question [of the able-bodied un-employed] oppresses me. I dream of it at night, I pray for light in the early morning, I grind, grind, grind, all the hours of the working day to try to get a solution. . . .

VOLUME 27

15 December. [41 Grosvenor Road]
I should like to begin this book with the end of the Royal Commission. But we are still slaving away. I am so fagged that I hardly do more than run after Sidney, who goes slogging along in his placid manner, looking neither to the right nor to the left, until he is through with it.

The poor old Commission – and it is getting more old and weary, if not actually senile, with every week's sitting. It is floundering about in its morass of a report. Everyone is disgusted with the report but no one dares get up and openly rebel. 'What is the alternative? Mrs Webb's draft dissent from the chairman's draft report,' says one disconcerted commissioner to the other. For our document stares at them in a fine blue cover; and though it is only Part I, yet there it is, three hundred pages of reasoned stuff with a scheme of reform at the end. . . .

Are all men quite so imbecile as that lot are? I sit and watch them and wonder. They play about, altering commas and capitals and changing the names of things, but leaving to mere accident whether or not the vagrants or the mentally defective are to be dealt with under the Poor Law. What puzzles me is that Provis goes into fits of laughter, and Loch is beginning to be hysterically hilarious, when the chairman is more than usually muddled and inconsequent. I should have thought that a report which everyone is waiting for is not quite a laughing matter. . . . If I ever sit again on a royal commission, I hope my colleagues will be of a superior calibre, for really it is shockingly bad for one's character to be with such folk. It makes me feel intolerably superior.

᥆ 1909 ᥆

1 January. [41 Grosvenor Road]
Our report is finished. . . . On Saturday we are all to attend and be photographed and sign a blank piece of paper. So ends the Commission of 1906–1909. I am in a state of complete exhaustion, made worse by nervous apprehension of more indiscretions in the press in the interests of the dissentient minority. The Minority Report has been pretty considerably read, and one or two copies are flying about. However, my colleagues will now melt back into the world at large and we shall know each other no more. The relation has not been a pleasant one, for either side.

17 January. [Longfords]
A scrimmagey meeting on Saturday ended the Royal Commission as far as I am concerned. I was dead beat, and in that state gave Duff a bit of my mind as regards the procedure of the Commission. We are all commanded to sign. But the report from which we had to sign our dissent is still in the making – a new piece of it came round today which apparently is to be inserted into the *signed* document without any meeting of the signatories. . . .

Meanwhile, everything looks favourable for the reception of the Minority Report. The majority are counting on the reviewers never getting to that document and damning it as socialist. We naturally are taking care, so far as we can, that they get at it not later than to the Majority Report. We believe that the Majority Report will get a bad reception from all sides. We shall see.

Now I am resting for a week with sister Playne before pulling myself together and clearing up all the mess left over by the report. Then we are going off for a month's holiday. The next months may be stormy. 'You have declared war,' wrote one of the inspectors of the Local Government Board, 'and war this will be.'

Looking back on those autumn months, I wonder how I managed to come through it. It was sheer will-power induced by prayer. Every morning I tramped out between 6.30 and 7.30 – an hour of sharp physical exercise combined with intense prayer for help to solve the problem before us each morning. And solutions *did* come to me in those morning walks. How they came I do not know, but by the time I sat down to work, the particular knot was undone. Now I am in a state of collapse because there is nothing to pray for, nothing particular to do, which seems *beyond* my power – for which I need inspiration. Perhaps there will be another 'Call'. I must be strong enough to answer 'Yes, we will come and do it.'

5 February. [41 Grosvenor Road]
Still in the depth of depression – the reaction from the pressure of the last eight months. But already I am beginning to foresee that presently I shall revive, and that I shall find myself back again in the quiet atmosphere of the student's life, with no public responsibilities, and with none of those horribly difficult questions of conduct that have been a sort of nightmare to me since I joined the Royal Commission. The plain truth is, that the position of a minority on a hostile royal commission is rather intolerable: it has no chance of fighting openly. . . . Throughout the whole business, Lord George has considered the Commission analogous to a government of which he was Prime Minister, and those who agreed with him secretaries of state, and the minority members sort of under-secretaries to be told as much, or as little, as he chose and to obey orders. This has led me to look elsewhere for my forces, and to undermine and circumvent the commissioners' will by calling on those forces. This, of course, has been 'not nice' on my side, and I

have from time to time felt horribly miserable about it – especially, I am afraid, when I have been found out! Such are the infirmities of half-civilized human nature! Sidney, of course, takes a different view and has no kind of qualms; he is *self-less* and does not mind doing what he decides it is right to do, whatever other people may think about it. And in all these ways he has a robust conscience. . . .

The Commission had sat for three years. Its members or their assistants had visited more than 200 Poor Law districts and over 400 institutions, heard 456 witnesses, received 900 statements of evidence, and produced 47 volumes reporting their proceedings. Both the Majority and Minority Reports were consequently massive. (The Minority Report alone amounted to 945 pages.) The reports were in agreement on the lax distribution of outdoor relief, the apathy and ignorance of many guardians, the incompetence of overworked and undertrained relieving officers, the need to prevent as well as relieve poverty without discouraging self-help. The Majority supported unemployment insurance, which the Webbs disliked, but had been reluctant to go so far as the Webbs' proposals for compulsory training for the feckless, public works geared to the trade cycle, and the creation of a Ministry of Labour. These were reasonable differences of emphasis and degree, not principle. But the two factions divided on one important point – the future of the Poor Law itself. The majority stood for its preservation, much modified: the Local Government Board was to retain central control of its policy and finances, and local public assistance committees were to be responsible for applying it, in collaboration with such voluntary agencies as the C.O.S. The Minority Report came out plainly for the break-up of the old system, the abolition of pauper status in any form, and the apportionment of the various categories of need to more capable and professional government departments. The issue was not resolved for many years, partly because the publication of two reports was an excuse for ignoring them both, partly because Lloyd George and Churchill introduced pension and insurance schemes which did not raise the same financial and political problems, and partly because the government became preoccupied with the struggle against the Lords.

18 February. [41 Grosvenor Road]
The day after the reception of the reports of the Poor Law Commission. We turned out to be quite wrong as to the reception of the Majority Report. So far as the first day's reviews are concerned, the majority have got a magnificent reception. We have had a fair 'look-in', but only in those papers who had got to know of the existence of a minority report before the issue late on Wednesday night. If we had not taken steps, we should have been submerged completely by the great length of the Majority Report, coupled with their revolutionary proposals, the largeness of their

majority and the relative weight of the names. Roughly speaking, all the Conservative papers went for the majority proposals, and the London Liberal papers were decidedly for ours. We secured, in fact, belligerent rights, but not more than that! The majority hold the platform. Perhaps we feel a trifle foolish at having 'crabbed' the Majority Report to our family and intimate friends, and exalted our own. That has certainly not proved to be the estimate of public opinion. . . .

In another fortnight we sail for Italy for a good five or six weeks' holiday. We need it to refresh us from the hard grind of these years, and to cleanse the thoughts that are in us – at least, I do. At present I am morbidly sensitive, quite unworthily so.

22 February. [41 Grosvenor Road]
I am recovering my equilibrium slowly. It is always interesting to analyse one's mistakes and successes. In our depreciation of the Majority Report and our false expectation of its failure to 'catch on', we overlooked the immense step made by the sweeping away of the deterrent Poor Law – *in name, at any rate*, and, to some extent, in substance – by municipalizing its control. Every now and again, I realized this, but then when I considered the chaotic proposals in the Majority Report, I lost sight of it in my indignation at their attempt to present a new appearance while maintaining the old substance underneath. In a sense, the Majority Report meant success to our cause, but not victory to ourselves. However, I am inclined to think the distinction between the two reports – the fact that only by distribution of the services can you obtain 'curative and restorative' treatment – will become gradually apparent to the nation. What is certainly most surprising is the absence of any kind of protest from the adherents of the old order, the believers in the Principles of 1834, against the iconoclastic effect of the Majority Report. That the Principles of 1834 should die so easily is certainly a thoroughgoing surprise. Even the *Spectator* acquiesces.

Wells always sent copies of his books to a large number of acquaintances. In a letter written on 10 February, Beatrice compared *Tono-Bungay* unfavourably with *The War in the Air*. Wells replied with a characteristically splenetic letter. On 24 February Beatrice sent an appeasing note, but Wells wrote back saying that she was 'wilfully unsympathetic', insisting that she and Sidney had 'the knack of estranging people', and implying that he was the object of a Webb conspiracy to tarnish his reputation. 'Don't shake us off altogether,' Beatrice replied on 28 February. 'It won't be good for either the Webbs or the Wells, and would be very bad for the common cause.'

24 February. [41 Grosvenor Road]
This letter from H.G. Wells is a real gem and I enshrine it with honours in my diary. It is, of course, H.G. at his worst; just now he is at his worst in anything that concerns the Shaws or us or the Fabian Society – conceit, bitterness, and an element of treachery to past intimacies. Will he get over it, I wonder? Or is he to become, as far as Fabians and Fabianism is concerned, a literary J.R. MacDonald, a persistent and furious hater of the dominant influence?

His two last books – *War in the Air* and *Tono-Bungay* – are amazingly clever bits of work. I have the bad taste to prefer the former. Both illustrate the same theme – the mean chaos of human affairs. But *War in the Air* is avowedly a sort of allegory, or a parody. In form, an extravagancy; it is, in substance, a realistic description of the lowest and poorest side of social life. *Tono-Bungay*, on the other hand, sets out to be a straightforward description of society as it exists today, a sober estimate of the business world. But it turned out to be a veritable caricature, and a bitter one. Moreover, it bores me because its detail is made up, not of real knowledge of the world he describes, but of stray bits he has heard from this or that person. There are quite a lot of things he has picked up from me – anecdotes about businessmen that I have told him are woven into his text, just all wrong, and conveying an absurd impression of meaningless chaos. But he is a useful missionary to whole crowds of persons whom we could never get at. It will be sad if he turns completely sour: if, after all, it turns out to be a misfortune to the cause we both believe in that we should have known one another. Also, I suspect that man is going through an ugly trouble, and I would like to help him through it, instead of serving as a source of bitterness and antagonism.

1 March. [41 Grosvenor Road]
Another letter from H.G., withdrawing the impersonal and emphasizing the personal aspect of his objection to the Webbs. I wrote back a soothing letter – I had apparently offended him by a careless letter about *Tono-Bungay* – stupidly worded because I admired *War in the Air* too much, and *Tono-Bungay* not enough. It is strange that he seems obsessed with the notion that we have some scheme to

undo his influence. Bless the man! we never think of him now he has resigned from the Fabian Society. While he was there we *had* to think of him, because he spent his whole energy attacking us. But – I can honestly say that our one thought was to stop him doing mischief, but to avoid doing him or his influence any harm. We wanted to keep him as an asset to the cause; but we could not let him simply smash the thing up without having the least intention of working out a new plan of campaign.

The Webbs went by sea to Naples, then to Rome and Assisi, and joined the Playnes in Florence.

20 April. [41 Grosvenor Road]
Home again, after the most refreshing six weeks' holiday . . . to find our little home cleaned up and re-decorated and our work awaiting us. Above all, I have a completely rested brain, and the Commission, with all its hateful friction, has practically ceased to concern me. Good intention is now dominant, and I have recovered the habit of prayer. What I have to avoid is all silly worry and self-consciousness. We have to go straight for our object – to clean up the base of society, single-mindedly, without thought of ourselves or what people think of us or our work. Sidney has this talent of unselfconscious effort: 'the soldier's pay if not the victor's mead' he is always content with, and our pay (he suggests), is a very handsome one! But I need to deliberately oust from my mind other feelings. Now that I am strong again and my brain thoroughly re-created with new thoughts and feelings, rested by thoughts about great things, unconnected with my own little spark of life, I can go back to my daily work with real enjoyment in the routine grind, and without thought of any other reward than the doing of the work itself, in loving companionship with my boy, and kindly intercourse with fellow workers. We may have another fifteen or twenty years of working life. May we use these years well, with zeal, discretion, kindliness and straightforward integrity.

25 April. [41 Grosvenor Road]
So far as we can foretell, the work of the next eighteen months will consist of (1) propaganda of the Minority Report, (2) bringing out of books connected with these proposals, and also (3) finishing up our eighteenth-century study of English local government. We are

starting a committee for pushing the Minority Report, and we are lecturing considerably: five days next week in the big North Country towns, and odd lectures in London, Oxford, etc. — all before we go for a week to the Fabian school in Wales. Beyond this work, I mean, during the next ten months, to turn my attention on to the Fabian Society and the School [L.S.E.] and to cultivate the young people who are members of either organization, more especially the Fabian Society. There is coming over the country a great wave of reaction against Liberalism and Labour, and the Fabian Society will probably lose in membership. The Minority Report, and the kudos which the Society has got out of it, will stay that reaction but not wholly prevent it. By our personal influence we have to keep the flag flying — the flag of steady, persistent pressure for levelling up the bottomest layer of society. We think that in the Minority Report we have a clear consistent scheme which can be worked out by any sensible and well-intentioned body of administrators. The wave of political reaction need not prevent this: the Conservatives are, for this purpose, quite as good as the Liberals and we have as much influence over them.

PART II

A Plunge into Propaganda
May 1909–May 1911

Introduction to Part II

FROM 1906 until she and Sidney left England on a tour of the East in 1911 Beatrice was preoccupied with the problems of the Poor Law Commission and the propaganda campaign which followed it, and despite her close association with Balfour, Haldane and other prominent politicians, there are few diary comments conveying the significance and intensity of the party struggle that was developing in Parliament.

The Liberals had won a massive majority in 1906 but they had been able to do little with it, partly because they were divided — Campbell-Bannerman had been more bent on retrenchment than social reform — and partly because they found great difficulty in passing the legislation they did want. They had carried the Trades Disputes Act in 1906, restoring the legal immunities that the unions had lost by the Taff Vale decision; they were introducing old age pensions; and they could claim that their Eight-Hour Act for the miners was the first statutory limitation on adult male hours of work. But it was becoming clear that Balfour was using the built-in Tory majority in the House of Lords to block any Bills the Opposition disliked. The Lords had already rejected Bills on plural voting, education, licensing and Scottish land reform, and it was obvious that they would take an even more intransigent line towards the reforms Churchill was proposing from his new Cabinet post in the Board of Trade and the redistributive taxes that could be expected with Lloyd George as Chancellor of the Exchequer. At the same time Asquith was under pressure from the radical wing of his party and from the labour movement as a new economic depression produced growing unemployment and signs of discontent in the country. The loss of eight by-elections in 1908 was a warning that something had to be done.

The House of Lords could vote out any Bill it pleased, but it was a parliamentary convention that the Upper House would pass Finance Bills. This offered a way to avoid the veto of the Lords, for social reform legislation could be linked to the Budget, but this device was likely to produce a constitutional crisis. It was Lloyd George's first budget that brought matters to a head. Faced by the heavy costs of the new old age pensions and increased naval expenditure, he raised death duties and income tax, introduced a super-tax and, a dramatic innovation, imposed land taxes which involved a valuation of all land in Britain. The Opposition reacted at once, seeing such measures as the beginning of the end of private property. Lloyd George, for his part, called this a People's Budget and dedicated himself to wage implacable warfare against poverty and squalor. He used all his powers of oratory to paint a picture of a country owned by 10,000 landlords who left 'the rest of us trespassers in the land of our birth'.

Thus provoked, the Lords threw out the Finance Bill at the end of November by 350 to 75, and so deprived the government of the funds to carry on its business. Parliament was dissolved and a general election called for January 1910. The great constitutional struggle – the Peers versus the People – had begun.

The result of the election was no more than an equivocal victory for the Liberals. They won 275 seats against 273 Unionists and thus had to depend on 40 Labour members and 82 Irish nationalists for their majority. After a year's unprecedented delay, the Lords accepted the mandate of the polls and passed the Finance Bill on 28 April 1910. The question of how to deal with their power remained.

On 14 April the Liberals introduced a Parliament Bill which deprived the Lords of any power over Money Bills, and provided that other Bills rejected by the Lords would become law after two years had elapsed since their introduction in the Commons. In the course of complex private discussions and public debates, it became clear that the lines were hardening on both sides. It was said that if the Lords continued to resist Asquith might try to use the royal prerogative and ask the King to swamp the Tories by a massive creation of new peers. On 6 May, during the parliamentary recess, the King died unexpectedly and the Prime Minister, cruising on the Admiralty yacht, returned on 9 May to face King George V, who had come to the throne ill prepared to cope with such constitutional complexities.

114

Asquith and the Liberals now sought a compromise solution by setting up a constitutional conference to work out more generally acceptable proposals. It consisted of leaders of both parties and representatives from the House of Lords led by Lord Lansdowne (1845–1927), a one-time Liberal who had defected over Home Rule, had been Balfour's Foreign Secretary in 1900–05 and leader of the Conservatives in the Lords since 1903. When no agreement had been reached by November, the Cabinet decided to call yet another election and before polling day Asquith elicited a promise from the King (who insisted that it should remain secret) that if necessary he would use his powers to pack the Lords with men who would vote for constitutional reform.

Parliament was dissolved on 28 November and by 21 December the new House was complete. Another high poll had produced little change. While the Liberals lost three seats and the Unionists (the name now given to the Conservatives) one, the Labour Party and the Irish nationalists gained two each. Despite the election some Unionists still pressed for the rejection of the Parliament Bill, regarding the King's rumoured promise as mere bluff, and Lord Lansdowne canvassed his own set of window-dressing proposals. At the beginning of March 1911 the Parliament Bill passed its second reading in the Commons by 368 votes to 273 and it reached the House of Lords in late June, the determination of the 'last ditchers' to hold out providing a disturbing background to the Coronation on 22 June.

By mid-July the King was advised that the moment had come for him to act but, reluctant to do so, he urged that the Lords should be given a last chance to face the reality of the situation. Although Lansdowne capitulated on 21 July and Lord Curzon urged his colleagues to give way, a nucleus of diehards held out. When the Bill was again presented in the Lords on 9 August, Lord Morley told them bluntly that rejection would mean the creation of peers to pass it. In the suffocating heat of an exceptionally hot summer, the Bill was passed on 11 August by 131 votes to 114.

The bitter confrontation of this struggle for power set the tone of politics for many years to come. The national restlessness erupted in a running fire of strikes, in the growing militant demands of the suffragettes, and an increasing polarization of the problem in Ireland.

115

ᴄᴎ 1909 ᴎᴗ

The Webb campaign provoked the supporters of the Majority Report into forming a National Poor Law Reform Association. This counter-campaign – together with the tactical advantage of the 'constructive' and more appealing slogan of 'a crusade against misery' – led the Webbs to change the name of their group to the National Committee for the Prevention of Destitution. Beatrice was confident that their efforts would 'convert the country to a policy of complete communal responsibility for the fact of destitution': for many years, she concluded, 'that responsibility will be imperfectly fulfilled, but it will never again be repudiated'. In this sense the Minority Report had a lasting influence and paved the way for the modern welfare state. Lloyd George had introduced 'the People's Budget' on 29 April.

15 May. [41 Grosvenor Road]
Enter the National Committee for the Break-Up of the Poor Law.

Started on our campaign of forming public opinion. My first attempt at organization. I am trying a new experiment – an executive committee for consultative purposes and a secretariat of young men and women who will initiate policy and carry it out, I acting as chairman and reporting to the executive committee. We start, with very little money and a good deal of zeal, on a crusade against destitution. It is rather funny to start, at my time of life, on the war-path at the head of a contingent of young men and women. What I have got to aim at is to make these young people do the work, acting as moderator and councillor and occasionally suggesting new departures for them to carry out. I have to teach them how to work, not work myself. All the same it is a horrid nuisance: I long to get back to the quiet life of research, and pleasant friendship, with the long days and weeks in the country we enjoyed before the Royal Commission came in to upset our life.

Leonard Hobhouse (1864–1929) was a cousin of Beatrice's brother-in-law, Henry Hobhouse. He was professor of sociology at London University. J.A. Hobson (1858–1940) was a radical economist and internationalist, author of *The Evolution of Modern Capitalism*. Gilbert Murray (1866–1957) was an eminent classicist, a Liberal and a strong internationalist. Graham Wallas (1858–1932) was a lecturer at the L.S.E., one of the early Fabians and an old friend of the Webbs'.

18 June. [41 Grosvenor Road]
A month's grind at preparing forms, letters, membership cards, leaflets, tracts and other literature, for the National Committee. It looks as if Sidney and I will be absorbed in directing the propaganda – probably entirely, for three or four months at any rate, and for most of our time for the next year or so. What I am trying to set on foot is a real comradeship in this crusade – an intensive culture of the membership with a view of enrolling others and getting everyone to give of their best. My band of volunteers are devoted; and we are trying to do the utmost with a small sum of money – £600. I have a vision of a permanent organization growing out of the temporary propaganda – an organization to maintain the standard of life in all its aspects, and to co-ordinate voluntary effort with the action of the public authorities responsible for each service. Time will show.

Meanwhile, we have been quite strangely 'dropped' by the more distinguished of our acquaintances, and by the Liberal Ministers in particular. I have never had so few invitations as this season, and this in spite of the advertisement of the Minority Report. No doubt this is partly due to our growing reputation for being absorbed in work, but largely, I think, because there is a return of active fear of socialism, or of being assumed to be connected with socialists, though Lord George Hamilton's bad word (and I hear he 'foams at the mouth' whenever I am mentioned) counts. Altogether I am rather in disgrace with the great folk!

In response to an invitation to dine, Haldane called yesterday – excused himself from dining here and asked us to come and dine that very evening with Elizabeth and himself alone. Last evening we told him, in a friendly way, of our new plunge into propaganda, and suggested that a crusade against destitution was a really fine complement to 'the Great Budget'. He welcomed neither the news of our work, nor the reference to the magnitude of his colleagues' success! Both displeased him. We gathered from what he said, or left unsaid, that he had become indifferent, if not actually hostile, to the minority scheme – or felt that the Cabinet intended to be so. There does not seem to be any chance of the majority scheme being accepted – rather an inertia and a willingness to accept John Burns's assurance at the Local Government Board that the *status quo* was the best of all possible worlds. Haldane actually stood up for J.B. as an efficient minister!. . . .

What the ill success of that evening proved to me was that my instinct to keep clear of the Liberal ministry was a wise one. It would have been better if I had *not* invited Haldane and had *not* accepted his *pis aller* invitation. For some reason which we do not appreciate, the Haldanes are constrained or estranged. Possibly because they feel obliged to go back on their former agreement with the Minority Report, possibly because they have heard that we admire Lloyd George and Winston Churchill and openly state that they are the best of the party. (I always put in a saving clause for Haldane, out of old affection.)

Unfortunately our estrangement from the Whigs does not mean comradeship with the Radicals: we are in the wrong and likely to become wronger with Lloyd George and Winston Churchill over immediate issues. We do not see our way to support their insurance schemes. We shall not go against them directly, but we shall not withdraw our criticisms in the Minority Report. If their schemes can be carried out, we should not much object. Both have good consequences. But we still doubt their practicability, and some of the necessary conditions strike us as very unsatisfactory. The *unconditionality* of all payments under insurance schemes constitutes a grave defect. The state gets nothing for its money in the way of conduct — it may even encourage malingerers. However, we shall honestly try not to crab the government schemes: they are thoroughly well-intentioned.

We remain friends with the Balfours. Arthur dined here a day or two ago and was as friendly as ever. Gerald has accepted the presidentship of the Students' Union of the London School of Economics — a very kindly action. But then they are not in office! and any agitation for the Minority Report does not affect them except that it may be an inconvenience to the Liberals and, therefore, welcome — so says the cynic. I am inclined to believe in their genuine friendliness.

As a set-off to the estrangement from the Liberal leaders, many progressives who have shunned both us and the Fabians are trooping in to the National Committee — Leonard Hobhouse, J.A. Hobson, G.P. Gooch, Wallas, Gilbert Murray, and H.G. Wells and others — and the Liberal editors are friendly.

What I have to keep intact is my health and my nerve. All this office organization, writing ephemeral tracts, preparing speeches and talking to all sorts of different persons, is soul-destroying; it excites but does not satisfy. There is none of that happy alternation of strenuous work and complete rest which made such a pleasant life. However, the life of an agitator lies before me for many months, perhaps years.

22 June. [41 Grosvenor Road]
I met Winston on the Embankment this afternoon. 'Well, how do you think we are doing, Mrs Webb?' '*You* are doing very well, Mr Churchill, but I have my doubts about your Cabinet; I don't believe they mean to do anything with the Poor Law.' 'Oh! yes they do,' said Winston. 'You must talk to Haldane about it, he has it in hand. We are going in for a *classified* Poor Law.' I muttered something about *that* not being sufficient, which he half-understood, and then turned the conversation. I had obtained the clue to Haldane's displeasure. He and Asquith have decided *against* the break-up of the Poor Law. We have a formidable fight before us. They are contemplating, not the majority scheme, but a new Poor Law authority of some kind or another. We shall have to fight that hard, and we may be beaten. We must not talk big, or boast or brag. We must just go persistently on, taking every opportunity of converting the country. Meanwhile, the less we see of the Liberal Ministers, the better. We had better not *know* they are against us. . . .

On 4 July the University of Manchester conferred the honorary degree of Doctor of Laws on Beatrice. Earlier in the year 200 Fabians had attended a testimonial dinner to the Webbs.

6 July. [41 Grosvenor Road]
A pleasant episode: delighted to get my doctorate, and from Manchester, the birthplace of my family as members of the governing class. Dear old father, how pleased he would have been!

22 July. [41 Grosvenor Road]
We are living in a veritable turmoil. The little office we took is crowded with literature and active workers: members are streaming in and a good deal of money. Sidney and I spend our lives writing, talking, organizing. After all, we are not far off the end of our working life, and if we could really start a great social drainage scheme before we leave the scene, it would be something for which

119

to die 'content'. It is no use shrinking from this life of surface agitation, from this perpetual outgiving of personality. We have just got to use ourselves up at it. I have taken to it too late to make more than a mediocre success, but I have our joint name as a sort of jumping-off place. It is a curiously demoralizing life, if one did not realize the essential conditions of it and guard one's mind from taking them otherwise than conditions that all agitators are subject to — the subservient and foolish admiration of followers. Just as during those last months of the Commission I was working in the atmosphere of perpetual hostility and disparagement, here I am working in the atmosphere of admiration and willing obedience to my will. One has to accept this atmosphere, even to foster it, otherwise an organization does not flourish. But one must be perpetually reminding oneself that the attitude of followers does not depend on one's own excellence but on the exigencies of leadership. . . .

The rumour that Wells and Amber Reeves were having an affair merged with gossip about his earlier involvement with Rosamund Bland, daughter of the pioneer Fabian journalist Hubert Bland and his novelist wife Edith Nesbit. Amber Reeves was now living at Woldingham, in Surrey, in a cottage paid for by Wells, who continued to visit her, although she had accepted a repeated offer of marriage from a Fabian lawyer, G. Rivers Blanco White (1883–1966), later Recorder of Croydon. Sydney Olivier had been appointed Governor of Jamaica in 1907. The Webbs were staying in a private hotel near the Fabian conference house.

Early August. [Brynlerion, Llanfair, Harlech]
The end of our friendship with H.G. Wells. A sordid intrigue with poor little Amber Reeves – the coming of a baby, and the run to cover of marriage with another man, a clever and charming young Fabian (Blanco White), who married her, knowing the facts, out of devoted chivalry. The story got about owing to Amber's own confidence to a Cambridge don's wife, and owing to H.G. Wells's own indiscretions. Moreover, after the hurried marriage, without the Reeves's knowledge, of Amber and Blanco, Amber and H.G. Wells insist on remaining friends – a sort of *Days of the Comet* affair. We hear of it late in the day and feel ourselves obliged to warn Sydney Olivier, who was over on a holiday, against letting his four handsome daughters run about with H.G. Wells. (Apparently H.G. tried to seduce Rosamund

120

Bland. If the Reeveses had only known of that, they would not have allowed Amber to stay with him [at his Sandgate home] for a month at a time.) So I think we were right to tell Sydney Olivier. But as a matter of fact H.G. had already told him that Amber was going to have a baby, that he was supplying the rent of the house, and that he had been madly in love with Amber and that 'we were much too timid about these things'.

For some reason that we do not understand, Sydney Olivier quoted us as his authority, and so we got these letters from H.G. Wells as well as a pathetic one from Reeves. It is a horrid affair and has cost us much. If Amber will let us, we shall stand by her as Blanco's wife and drop H.G. Wells, once for all, as he no doubt will drop us. He will doubtless drift into other circles – probably the only person of his own *ménage* who will suffer is his patient and all-enduring little wife, who, having entered into that position illicitly herself at the cost of another woman, cannot complain.

But the whole case, and the misery that seems likely to follow, is a striking example of the tangle into which we have got on the sex question. We accepted Wells, in spite of his earlier divorce case, on grounds of tolerance. He and his wife were happy – the other wife had married again, and there seemed no reason, on ordinary enlightened principles, for us to hold back or object. The Reeveses knowing all these facts, and Mrs Reeves claiming to be 'advanced' in her opinions (she did not object to *In The Days of the Comet*), were very intimate with him and allowed him to become Amber's guide, philosopher and friend. Amber being a little heathen, and H.G. being a sensualist, they both let themselves go, and start a surreptitious liaison. At first, both of them think that they will stand it out. But Amber gets into a panic, and marries the first faithful swain who will let himself be married to a lady with a 'past' of an imminent character. But apparently there is no breach; and the household goes on being of a very mixed sort – the Reeves parents looking on in tragic sorrow, and Reeves calling H.G. a 'vile impudent blackguard'.

And all this arises because we none of us know what exactly is the sexual code we believe in, approving of many things on paper which we violently object to when they are practised by those we care about. Of course, the inevitable condition today of any 'sexual experiments' is deceit and secrecy – it is this that makes any divergence from the conventional morality so sordid and lowering.

That is why upright minds are careful not to experiment, except in the 'accustomed way' (i.e. with prostitutes). It is hardly fair to become intimate with a young girl, fresh from college, on the assumption that you believe in monogamy, and then suddenly to propose a polygamous relationship without giving her guardians and friends any kind of notice. That is not playing the game of sexual irregularity even according to the rules of a game full of hazards, at any rate, for the woman.

Oddly enough, Sidney had long had a settled aversion to H.G. Wells, thought him a purely selfish creature, with no redeeming motive, nothing but his cleverness to recommend him.

What we regret is the possibility of adding to W.P. Reeves's grief, or doing anything to lessen the bare chance of a happy marriage between Amber and Blanco. If either of us is to blame, it is I, and it is Sidney who seems likely to get the blame from Reeves and others.

Anticipations, published in 1901, was an extremely successful 'prospectus' on life in the new century. The Sassoons were a wealthy and socially smart dynasty of merchants in the India trade, who had a house at Hythe noted for its lavish entertainment. Edward Sassoon (1856–1912) was the M.P. for Hythe when Wells was living at Sandgate, and Wells was frequently invited to the Sassoon house. Taplow Court, near Henley-on-Thames, was the country house where Lady Desborough entertained the fashionable world.

22 August. [41 Grosvenor Road]
All is right between us and Reeves, and we have opened friendly relations with Amber. We will make a real, honest effort to get a hold over her and prevent the 'rot' going further. She is a little liar, she is superlatively vain, and she has little or no pity in her nature – but this triad of bad qualities may be but one of her personalities. She has a fine intelligence and considerable will-power – these qualities *may* suffice to keep her 'straight' in the eyes of the world. Whether there is something finer and nobler deep down in her nature, which can be appealed to or drawn out, remains to be seen. If there is not, I fear her intelligence will not save her from a 'ruin' that will be apparent to the world.

The rise, grandeur, and decline of H.G. Wells is an interesting study in human nature. When first we made his acquaintance some eight years ago, he was decidedly on the up-grade, not merely in position but, I think, also in character. Now he is most distinctly on the down-grade, and unless he can pull himself up he will soon be little more than a ruined reputation. What have been the intermediate stages?

I so well remember our first visit to Sandgate. We had been struck with the force and illumination of *Anticipations*, combined with the ignorance the book showed with regard to the social factors of industrial life. In particular, the doctrine that the whole manual working class must be allowed to sink deeper and deeper into the morass of misery and eventually to extinguish itself, seemed to us to mean a bad form of reaction. The idealization of the scientifically educated materialist lower-middle-class man, as the future governor of society, was also the sort of crude gospel that would lower the demand for careful study of the facts of sociology and psychology as distinguished from physical science. So we opened up communication with Wells.

He was then a pleasant, breezy person eager to establish himself among interesting folk. Very wisely, he and his wife had made for themselves a refined and charming home, and had carefully trained themselves in dress and 'table manners' – unostentatiously but with considerable skill, so as to be fit to associate with the greatest gentlemen in the land. There was a remnant of humility – and yet a guileless frankness as to their antecedents and about their attitude towards new acquaintances. He never told us about the divorce case, but he told GBS – who he knew would tell us. To the Reeveses he seems to have told the whole story. 'I don't want to be self-conscious and I am not ashamed about my past but I wish you to know,' was his style of address. I am inclined to think H.G. was at that time living a perfectly self-respecting open life, absorbed in his babies, working hard at his art, and beginning to observe, with a desire to *understand*, other classes of society and other ways of looking at life.

Exactly when the tide turned towards evil I do not know. Unwittingly I did H.G. a bad turn when I introduced him to the Elcho–Balfour–Desborough set. That whetted his social ambition and upset his growing bourgeois morality. His rise to literary fame and his growing conceit accentuated the irresponsible and wilful side to his nature. He began to fancy himself a Goethe, who was going to experiment in life. His excursion into the affairs of the Fabian Society was also extraordinarily unfortunate. He went in, blown out with self-conceit, inflated with a somewhat windy social enthusiasm, determined to become the boss of a new socialist movement. He began to look on Webb and Shaw as 'back numbers'. The Webbs had taken to abstruse history, Graham Wallas had left the Society, Sydney Olivier was becoming a colonial administrator, GBS had become a fashionable buffoon, all were getting old and indifferent. Forgetting any ties of friendship, he made up his mind that he would depose the Old Gang. Then came the humiliating failure and the pricking of the bubble by GBS. Wells retired, furiously angry, convinced that his failure was due, not to his own incapacity or bad comradeship, but to a deep-laid intrigue on the part of Webb and Shaw – a secretive wily opposition to the worldwide appreciation of this Great-Souled-Personality. From that day, Wells ceased in his own mind to be our friend.

What exactly happened to him after that, I do not know, as whenever we met he was suspicious and hostile. He revolted against the puritanism of the leading Fabians and was more and more attracted by the charm and glamour of smart society. We heard of him at the Sassoons, and at Taplow Court, dining with duchesses and lunching with countesses. I imagine he let himself go, pretty considerably, with women. At any rate, he dropped completely out of our set and preserved an attitude of contemptuous hostility towards us and our work. Meanwhile he and Amber were becoming intellectual comrades and he was evidently considering the advantages to their respective development of a polygamous relationship. His wife had no hold on him. What he desired to do, and what he evidently thought he could do, was to lead a double life – on the one hand to be the respectable family man and famous *littérateur* to the world at large, and on the other, to be the Goethe-like libertine in selected circles. Now he is raging because he is found out and his card castles are tumbling down round about him. In his rage, he is hurling insults at everyone, giving his friends and acquaintance good excuses to drop him. As likely as not he will pursue his relations with Amber, in which case he will disappear, for good, from reputable society. And as is often the case, it will not be altogether the worse part of him which will be his undoing. His courage, his frankness, his desire to give Amber comfort and luxury, all these motives will contribute to his ruin. For once H.G. sinks in his own estimation and in the estimation of those 'who count', he will be *supremely and permanently* wretched. I doubt whether he will keep his health – and he may lose his talent. It will be the tragedy of a lost soul.

What is the alternative? A complete breach with Amber and a year's absence from England would re-establish him – on a lower level of social estimation, it is true, but with his literary fame intact and with the multitudes of friendly acquaintance which such literary fame always brings with it. And since life is busy and there are plenty of agreeable pleasant folk in the world, his daily life would not be much different from his daily life of years ago. He might even go regularly to Taplow Court, though the chances of his wife being accepted would become more and more remote! Will he have 'the manners and the patience' to take this course? I trow not.

The 'People's Budget' was greeted by a storm of abuse, and the Opposition began a long-drawn-out struggle against it. The Finance Bill was only passed by the Commons on 4 November 1909, after 554 divisions, and when it was sent up to the Lords they rejected it, thereby precipitating a constitutional crisis that lasted until 1911.

27 September. [41 Grosvenor Road]
The plot thickens round the tragic Wells–Blanco White–Reeves affair; and the Reeveses are coming in their misery to us for counsel and sympathy. The blackguardism of Wells is every day more apparent. He seduced Amber within the very walls of Newnham, having been permitted, as an old friend, to go to her room. He continued the relationship during her visits at his own house, apparently with the connivance of his wife, whilst he was on the most intimate terms of friendship with her parents. He taught her to lie, and to spend, and to grasp every enjoyment and advantage for herself, independently of its effect on other people. He ended by decamping with her to France, writing an impudent letter to Reeves to tell him of his adventures and actually suggesting that Mrs Reeves, by her admiration of *In the Days of the Comet*, had condoned the intimacy! Then, when he discovered that Amber was going to have a baby, he pushed her into a marriage with Blanco, but persuaded the latter to let his young wife carry on 'business relations' with him until the birth of the baby. Here both Reeves and Blanco White seem to have been monuments of folly, shutting their eyes and allowing themselves to be gulled by Amber's audacious lying. Anyway, the position now is that Amber is living in a cottage that has been taken by Wells, and is receiving frequent visits from him while her husband lives in his chambers in London. And poor Reeves is contributing £300 a year to keep up this extraordinary *ménage*!

Our advice to father and husband is to break off all negotiations with Wells, to employ a solicitor in dealing with him and to insist that Amber returns to her family's home if she refuses to live with her husband. If she insists on staying with Wells, to threaten divorce proceedings and to carry them through directly after the birth of the child. For if they fail to grapple with the situation, they will presently discover that H.G.W. has escaped without punishment and without financial liability, and that poor little Amber is in the gutter, probably consorting, in her despair, with some other man – a ruined woman, doomed to sink deeper in the mire with every fresh adventure. And in the list of co-respondents of the eventual divorce case, H.G. Wells will not be. That is *what he is playing for* – and playing for with impudent audacity.

The whole political world is convulsed with excitement as to whether or not the Lords will throw out the Budget. No one quite knows what will happen to the finances of the country if they do – the tea duty and the income tax will lapse, and unless the government takes some extraordinary measures the public revenue will be in the most amazing confusion. That in itself seems to prove that the constitution does not provide for the Lords throwing out a Budget! Hence, wiseacres who are not party men – like Courtney and Sidney – say the Lords won't throw out the Budget. On the other hand, two considerations drive them to do so – the exigencies of tariff reform and the fear of future onslaughts on their power over Money Bills. All advance of socialism might, perhaps even must, take the form of Money Bills now that the cleavage between parties is chiefly a cleavage with regard to the ownership of property. Hence, if the Lords do *not* throw out the Budget, they admit that they are powerless to fulfil their main function – the protection of property and the *status quo*. On the other hand, by throwing out the Budget they raise the old, old issue of the right of the Commons to tax the commonalty – an issue that dates back to Charles I and Hampden; they also set themselves against the rapidly growing feeling against great holdings of land and capital by individuals. And if the country declares overwhelmingly against them they may lose their veto, not merely over Money Bills but over all legislation whatsoever. In forcing the Lords to fight on a Budget, and a Budget which taxes land and great accumulations of capital, the Liberals have chosen the only position from which they may win a victory. And even if they were to lose, they have a splendid question upon which to work up democratic fanaticism against a *tax-the-food-of-the-people* government. I am inclined to think that, whatever the result of an election on the Budget, it will land the Lords in their last ditch. But have they an alternative?

Meanwhile, our agitation booms along in its own little way. Our membership rises rapidly – a good deal of fluff, of course, but a good deal of good material mixed in with it. The manufacture of this movement is really like the manufacture of the School of Economics – it depends on untiring ingenuity in organizing power, perpetually inventing new devices, stepping from stone to stone. Though the blatant Budget agitation overshadows our propaganda in the public mind, I am not altogether sure that this is not something of an advantage. We don't seem to belong to any party, and each party is inclined to look at us beneficently. We are, in fact, creeping into the public mind much as the School of Economics crept into the University, into the City, into the railway world, into the civil service, into the War Office – before anyone was aware of it.

Our little office, wedged between the Fabian Office close on its right, and the London School of Economics a few yards to its left, is a sort of middle term between avowed socialism and non-partisan research and administrative technique. The staff of the three organizations and the active spirits of their management are all the same persons, and they exchange 'facilities' with the utmost free-dom. It is only in London that this triangular activity of the Webbs could occur – London, with its anonymity, with its emphasis on personal likings, and its contempt for intellectual principles – a state of things which favours a rapid but almost unconscious change in the *substance* of the structure of society. . . .

4 October. [41 Grosvenor Road]
At her own request I went down to see Amber Blanco White, living in the charming little cottage which H.G.W. has taken for her. She was in a quiet and restrained state of mind, and impressed me far more favourably than ever before. She had lost the deceit and the artificiality of former days and was absorbed in her care for H.G.W. and her affection for his and her coming child. The two are taking up a quite impossible position, according to current morality. Having married Blanco White, she now expresses a loathing of him and refuses to have him near her. And she persists

127

on seeing Wells and living her whole intellectual and moral life with him. And she demands that her father shall go on with the allowance of money, and her husband continue the allowance of his name. When an alternative is presented to them that either they must break off, or be repudiated, they both decide to be repudiated. H.G. is to support her entirely, they are to have a chaperone, and thus avoid a divorce.

Of course, unless they mean to have a divorce, the proposal is lunacy. Meanwhile, GBS has intervened and is trying to persuade the father and the husband to condone everything and accept the situation in order to avoid a public smash! He has even suggested to Reeves that he should entertain all three to dinner every week to show his approval! That merely enrages the poor conventional father, who now takes up an almost melodramatic attitude of furious indignation against the 'blackguard Wells and his paramour'. We go on pressing Reeves to put himself in the hands of an experienced solicitor who could talk to each party from a cool detached point of view. It is useless to raise the ethical issue in a manner which is insulting, when the parties have no common basis. 'What will actually happen if you do this or that?' is the only basis of hopeful discussion. Amber and H.G. are so far cleverer and more unscrupulous than the others that they may remain as they are at present, masters of the situation in the sense that they are living the life they please in spite of the misery they are inflicting on all others concerned. But there is usually a limit to this, and clever and unscrupulous people generally end by over-stepping it, and find themselves in the worst position – a position made all the more intolerable by their former success.

Meanwhile H.G.W., apparently with Amber's consent, publishes a new novel [Ann Veronica] descriptive of his relations to her, or rather of her portrait of him – which adds a roar of insult to his injury of the Reeves family.

I believe he is now engaged in satirizing us in his New Machiavelli.

The following entry is misdated. It should probably be 3 November.

[?] 3 October. [41 Grosvenor Road]
Winston and his wife dined here the other night to meet a party of young Fabians. He is taking on the look of the mature statesman –

bon vivant and orator – somewhat in love with his own phrases. He did not altogether like the news of our successful agitation. 'You should leave the work of converting the country to us, Mrs Webb; you ought to convert the Cabinet.'

'That would be all right if we wanted merely a change in the law; but we want', I added, '*really to change* the mind of the people with regard to the facts of destitution – to make them feel the infamy of it and the possibility of avoiding it. That won't be done by converting the Cabinet – even if we *could* convert the Cabinet, which I doubt. We will leave that task to a converted country!'

James Seth (1860–1925) was professor of moral philosophy at the University of Edinburgh. Balfour wrote to Lady Elcho about the Webb visit: 'The talk was abundant but strenuous, Mr and Mrs W. being little moved by the more frivolous side of life. But they were extraordinarily pleasant and interesting.'

14 November. [41 Grosvenor Road]
We are carrying on a 'raging tearing propaganda', lecturing or speaking five or six times a week. We had ten days in the North of England and in Scotland – in nearly every place crowded and enthusiastic audiences. In Scotland our special end was to establish the Scottish National Committee. That is a somewhat difficult task, as we have no personality as yet in the movement, except perhaps that gentle and intellectual Professor James Seth. And the Scottish people are cautious, and wait to have the 'credentials' of a new movement before they join. But so far as interested and enthusiastic audiences are concerned, and large sales of literature at our meetings, we could hardly have done better. In some ways Scotland is more ripe for our scheme than England. . . .

We had a delightful three days at Whittingehame with Arthur Balfour, Lady Betty, Miss Balfour and Professor Lodge. Sidney had far more talk with A.J.B. than ever before. He was more than sympathetic about the Minority Report. I made him read the whole of the latter part of the Scottish Report and he asked Sidney what could be said against the minority scheme – it almost seemed self-evident. Of course, we must not build too much on such sympathetic sayings from a man of Mr Balfour's temperament. But it means that if the Liberals did bring in a new Poor Law, they would probably be opposed by the Labour Party and by the Front Opposition Bench, only too glad to find itself 'advanced'. . . .

129

When the Lords rejected the Budget on 30 November, they forced Asquith to call an election in which the only issue was 'a breach of the Constitution and a usurpation of the rights of the Commons'. The fortnight's polling that began on 15 January ended with a muted Liberal victory. Asquith, was now to find the Irish pressing Home Rule as a price for support of the Liberal plan to limit the veto power of the House of Lords. Alfred Lyttelton was married to Balfour's sister Edith.

1 December. [41 Grosvenor Road]
Another two spells of lecturing – Sheffield, Leeds, Bradford and Hereford last week, Bristol, Newport, Cardiff this week, Worcester, Birmingham, Manchester next week – a wearing sort of life, but we do seem to be impressing the Minority Report on those who are interested in the poverty problem.

Meanwhile, we are on the eve of the great political match: Lords v. Commons. I am inclined to think the Lords are in for a bad beating; and, through them, the tariff reformers are going to get a set-back. To the onlooker it looks rotten business for the very section of the party, the extreme tariff reformers, who have pushed the Lords over the precipice. Tariff reform would have won handsomely at the next general election, coming in its ordinary course. But, allied with Lords and land monopoly, I cannot conceive that the tariff reformers will get any better result than some considerable reduction of the government majority, which will leave the government in power for another five years, and Lloyd George and Winston Churchill in command of the government majority with the backing of the Labour Party. . . . If by any chance the Tories come in, we think that the personal friendship of A.J.B. and Lyttelton, combined with the anxiety of the tariff reformers for an advanced programme, will entail a continuation of the 'breaking-up' process, even if they do not deliberately adopt the whole scheme straight away. . . .

J.L. Garvin (1868–1947) was an extremely influential journalist who edited the *Observer* 1908–42; he wrote the authorized life of Joseph Chamberlain – 'the old politician of Highbury'. Alfred Cripps, Liberal M.P., was the widower of Beatrice's sister, Theresa. Seddon (1882–1977) was their eldest child. Stafford (1889–1952) was the fifth and youngest; a successful barrister, he was a leading member of the 1945 Labour government. George Curzon (1859–1925) was a foreign affairs specialist in the House of Lords, where he played a decisive role in getting the Lords agreement to the Liberal proposals of reform.

20 December. [41 Grosvenor Road]
Spent Sunday with Alfred Cripps. Parmoor grows in luxurious comfort and charm year by year. Seddon, who has taste, is allowed to lavish money on each separate room to bring it up to a high standard of ease and elegance. Both Seddon and Stafford look pasty and slack, overfed and underexercised in body and mind; but they are agreeable lads and dutiful to their father. Stafford has distinct talent, if not a touch of genius, and would naturally be strenuously ambitious. But the indefinite ease of the life, and the very slight demands made on him, are loosening his moral and intellectual fibre. It is odd that exactly the 'school' that thinks the most terrible struggle against fearful odds is good for the poor, take steps to prevent young persons of their own class from having some kind of struggle − even for the pleasures of life! It is strange that these excellent persons should not see that their self-contradictory philosophy of life strikes the ordinary Labour man as hypocritical. The more I see of this conscienceless use of other people's labour by the rich, the more it seems to me that the worst kind of denunciation of the socialist is justified − except that it does no good! . . .

We are all awaiting breathlessly the issue of the great battle. The progressives of all shades are in mind united; however, Labour and Liberal party exigencies may make them fight among themselves in particular cases. To the outside observer, it is amazing that the Lords should have dared democratic feeling at one and the same time on the political and economic side! Those who have led them − men of the type of Hewins, Milner, Garvin, Curzon (encouraged by the old politician of Highbury) have apparently relied on the ignorance and snobbish prejudice of the non-political elector, the man *without social purpose* of any kind, the reader of the *Daily Mail* and *Express*, intent only on keeping all he has, and leading his life undisturbed by social obligations. No one knows how big this class is; how many persons are actually without any social purpose and can be swayed by vulgar cries of alarm for their property or their personal freedom, or by admiration for the 'sporting lord'. We believe that English public opinion is still sound and healthy, and that there will be at the polls a considerable majority in favour of steady popular control over the life of the community. Even if the polls go against us, the battle will have only just begun and will be [one] of the longest and bitterest that England has experienced since the first Reform Bill. The wisely moderate man should dread a

Tory victory. The whole Liberal Party would become extremists. There would be no turning back for the Greys and the Haldanes — the lines would be drawn; political radicalism would be finally merged into economic collectivism. The Fabian Society would be, in fact, triumphant. Perhaps it is an instinctive perception of this fact that has made both Courtney and Henry Hobhouse throw in their lot with the Liberals. The moderate men must, if wise, desire a moderate Liberal victory. That alone will keep the Liberals, for another spell, from falling into the arms of the socialists.

The reception of *Ann Veronica* was affected by the gossip about Wells and Amber Reeves. The novel appeared when a national campaign for moral purity was reaching its peak, and the *Spectator* (whose editor, St Loe Strachey, was aware of the scandal) led a hue and cry for censorship of 'literary filth', denouncing this 'poisonous book' in which ' a community of scuffling stoats and ferrets' had been dredged from 'the muddy world of Mr Wells's imaginings'. Wells at last agreed to give up the relationship with Amber, but the episode was to be a turning-point in his career. Though he continued to write novels, he became more of a publicist and popular educator. Amber gave birth to a daughter on 31 December. The Shaw play was *Misalliance*.

27 December. [41 Grosvenor Road]
The Reeveses dined with us last night, both of them shrivelled up with the pain of their daughter's past(?) relations to Wells. Just at present there is a lull in the episode. Amber and H.G.W. have contrived to make both the Reeveses and Blanco White believe there is a permanent separation between them. After all his insolent bluster, H.G.W. has backed down and agreed to keep away for two or three years, at the same time repudiating all financial liability for Amber's confinement and the infant's keep. He was frightened into better behaviour by the way in which one friend after another was shunning, sheering off, and by the damning review of his book in the *Spectator* — a review which was really an exposé of his conduct under the guise of criticism of a 'poisonous book', written clearly with knowledge and intent. Amber, too, professes to have given up all thought of seeing him. She is now in the nursing home awaiting her baby. It may be that she is seeing H.G.W. every day, unbeknown to her husband or parents. Most likely this repudiation of the financial responsibility by H.G.W. is a mere device to screw every farthing they can out of her parents and to keep his money for more luxury and freedom for her. They

wanted to make the Reeveses support an overt relation; they will now make them support a surreptitious one. How long, I wonder, will the deception last?. . . .

GBS read his new play to us the other night – a good three hours. It is amazingly brilliant – but the whole 'motive' is erotic, everyone wishing to have sexual intercourse with everyone else – though the proposals are 'matrimonial' for the most part, and therefore, I suppose, will not upset the Censor's mind. I don't see any good in the play except intellectual brilliancy. There is a reflection of the Amber-Wells philosophy of life – I think probably the revelations in the H.G.W. various sexual escapades have largely suggested the play – and the leading woman is Amber, with a rather better excuse than Amber had for pursuing men, since this lady had no other outlet for her energies. Sidney and I were sorry to see GBS reverting to his studies in anarchic love-making. Now cramming these episodes into *one scene* gives an almost farcical impression of the rabbit-warren as part of human life. I don't think a rabbit-warren would be much improved by intellectual brilliancy.

Sidney was speaking for the Fabian candidate for Portsmouth and the Webbs then spent three days walking in the Isle of Wight.

New Year's Eve. Southsea
Very happy we have been, since the close of the Commission and our Italian holiday. Since we took up this propaganda we have had a straightforward job, with no problems of conduct, but with a great variety of active work – organizing office work, public speaking and personal persuasion of individuals, work which absorbs all one's time without any severe strain on one's nerves. I enjoy it because I have the gift of personal intercourse and it is a gift I have never, until now, made full use of. I genuinely *like* my fellow mortals, whether as individuals or as crowds – I like to interest them, and inspire them, and even to order them, in a motherly sort of way. Also, I enjoy leadership. Everyone has been kind and appreciative; and money has come in when I asked for it, and volunteers have flocked around us. . . .

Sidney has also been thoroughly happy – partly because our comradeship has never been so complete. Hitherto, we have had only one side of our work together – our research and book-writing. But this last year we have organized together, spoken

133

together, as well as written together. And he has been extraordinarily generous in not resenting, in the very least, my having nominally to take the front place, as the leading minority commissioner, and ostensible head of the National Committee. Fortunately, in spite of his modesty, everyone knows that he is the backbone of the Webb firm, even if I do appear, on some occasions, as the figurehead.

∽ 1910 ∾

27 January. [41 Grosvenor Road]
After the elections. The Coalition back with something over one hundred majority – a clear anti-Lords majority and, abstracting the Irish, a majority for the Budget.

What is remarkable is the dividing of England into two distinct halves, each having its own large majority for its own cause: the South Country – the suburban, agricultural, residential England – going Tory and tariff reform, and the North Country and dense industrial populations (excluding Birmingham area) going radical socialist, a self-conscious radical socialist. The conversion of Lancashire from chronic Conservative to Liberal-Labour is a big fact; the fidelity of Scotland, in spite of the scare of socialism, to the anti-Lords-pro-Budget party, is another asset for our party. On the other hand, tariff reform has got hold of large masses of workingmen and lower middle-class men and has become the shibboleth of the upper, and upper middle classes. . . .

We are considering 'mending our fences' on the tariff reform side. The more active spirits see that they must find something that will take with the industrial classes, other than tariff reform. By sheer ignorance, they *might* plunge on Poor Law reform. We must see to it that they do not do so. These troubled waters are somewhat disturbing to our little bark; but if she be skilfully steered into the right currents of party interests, she will get all the quicker into harbour.

Lord Salisbury (1861–1947), eldest son of Lord Salisbury, the Prime Minister, was president of the Board of Trade in 1905 and an opponent of the Finance and Parliament Bills. George Wyndham (1863–1913), a 'Soul' who was a close friend of Balfour, had been Chief Secretary for Ireland 1900–05. Lord Hugh Cecil was one of the leaders of the 'ditchers' who fought the Parliament Bill to the last, as opposed to the 'hedgers' led by Curzon, who favoured a compromise. The 'Hotel Cecil' was a gibe from the days when Salisbury and Balfour had filled their governments with relations and friends of the Cecil family. Beatrice was lecturing at Plymouth, Exeter and Falmouth.

15 February. [41 Grosvenor Road]
A week-end at Stanway with A.J.B., the Salisburys, Hugh Cecil and George Wyndham – a real 'Hotel Cecil' party. All these, including the leader, were anxious to understand the reason of the rout in Lancashire and Yorkshire. We naturally improved the occasion and tried to awaken them to the evil consequences of letting tariff reform be associated with anti-social reform. But Hugh Cecil (who is an attractive creature) was already desperately alive to the peril to their souls of any alliance with reformers of our colour. We shall not get the tariff reform party to take up the Minority Report. All we shall do is to prevent them from throwing their whole weight *against it*. To many of the more upright minds, failure at the polls would be the lesser evil compared with the downward course towards a collectivist organization. They have almost a *blind* fear of any increase of social responsibilities, and, if they are to accept any measure of it, they would positively prefer to hide their heads in the sand and *refuse to see it*. Arthur Balfour is, if anything, attracted by our scheme, but he is too unconcerned and sceptical to be more than *negatively beneficent*. . . .

Sometimes, in moments of physical depression, I wonder whether we can keep up this agitation, all of which revolves round our joint personality. On Friday I start off for six days' continuous lecturing in the West Country, whilst Sidney is dashing about in other parts of the country. Shall we be able to keep it up?

The Webbs first stated their idea of a 'National Minimum' in living standards in *Industrial Democracy* (1897).

1 March. [41 Grosvenor Road]
. . . This week Sidney quietly slips out of the L.C.C. to which he has devoted so much time, thought and feeling. The last three years the L.C.C. has been rather dead to him. The Progressive movement which the Fabian Society started in 1889 has spent itself. The machine that has been created goes grinding on all in the right direction, but it

has become more or less automatic. A fresh impetus will, I think, come from our propaganda, from the new principle of the National Minimum and the joint responsibility of the individual and the community, for a given standard of individual life. Possibly he may return to the council to carry out such a programme, but for the present we can do more in persuading of the country at large than in the administration of London's municipal business.

On 13 April the Cabinet decided to advise the King to create enough peers to pass its measures through the Lords, or to resign and let Balfour try to govern without a parliamentary majority. The 1909 Budget, having passed the Commons again on 27 April, was accepted by the Lords next day, Lord Lansdowne agreeing that the January election had settled the Budget, though not the larger constitutional issue. Constantine Benckendorff (1880–1959) was a friend of the Asquiths'.

13 March. [41 Grosvenor Road]
We met the Prime Minister, Grey and Birrell at dinner the other day. Interesting to note that we had met none of these personages since they were in office. Grey I had not seen for years. We neither of us spoke to any of them, though it was a small party. Asquith was somewhat marked in his non-recognition of either of us. He is much older, and, in a sense, commoner, in appearance. . . . Grey looked the same charming aristocrat that he has always been, slim in figure and young and refined in expression, but somewhat of 'a stick' in general attitude. Birrell was the same jovial *littérateur*, pleasantly sparkling about nothing with a group of admiring women. I was quite entertained with a thoughtful Russian (Count Constantine Benckendorff, son of the Russian Ambassador) at dinner, and Raymond Asquith afterwards. But it was a somewhat odd sensation to see these three ministers for the first time since they were in office, to be conducting an agitation in the country which must eventually affect their policy, and yet not have even a 'good day' from them! Each one of them would, I think, have been supremely bored to have exchanged one little word about Poor Law or any other social-economic question. Contrasting it with the talk down at Stanway, even with the interest shown in all these questions by Lord Salisbury and George Wyndham, the Liberal Ministers' indifference, not to say distaste, is amazing and makes one wonder what exactly is happening to the 'leaders' of the Liberal Party. Here we are, making the bed they will have to lie in, and yet they seem

wholly unconcerned with this happening. Strange!

I went to Granville-Barker's *Madras House* this afternoon. After listening to this and to GBS's *Misalliance*, one wonders whether these two supremely clever persons are not obsessed with the rabbit-warren aspect of human society? GBS is brilliant but disgusting; Granville-Barker is intellectual but dull. They both harp on the mere physical attractions of men to women, and women to men, coupled with the insignificance of the female for any other purpose but sex attraction, with tiresome iteration. That world is not the world I live in, or, indeed, think to exist outside a limited circle at the top and at the bottom of the social strata. In the quiet intermediate area of respectable working-class, middle-class and professional life, and in much 'gentle' society, there is not this over-sexed condition. The women are almost as intelligent as, and certainly a good deal more spiritual than, the men, and their relations to the other sex are those of true friendship and intelligent comradeship in the transaction of the affairs of life, and in the enjoyment of the interests and beauty of life. *The male and the female have become the man and the woman.* It is mischievous to be perpetually drawing society as even worse than it is, just because most persons are stupider than such clever mortals as GBS and Granville-Barker, and fail to express their good thoughts and feelings otherwise than in [stereotypes] and banal phrases which bore these clever ones. . . .

Where I think GBS, Granville-Barker, H.G. Wells, and many other of the most 'modern' authors go wrong, from the standpoint of realism in its best sense, is their complete ignoring of religion. By religion I mean the communion of the soul with some righteousness *felt to be outside and above itself.* This may take the conscious form of prayer, or the unconscious form of ever-present and persisting aspiration – a faith, a hope, and a devotion to a wholly disinterested purpose. It is this unconscious form of religion which lies at the base of all Sidney's activity. He does not pray, as I often do, because he has not acquired so self-conscious a habit. But there is a look in his eyes when he patiently plods on through his own and other people's work, when he unwittingly gives up what other people prize, or when he quietly ignores the spite or prejudice of opponents, that tells of a faith and a hope in the *eventual* meaning of human life – if not for us, then for those who come after us. He refuses to put this aspiration into words, because he would fear the untruth that might be expressed in those words. He has a dread of being even remotely irrational or superstitious. But, for all that, he believes.

Not one of GBS's men or women, or Granville-Barker's or H.G. Wells's, have either the conscious or unconscious form of religion. The abler of these puppets of their thoughts deny it: the stupider are oblivious of it – a few are blatant hypocrites. And, that being so, there is nothing left for them to be but intellects or brutes, and for the most part they are both. It is strange that, whatever these clever men may think and feel themselves, they don't perceive that there *is* such a thing as religion and that it is a force which moulds many lives and makes the mere rabbit-warren an inconceivable horror.

Churchill, now Home Secretary, acknowledged the influence of *Justice* by John Galsworthy (1867–1933) on the prison reforms which he was initiating.

15 March. [41 Grosvenor Road]
Sidney and I went to Galsworthy's *Justice* – a great play, I think, great in its realistic form, great in its reserve and restraint, great in its quality of pity. Its motive, that all dealings with criminals should be treatment *plus* restraint in the interests of the community, is all worked in with the philosophy of the Minority Report.

20 March. [41 Grosvenor Road]
Blanco and Amber White came to lunch today. Apparently that bad business is at an end. H.G.W. has been frightened off and has definitely broken off the relationship. Amber is settling down with her husband and is absorbed in her baby. She was shy and subdued, and certainly her expression was both sweet and frank. Blanco watches her with affectionate concern. We are prepared to stand by them and let the past be forgotten. I think the world will do likewise. It is one of those rare cases where the punishment will fall far more heavily on the man than on the woman. Amber, if she behaves well, will be taken back by her friends. H.G. and his wife will be permanently dropped by most of his old acquaintances. He is too old to live it down. The scandals have revealed the moral rottenness of his life. I am sorry for Jane Wells, but she pandered to him and deceived friends like the Reeveses. I wish we had never known them.

Asquith was at Gibraltar on a holiday cruise when, on 7 May, he heard that King Edward was dead. He reached London on 9 May, and began a long series of consultations in the hope of reaching a compromise acceptable to the new and inexperienced George V. There were twelve meetings between Asquith and Balfour (and their closest colleagues) between 17 June and the end of July, and more discussions through the early autumn. But the effort to distinguish between financial, ordinary and constitutional legislation, and to give the Lords different powers in each case, came to a dead end on 10 November. One of the most intractable issues was the definition of Home Rule measures, for Lansdowne spoke for the diehard landowners who sustained English supremacy in Ireland. It was on 16 November that George V privily and reluctantly agreed to create peers to force through the Parliament Bill, and the scene was set for the protracted last act of the crisis.

19 May. [41 Grosvenor Road]
The King's death has turned politics topsy-turvy and robbed the Liberals of their cry. Whether they will be able to get up the steam again seems very doubtful. London and the country generally is enjoying itself hugely at the Royal Wake, slobbering over the lying-in-state and the formal procession. Any collective thought and feeling is to the good; but the ludicrous false sentiment which is being lavished over the somewhat commonplace virtues of our late King would turn the stomachs of the most loyal of Fabians. But is it possible for a *crowd* to be anything but exaggerated in its manifestations, with a popular press playing up to it? . . .

27 May. [41 Grosvenor Road]
It is just one year since we started the National Committee. . . . We have done what we set out to do. A year ago the Minority Report was one among many official documents: now it is a movement which is obviously spreading, from one section to another. . . . And we do seem to be attracting the devoted service of a large body of volunteers. We are moving out of our five little rooms into more spacious offices, and we are developing a highly organized staff out of the salaried workers and some thirty or forty unpaid office helpers and some four hundred lecturers. . . .

Now the question is: can we develop this organization into a really big national movement to do away with destitution as a chronic and wholesale state of millions of our people? Here seems an opportunity. The Minority Report has the extraordinary advantage of being a platform at once concrete, comprehensive, and yet unconnected with any one political party. It has a philosophic basis in the whole theory of an enforced minimum of civilized life; and yet it is part and parcel of an urgently needed reform which must come up for consideration by whichever party is in power. But, at present, the whole organization depends on us, and is limited by the defects of our joint personality and the prejudices which this personality arouses. So long as this is the case, the life of the movement will be precarious, not merely because our strength and means might fail, but because the distrust and dislike of us might blaze out into a powerful hostility to the spread of the philosophy which lies at the base of the minority scheme.

Sidney and I *are* socialists; there is no denying that fact. In Scotland this fact has prevented the Minority Report making any substantial headway with the upper and professional classes, and that means no money for propaganda. Owing to our social prestige and Sidney's administrative reputation – largely owing to Arthur Balfour's personal friendship – this 'stigma of socialism' has not stood in our way in England. But, at any time, the fear of socialism might deplete our moneyed membership, and then our organization would necessarily collapse. The problem before us in the next few months is: can we give this organization an existence independent of our leadership – exactly as we have done in the case of the London School of Economics? If not, it will have its day – a quite vigorous and useful day – and then be wound up with the first instalment of the reform of the Poor Law on the lines of the Minority Report. . . .

I often wonder whether I like this life of propaganda or not. I enjoy the excitement of successful leadership, I like the consciousness of the use of faculties which have hitherto been unused – the faculty for public speaking and the faculty for organization. On the other hand, I feel harassed, I don't like financial responsibilities, I am perpetually haunted by the fear of failure to live up to the position I am forced into. And I grudge the quiet study and thought, with its output of big books. I sometimes wonder whether the expenditure of money and energy on mere passing propaganda is as socially useful as research. And I positively dislike the feeling of being dragged along by the movement we have created, almost mechanically dragged along, not able to refuse to respond to a demand we have ourselves stimulated. And now and again, I wonder with regard to the unemployment scheme whether we could really carry it through. One ought never to propose any public action which one could not, *if called on*, carry out. About the non-able-bodied part of our scheme, I am supremely confident in that we are almost *blatantly right*. But with regard to certain parts of the unemployment scheme, I am not quite so sure: e.g., the regularization of government work and the technique of training establishments both give me pause. Also, I am convinced that Sidney underestimates the expense. However, that last point does not upset me. The more of the national wealth we can divert from the rich to the regular outgoings of the poorest class — *so long as it is accompanied by the increase in personal responsibility on the part of these benefited classes* — the wholesomer for the state. Only one does not like to mislead the public, even for its own good!

The Webbs took a month's holiday in Switzerland in June. Beatrice was now considering how to transfer the research, organization and publicity generated by the campaign to a more permanent organization — possibly a reconstituted Fabian Society. Caermeddyg was one of the two 'overflow' houses rented to accommodate the Fabian summer school. This summer school was profitable enough to pay off the Fabian accumulated debt of £191. On this occasion Beatrice was the formal director of the school.

19 August. Caermeddyg, Llanbedr
Half through the very exhausting performance of directing the Fabian summer school.

On the whole, more satisfactory than I expected. The first fortnight, with the somewhat remarkable party we had here and the many interesting and influential persons who had congregated at the national conference [of the Poor Law campaign], was really profitable from the standpoint of propaganda and personal influence. But I cannot say that even this fortnight was exactly 'enjoyable'. To keep house for twenty persons and be accessible to another hundred, as well as lecturing three or four times in the week, is a strain on nerves. Since our more especial friends and supporters have left, we have been surrounded by a miscellaneous crowd, all kindly and well-bred and interested, but not exciting in themselves, and some of them ugly and crude in mind and manners. Still, my dominant impression is the 'well-bredness' of this extraordinarily mixed assembly: I.L.P. organizers, medical officers of health, teachers, minor officials of all sorts, social workers, literary men, journalists and even such out-of-the-way recruits as auctioneers and un-registered dentists, all living in extremely close quarters, and yet not getting on each others' nerves through a too great a disparity of speech and behaviour. It is a wonderful instance of the civilizing effect of a common purpose and a common faith. . . .

What appals me is the fear that we may never be able to get quit of leadership again. Is our existence going to be one perpetual round of talking and organizing for the rest of our working lives? It is a terrifying prospect! The two of us, taken together, seem to constitute a leader at the time when the English political world is singularly without definite leadership on social and economic quest-ions. And no one has yet attempted to make a political movement without being in politics or desiring to be in politics. I wonder whether it will succeed' . . .

Clifford Allen, later Lord Allen of Hurtwood (1889–1939) was a Fabian, a member of the I.L.P. and a prominent spokesman for the conscientious objectors in the First World War. W. Foss, of Emmanuel College, was the current secretary of the Cambridge University Fabian Society. Mary Hankin-son was a gymnastics instructor; she captained the Fabian cricket team, and for many years managed the Fabian summer school. Mabel Atkinson (d. 1959) was a Fabian journalist on the *Daily News* and an economics lecturer who later emigrated to South Africa. The weather in August was particularly wet.

4 September. [Llanbedr]
Within sight of the end of our six weeks' directorship of the Fabian school – only one more week and the ordeal is over.

The attempt to attract university Fabians has failed. . . . A little group of half-a-dozen Cambridge men – Dalton, Rupert Brooke, Strachey, Clifford Allen, Foss, came for a week, and Clifford Allen has stayed on as our guest. One or two other university or ex-university Fabians dribbled in from Edinburgh, Manchester, London, but at the most liberal calculation there cannot be more than forty or fifty university men and women here. Hence, the rather elaborate programme of two discussions every day has been a frost bordering on the ridiculous. We have had interesting and useful talks with these young men – but the weather, being detestable, must have made the trip appear rather a bad investment for them, and they are inclined to go away rather more critical and supercilious than they came. Quite clearly, we must not attempt it again unless we can ensure the presence of twenty or thirty leading dons and attractive celebrities. 'They won't come unless they know who they are going to meet', sums up Rupert Brooke. And I gathered that even if they *did* come, they would only talk together and to us. So that it would not be much use. They don't want to learn, they don't think they have anything to learn. They certainly don't want to help others; unless they think that there is something to be got in the way of an opening and a career, they won't come. The egotism of the young university man is colossal. Are they worth bothering about?

Apart from this specific failure, what is apparent from this six weeks' experience is that there are two conceptions of the school which are really incompatible with each other — the Webbs' conception, and that of the general manager, Miss Hankinson. She and Miss Atkinson desire a co-operative country holiday made up, in the main, of organized games, excursions and evening entertainments, with a few lectures and discussions thrown in to give subjects for conversation. Our conception is that of an organized school — teaching, learning and discussing, with some off-days and off-hours for recreation and social intercourse. . . . For the first fortnight *our* conception was carried out; for the second fortnight, there was a rather unsatisfactory compromise. But this third fortnight has been practically given over to Miss Hankinson's 'pleasuring', and the lectures and discussions have suffered in consequence. . . .

One thing stands out as the net result. If we again think of undertaking this sort of business, we must run it deliberately ourselves, with our own staff. Miss Hankinson is most valuable as an organizer, but she is, in a sense, too much of the expert, and will not carry out any policy but her own. Secondly, six weeks is far too long. We must limit the session to a fortnight or three weeks, at most four weeks. Thirdly, we must try and solve the question of a compromise between studiousness and a certain amount of carefully devised entertainment. It is *not* desirable to exclude games, exercise, music, but these must not be permitted to absorb the whole energies of any section of the company. And for this reason I am rather against having professional gymnastic instructors, or letting any lively man or woman absorb a large part of the company in a play or a pageant. Exercise, like walking, cycling, golf, bathing, tennis, is all right if it is taken when convenient. But regular lessons or highly organized games, the learning of parts in plays and the preparation of dresses and scenery, become occupations in themselves and turn the mind away for good and all from listening to

143

lectures and quiet fireside discussion. Hence, another time we must, somehow or other, select our staff and even our guests, and take a great deal more trouble to plan out an intellectually varied bill of fare, and a far more *technical* and *specialized* kind of discussion which will attract a better type. . . .

W.V. Osborne, a minor official in the Amalgamated Society of Railway Servants, sought a judgment that it was unlawful for a trade union to spend its funds on political purposes. When the House of Lords upheld his claim in December 1909, the Labour Party was faced with a financial crisis. In spite of frequent deputations the government did nothing, and in September 1910 MacDonald warned that its attitude was 'tantamount to a declaration of war'. The situation was relieved by an Act of 1911 which provided a salary of £400 for M.P.s and by an Act of 1913 which permitted unions to set up a distinct political fund. In a talk to the A.R.S. Executive, Sidney commented unfavourably on the court decision, and three governors of the L.S.E. (one a brother of Lord George Hamilton) resigned. The Osborne Judgment was an important factor in the rise of the syndicalist doctrine of social change through industry-wide strikes rather than parliamentary action. A shipbuilding lock-out in September, a cotton lock-out in October and a strike in the South Wales coalfield exemplified the new militancy. Tom Mann (1856–1941) was an engineer, a leader of the 'New Unionism' who had a prominent part in the 1889 dock strike. He was an I.L.P. propagandist who became the main spokesman for the syndicalist movement. The Independent Labour Party in the country and in Parliament was still the main means for individuals to join the federally organized Labour Party, and its branches were the main focus for left-wing propaganda. The strain between the I.L.P. enthusiasts and the Labour leadership was to grow to breaking-point in the next two decades.

17 September. [41 Grosvenor Road]
Position in the political world is most unsatisfactory for the progressive movement. The financial basis of the Labour Party has been smashed by the Osborne Judgment. The Labour M.P.s are being attacked by a considerable section of the I.L.P. The trade union movement is distracted by the insurrection of large bodies of its members against their officials – an ·'insurrection' which involves repudiation of agreements made by the officials.

Meanwhile, Tom Mann, recently returned from Australia, is preaching general trades unionism and the general strike and running down political action. And behind it all there is the likelihood of a compact between the Front Benches which will keep the Liberal Cabinet in power, in spite of the Labour and Irish parties, till after the Coronation, and bring the tariff reformers back in strength at the next election. It looks as if Asquith and Co. had rucked up, and were determined to ally themselves with the Tories rather than let themselves be goaded by Labour. However, there will be old age pensions, the Budget, and a weakened House of Lords as the net result. No break-up of the Poor Law. I doubt the passing of the insurance schemes. Neither Labour nor the Tories will accept them. And if Labour breaks away, many Radicals will follow. The Liberal Cabinet will have to depend on Tory support, and will, therefore, if it remains in, sit still. More probably, there will be an explosion in November and an election in January. Balfour may come in: but not with a *bona fide* tariff reform majority. In fact, my impression is that tariff reform itself has lost ground these last months and that a Conservative majority will be simply an anti-Liberal Cabinet majority. The time might come for a genuine socialist party if we had this sort of smash-up of the Liberal Party.

9 October. [Cloan] Auchterarder
Started on our autumn campaign. After lecturing at Bournemouth and Southampton, I returned to London for three days and then journeyed to Hull, Middlesbrough and Darlington, arriving here on Saturday and leaving again on Monday for Inverness. . . . Now I am spending the Sunday with the Haldanes before opening the Scottish campaign at Inverness and Edinburgh.

I find the Haldanes as kindly as ever; the dear old lady is very frail – Elizabeth is the same sturdy, kind and direct woman. R.B.H. is rapidly ageing and looks as if he were on the verge of another breakdown. He is terribly stout and pasty, and eats enormously and takes no exercise. He is worried and depressed about his War Office administration – in a very different state of mind from the buoyant self-confidence and delight with which he undertook it. He is conscious of hostility to his beloved Territorials from the National Service League, of indifference from his own party, and of limpness and inefficiency in the War Office itself. 'I can't depend on my orders being carried out – there is slackness directly I turn my back'. . . .

What makes one despair is the atmosphere in which these leaders live. Their lives are so rounded off by culture and charm, comfort and power, that the misery of the destitute is as far off as the savagery of central Africa. . . . They don't realize either the

145

misery itself or the possibility of preventing it. And the atmosphere of Cloan is practically identical with that of Whittingehame. There is no difference at all in the consciousness of the Front Benchers. What differs is the rank and file behind them, one made up of ·reactionaries, and the other of progressives. But as a set-off, the Tory Front Bench have complete control of their party and they have no effective opposition to any of their schemes, *if they are progressive*; whilst the Liberal Front Bench has always the Tories and the House of Lords to stem their progress. So really I don't know from what party we shall get the most. We may have, in the end, to establish a real socialist party if we want rapid progress.

George Wyndham, also a guest at Whittingehame, wrote to Mary Drew: 'I told Mrs Webb that, much as I liked Mr Webb, I always see a bunch of big steel keys hanging from his girdle.' Wells interpolated a mischievously clever character sketch of the Webbs into *The New Machiavelli*. Oscar and Altiora Bailey, he wrote, were 'active self-centred people, excessively devoted to the public interest': Altiora's soul, he added, was 'bony', and 'at the base of her was a vanity gaunt and greedy'. This remains one of the most effective (though hostile) descriptions of the Webbs and their circle at the peak of their careers. The novel first appeared as a serial in the *English Review*.

5 November. [41 Grosvenor Road]
. . . The Scottish tour has, I think, been an unqualified success. We have got through the whole programme and the new lectures on voluntary agencies, unemployment and education, which I was rather dreading, were the most successful of those which I gave. . . . One Sunday we spent at . . . Whittingehame with that most charming of families. A.J.B. and I had a long argument as to whether the stately charm of Whittingehame was compatible with either feeling or knowing about the problem of destitution. As a 'holy-day' it is extraordinarily refreshing – there is a delightful atmosphere of intimacy, a freedom to say anything to anybody, to be yourself. Sidney feels it just as much as I do, so evidently do the other guests. But Lady Betty realizes that it is gained at the expense of aloofness from the world, from the countryside, from the world of experts and administrators, even from the world of Conservative politicians. A.J.B. works hard as a politician, is nearly always in his place, dominates his Front Bench, gives distinguished, if not powerful, platform speeches; but, save for this work, he is as aloof from all intercourse as if he were a lonely college don. Gathered

around him are his family, his intimate friends, and every now and again a newcomer chosen for some personal charm or interest. Within this circle all is friendliness, frankness and equality – without it, all men and women are kept at an equally remote distance, not from any feeling of superiority – A.J.B. is far too philosophical to be conscious of class – but merely from sheer indifference. 'No doubt these people are as nice as any others, but life is not long enough to think of knowing them,' is the sort of attitude he takes towards the whole world outside the little circle of friends.

H.G. Wells's *New Machiavelli* is now all published in the *English Review*. We have read the caricatures of ourselves, the Trevelyan brothers and other old acquaintances of H.G.'s with much interest and amusement. The portraits are really very clever in a malicious way. What interests us most, however, is the extraordinary revelation of H.G.'s life and character – idealized, of course, but written with a certain powerful sincerity. Some of the descriptions of Society and of the political world, some of the criticisms of the existing order, are extraordinarily vivid; and the book, as a whole, to a large extent compels agreement with its descriptive side. But it lays bare the tragedy of H.G.'s life – his aptitude for 'fine thinking' and even 'good feeling', and yet his total incapacity for decent conduct. He says in so many words that directly you leave your study you inevitably become a cad and are indeed mean and dishonourable and probably cruel. As an attempt at representing a political philosophy the book utterly fails, swaying between a dreamy and inconsistent utopianism and a complete and dreary cynicism as to the possibility of any other motive but self-interest, tempered by class bias. All parties are in turn rejected and no measures are indicated but a vague proposal to endow mother-hood! 'Love and fine thinking', which Remington advances as his motto, is in the end effectively countered by the drunken little don's demonstration that all political parties are based on 'hate and coarse thinking'. And H.G. leaves you guessing that in his heart he agrees with this summing-up of the whole business. You are left wondering also whether, having betrayed Margaret, he will not presently cut off Isabel. Why not?

One small matter interested us. In his description of acquaint-anceship with the 'Oscar Baileys' he shows that he never really liked us – at any rate after the first blush of the intimacy. What annoyed him was our puritan view of life and our insistence on the fulfilment of obligations. There is even a passage in which he distinctly says that he was irritated at our blindness to the fact that he was leading a sexually irregular life – that we *would* assume him to be a conventionally respectable man! Of course, that is absolutely true. He and Jane Wells had all the appearance of a devoted husband and wife, and it never occurred to us to doubt their monogamy. For a little while I think we influenced him, at any rate in thought, and the Samurai of the *Modern Utopia* was the literary expression of this phase. But he passed back again to the theory and practice of sexual dissipation and vehemently objected to and disliked what he knew would be our judgement of it. He was, in fact, deceiving us and the Reeveses and a host of other respectable folk, and he began to hate us without knowing why. Then came the failure to carry the Fabians, and the hatred blazed out, all the more that he was conscious of his own baseness in having Amber as his demoralized mistress at a time when he was on intimate terms of friendship with her parents. The idealization of the whole proceeding in *The New Machiavelli* is a pretty bit of work and will probably enable him to struggle back into distinguished society. I find myself feeling that, after all, there is a statute of limitations, and that I shall take no steps to prevent this so long as no one expects us to meet him on terms of friendship.

Discussions with the Opposition to resolve the problem of the powers of the House of Lords had broken down on the Irish question, and Asquith dissolved Parliament on 28 November.

30 November. [41 Grosvenor Road]
The autumn lecturing is well nigh over – only four more lectures before Xmas – another four in January (put off on account of election), and we shall have carried out the whole programme of eighty meetings for the two of us in two and a half months. . . .

Meanwhile, we are again in the turmoil of an election. The sensational counter-stroke of the Lords is a clever dodge which will, if it does not succeed, do much to damage their prestige as sober folk. The violent abuse by the Tory press of the Liberals and Lloyd George on the ground of socialism and Irish nationalism is an old game which everyone tires of. But it is hardly to be expected that Liberals will do more than hold their own. . . .

The big thing that has happened in the last two years is that Lloyd George and Winston Churchill have practically taken the *limelight*, not merely from their own colleagues but from the Labour Party. They stand out as the most advanced politicians. And if we get a Liberal majority and payment of members, we shall have any number of young Fabians rushing for Parliament, fully equipped for the fray – better than the Labour men – and enrolling themselves behind these two radical leaders.

Balfour had proposed a referendum on the Parliament Bill. The Liberals neatly suggested that he accept the same device for a poll on tariff reform, and on 29 November he appeared to agree, no doubt seeing this as a means of escape from the Protectionist pressures in his own party. Nothing came of the proposal but it angered the Unionist extremists, who were already criticizing his reluctance to oppose the Parliament Bill to the bitter end, and his days as their leader were now numbered.

1 December. [41 Grosvenor Road]
Balfour's sudden advocacy of the referendum (whatever effect it may have, at the eleventh hour, on the election) completely alters our constitutional system. Now that a responsible party has proposed the referendum, it will have to come; unless, of course, the responsible party were to drop it, which it will not. It is not a bad method of government, if the country could trust its representatives to play fair. But elections have been run on such rotten issues lately that the referendum may be the only way out of the difficulty. And from the point of view of the leader of a party, it has one inestimable quality. It delivers him from the domination of a political sect that has got hold of the caucus. That advantage must appeal to A.J.B., who has been suffering from having had tariff reform foisted on him. It is the last move in his duel with Chamberlain: it is a final checkmate to tariff reform. And it is a superlatively fine stroke in his duel with Asquith, though may be it has been delivered too late for this time.

What other effect will the referendum have on our political life? If we have it coupled with the payment of members, it will hasten the advent of a class of expert representatives paid to carry out the will of the people. It will be the death knell of the caucus supported only by small and energetic minorities capable of making themselves troublesome to the elected representatives. It will therefore delay some types of social reform – the more recondite advances in social control, unless the advocates of these can get them *accepted by both parties*. And will it not delay indefinitely women's suffrage?. . .

10 December. [41 Grosvenor Road]
Sidney and I are both feeling weary and somewhat dispirited. In spite of all our work, the National Committee does not seem to be gaining many new members and our friends are beginning to melt away. One wonders whether we have not exhausted the interest in the subject and whether our dream of a permanent organization inspiring a large sustained movement on a broad philosophical basis is possible at present? Is public opinion ripe for a synthesis taking the place of chaotic endeavours of public authorities and voluntary agencies? We shall go on steadily for another six months, devoting ourselves for the next two months to collecting money sufficient to carry the National Committee through our absence, and to organizing the national conference at Whitsun. . . .

Clifford Sharp (1883–1935), the founder of the Fabian Nursery in 1906, was the most active of the young people who worked in the Poor Law campaign. He was the political editor of the *New Age* in 1908 and then editor of *The Crusade*, the monthly organ of the campaign; he was a natural choice as editor of the *New Statesman*, which the Webbs founded in 1913. In 1909 he married Rosamund Bland. W. Arthur Colegate (1883–1956), another member of the Fabian Nursery, had been the organizing secretary of the Poor Law campaign, and was now a civil servant in the Board of Trade. He later became a Conservative M.P. and a director of the chemical combine, Brunner Mond. W. Mostyn Lloyd (1878–1946) was a Fabian, Guild Socialist and an energetic worker in the Poor Law campaign. He later became head of the social science department at the L.S.E. and for many years a member of the *New Statesman* staff.

30 December. Fisher's Hill, Woking
We are spending a fortnight in the charming house of the Gerald Balfours, lent us whilst they are at Whittingehame. I have been lazing (Sidney working as usual), alternating long walks – twelve to fifteen miles – across the Surrey hills with days writing casual letters, reading, and talking to a succession of young friends we have had with us.

There is Clifford Sharp and his little wife, Colegate, Lloyd, and the Blanco Whites (Amber seems to have settled down with her husband and apparently made up her mind to play straight).

Meanwhile I have been carrying on a lively correspondence with Whittingehame about the election. . . . If A.J.B. would only come out with a really great programme of social reconstruction on the basis of a Zollverein Empire, he might yet come back with a big majority. . . .

The Webbs continued to antagonize the government by their opposition to the policy of Lloyd George and Churchill. Their objection, as they stated in *The Prevention of Destitution*, was that it was a wasteful and potentially demoralizing alternative to the prevention of poverty, giving costly benefits to the better-off workmen and doing least for the poorest and sickest. The second of the general elections of 1910 made the Liberals the first party to win three successive contests since the Reform Act of 1832. The result was close to that of the previous January but it gave the Irish two more seats to increase the majority for the Parliament Bill and for Home Rule.

∽ 1911 ∾

[?] *January*. [41 Grosvenor Road]
The general election has brought the Liberals back with far greater power, because they have not lost but slightly gained on balance. They have also got a clear mandate in favour of the Veto and Home Rule, payment of members and a complete reform of the constitution. As Lloyd George said to the press interviewers, we are in for a period of rapid social reconstruction unless foreign complications turn the nation away from its quarry. Whether the complete supersession of the Poor Law will be one aspect of that reconstruction depends on whether or not John Burns stays at the Local Government Board. And the schemes of insurance are not really helpful to our scheme. Doling out weekly allowances, and with no kind of treatment attached, is a most unscientific state aid, and if it were not for the advantage of proposing to transfer the millions from the rich to the poor, we should oppose it root and branch. As it is, we shall stand by, quietly suggesting criticisms of the schemes to the Labour Party and the Conservatives. The unemployment insurance might bring inadvertently the compulsory use of the labour exchange and the standardization of the conditions of employment. But the sickness insurance . . . is wholly bad, and I cannot see how malingering can be staved off

151

except that the amount given is so *wholly inadequate* that it will be only the very worst workmen who will want to claim it and remain out of work. (The low-paid women, by the way, and the inhabitants of Irish and Scottish country districts, may find it better than their wages, especially as it will be impossible to prevent their doing home-work.) The invalidity scheme may be only an extension of old age pensions, to which there could be no objection. What the government shirk is the extension of *treatment* and *disciplinary supervision* – they want merely some mechanical way of increasing the money income of the wage-earning class in times of unemployment and sickness. No attempt is made to secure an advance in conduct, in return for the increased income. What we should like would be for Lloyd George to make the financial provision, but to find his scheme so criticized, that he had to withdraw it for reconsideration. Of course, we are handicapped in our criticism by the fact that Lloyd George and Winston are the most favourable to the supersession of the Poor Law, and that it is these Ministers who are responsible for the insurance schemes. We have to dance on eggs without cracking them. We shall have to try and invent some way out for Lloyd George.

16 January. [41 Grosvenor Road]
. . . After our Eastern tour, I should like to get back to our research and finish up all those volumes [of local government history]. And there may have come the time for a big campaign for a socialist party with a self-conscious collectivist programme. Payment of members and election expenses may entirely revolutionize English politics. Hosts of able young men, well trained in Fabian economics and administrative lore, will be crowding into the political arena, and if they succeed in squeezing themselves through a many-cornered election they will make Parliament hum! The young men are with us.

VOLUME 28

William O'Brien (1852–1928), an Irish nationalist and journalist, was M.P. for Cork 1910–18. Dr R.A. Lyster, an expert on public health, was Medical Officer of Health for Hampshire 1908–29.

6 March. [Eastbourne]

Let our house for one year to the William O'Briens, in order to get it off our hands for our Eastern tour, and retired first to a little house here for five weeks, then to Luton Hoo for two-and-a-half months.

It is a relief to get out of London, with its perpetual whirl of talking and organizing, and occasional lecturing. After two lectures this next week I am free to turn to the writing of our little book on *The Prevention of Destitution*, summing up all our lectures of the last two years, to be left as a legacy to the National Committee for the next session's propaganda.

Since Xmas we have been seeing a good many political personages – we have had both Haldane and Churchill to dinner; we have breakfasted with Lloyd George and had A.J.B. to meet various M.O.H.s. The Front Bench Liberals have, in fact, been softening towards us, partly because we are going away, and partly because we could, if we chose, wreck their schemes of insurance by rousing the Labour hostility to them. What we are trying to achieve is to direct the sickness insurance scheme into a big reconstruction of public health. It is clear that public opinion has got firmly into its silly head that insurance has some mystical moral quality, which even covers the heinous sin of expenditure from public funds. It is an amazingly foolish delusion. The only moral advantage of insurance was its voluntary character; when that is superseded by compulsory contributions all the moral characteristics vanish, and you are left with a method of provision which is provocative of immoral motives. But there comes a time when it is useless to argue with an obsession of the public mind; you have to accept it, and by skilful devising of the scheme see that it does as little harm as possible. In the public health scheme, which we have put into the hands of the M.O.H.s to press on Lloyd George and to give to leading politicians in the three parties, we have accepted the contributory side of insurance and attempted to supersede the provision characteristic of insurance, by the provision characteristic of public health administration. We talked to Lloyd George about it, and then suggested that he should see persons who were more expert than ourselves – the little group of M.O.H.s who are in our confidence. Meanwhile, the scheme is published simultaneously under Lyster's name in the *British Medical Journal*, *Public Health Journal* and *The Crusade* of this month. It has been given to all the

153

Cabinet Ministers favourable to our views; to A.J.B. and the Labour Party and to Llewellyn Smith and other officials.

There was a new crisis in the Fabian leadership. The Webbs were going abroad, Shaw was now absorbed in the theatre, Olivier (recently knighted) was posted overseas, Bland was in poor health, and Pease was a tetchy bureaucrat disliked by the younger members. 'Apart from pure routine there has been absolutely no *raison d'être* for the Society,' Shaw wrote on 22 March 1911.

7 March. [Eastbourne]
Last night I was dead tired when I gave my last lecture in London. Tomorrow I have to speak to the Free Church Council at Portsmouth. After that I am free from this strain of public speaking. For the remainder of our time in England I shall be writing, and, to a small extent, organizing. And then our holiday, that supreme luxury of the propertied brainworker! If the national conference turns out a success, I believe we shall have practically converted England to the obligation of preventing destitution. What will remain is seeing that the obligation is fulfilled by the different public authorities, and the voluntary agencies attached to them. But oh! I am tired, deep down tired. I shall just last out, but not more than last out.

The Fabian Society is going through a crisis, not of dissent, but of indifference. Sidney thought that, as he was leaving England, he had better resign [from the Executive] for a year. Thereupon GBS not only announces his intention of resigning, but persuades some half-a-dozen others of the Old Gang to resign also. All with the view to making room for young men who are not there! Clifford Sharp, who is a loyal and steadfast member of the Executive, is in despair, and Sidney is remaining on if GBS and the others persist in going. Charlotte Shaw told Sharp that GBS had got sick of the Fabian Society and cared for nothing but his own productions, that he felt himself too important to work in harness with anyone else. It is largely her fault, as she has withdrawn him from association with us and other Fabians in order not to waste his intellectual force in talk and argument. It is clear to me that the Fabian Society has to get a new impetus, or gradually dwindle to a mere name. I am not sure that the time may not have arrived for a genuine socialist party with a completely worked-out philosophy, and a very detailed programme. When we come back from the East we will see how the land lies. If the prevention of destitution movement is safely in other hands, I am not sure whether we had better not throw ourselves into constructing a party with a religion and an applied science. In that case, I should devote half the year to public speaking and organizing, and half the year to thinking and writing.

8 March, 4 a.m. [Eastbourne]
The non-brainworker has little conception of the misery of the over-excited brain. Yesterday night I lay right through the long hours twisting every domestic detail or incident of our organization into a giant of evil, a monster of unpleasant things. And it is in the night that I suffer from remorse for lack of consistency between conduct and conviction. All my little self-indulgences – the cup of tea or occasional coffee after a meal, the regular five or six cigarettes consumed daily, the extra expenditure on pretty clothes – all seem sins from which I can never shake myself free. Ought one ever to do anything that is against an ideal of perfect health, equality of income and the noblest use of money? When the morning comes and one returns to the rough and tumble of a hard day's work, or the necessities of human intercourse, these scruples seem mere weaknesses, and one goes forward without thought of justification with the habits and customs of one's daily life. Still, there lies at the back of one's mind a discontent with these compromises, a longing to be completely at peace with one's own ideal even in the smaller details of life.

To a great extent, Sidney and I are at peace with our ideal. In all the larger determinations of our life we do conform to our perception of what is best for the community, and we have the extraordinary joy of complete agreement as to this purpose. But I still fail in some of the minor matters because I am not sufficiently convinced of the wrongness of the action to overcome my self-indulgence. As for Sidney, he sweeps on one side as irrelevant and foolish all consideration of these trifles! By nature and training economical in personal expenditure, abstemious without being faddy, untroubled by vanity or large appetite, he goes on his way of sane temperance, without temptation or scruple, and with one settled opinion that he wants *me* to indulge myself to the top of my bent! He is the most perfect of lovers, by night and by day, in work and in play, in health and in sickness!

155

12 March. Eastbourne

Sidney has gone up to London, summoned by the M.O.H.s to counsel them what next to do. They had a formal interview with Lloyd George, Buxton and Masterman, at which Lloyd George explained his scheme of wholesale subsidy to friendly societies; and, for the excluded residuum, an artificial friendly society managed by the state nominees, with far lower benefits relatively to the contributions. They report that Masterman seemed a bitter opponent of the public health administration, and that he even suggested that the Poor Law was not 'half bad'. Lloyd George, having explained his scheme, asked the M.O.H.s to consider it and send him a memorandum on it, and he would see them again. So they wrote begging Sidney to meet them and draft the memorandum. They have now their chance. Alone among medical men they have been consulted. It is characteristic of the public contempt for the medical profession that it should be so, a contempt largely justified since the B.M.A. has only one idea – to protect the pecuniary interest of the worst type of medical man by a futile insistence on free choice of doctors by the beneficiaries of state insurance – an obvious administrative absurdity, as absurd as free choice of teachers by the schoolchildren or their parents; rather more so, as the parents would be a better judge of a teacher than of a medical man as they would have *far less reason for choosing a bad one*.

The whole attitude of the government about the destitution question, together with the leaderless state of the democratic movement, makes me feel more strongly every day that our duty, when we return, *may be* to throw ourselves into the democratic movement. Hitherto Sidney and I have kept ourselves almost exclusively for the work of expert guidance of the expert. Sidney has had a repulsion for public speaking and public agitation, partly because he is impatient of stupidity, and partly because he really hates putting himself forward; he far prefers working quietly in the background and he does not like the intercourse entailed by leadership. The life he really enjoys is to sit in a room and draft things for other people, and then to spend his spare time reading endless books and being with me without anyone there to bother him. Added to that, he would like to go on writing great books of wisdom and research, and enjoy the mild pleasure of an academic reputation. Popular approval he does not enjoy, it bores him; he has no glow of satisfaction at the applause at a public meeting. He is the ideal 'man at the desk' – thinking, devising, scheming and drafting ideas and devising actions for subordinates to carry out, and other public speakers to advocate. And this is in spite of the fact that he is a most persuasive advocate and speaker himself, and if he had chosen to push forward, might have been a notable leader of public opinion and acknowledged as such in his own generation. . . .

Fanny's First Play was a commercial success and ran for 624 performances when it was put on in 1911. A biography of Shaw by Archibald Henderson had just been published. Shaw rebuffed suggestions that the Irish Catholic impresario George Vandeleur Lee (*c.* 1831–86) might be his natural father.

21 April. The Hermitage, Luton Hoo

In retreat here, toiling at our book on destitution and finding the task a tediously stale one. But we had to present the old story in a new form, with all the main objections answered and all the new developments noted. . . . If we were quite certain that our proposals would be accepted if we withdrew ourselves and our book, we would retire at once, and for good and all, and devote our energies to pushing on further up in the socialist movement. In fact, that is what we rather hope may happen during the next year or so. . . .

We spent a Sunday with the Bernard Shaws and he read us his last little play (*Fanny's First Play*). A brilliant but slight and somewhat futile performance. He and Charlotte are getting every day more luxurious and determined to have everything 'just so' without regard to cost or fitting in with other people's convenience. But they are neither of them quite satisfied with their existence. GBS is getting impatient and rather hopeless of his capacity to produce anything more of value; Charlotte is beginning to loathe the theatrical set and is even turning to us to try and interest GBS again in socialism. He and Sidney really like and appreciate each other and they might be, as they have been, of great value in mutual [stimulus?] and criticism. But GBS is bored with discussion; he won't give and take; he will orate and go off on to the sex question, which does not interest Sidney as GBS has nothing positive to propose. Then, Charlotte does not really like me and I do not really care for her! We respect but do not admire each other. As a matter of fact there does not seem much reason for meeting – and therefore we seldom meet, and when we do, the conversation

157

tends to be made-up and not spontaneous. Which is somewhat sad, as he and Sidney have always cared for one another: they are perhaps each other's most long-standing friends. Possibly if we throw ourselves into the work of the Fabian Society I might increase my intimacy with Charlotte and therefore of the two of us with Shaw.

About Shaw's parentage. The photograph published in the Henderson biography makes it quite clear to me that he was the child of G.J.V. Lee – that vain, witty and distinguished musical genius who lived with them. The expression on Lee's face is quite amazingly like GBS when I first knew him. One wonders whether GBS meant this fact to be communicated to the public?

Lloyd George introduced the National Insurance Bill in May but its acceptance was delayed until the autumn because of the constitutional struggle. A Bill enacting unemployment insurance became law as Part 2 of the National Insurance Act. George V's coronation took place on 22 June 1911.

13 May. [The Hermitage]
The splendid reception by all parties of Lloyd George's scheme of sickness insurance is a curious testimony to the heroic demagogy of the man. He has taken every item that could be popular with anyone, mixed them together and produced a Bill which takes some twenty million [pounds] from the propertied class to be handed over to the wage-earners *sans phrase* to be spent by them, as they think fit, in times of sickness or unemployment. If you add to this gigantic transfer of property from the haves to the have-nots the fact that the tax is to be collected in the most costly and extravagant fashion, and that the whole administration of the fund is to be put into the hands of the beneficiaries who are contributing only one-third, there is enough to make the moderate and constitutional socialist aghast.

The first asset he started with was the word *insurance*. To the governing class, insurance has always meant the voluntary contributions of the persons benefited – a method of raising revenue which has saved the pockets of all other persons. During the controversy about old age pensions, insurance gradually acquired a compulsory element, and the Conservative Party became pledged to raising money from wage-earners, employers and the general taxpayer, as an alternative to non-contributory pensions. Hence, by using this word Lloyd George secured the approval of the Con-

158

servative section of the community. Then there were the friendly societies who stood in the way. So he puts them into possession of the whole machinery of distribution: a fund that is mainly contributed by non-beneficiaries is to be wholly administered by the beneficiaries. This scheme has the adherence of the friendly society world and of the larger part of the working class. . . .

Now the question is: can he hustle it through this session? If he does not, the scheme won't survive the criticism of all the interests imperilled by it. He has extraordinary luck. The Coronation shortens the time, distracts the attention, and makes everyone inclined to a sentimental gift to the working class. The Parliament Bill paralyses the Opposition – they dare not oppose any popular scheme. The Labour and Irish parties stand to gain – the Liberals are naturally averse to even criticizing their leader's magnificent demagogy. If the Cabinet backs him up, the scheme will go through. The only way of stopping it would be for all the outraged interests to make the ordinary M.P. feel that he would lose votes heavily. But they have precious little time to organize this pressure.

Sidney, on the whole, wishes the Bill to go through. I am not sure that I do. He believes that the big and difficult matter is to get the money voted, and that the inanities of both the method of raising the revenue, and the character of the provision given, could and will be altered by subsequent legislation. I fear the growth of malingering and the right to money independently of the obligation to good conduct. I cannot dismiss my rooted prejudice to relief instead of treatment. . . .

The Unemployment Bill is on quite a different basis. If it is carried through, it will lead to increased control of the employer and the wage-earner by the state. We are not against this, so long as this control is exercised on the wage-earners' behalf. On the other hand, it might smash up trade unions and not give anything in return. I should imagine the Opposition will concentrate on this far more statesmanlike proposal, just because it is statesmanlike. Public opinion takes the sloppy and sentimental schemes and dislikes anything that looks like increased efficiency and control. Even the propertied class are ready to spend public money, but they are not ready to exact the corresponding conduct, even when it is the conduct of the non-propertied class on whom the money is being spent. Administrative nihilism has its partisans; slovenly administration has its adherents; good administration has no public opinion on its side. That is the principal danger in front of us. . . .

After holding the successful National Conference on Destitution in Whitsun week at the Albert Hall, Beatrice and Sidney left for their long journey through Asia.

26 May. [The Hermitage]
George Lansbury was down here consulting with us about the amendment or postponement of Lloyd George's rotten scheme of sickness insurance. The more we examine, the less we like it, both for what it does and what it omits to do. We have written in our new book what is virtually a scathing indictment of insurance in general and the government scheme in particular – but it will come out after the Bill is well in committee and will probably not be much attended to except by our own followers. Lansbury told us that Masterman came up to him after Lloyd George's triumphant exposition of his scheme with a pleasant jeering expression: 'We have spiked your guns, eh?' – showing that he is hostile to the whole conception of the Minority Report and that the government schemes are intended as an alternative method of dealing with the question of destitution. John Burns also goes about saying that insurance has finally 'dished the Webbs'. All of which is interesting. What remains to be seen is whether the Minority Report has come too late to stop insurance, or whether the government scheme of insurance has come too late to stop the Minority Report! The issue is fairly joined – complete state responsibility with a view of prevention, or partial state responsibility by a new form of relieving destitution unconnected with the Poor Law, but leaving the Poor Law for those who fall out of benefit. It is a trial of strength between the two ideas. In our new book we have said our say. By the time we get back from our holiday, the matter will probably be settled one way or the other – possibly for a generation. . . .

PART III

Round the World and Back Again
June 1911–July 1914

Introduction to Part III

BEATRICE AND SIDNEY spent almost a year on the world tour which took them to Canada, Japan, Korea, China, Malaysia, Burma, India and Egypt. It was a journey that was at once more ambitious and more adventurous than their previous sabbatical voyage to New Zealand and Australia, and their composite account of it survives as a typed and still unpublished manuscript of more than five hundred pages. It was not, in fact, a proper personal part of Beatrice's diary, though it runs over three volumes of the set – 29, 30 and 31. She never made intimate entries when she was travelling with Sidney, and in any case it was he who wrote many of its routine descriptions and impressions. All the same, this was an important year for both of them and the diary records significant changes in attitude. Temperamentally and in their work they had always been an insular couple, and this protracted progress through Asia showed them what British imperialism meant in practice and taught them something of the old cultures of the East. Beatrice was particular affected, finding contact with oriental religion as fascinating as the new nationalisms – forms of belief and action which seemed to intensify the radical impulses aroused by the Poor Law campaign and to give her a sympathy for young and rebellious spirits which she never lost.

The Webbs were élitists, with a conventional belief in the superiority of the civilized races and especially the educated classes which emerges in many thoughtless asides. At the same time Beatrice was sensitive to exploitation and racial discrimination. Even in the first accounts of Quebec, where they landed at the end of June, she objected to 'the universally contemptuous and often abusive tone in which the Protestant Canadians refer to the Roman Catholics', declaring that Quebec was 'the only part of Canada which has a metaphysic of any kind; or any self-conscious standard

163

other than that of breezy, virile money-making'. The railway magnates and bankers they met in the Mount Royal Club were 'naïvely ignorant' individualists, whose opening of the West had provided 'rough comfort' for the working-man and a rough-and-ready assimilation of 'the lower races of Europe' who were now streaming up the St Lawrence to settle land that could well have been taken by poor or workless men from Britain. But for all the heat of a Canadian summer Beatrice liked the country and the easygoing hospitality they found in Ottawa, Toronto and Winnipeg, on the farms they visited on the prairies and in the fruit-growing Okanagan Valley beyond the Rockies – where they suffered the 'terrible affliction' of a day-long visit of a pair of migrant Marxists, who were nearly as tedious as the American electoral reformers who insisted in whisking them off to a dreary convention in Seattle. As they sailed away from Victoria, on the Japanese steamer *Inama Maru*, she reflected that Canada was a place of 'extraordinary beauty', in which the people worked with American energy to acquire wealth and spend it on material pleasures. 'From the standpoint of collective action', she sadly reflected, the Canadians were 'at present the most hopeless of any nation'.

From the moment Beatrice sailed on the sixteen-day crossing to Yokohama she found herself making comparisons that favoured the Japanese: there was 'more democracy and better manners' on the ship than on a comparable British liner, and almost all those the Webbs met during their three-month stay seemed more attractive than the Americans and Europeans who 'disliked and despised' them. The Webbs, of course, were well disposed from the start. They had been much impressed by the resounding Japanese successes in the war against Russia; like H.G. Wells, who had named his governing clique of scientists after the Samurai, they had seen Japan as an attractive (and neo-Fabian) combination of benevolent authority and efficiency and, with some tartly critical exceptions, they were not disappointed either by their hosts or by a social system they thought had great potential for the future. Arriving with excellent introductions from the Japanese Ambassador in London, they started by meeting the outgoing Prime Minister, the vice-minister of foreign affairs, a financial magnate and a scattering of university professors. As they travelled through the country they were handsomely received, and they reciprocated with grace. Within a few days, Beatrice noted, officials remarked 'with both pleasure and amusement on the perfection of Sidney's elaborate bowings and polite ceremonial speeches'.

They made a sixty-mile walk across the mountains from Nikko to Ikao, both for pleasure and to observe the Japanese methods of cultivation and rural industry. For all the prevalence of Shinto and Buddhist shrines, Beatrice noticed, there was 'no priestly intervention in the common person's life': it was reverence rather than religion that seemed to regulate all social relationships. 'There is perhaps one characteristic of the Japanese race that we have not emphasized sufficiently because it is not so much a definite quality as the whole atmosphere of their lives, and that is their capacity for reverence,' Beatrice reflected in an entry dated 25 October. 'Children reverence their parents, women reverence men, students reverence their teachers, soldiers reverence their officers, the layman reverences the official, and the whole race reverences and even worships the Emperor. The only persons who appear to inspire no reverence as such are women and priests! . . . It is perhaps a result of this atmosphere of reverence that the Japanese are an intellectually modest race, are always in the attitude of learners. When one thinks of the conceit of the ordinary Englishman, still more of the childish vanity of the American, the modesty and anxiety to improve themselves of the Japanese is very remarkable. With their growing success and prominence, will they lose this quality?'

Attracted, engaged, spending most of their time with Japanese guides, officials, politicians, businessmen and teachers, the Webbs were assured and indefatigable travellers. They went to schools, to Buddhist orphanages and monasteries, to silk mills where the women workers were kept in 'practical bondage to a life of monotonous toil', to a prostitutes' quarter where Sidney was sent off (with payment at the normal rate) to interrogate one of the girls about her conditions of work, and to a geisha dinner, given by a wealthy banker, where the presence of Beatrice and the chaperoning banker's wife caused some embarrassment. The geishas, Beatrice wrote, 'were evidently rather glum at the presence of ladies, and at the kind of conversation, for we discussed banking problems across the room.'

Half-way through the tour Beatrice had already found much to approve. She was very taken by 'the practical freedom of the villagers in their daily life . . . the patriarchal relationship with the resident landlord . . . and, in spite of incessant work in the summer months, and a universal hard toil for men and women alike, the essential civilization of the whole people . . . a centralized government of remarkable efficiency . . . abundant and apparently quite good primary schools . . . some beginnings of medical and sanitary service, good post, telegraph and telephone services, an ever-extending railway and a very efficient police'.

There were breaks in this run of praise. The Webbs were scathing about the working conditions in an oilfield they visited, and about the grinding exploitation in some of the textile mills they saw. Both here and in India they spoke nostalgically about English factory regulations and inspectors, and disparagingly about some of the industrial towns, with their slums and their lack of municipal amenities. 'Will Japan learn to prevent the degradation of the standard of life in time to obviate the growth of a demoralized working class?', Beatrice asked. She thought too little was done for secondary and higher education, noted the complaints of a professor who told her that Japanese history 'cannot be frankly and scientifically dealt with . . . because the current myth as to the divine descent of the Emperor must not be disturbed,' and concluded that 'there is evidently no desire to teach people to think, and a steady repression of unpopular opinions.' And yet, as their tour came to an end with ten crowded days of receptions and entertainments in 'the ugly wilderness' of Tokyo (and a 'first-rate' public lecture by Sidney on 'How the administrative experience of the British Empire might be made useful to Japan'), Beatrice struck a respectful rather than critical balance of all they had seen.

'On the shores of the Inland Sea,' Beatrice wrote after she had reached Seoul on 19 October, 'our last impression of Japan was one of extraordinary grace and beauty – of untiring industry, of sensitiveness and open-mindedness. And there is something pathetic in the impression one gathers of the stress and strain through which the whole Japanese race is now passing. In physical form and constitution, and in their mentality, they seem too slight and frail for the terrific task of taking their part among the great governing races of the world – alone among the coloured races – and subject to the hostile criticism of the Western peoples. For Japan not only possesses her own country but she is entering into the arduous heritage of a race of colonizers and conquerors. To watch her in this capacity we find ourselves in Korea, on our way to Mukden. And whilst we travel we hear the rumblings of the revolution in

China, which may mean the break-up of the Chinese Empire, and more work for gallant little Japan.'

Beatrice's euphoric reaction to Japan persisted as she looked at the recently annexed Koreans, 'a degraded and disagreeable people' whose decline seemed to be due to 'the insidious effect of several centuries of continuously arbitrary and uncertain taxation . . . a striking example of how a whole nation may take a wrong turn, a steady decline in civilization with accelerating speed, until nothing is left but barbarism' – a fate, Beatrice added, from which the Koreans might only be rescued by the 'far-sighted energy' of their Japanese rulers.

In Mukden, as the Webbs swung north through Manchuria on their way to Peking, Beatrice decided that the 'immeasurably inferior' Chinese officials could learn much from the 'active, open-eyed, self-controlled little Japanese men'; they were 'a self-indulging, indolent-looking lot who seem to be perpetually smoking and drinking tea, and who are only too ready to leave their offices on any account'. The 'general appearance of inefficiency and drift', as the Ch'ing dynasty tottered to its end, was so pervasive that Beatrice had already come to a gloomy conclusion. 'We do not see much ground for hope in a New China,' she wrote on the twenty-four hour train journey down to Peking, 'or for belief in a possible regeneration of the race.'

The late autumn of 1911 was none the less 'a most exciting moment' to reach Peking, for no one knew whether or when the capital would fall to Sun Yat Sen's army; and in such a time of tension, when the Court and many officials were preparing for flight, it was difficult for the Webbs to go on their usual round of well-regulated visits to schools and other public institutions. Some Chinese graduates of the London School of Economics helped them to meet harassed officials. They were entertained by English newspapermen, American bankers, French contractors. They managed, despite the approach of the revolutionary troops, to go on a two-day visit to the Ming Tombs and the Great Wall, to visit the Summer Palace, and go through a lamasery, where the monks were so repulsive that 'you would think you were passing through a convict establishment suddenly denuded of warders . . . a mass of putrefying humanity – indolence, superstition and sodomy seeming to be its main characteristics . . . it is this rottenness of physical and moral character that makes one despair of China – their constitution seems devastated by drugs and abnormal sexual indulgence.'

Writing as they went along, Beatrice did not try to resolve the paradoxes and contradictory impressions that broke into the diary notes. This sweeping and savage comment on Chinese morals, for instance, was followed by others in which she sharply condemned the contempt with which most Europeans and Americans regarded the Chinese. 'Never judging them by the same standards or really considering them as human beings at all. . . . It never occurs to them to estimate the Chinese as a nation, on a par with European nations, having a civilization of its own and entitled to equality of consideration and treatment.' Whatever Beatrice thought of the subject races as she passed through Asia (and dislike of indolence and 'unnatural vice' struggled with her interest in old cultures and religions) she was caustically critical of the arrogant stupidity of their white overlords, few of whom came up to her notion of what a civilizing imperial class should be like.

The Webbs got safely away from Peking as the Manchu regime collapsed, scrambling on to a refugee train to Tientsin with the help of an English guard – an I.L.P. supporter who recognized Sidney from an illustration in a *Labour Leader* posted on from home; and a coastal steamer took them on to Shanghai, seized by the rebels without much obvious sign of change, to catch the boat for Hong Kong. From the island colony, where a short and pleasant visit was marred only by more examples of British racial condescension, they sailed up to Canton, also in the hands of the revolutionaries. The city, Beatrice remarked, was 'a sort of nightmare – this million of blue-clad human ants inhabiting an apparently endless series of dark and dirty cells . . . with the animated motion, the uniformity and the perpetual repetition of identical parts of an anthill.' They came back by way of Macao, run by a 'curiously degenerate' Portuguese government, 'which keeps the town clean and tidy, but otherwise lets the Chinese do as they choose', and then they were off to Singapore and a thoroughgoing journey up the Malay peninsula through Serentam, Kuala Lumpur and Penang. Once again Beatrice found fault with the pro-consuls of the colonial service, blaming them for the poor education and lack of social amenities for the native population. 'One cannot help feeling that the English official has been in earnest only about maintaining law and order and administering justice in an amateur, country-gentleman way. He has not really tried to educate the Malay, or even to make the country healthy for him. When revenue became abundant it was spent on magnificent roads, on which presently the officials' and planters' motor cars were everywhere to be seen.'

In Burma, where the Webbs spent a fascinated eight days in Rangoon and Mandalay, Beatrice at first noted 'a great and almost universal prosperity', with the ordinary Burmese on their rice plots 'undeveloped, or at least unspoilt by British rule . . . the tiny hamlet of a score of bamboo huts represents their highest form of social organism'; and she was intrigued to find that the people who lived in these rude huts, 'dirty and devoid of furniture and convenience of any kind', were 'gentle and courteous in manner, pleasing in countenance and beautifully dressed'. But the picturesque impression gradually gave way to a feeling of 'positive depression'. Despite the outward show of Buddhism, which Beatrice respected, she decided that the religion of the multitude was simply a rag-bag of sorcery, soothsaying and astrology – a degree of superstition she thought insulated the Burmese from modern science as much as their belief in reincarnation inhibited worldly effort. The result was a kind of 'indolence and apathy' that disgusted her.

India was too large and its affairs too complicated to be so summarily dismissed. The Webbs arrived in Calcutta at the beginning of January 1912, when official India was preoccupied with the visit of George V and Queen Mary for the great Durbar; and this was to their advantage, for Beatrice found the Indians more congenial company and she was saved from too much irritating contact with British officials whom she found professionally wanting and socially far from agreeable. They began with a visit to the sessions of the Indian National Congress, which was meeting in Calcutta, and found them 'rather a frost'. They were poorly attended, and the clique which ran the nationalist movement in a 'cut-and-dried' fashion seemed to be keeping the younger men down for fear of encouraging sedition: the proceedings were little more than a series of orations, Beatrice noted, as she watched these lawyers, editors, landlords and capitalists conferring. The conference achieved little, she decided, apart from exposing 'the real and growing discontent of the educated class of India at being virtually excluded from deciding on the policy of the government of their country'. As she travelled across India, and saw a great deal of its wealthy, educated and professional men, she kept coming back to her first impression of a needless and wasteful gulf between them and the British bureaucrats – 'all cast in the same mould as to dress, manners, language and habits, and . . . also opinions and prejudices'; and utterly unaware that 'in spirituality, in subtlety of thought and in intellectual humility' the Indian might be superior to them. 'A stupid people find themselves governing an intellectual aristocracy.'

In the high noon of the Raj the shadow of eventual independence had begun to fall across India, and everywhere the Webbs went they were aware of it – though Beatrice felt that national freedom would come only when the Hindu majority could overcome the other-worldliness of its religion (which she admired as much as she disliked its 'promiscuous idolatry' and 'grotesque lewdness') and its indifference to effort and organization. She and Sidney were therefore fascinated to meet their old Fabian acquaintance Annie Besant, who had founded the Hindu Central College at Benares. This was 'the most hopeful institution we have seen', Beatrice wrote home on 15 January. The extraordinary Mrs Besant had moved on from secularism and socialism to preach the 'New Hinduism' and to play a decisive part in the founding of the Indian National Congress, and though Beatrice had doubts about this latest of many enthusiasms ('I cannot in talking to Mrs Besant quite believe in her intellectual sincerity'), she recognized the old campaigner's ability 'to call out the patriotism and the self-respect of the educated Hindu public, and she has combined Hinduism with liberal views, and a faith in conduct as a necessary element in life. . . . It is strange that the dominant personality of an English woman is the only chance of securing common action among Hindus for the teaching of the National Religion.'

This uplifting dedication was in marked contrast to what she considered the 'faintheartedness' of the British bureaucracy in anything other than the maintenance of law and order and ring-keeping for the commercial interests. 'We have been at it for half a century,' she wrote about popular education, 'and only a tiny proportion of boys and a handful of girls are, even now, getting any decent education in the primary grade, let alone in the higher – a situation aggravated by the half-hearted indecision of the civil service as to whether they want to educate the Indians or not, and how they want to educate them.' Little was done for social and public services: the Webbs went 'in camp' with a Collector in the United Provinces, who took them through a district where he had £20,000 to spend on roads, bridges, schools, sanitary and medical provision for a population of more than three million. They admired this man, who became a lifelong friend, for he taught them much about rural life; and they learned more from a forest administrator who took them elephant riding up to the Nepalese border. But everything they saw led to the same conclusions. The British could neither make the most of India, nor enlist the help of the Indians. The central government could not raise sufficient funds, once the opium monopoly was abolished, because it did not want to annoy the Europeans with high import duties, compete with private interests, develop its forest and mineral resources, and invest in new and profitable enterprises. Moreover, its own individualist dogmas were matched by Indian inhibitions. Hindu family custom made death duties unacceptable, Hindu religion meant that taxes on alcohol, tobacco and coffee produced little revenue, and Indian wiliness made income tax ineffective. So long as the Raj survived, India would stagnate economically and socially, the national movement would gather strength, and potentially disruptive tension between the Hindu and Muslim peoples would increase.

The Webbs were seeing a great deal of India: their tour took them to Allahabad, Lucknow, Delhi, Amritsar, Lahore, Peshawar and the Khyber Pass, and back through the princely states of Rajputna to a last few days in Bombay before they sailed for home. And the longer they stayed, the more they came to like the Indian politicians and teachers they met. Beatrice was particularly impressed by the monastic commitment of the Arya Somaj (Servants of India), a small group of dedicated men preparing themselves for public service like dedicated Positivists; the order founded in 1875 to revive Vedic teaching. Characteristically, she praised its 'insistence on extreme austerity in restraint of animal passion, its inculcation of public spirit, and patriotism, and its proselytizing fervour', as well as its belief that Hindus had to fit themselves for political freedom by 'an advance in personal character'. That was the rule of conduct by which Beatrice herself tried to live, but she believed that it must be combined with the scientific method applied to social problems, and this is where she found her new Indian friends deficient. She gives a touching account of a visit

171

to the Maharajah of Chhatarpur, a weak and sickly man who read Comte, Herbert Spencer and Marie Corelli with equal pleasure, and was captivated when Beatrice explained to him the difference between science and religion. On Beatrice's advice the impressionable man at once sent off for the works of Henri Bergson and William James.

Other Indian princes proved equally engaging. The Gwaekar of Baroda, who governed a progressive state 'enormously ahead of the rest of India' in providing nearly universal education, had fallen out with the Delhi government and was afraid that a display of bad manners and dissident political opinions might lead to his banishment, and at the very least to the reduction of the number of guns in his royal salute. The Jam of Nawanagar, better known to English cricketers as the great Ranjitsinji, had overspent and was being sent off to live in Europe while the British Resident set about restoring his bankrupt state's finances. The Begum of Bhopal, the only woman among the native rulers, had by contrast 'a great reputation as perhaps the most dutiful and statesmanlike' of them all: able, most agreeable, believing that the world would be better governed if all rulers were females, 'her main preoccupation' was the education of women, and she had given practical proof of her belief in her sex by importing women doctors, starting schools for girls and encouraging the translation of modern works into Urdu and Hindi.

From time to time Beatrice made comments on the women she met or saw about their normal occasions. She thought little of the women in Japan, who were either dolls or toiling peasants, bonded workers slaving in textile mills or the caged prostitutes who were little more than 'Human Beasts being visited by other Human Beasts'. She got the impression that in Burma the women 'enjoyed equal rights and separate property, and are in practice well-treated, with at least equal influence'. She met interesting and appealing Indian women both in and out of purdah, especially in Calcutta and Bombay, where she found the whole set of wealthy Indians 'attractive, cultivated persons, enlightened and discreetly patriotic, the women . . . good-looking, charmingly dressed and highly educated', and in all respects preferable to the British officials and their snobbish memsahibs who systematically snubbed them.

On 16 April, homeward bound, the Webbs tried to sum up their feelings. First, about India: 'The more we saw of India,' Sidney wrote for them both, before the heat and a screaming baby distracted him, 'the more we learned about the government and the officials, *the graver became our tone* and the more subdued our optimism.' Then Beatrice took over, concluding that despite the common institutions they had seen in Japan, China and India – the close-knit family, with 'its subordination of women and its community of property', the prevalence of the small cultivator, the underlying similarities of religions affected by Buddhist teaching – there was 'deep-down unlikeness'.

The Japanese are a race of idealists, but these ideals are fixed and amazingly homogeneous and are always capable of being translated into immediate and persistent action. They are, in fact, perhaps the most executive race in the world – the most capable of discovering the means to the end – and the most self-contained and self-disciplined in working out these means, and therefore in attaining their ends. One sees, in front of them, the danger of becoming vulgarized by their success as practical men, of losing the substance of their ideal in the shadow of accomplishment. About the Chinese I do not feel competent to speak as I dislike them so heartily. But the very fact that they excite our dislike, whilst the Japanese excite our almost partisan admiration and the Indians our real affection, shows how very different the Chinese race must be. . . . As for the Hindus, they strike us as an essentially lovable race. . . . That terrible coarse-grained self-satisfaction and self-absorbed sensuality and self-conscious respectability consciousness of God's Own Englishman as the King of the Universe – which makes some good-hearted and capable Englishmen so horrid to live with, or even to talk to, is not to be met with among Hindus. All Humanity is a pitiful business to the philosophical Hindu, and the greatest one on earth is inferior to the humblest ascetic on the straight way to final emancipation from the Wheel of Human Desire. It is this quality of intellectual perspective that makes the Hindu a delightful and refined intellectual companion. . . . In the finest form of Hinduism, we watch an almost perfect relation between religious emotion and intellectual life. Here all ratiocination is left free and untrammelled by religious dogma – you can think what seems to you to be true in any particular case. Religion concerns itself with the purity and nobility of your *purpose* in life, with the self-discipline which will enable you to maintain it intact. Even the control over your physical instincts which is enjoined is to be guided by a scientific knowledge of the laws of health, and is to be varied and developed according to any new knowledge attained by scientific discovery.

It was clear that Beatrice had been as entranced by the spiritual attractions of Hindu thought as she was 'converted to the nationalist position' on India's economic problems and political prospects; and

173

after a long digression on land tenure she came back to consider whether there was any justification for the practice of Yoga. 'Our Western ideal,' she wrote, 'is the fullest possible development of human faculty among the whole people. . . . But it is clear that this ideal is wholly antagonistic to the Eastern ideal of restricting activity and assiduously cultivating a state of mind which seems to us to resemble blankness. . . . I had hoped that our journey to the East would have enlightened this fundamental question, but I come back as mystified as ever. Mrs Besant's coquetry with Yoga, and the sight of the Saddhus who are supposed to practise it, leaves me in a state of cold scepticism — testifying to my continued ignorance of what may be behind this old world wisdom.'

With such speculation swaying through her mind to the slow rhythms of the boat, and the prospect of picking up the remnants of the Poor Law campaign and giving some focus to the disparate Fabian factions, Beatrice paid little attention to Egypt. 'A pale reflection of India,' she noted after a week-long visit to Cairo. 'No one is responsible for the good government of Egypt and the development of Egyptian character. By our financiers and our engineers and our police we have enormously increased the material prosperity of Egypt. It seems more doubtful whether we have added one iota to her moral and intellectual development.'

The face of British politics had changed dramatically by the time the Webbs returned to London in May 1912. Their friend Arthur Balfour had resigned the Tory leadership in November 1911. He had long been unpopular with the tariff reform faction and he was the inevitable scapegoat after his party's humiliations in the constitutional crisis over the House of Lords. 'Balfour Must Go' was the battle cry. He was replaced by Andrew Bonar Law (1858–1923), a mediocre man supported by the tariff reformers and the Ulster wing of his party. In the struggles that led to the Parliament Act in August 1911 the constitutional system had been strained almost to breaking point, and the period of the 'Great Unrest' which followed was marked by a militancy and violence unknown since Chartism had collapsed seventy years before. Ireland was drifting into civil war. The failure of the Liberal government to make any concessions on women's suffrage had driven many of its frustrated supporters to back Emmeline Pankhurst and her daughter Christabel when they resorted to window-breaking, arson, disruption of the House of Commons and other forms of direct action. And while the Webbs had been away one great strike had succeeded another. In 1911 the seamen struck successfully. They were followed by the dockers (troops were called out to stop the rioting in Liverpool and the cruiser *Antrim* was sent up the Mersey), a national stoppage by the railwaymen, and a bitter strike by the coalminers that began in February 1912. All these disputes, moreover, were coloured by the new class-war slogans of syndicalism and industrial unionism which Beatrice heard in such strident tones that autumn at the Newport meeting of the Trades Union Congress. Though different in origin, for syndicalism came from France and was much influenced by George Sorel's theory of the insurrectionary strike, while the idea of One Big Union was the watchword of the Industrial Workers of the World in the United States, these two doctrines were not very different in kind. They were used more or less interchangeably by their most passionate advocate, Tom Mann, now editing *The Syndicalist* and stumping the country for direct action.

Beatrice could see that new developments required a new response and though she was exhausted from the long journey she found the energy and will to do it. She gave two lectures on syndicalism to the Fabian summer school on her return, and during the summer weeks that she and Sidney rested at a rented rectory at Madehurst, near Arundel in Sussex, they began calling in friends to discuss their plans. They needed a means to speak directly to the heterogeneous group of reformers who had emerged in the Poor Law campaign – the middle-class 'Stage Army of the Good', the journalist Henry Nevinson called them. During the campaign Clifford Sharp had edited *The Crusade* for them. When that monthly was wound up in March 1913 he went on to run the *New Statesman* as a non-party political and literary review, much like the *Nation*, which was edited by the high-minded Radical journalist H.W. Massingham, and the *New Age*, which A.R. Orage (1873–1934) had made the brilliant spokesman for all the dissident causes of his day.

At the same time the Webbs saw that a revived Fabian Society was the only organization left to them once they had wound up the collapsing National Committee for the Prevention of Destitution. 'We had no influence over the Liberal Cabinet,' Beatrice wrote in May 1918; 'we had not even any influence with what there was in the way of a Labour Party; we had lost any footing we had with a certain class of Tories.' Without any significant political allies they had no choice but to strengthen their own forces. The Fabian Society was indeed in a somewhat demoralized state, for the Webbs had left it to drift after the row with H.G. Wells and they had carried off some of its more energetic members into their Poor Law campaign. The remainder had spent their time in irritating constitutional disputes, on arguing about their attitude towards the I.L.P., the Labour Party, the need for a genuinely socialist party, women's suffrage, and the Webbian collectivism which had lately become unfashionable on the left.

Once Beatrice had made up her mind to rally the Fabians she had no patience for such a talking shop. Throwing herself actively into their affairs for the first time (she only became a member of the executive on her return from Asia), she drafted a 'scheme of work'. There were to be two committees of enquiry, one on Rural Problems, which published its report a year later, and the other on the Control of Industry, which was to become an ambitious and open-ended discussion of all forms of industrial organization. Beatrice hoped to involve the clever young university Fabians whom she had met at the summer schools in these enterprises, but getting their co-operation proved to be tiresomely difficult. The founders of the Fabian Society had all been rebels in their time, and like had attracted like – especially in the kind of family-style society the Fabians had been from the first – so that each generation of recruits sought to establish its identity by a conflict of wills with its elders. As the members of the Old Gang dropped away from active leadership, only the Webbs were left to play the parental role.

A group of Fabians from the Oxford University society, led by G.D.H. Cole (1889–1959) and William Mellor (1888–1942), were especially articulate. These clever, energetic and arrogant young men had no time for the reformist tactics of the Labour Party or the old-style trade union leaders. They were devotees of an intellectual fad called Guild Socialism, an offshoot of the newly popular ideas of syndicalism. In 1906 the Christian Socialist architect A.J. Penty (1875–1937) had followed up the neo-medievalism of William Morris in a book called *The Restoration of the Gild System*, which exalted craftsmanship over crass commercialism. S.G. Hobson (1864–1940), a temperamentally rebellious Fabian, joined A.R. Orage in giving a modern twist to this art-

and-craft doctrine, and the *New Age* began to argue for an industrial system owned by the state, dedicated to worthwhile workmanship, and democratically controlled by self-governing Guilds developed from the conventional trade unions operating in each industry.

It was an appealing theory for socialists brought up on John Ruskin and William Morris; it had a kind of timeliness in the heyday of syndicalism; and it provided an outlet for the group whom Margaret Cole later called the 'natural insurrectionists' among the younger Fabians. They were particularly critical of the Webbs, lampooning them with much the same vigorous (though less talented) invective that H.G. Wells had used in *The New Machiavelli*. Between 1913 and 1915 they tried and failed to capture the Fabian Society. But they did manage to take over the Fabian Research Department which Beatrice developed out of the Enquiry into the Control of Industry. This venture proliferated specialist sub-committees and acquired so many members (85) and consultants (66) that it became a sizeable organization in its own right, and it soon received formal recognition as a Fabian group with the right to handle its own finances. The Guild Socialists (who were obsessed by the structure of capitalist industry and the role of trade unions in changing it) now had the chance to show their mettle. And though Beatrice criticized their boorish behaviour in the privacy of her diary she recognized their ability and publicly supported them, for they had the kind of dedication she admired. In years to come, indeed, G.D.H. Cole and his wife Margaret were to become the political heirs of the Webbs and their successors in Fabian esteem.

VOLUME 32
∽ 1912 ∾

5 September. Newport Trades Union Congress
It is now over three months since we got back to England and not a
word have I written. It took me at least two months to get over the
effect of the tropical climate and perpetual journeyings – my nerves
were all to pieces, and waves of depression and panic followed each
other. Now I am all right again and in good working form.

I am writing now in the early morning of my third day at the
Trades Union Congress. Not substantially different from the
congresses of twenty years ago. The extreme left of those years, the
state socialists, are now on the defensive against the new left – the
syndicalists. The bulk of the delegates are the same solid stupid folk
they have always been, mainly occupied with their trade union
work, their own eating, drinking and smoking, and their family
happenings: they take a placid, good-humoured and somewhat
contemptuous interest in this or that 'new talk', very much as a city
man discusses the new toys that are sold on the pavement, or the
members of a congregation listen to the particular theological
doctrines of the new preacher. But there is one change of outlook.
The ordinary trade unionist has got the National Minimum theory
well fixed in his slow solid head: it has taken twenty years to mature
but there it stands at last, the substance of his political desire. And I
think the idea of nationalizing the great public services is just
emerging out of the shibboleths of a minority into the settled
intention of the majority. But here the syndicalist enters a caveat –
the protest of the idealist against what actually happens when
services are nationalized and worked by officials having the same
assumptions as the ordinary capitalist in respect of remuneration
and status of the wage-earner.

The Fabian Society and the I.L.P. started joint agitation for a legal minimum
wage under the slogan 'War against Poverty'; it was in some ways a continuation
of the Poor Law campaign. Sidney chaired the conference at the Memorial Hall
on 11 October. Beatrice, Sidney, Shaw, Lansbury and Mary Macarthur
(1880–1921), a trade union organizer and I.L.P. official, were speakers at an

Albert Hall rally that evening. The new weekly was the *New Statesman*. The Webbs were among the twenty-six original shareholders but the main capital was provided by Shaw; Ernest Simon (1879–1960), later Lord Simon of Wythenshawe, a Manchester industrialist who became a Liberal M.P. and chairman of the B.B.C.; Edward Whitley (d. 1945), a prosperous research chemist and supporter of the Poor Law campaign, and Henry Devenish Harben (1874–1967), a Tory turned Labour who came into a substantial share of the family fortune from the Prudential Insurance company. He used it to support the militant suffragettes, the syndicalist *Daily Herald* and other left-wing causes. Successive loans from these men, and from the Webbs themselves, were gradually converted into shares until the paper finally began to pay its way. Shaw, despite his help, was dubious about the scheme, and he proved a troublesome contributor. The clever young men who were to help Sharp establish the paper included the literary editor John Collings Squire (1884–1950) and the drama critic Desmond MacCarthy (1877–1952). Henry Schloesser (b. 1883), later Lord Slesser and a distinguished judge, was the chairman of the Fabian Reform Committee. Philip Snowden (1864–1937) was the chairman of the I.L.P. until he became a Labour M.P. in 1906. *The Story of the King's Highway*, Volume V of the Webbs' history of local government, was published in 1913.

11 October. [41 Grosvenor Road]
Since we returned to London I have been in a whirl of work – a fine mix-up of activities – the winding up of the National Committee, the I.L.P. and Fabian campaign on the National Minimum; our own course of lectures on the Control of Industry, and the starting of the Fabian Research Department. In all these enterprises Sidney has been helping by counsel and drafting, by writing tracts and taking his share of public speaking. Meanwhile he has been finishing, without help from me, the book on Roads, one of the innumerable fragments of our unfinished work. It is annoying not to be able to complete that big task of historical research to which we devoted so much time and money. But there seems to be a clear call to leadership in the labour and socialist movement to which we feel that we must respond. For that purpose we are starting a new weekly next spring, and the planning out of this organ of Fabianism is largely devolving on Sidney. It is by far the most risky of our present enterprises – we start with a quite insufficient capital: £5,000 (Shaw, Whitley, Harben and Simon each £1,000 and £1,000 more in small sums), without the advice of any one who understands newspaper production. To the experienced journalist it must seem a mad adventure, and we ourselves hardly expect more than a run for other people's money and our own hard work. But

then the London School of Economics did not seem much more promising, and today it rolls on majestically from success to success. Sidney has not even troubled to become chairman again, realizing that the School has now a life of its own. He still watches over the growing library and is always on the look-out for new endowments or new opportunities for work.

The Fabian Society, which we found in a state of disruption, has settled down with admirable good temper to the work of research and propaganda. The troublesome Reform Committee, led by Schloesser, which had got absurdly on the nerves of the Old Gang, has formally dissolved itself and we are all the best of friends. The Standing Committee of the I.L.P. and Fabian Society is a success and is controlling the policy of the labour and socialist movement in this country – in so far as this movement has any policy. What annoys me is the absence of any relation, good or bad, between the Labour M.P.s and the labour movement in the country. The Labour M.P.s seem to me to be drifting into futility, a futility that will be presently recognized by all whom it may concern. J.R. MacDonald has ceased to be a socialist, the trade union M.P.s never were socialists, Snowden is embittered and Lansbury is wild. At present there is no co-operation among the Labour members themselves nor between them and the trade union leaders. We personally have no relations either with the Parliamentary Party, or with the trade union or co-operative movements; our only connections are with the I.L.P. branches and individual Fabians throughout the country. All the Labour members seem to me to have become cynics except Lansbury, who has become a raging revivalist preacher of general upheaval. All one can do is to go steadily forward without considering the likelihood of results.

The National Minimum campaign published a number of pamphlets and held conference rallies in provincial towns. As part of the campaign Beatrice chaired a London conference on 'The Underpayment of Women' organized by the Fabian Women's Group: it called for legal measures to provide equal pay for equal work. Beatrice also spoke on the National Minimum at the Memorial Hall on 20 December, as one of the regular Fabian autumn lectures. George Lansbury had been elected as Labour M.P. for Bow and Bromley in December 1910. Two years afterwards, when he resigned to fight a by-election on the issue of women's suffrage, his majority of 863 wilted into a defeat by 731 votes: it was attributed in part to a public reaction against the militant wing of the movement. Soon afterwards Lansbury took over the *Daily Herald*, the struggling syndicalist newspaper which had started as a strike sheet during a printing dispute, and made it the champion of every left-wing cause. The British Socialist Party (B.S.P.) was a Marxist group which had succeeded the Social Democratic Federation.

1 December. St Vincent's Hotel, Clifton [Bristol]
Down here for a conference and public meeting on 'War against Poverty', an afternoon PSA [Pleasant Sunday Afternoon] on syndicalism, and a Free Church council meeting at Bath on the National Minimum. I came down exhausted, but the isolation from work in this pleasant and quiet hotel has counterbalanced the fatigue of speaking. The conference was successful; about 150 delegates from trade unions and socialist societies. The majority of these men were silent; they passed the resolutions, listening attentively to what was said: whether they understood the issues or were really in favour of the resolution, I do not know. There are backwaters in those men's minds: fear that a particular mine or factory will be shut up by an increased wage, fear that shortening of hours will result in lessened wages, distrust in the capacity of the working-man to govern anything, real admiration for the 'Boss' just because he is 'Boss', pious anxiety that religion and morality may be threatened, hereditary loyalty to the Tory or Liberal cause. All these doubts and hesitations may not give them sufficient conviction to speak or vote against resolutions at working-class meetings, but it prevents them from joining in any vigorous action on behalf of the policy. The majority of the Bristol delegates were, I believe, Liberals; they showed no approval of abuse of the Liberal government and in their hearts they acquiesced with the Insurance Act, though they passed a resolution for its drastic amendment. There was a little knot of extreme socialists and syndicalists, who wanted to tack on or substitute the usual class-conscious revolutionary resolution. As a compromise I drafted a socialist declaration to wind up the meeting and the whole conference voted for it, after they had altered the word 'nationalization' to 'socialization' at the request of the syndicalists.

Syndicalism has taken the place of the old-fashioned Marxism. The angry youth, with bad complexion, frowning brow and weedy figure, is now always a syndicalist; the glib young workman whose tongue runs away with him today mouths the phrases of French syndicalism instead of those of German social democracy. The inexperienced middle-class idealist has accepted with avidity the ideal of the syndicalist as a new and exciting utopia. But to the trade union organizer or to the Labour member of a municipal council, syndicalism appears a fantastic dream barely worth considering. So far as we can foresee, syndicalism will disrupt the British Socialist Party, it will detach some of the branches of the I.L.P. and some impatient Fabians; it will increase discontent with the Labour Party; but it will have no appreciable effect on the larger currents of trade unionism.

George Lansbury's defeat at Bow and Bromley has, I fear, turned him into a wrecker of the Labour Party. He always had a sentimentally disruptive mind, forceful feeling, unguided by reason, and the atmosphere of syndicalist philosophy justifies this personal predisposition. A strain of outraged vanity – a strain present in all of us – will prevent his realizing the folly of resigning his seat and add to his bitterness against MacDonald and Henderson. I shall try and maintain my friendship with him.

The plain fact is that Lloyd George and the radicals have out-trumped the Labour Party. They have dealt out millions of public money, they have taken up semi-socialist devices like compulsory insurance, which cannot be easily opposed even by the Conservative Party. By no other measure could £25 million have been raised and spent on sickness. The fact that it will be wastefully collected and wastefully spent may condemn it to the thoughtful socialist or to the economically-minded citizen, but to the ordinary elector it makes no difference, since he is too dull-witted to understand that it will be so. And given the fact that the money could not be got otherwise there is much to be said for the acceptance of the scheme by the Labour Party, especially as they had not the wit to offer an alternative. Who cares that a large part of the Workman's Compensation Fund is wasted, that industry is heavily taxed without benefiting the injured or their dependants?

But we must make the best of the Insurance Act, and use to the full all its incidental advantages – it is something to have got the whole of the working population registered from the age of sixteen; it is a step forward to have some sort of machinery for paying out weekly pensions to the sick and invalided without the stigma of pauperism; and the statistics of illness automatically collected will be of great value. The big fault of the Act is the creation of huge vested interests – the Industrial Insurance companies' method of collection and the Panel system of medical attendance. These vested interests mean not only waste of public money and financial chaos in the relative insolvency of the different societies, but wholesale demoralization of character through the fraudulent withholding or the fraudulent getting of benefits. Trade unions will be turned into great insurance societies and their leading men, already too much distracted by politics, will be further diverted from their special work by being made responsible for the technique of insurance. It would be far better if the Co-operative movement undertook all insurance and the trade union leaders devoted themselves to their function of securing good conditions of employment. With trade unions as associations of consumers (of insurance benefits) there will be some unedifying disputes with their new staffs of calculators and clerks!

William S. Sanders (1877–1942) had been factotum to John Burns in Battersea, then assistant to Pease at the Fabian office, succeeding him as general secretary when Pease retired on inheriting £28,000. He also took the place reserved for the Fabians on the Labour Party Executive and was replaced there by Sidney Webb in 1916 when he was recruited into intelligence work. William C. Anderson (1878–1919), an able and likeable I.L.P. member of the House of Commons, died in the influenza epidemic. Francis Johnson (b. 1878), was the secretary of the I.L.P. 1904–23. James Parker (1863–1948) was an I.L.P. organizer elected for Halifax in 1906. Tom Richards (1859–1931), secretary of the South Wales Miners' Federation, sat for Ebbw Vale from 1904. James O'Grady (1866–1934), president of the National Federation of General Workers, was elected for East Leeds in 1906.

Xmas. Weymouth

Gaining strength and energy for the next year's work, walking from ten to fifteen miles a day, with a day's rest now and again. C.M. Lloyd and his young wife with us. Long days in the sea air, even if it be in wind and rain, too tired to think and not too tired to sleep, is the best of recreations.

Our plans for the coming year are already cut, I will not say dried – they are still moist with uncertainty as to detail. First there is the starting of the *New Statesman*. During the next three months we have to get, by circularization, a large number of postal subscribers; if we can get 2,000 the success of the paper is secured; if we get only 500 it is extremely doubtful whether it can survive two years. Then Sidney and I have to contribute the long series of articles on 'What is Socialism?'. We have also to help Sharp to get other contributors.

Secondly, we have to complete the enquiry into the control of Industry and draft the report, probably as a supplement to the *Statesman*. I don't feel anxious about this seemingly gigantic task – we could write the report now; and getting the new material is largely a method of educating our young people. Finally, I have to take my share in organizing the next I.L.P. and Fabian campaign, a difficult business as the Labour M.P.s are stupid, suspicious and timid, and we have to work with them. There are lectures to be given at Cambridge, Edinburgh and Glasgow – the remainder from last autumn's campaign. And if there is energy left over we have to complete the eighteenth-century books on local government. A formidable programme.

Sanders, Schloesser, Anderson, Johnson and I had an important interview with a committee of the Labour M.P.s (Parker, Snowden, Richards, O'Grady and Henderson) about promoting Bills embodying the 'War against Poverty' campaign, and deciding on the subject for next autumn's propaganda. . . . The interview ended by a proposal from Henderson that we should have a regular meeting for the discussion of policy between the [I.L.P.–Fabian] standing committee, the Parliamentary Committee, the Labour Party and the Labour members. In the meantime they would introduce some, if not all, of our Bills. These Labour M.P.s are not a strong body of men, and they are plainly enervated by the atmosphere of the House, and MacDonald's astute but over-cautious and sceptical leadership – sceptical of all the reforms which he is supposed to believe in. If we could see into MacDonald's mind I don't believe it differs materially from John Burns's mentality. But the Labour Party exists and we have to work with it. 'A poor thing, but our own.'

Hilaire Belloc (1870–1953) was a radical anti-socialist and Catholic writer who wrote *The Servile State*, a popular attack on bureaucratic collectivism. His friend and co-editor of the *New Witness*, which ran a strong line in political scandal, was G.K. Chesterton (1874–1936), a better-natured novelist, poet and social critic. Shaw called the two men 'the Chesterbelloc'.

184

◡ 1913 ◠

[?] *January.* [41 Grosvenor Road]
For the last fortnight I have been exclusively engaged in circular-
izing for postal subscribers to the *Statesman*. We start with the
clientele of the Fabian Society, and the National Committee, and
upon this we are building a card catalogue of 20,000 possible
subscribers to the paper. To all the most promising of these we send
out personal, to the less promising manifolded, letters from me:
GBS and Sidney are appealing to the Fabians who are not members
of the National Committee. We have secured some 150 subscribers
— I doubt our getting 1,000. To make the paper pay we must get a
circulation, postal or trade, of 5,000.

We heard from Colegate the opinion of the *Nation* group with
regard to our chance of success. They put the lowest sales at which
the paper can keep going at 3,000, and the maximum that we
might get at 5,000. (Something between these two figures is, we
think, the circulation of the *Nation* itself.) This cannot be done,
they argue, unless we attract a good many different groups of
readers. GBS, they think, is good for 500 to 1,000, the Webbs for
200 to 300, and Squire, if you please, for 100, making up 1,000 to
1,500 in all. Hence the venture is bound to fail. The paper that
will be turned out will be one-idea-ed: the Webbs only know the
social and economic question, and they will always be hammering
at it exactly like Belloc and Chesterton hammer at the one theme of
political corruption in the *New Witness*. How can they get a really
well-informed article on Persia, for instance? The paper will be the
Webbs, flavoured with a little Shaw, and padded with the contributions of a few cleverish but ignorant young men. People may
take it in, at first, out of curiosity, but they will soon drop it.

There is truth in this criticism. The group of men who write in
the *Nation* are an able, experienced and fairly versatile lot, who
have worked together for many years. Massingham is an exceptionally brilliant journalist and editor. But I think that Sidney and I are
not quite so one-sided as we look. We have never written on other
questions, but Sidney has an encyclopaedic knowledge and we have
seen a few things. GBS, if he really throws himself into it, has a far

185

larger public than is thought by the Liberals, and I believe we can attract around us able persons of quite different interests and outlook and in harmony with our general position. And though we are wholly inexperienced on the business side we have initiative, persistency and audacity, which more conventionally experienced persons lack. So I think that our friends of the *Nation* may be unpleasantly disappointed. However, they are obviously better judges than we are and the chances are that they are right. In that case we shall have spent our money and our time, not exactly in vain because we shall have raised the standard of socialist journalism. If I were forced to wager I should not back our success. I do not feel sufficiently confident in Clifford Sharp's ability or in our capacity to supplement his deficiencies. He has method, sound sense and good journalist manners, but he is slow and somewhat timid. GBS, on the other hand, is somewhat risky – how many persons will he offend?

[*Beatrice inserted this additional note in August 1918.* The event proved that both the elderly critics and the elderly promoters calculated without the young men of the *New Statesman*. Bernard Shaw was a failure and left the staff before the paper gained its present unique position. I also soon ceased to write for it. To Sidney it owes a good deal, not only on account of his weekly article on political-economic questions, but also to his tact and ability as chairman. But the success is principally due to Clifford Sharp and Jack Collins Squire and the group of younger thinkers that they (and not we) attracted as contributors. And oddly enough it is in foreign affairs that the unexpected success has principally been made. Owing to the preposterous price of paper in this, the fifth year of the war, the *New Statesman* still runs at a loss. But it is unlikely to cease on this account, and Fleet Street and Whitehall count it as a great success. The circulation is now well over 6,000 and rises steadily.]

3 April. [41 Grosvenor Road]
Our promoting is at an end and we start with 2,300 postal subscribers, a notable result. We are now at work on the series of articles on 'What is Socialism?', for the first twenty numbers of the paper. Sidney is booked for a weekly article on his own range of expertise. GBS has surprised and disconcerted us by refusing to

186

sign any articles, but sends us three for the first number, and apparently means to write regularly. The first number will be brilliant but it cannot be good. . . .

Meanwhile the Report on the control of industry oppresses me and I regret starting the idea. We shall get it done, but it will mean a horrid grind for us. I doubt whether the committee will justify its name of Research Department: I have not the strength to run it, and there is no one in the Fabian Society capable of doing it but ourselves. What may happen is the development of a semi-research department in connection with the *New Statesman*.

25 May. [41 Grosvenor Road]
I find it increasingly difficult to find time or energy to write in my diary. The *New Statesman* absorbs both. We started with 2,450 postal subscribers. How many of these we shall keep depends on the uniqueness of the paper. There are all sorts of conflicting criticism. The paper is dull: it is mere brilliant writing and there is not enough solid information; the political articles are good but the literature 'rot'; the literary side is excellent, but the political articles not sufficiently constructive.

Our main difficulty is with Bernard Shaw – a difficulty which we always knew would arise in one way or another. He won't write over his own signature and some of the articles and notes that he sends are hopelessly out of keeping with our tone and our methods. And in order to threaten us, he writes signed letters to the *Nation*, Massingham of course trying to capture him from us. However, we have just to go on making the paper valuable. Sharp is turning out a good man of business, a safe though not distinguished writer. What he lacks is personal magnetism; in some ways he is too doggedly sincere.

Leicester had two parliamentary seats, one held by a Liberal and the other by Ramsay MacDonald. In 1913, when the resignation of the Liberal M.P. caused a by-election, the local Labour Party was keen to contest the vacancy. The Labour leadership, knowing that such a challenge would destroy the arrangement which gave MacDonald a clear run and a safe seat, forced the local members to withdraw. The decision rankled, and much of the local party bolted to support a candidate from the British Socialist Party who ran a bad third. MacDonald's seat was saved, though many thought it had been done by cowardly and unprincipled means.

5 July. [41 Grosvenor Road]
GBS has in fact injured the *New Statesman* by his connection with it; we have had the disadvantage of his eccentric and iconoclastic stuff without the advantage of his name. Lots of people will think any article brilliant that they know is by him, whilst dismissing his anonymous contribution as tiresome and of no account, or as purely mischievous. And in all the details of his arrangements he is grossly inconsiderate, refusing to let Sharp know whether or not he was going to write, and what he was going to write about, until, on the day the paper goes to press, there appears on Sharp's table two or three columns – sometimes twice that amount – on any subject that he (Shaw) happens to fancy. Sharp has now decided that if Shaw insists on these terms we are better without him. Meanwhile, persons who subscribed for their weekly portion of Shaw are angry and say they were got to subscribe on false pretences. The *New Statesman* is in fact the one weekly in which Shaw's name never appears, and it is Shaw's name that draws, not his mind. He may become more considerate: he means to be kindly, but he is spoilt – spoilt by intense vanity and intellectual egotism. He will not co-operate on terms of equality.

Our attempt to connect up with the Labour Party in the House of Commons has failed. The Labour members, guided by Henderson, tried to persuade the joint committee of the I.L.P. and Fabian Society to give up its separate propaganda and merely contribute its funds and its speakers to the Labour Party campaign. Anderson and I objected, and though we have patched some sort of consultative committee, it is clear that we are not going to work together. The Labour Members, either from stupidity or ill will, have failed to introduce our Bills, which they distinctly promised to do. The Parliamentary Labour Party is, in fact, in a bad way. The Leicester electoral fight has further discredited it and even the I.L.P. has been seriously injured by its connection with it. Within the Fabian Society there is growing up an anti-Labour Party section, in direct conflict with the late rebels who wanted the Fabian Society to bind itself to the Labour Party; the Executive holding the balance between the old faction and the new. The Parliamentary Labour Party has, in fact, not justified its existence either by character or by intelligence and it is doubtful whether it will hold the trade unions.

The labour and socialist movement is in a state of disruption; there is more evil speaking and suspicion than there has ever been before and there is less enthusiasm. As a matter of fact the Fabian Society is the only socialist society that has increased its membership and income during the last year, and we should have been stronger if we had kept clear of the Labour Party. George Lansbury is preaching alternately universal goodwill and universal revolt, whilst the British Socialist Party is rent asunder by the rival impossibilism of the old-fashioned Marxist and the new-fashioned syndicalist. . . .

Shaw had become infatuated with the successful actress Stella Campbell (1865–1940), known as Mrs Patrick Campbell or 'Mrs Pat'. She had made her mark in Pinero's *The Second Mrs Tanqueray* in 1892 and Shaw wrote the part of Eliza Doolittle in *Pygmalion* with her in mind. His flirtatious letters, which he had been writing for a year while working on the play, confirm Beatrice's remark that in middle life Shaw was reverting to the philandering manner of his youth. Although the 'affair' reached its climax in August 1913 they continued to correspond. Audrey (Ada) Wallas (1859–1934), wife of Graham Wallas, had a modest gift as a writer. The new Fabian Research Department was in the Norfolk Street offices of the Poor Law campaign, and the Fabian Society was close by in Clement's Inn, across the Strand. The Fabians soon after moved to Tothill Street, Westminster.

13 July. [41 Grosvenor Road]
Charlotte Shaw asked me to come and see her one day last week. She has been ill, off and on, ever since we returned from India. She was lying on the sofa looking unusually gentle and attractive. She told me, in a singularly gentle and dignified way, that GBS had fallen in love with Mrs Patrick Campbell and that most people knew it, that he was really obsessed by it and had fallen completely under that somewhat elderly witch's spell. (*She* did not call her an 'elderly witch'!) I was not surprised. When he was with us last November he talked incessantly about Mrs Pat and told me a lot of stupid stuff about her past relations with her husband, children and with the stage, as she imagined them to have been, and he repeated her silly and insolent remarks about Charlotte's big waist. I paid little attention to it, one is so accustomed to GBS's vanity and egotism. One used to watch these faults leading to all sorts of rather cruel philanderings with all kinds of odd females. But I had certainly thought he had outgrown this business. Though I was alarmed by it as a symptom of intellectual deterioration, it never occurred to me that it meant emotional disturbance.

189

From what I recollect of GBS's chatter about Mrs Pat the relationship is one of gross mutual flattery, each pandering to the other's morbid craving for the recognition of unique genius. It is remarkable how long Charlotte has kept his volatile nature attached to her and I am not sure that he won't [will] return to her. The present obsession, reacting on declining vigour, may be more serious. Formerly he was always quite detached and he could pull himself up when he chose. He allowed himself to be adored, I never knew him adore. In this case I gather that he is the fly and the lady the spider.

We are unhappy about Shaw. About five years ago I thought he was going to mellow into deeper thought and feeling, instead of which he wrote *Fanny's First Play*! He used to be a good colleague, genuinely interested in public affairs and a radically kind man. Now he is perverse, irate and despotic in his relations, and he is bored with all the old questions. And the quality of his thought is not good. One of our difficulties on the *New Statesman* is that his work, unsigned, is not good enough – the literary quality is not distinguished enough to carry the poor and petulant reasoning, the lack of accuracy, logic and dignity. For the last year or so we have found it increasingly difficult to discuss with him; he no longer tries to meet another person's points. He merely orates, and all his talk revolves round persons and not ideas. In political theory he is inclining towards Belloc and Chesterton, and the propaganda of revolt. Now and again he has a brilliant flash of illuminating thought, but it is over before one has had time to fit it in to the rest of his philosophy of conduct.

Old friends drift apart. We sometimes see Graham Wallas and I am more friendly with Audrey than ever before, but there is no common work and our meetings are rare. Sydney Olivier has been in London as permanent head of the Board of Agriculture for eight months or more, and we have only seen him twice. We have dined twice with Haldane since we returned from India, and Herbert Samuel has dined here once – otherwise we have not even said 'good-day' to a Liberal minister. Of the smattering of 'Society' I used to see, Betty Balfour alone remains – with A.J.B. as an occasional guest. Sidney still keeps an eye on the School of Economics and is good friends with Reeves and all the staff. On the other hand the L.C.C. is in the far distance and we never hear of its internal doings. My sisters I often see, and our relations with them are of the most affectionate. But the centre of our lives are the three offices, of the Fabian, the National Committee and Research Department, and the *New Statesman*; and it is with the inhabitants of these that we spend our outdoor life, whilst there streams through our little house the usual assortment of students, travellers and fellow workers. It is remarkable how limited one's circle becomes when one is at once elderly and hard-working. Our close comradeship, our day-by-day joint work, the long enduring honeymoon of our holidays, in fact the ideal marriage, dwarfs all other human relationships. And as personal life draws quietly to its end, one's thought concentrates on the future of the race and the search for the purpose of human life.

After adjourning to Saas Grund in Switzerland in 1911, the venue of the Fabian summer school had now moved from North Wales to Barrow House on Derwentwater in the Lake District. The Webbs had taken the Hampshire house for their customary summer retreat. The National Administrative Council was the governing body of the I.L.P., which Beatrice had joined on her return from Asia.

28 September. Innesfail, Ropley, Hants
We spent two exhausting weeks at the Fabian summer school at Keswick. The large, ugly bare and somewhat dirty house, the punctually provided but scrimmagey meals, the strange medley of guests: these standing features of the institution were dignified by the atmosphere of hardheaded discussion on definite points in the theory and practice of socialism, in the two successive conferences – that of the Research Department and that of the joint committee of the Fabian and the I.L.P. Perhaps the fact that, owing to these conferences, the company was three-quarters male instead of three-quarters female improved the occasion. For six days, for five hours a day, sat I in the chair, directing the various discussions on the material gathered together by the department. The conference with the National Administrative Council [of the I.L.P.] was more disjointed. The I.L.P. was absorbed in its own meetings and more inclined to holiday-making than the sterner Fabians. Both conferences were voted a great success and are to be repeated . . . .

4 December. [41 Grosvenor Road]
GBS is making an effort to keep in with the Fabian Society and ourselves and he has attended every one of our six public lectures,

and taken the chair twice. Also he has been most kind in doing things for the Fabian Society. He no longer writes for the *New Statesman*, though he is quite friendly and asks whether we want more money. Apparently he keeps away from Mrs Pat, and he and Charlotte are outwardly on the best of terms. The two plays he had on the English stage were not a success, but this has been compensated by Continental and American 'big runs' – especially of *Pygmalion*.

Beatrice divided people into A's and B's. The B's were benevolent, bourgeois and bureaucratic. 1913 saw a hardening of attitudes and an increase in direct action on the Irish and labour questions and women's suffrage.

[?] *6 December. Midland Hotel* [Burnley?]
On a short lecturing tour, Bradford, Liverpool and Burnley, five lectures in four days. . . .

The labour movement, indeed the whole of the thinking British public, is today the arena of a battle of words, of thoughts and of temperaments. The issue is twofold: are men to be governed by emotion or by reason? Are they to be governed in harmony with the desires of the bulk of the citizens or according to the fervent aspirations of a militant minority in defiance of the will of the majority? Two quite separate questions but each of them raising the same issue: the validity of democratic-government. The Webb conception of the relative spheres of intellect and emotion on the one hand, and, on the other, of the right relation of the leaders to the average sensual man, is vehemently objected to by all the 'A's', by the Artist, the Anarchist and the Aristocrat. Our answer to the first question is that the idealist chooses the purpose of life, whether of the individual or of the community, whilst the man of science thinks out the processes by which this purpose can be fulfilled; our answer to the second is that leaders, idealist or man of science, *propose, but that the ordinary man* (in his collective capacity of being the mass of the people) *disposes, and that it is right that he should dispose.* We uphold the authority of the mass of the people and object to any defiance of it or any tricks of evasion. The minority must submit until they have succeeded, by the magic of their idealism, or by the verification of their reasoning, in persuading their fellow men to accept their aims or their methods of reaching those aims. . . .

This philosophy postulates deliberate division of labour; it demands patience, discipline and tolerance – characteristics which do not appeal to either the revolutionary or the reactionary. That is why the Webbs are so hated – all the more so because we seem so 'damned sure' of our conclusions. We are extraordinarily unpopular today, more disliked, by a larger body of persons, than ever before. The propertied class look upon us as their most insidious enemies; the revolutionary socialist or fanatical sentimentalist, see in us, and our philosophy, the main obstacle to what they call enthusiasm and we call hysteria. Our one comfort is that both sets of opponents can hardly be right. . . .

Sir Richard Holt (1868–1941) was Lallie's eldest son. Lawrence (1882–1961) was the youngest of her eight children. The other sons were Robert (1872–1952), Philip (1876–1958) and Edward (1878–1955). John Hobhouse (1893–1961) was the sixth of Margaret Hobhouse's seven children.

8 December. 54 Ullet Road [Liverpool]

. . . I am staying at dear old Lallie's old home (my generous but tragically unselfcontrolled sister), seeing the life of her children and their mates, in the intervals of giving two lectures in one day. It is significant of the small repute of the Webbs that not one of the eight nephews and nieces or any member of the clan came to either of my lectures. I am regarded with kindly tolerance as a crank, perhaps by some of them as a mischievous crank. One or two of the connection, do, however, take in the *New Statesman*.

R.D. Holt M.P., destined at no distant date to become Sir Richard Holt, is a stout, straightforward businessman. . . . As the senior partner of the Blue Funnel Line he has the status, if not the capacity, of the great business organizer. . . . The young brother, Lawrence, has I think slightly more originality and decidedly more social compunction; he worries over casual labour and feels to some extent responsible for its existence. But he is a prig and almost pathologically self-centred. The other two brothers are just commonplace philistines, cotton brokers by profession. . . . To this family party has been lately added Jack Hobhouse, the only one of Maggie's sons with the profit-making instinct, a pleasant, handsome, clever lad, honestly intent on 'getting on' and presently to be a partner in the Booth-Holt line. . . .

∾ 1914 ∾

2 January. Minehead
A fortnight's walking and motoring tour in Cornwall and Devon, with GBS (and Mellor of the Research Department for the first week). It has been a delightful and luxurious holiday, our first intention of tramping round the coast, with knapsack and mackintosh being transformed, by the advent of GBS, into walking over ten or thirteen miles of picked country with the motor car in attendance to take us, when tired, to the most expensive hotel in the neighbourhood. Our old friend and brilliant comrade is a benevolent and entertaining companion, but his intellect is centred in the theatre and his emotion in his friendship with Mrs Pat. He is still fond of Charlotte and grateful to her, but he quite obviously finds his new friend, with her professional genius and more intimate personal appeal, better company. He is self-complacent – feels himself one of the world geniuses and is mortified by the refusal of his generation to take him seriously as a thinker and reformer. He is getting rapidly old physically, and somewhat dictatorial and impatient intellectually, and he suffers from restlessness. We talked more intimately than we have done for many years. He is interested in the newer developments of Fabianism, not at all impressed with militancy or syndicalism, a good deal less anxious to conciliate the newcomers than we are. He is in fact more rigid in his adhesion to his old doctrines. He is estranged from the *New Statesman* and Sharp, but he is not at all hostile. 'It is not my organ, but it may be none the worse for that.'

The mining and textile trade unions, many of whose officials had sat as 'Lib-Lab' M.P.s, had been slow to affiliate to the new Labour Party; and they saw the party as little more than an ally of the Liberals. The I.L.P., perennially critical of the moderate unions and of the parliamentary leadership, wanted a distinctively socialist policy. The unions, which had a strong geographical base (coal, steel and textiles), understandably favoured the first-past-the-post electoral system, which gave them all the seats in such areas rather than a proportion of them. Local parties with no prospect of an outright majority were more sympathetic to schemes of proportional representation. In the early years of the *New Statesman* the paper carried several supplements a year summarizing or reviewing government publications.

6 February. [41 Grosvenor Road]

. . . . The Labour Party conference was a personal triumph for J.R. MacDonald. The first day's criticism, in which Sanders took a leading part, was steam-rollered by the platform. There was much discontent among the I.L.P. delegates, but the solid phalanx of miners and textiles don't want the Labour members to cut loose from the Liberal Party, and MacDonald knows it. The other big controversy, proportional representation (what a subject for heated discussion at a Labour Party conference!), was also dominated by the sectional interests of industries massed in narrow areas. MacDonald, with his romantic figure, charming voice and clever dialectics, is more than a match for all those underbred and undertrained workmen who surround him on the platform and face him in the audience. So long as he chooses to remain leader of the Labour Party he will do so. In his old-fashioned radicalism, in his friendliness to Lloyd George, he represents the views and aspirations of the bulk of trade unionists. Owing to his personal distinction and middle-class equipment he is superior to all his would-be competitors.

The British workman has been persuaded by the propaganda of the I.L.P. that a Labour Party is useful, that some of his class ought to enjoy the £400 a year and the prestige of the M.P.'s position, but the closer the Labour member sticks to the Liberal Party the better he is pleased. So far as he has any politics he still believes in the right of the middle and professional class to do the work of government. He does not believe his own mates are capable of it, and roughly speaking he is right. The landslide in England towards social democracy proceeds steadily, but it is the whole nation that is sliding, not the one class of manual workers.

Our present anxiety is the chance of renewal of the 2,400 postal subscribers to the *New Statesman*. We gathered these up by all sorts of understandings and misunderstandings, curiosities and expectations. We shall probably lose one half of them and start the second year of the *Statesman*'s life with 1,500 or 2,000 annual subscribers. Our other sales are 2,000 or over, that would mean a circulation of 4,000 and would warrant a determined effort to keep the paper in existence. If, on the other hand, we lost 2,000 of the postal subscriptions, the position would be hopeless. . . . In the supplements, I think, we have found quite a new and permanent attraction, but an expensive one to maintain. . . .

James Keir Hardie (1856–1915) was the founder of the I.L.P. in 1893 and the first leader of the Labour Party in the House of Commons. F.W. Jowett (1864–1944) was a Bradford socialist, elected to the House of Commons in 1906, who played a prominent part in the I.L.P. for many years.

18 February. [Edinburgh]
Sanders, who is now on the Labour Party Executive in succession to Pease, gave me a depressing account of the Labour members. Apart from MacDonald, and with the exceptions of Snowden, who has intellect but is a lonehander, and Keir Hardie, who is now little more than a figurehead, the Labour members are a lot of ordinary workmen who neither know nor care about anything but the interests of their respective trade unions and a comfortable life for themselves. He makes an exception for Arthur Henderson, who feels that the Labour members ought to take a more distinctive line and whose uneasiness has a bad effect on his temper. MacDonald rules absolutely and the other Labour members stick to him as their only salvation from confusion. Whenever anyone, like poor little Jowett, wants to strike out in the constructive socialist direction, MacDonald quietly proves that his proposed action is 'out of order'. MacDonald, himself, does not want anything done in particular. He honestly disapproves of nearly all the planks in the ostensible party programme. His political policy is to fight eternally on the 'right of combination' and the 'right of free speech' and any other old Radical shibboleth. He abhors and despises the 'rebels' and dislikes and distrusts the 'reformists'. He is bored with his Labour colleagues and attracted to Front Bench Liberals. But he feels it difficult to go back on his past. So he remains the Parnell of the Labour Party – but a Parnell who does not believe in his cause. His aloofness is, in fact, restricted to his own followers: with the Liberal leaders he is on terms of personal friendship, and they always address him, in the House, as 'Honourable Friend'. From the standpoint of the Liberal Cabinet he has been better than Burns, as they have his steady support without giving up place or programme. The one drawback to the existence of a Labour Party are the three-cornered contests. J.R. MacDonald would like to stop them: this he cannot manage because of the genuine faith in a Labour Party instilled, by years of propaganda, into the rank and file, and reinforced by the ambition of every local Labour leader to get into the House of Commons.

The middle and working-class socialists are in a quandary. They are hopelessly outnumbered within the Labour Party, and whenever they protest they are voted down. They have pledged themselves to working-class representation as part of the process of making the manual labourer conscious of his disinherited condition, and of arousing, in the working class, faith in the class struggle. But they are, by their adhesion to the present parliamentary party, bolstering up a fraud, pretending to the outside world that these respectable but reactionary trade union officials are the leaders of the social revolution. Moreover, by belonging to the Labour Party they are, to some extent, hampered in the old Fabian policy of the permeation of all parties, this policy demanding that socialists should be free to work inside all social sets and political parties. But to go back on the creation of a Labour Party would be to admit failure.

The International Socialist Bureau [I.S.B.] tried to persuade the contumacious socialist organizations in Britain to unite – a move that in practice would have meant the absorption of the British Socialist Party into the Labour Party. Sidney was chairman of the meeting of the various executives. Beatrice favoured the move but nothing came of it. H.M. Hyndman (1842–1921) was an admirer of Marx who had founded the Social Democratic Federation and led the B.S.P. that emerged from it. H.J. Gillespie, a militant suffragist and Guild Socialist, was currently the secretary of the Fabian Research Department. He and Cole were trying to persuade the Fabian Society to disaffiliate from the Labour Party on the grounds that its function was 'primarily to conduct research'. Sidney Webb's counter-motion was carried by one vote but Cole continued his campaign to change the Society's constitution.

8 March. Newcastle
Here for a socialist unity meeting with Hyndman and Keir Hardie. . . . Though our main work is the preparation of reports for the Fabian Research Department, our main anxiety is the financial position of the *New Statesman*. We have used up the larger half of the capital with which we started, and unless we can pull up the advertisement revenue and a larger circulation, or get another heavy subsidy from rich friends, we cannot carry on. The three rich Fabians – Harben, Whitley and Shaw – volunteered another £500, and E.D. Simon was almost forced to follow suit. This means financial safety for another year.

In one direction our plans have turned out better than we

197

expected. When I started the Fabian Research Department I did not realize that it would be extraordinarily useful in providing supplements for the *New Statesman*. It seems that the only chance of success for the *New Statesman* lies embedded in these supplements. If it survives, it will become primarily an organ of research and secondarily a general weekly paper. Fortunately, GBS has taken a sudden fancy to research as the primary purpose of the Fabian Society. At the members' meeting at which the new group of rebels (G.D.H. Cole, Mellor and Gillespie) tried to alter the basis and upset the policy of the Fabian Society, Shaw supported the resolution, moved by them, to limit the Society to the work of research, as against Sidney's amendment that research was one of the principal functions of the Fabians. The situation is certainly humorous. The Webbs have not been behind in the work of research, indeed we have been up to now the only Fabians who have been noted for research. Of course, what the little knot of rebels are after is not research at all, but a new form of propaganda and a new doctrine which they believe themselves to be elaborating with regard to the control of industry.

My purpose is to connect the Research Department with the international socialist movement and thus bring to bear, on all the problems that confront the socialists, the finer intellects of our German, Belgian and Dutch comrades. We ought to have an international programme and an international literature, and the Fabian Research Department ought to be the centre. But who is to do the heavy and highly skilled brainwork involved? The young men talk but they do not get through much work, and they are fanatical and one idea-ed. Mellor is not an ideal secretary, and yet I see no other means of livelihood open to him. However, he is very much alive, and if he does not produce light, he produces heat.

On 9 March Asquith moved for the third time the second reading of the Home Rule Bill, first introduced in 1912, which put a time limit on Ulster's right to stay outside the parliament in Dublin. The proposals provoked threats of rebellion and secession from the Ulster Protestants as well as a defiant near-mutiny on 20 March from army officers serving on the Curragh in Ireland. Andrew Bonar Law, now leader of the Conservative Party, was inciting the Ulster rebels in terms close to a threat of civil war. Colonel J.E.B. Seely (1868–1947), the Minister of War, resigned, and Asquith took over the War Office on 30 March. *Parsifal* was being performed for the first time in England at Covent Garden. E.S. Montagu (1879–1924) was a banker and Liberal M.P.

1906–22. He was Asquith's private secretary 1906–10 and financial secretary to the Treasury 1914–16. Dr Christopher Addison (1869–1951), then parliamentary secretary to the Board of Education, became Minister of Reconstruction in 1917, and later held office as a member of the Labour Party. Margaret Bondfield (1873–1931) was an organizer of the Shop Assistants' Union, and in 1924 she became the first woman to hold a government post. Camille Huysmans (1871–1968), the Belgian socialist, had been Secretary-General of the Labour and Socialist International Bureau since 1904. He became Prime Minister of Belgium in 1946. Mrs Patrick Campbell married the soldier and author George Cornwallis West (1874–1951) on 6 April, six days before the opening night of *Pygmalion*.

23 April. [41 Grosvenor Road]
The turmoil over Ulster and the recalcitrant officers loomed large at Westminster, and in the party papers; and among little cliques of the fashionable and wealthy the talk was of civil war and revolution. For about three days, members of the governing class glared at each other and social entertainments were boycotted by one of the party clans or the other. In the end, Asquith came out on top by his bold bid for confidence as War Minister. The Hyde Park Ulster demonstration was merely a festival day for city men and their clerks and the hangers-on of the Conservative associations. Bonar Law is proving himself a contemptible leader. If it were not for the unpopularity of the Insurance Act, the Liberal ministry would be stronger than ever. But that is proving an even bigger blunder than we foretold.

We have resumed relations with two of the Liberal Ministers – Lloyd George and Herbert Samuel. At a performance of *Parsifal* Sidney and I ran up against them during the long interval in the outer hall and presently found ourselves heatedly discussing, surrounded by an ever-widening circle of amused and interested listeners, the excessive sickness of married women under the Insurance Act owing to the humorously ignorant omission by the government actuaries of the 'risk' of pregnancy. As we hurried back to the gloriously dramatized religious service, Lloyd George appealed to us to help him to get out of the financial hole. The result was a breakfast at 11 Downing Street, with Montagu (Financial Secretary to the Treasury) and Dr Addison as fellow guests; and a dinner at Grosvenor Road to enable Lloyd George to meet Margaret Bondfield and Mary Macarthur. It is certainly to his credit that he bears no malice for our criticism – perhaps it is to our credit that we, also, are willing to let bygones be bygones in order to get the best out of the situation. . . .

We attended the gala days of the I.L.P. conference (the twenty-first anniversary of its existence) as fraternal delegates from the Fabian Society, and listened to endless self-congratulatory speeches from I.L.P. leaders and a fine piece of oratory from Huysmans, a man of far finer calibre than our British leaders. When the conference settled down to business the I.L.P. leaders were painfully at variance. J.R. MacDonald seems almost preparing for his exit from the I.L.P. I think he would welcome a really conclusive reason for joining the Liberal Party. Snowden is ill, some say very ill, at once bitter and apathetic; Keir Hardie is vain and egotistical, 'used up', with no real faith left in the labour movement as a revolutionary force. . . . The cold truth is that the Labour members have utterly failed to impress the House of Commons and the constituencies as a live force, and have lost confidence in themselves and each other. The labour movement rolls on – the trade unions are swelling in membership and funds, more candidates are being put forward; but the faith of politically active members is becoming dim or confused whilst the rank and file become every day more restive. . . .

[*Beatrice inserted this additional note in August 1918.* Like all characterization arising out of current events, this is an untrue description of Keir Hardie. I am not qualified to describe this Labour leader (become, since his death in 1915, the canonized founder of the I.L.P.), as neither Sidney nor I ever worked with him or even talked with him intimately. When I came across him in 1913–14 he had become the picturesque prophet of the labour movement. But he was a disheartened prophet. To him the regeneration of the world by the upheaval of the manual working class throughout the world had been a religion, and unlike other leaders, notably MacDonald, he had kept himself unpolluted by personal ambition or desire to temporize with the authorities that be. He was a cultivated man – he knew his Bible, his Shakespeare and his Burns in a way that ennobled his thought and feeling and gave real distinction to his spoken and written word. But he had no administrative experience, and still less scientific knowledge of the subjects about which he dogmatized and enthused. When it became clear to his sincere but limited mind that Labour leaders in

Parliament were not different from aristocrats and plutocrats in their disinclination to propose revolutionary measures, and were less capable of devising them, Keir Hardie lost all his old vim. Being a loyal man he did not turn against the Labour Party, but he spent most of his time in travel in India and the Colonies, and walked through his part, as star performer, at party conferences and gala Labour festivals. The war literally 'finished him', and his devoted followers declared with some justification that he died of a broken heart.]

We had six days of walking and motoring with GBS after the I.L.P. conference. He was hard hit by Mrs Pat's marriage, but he has taken it in the best possible manner and has been doubtless consoled by the success of *Pygmalion*. He is making piles of money – which is fortunate for the *New Statesman* – and he seems most friendly in his intentions towards Fabianism and all its works.

Meanwhile I am desperately tired. Even the six days walking in glorious weather did not rest me. I have come back more tired than when I left London. Irritable and depressed: a wicked state of mind for one endowed with an extravagant share of all that is fortunate in human relationships and material circumstances.

The renewal of the original subscriptions to the *New Statesman* are extremely satisfactory – some 1,800 out of the original 2,800 and others coming in day by day; we shall probably start the second year with at least 2,000 postal subscribers. What is unexpected is the trouble and cost of the renewals – due, no doubt, to lack of method in cataloguing. Now we have to make a success of the meeting of subscribers and I have to prepare a short address on 'The Contempt of Women in the Press of Today'. But oh, how tired I am; I should like, at least, a fortnight's complete rest, with nothing to do or think about.

Will Dyson (1880–1938) was the Australian-born cartoonist of the *Daily Herald*.

3 May. [41 Grosvenor Road]
Harben and Lansbury, now respectively the proprietor and editor of the *Daily Herald*, rich man and rebel, excited and enthusiastic, controlling a team of clever and intellectually unscrupulous young journalists with Will Dyson, the cartoonist, at their head and Lansbury exercising an emotional paternal influence. Mellor, late

secretary of the Research Department, a very determined rebel, has joined them, much to our relief.

George Lansbury has lost his old friendly *bonhomie*. He is prematurely grey-headed and suspicious, with his hand against every man, claiming to be respectable. . . . He is steadily losing popularity because working-men are beginning to doubt his good-heartedness. Lansbury is not sufficiently able to succeed except as a saint. He has splendid self-devotion and disinterestedness – but he is conceited and vain, and recent rebuffs have turned him sour. Patience, tolerance, kindliness and steadfast and persistent faith and industry are qualities most needed in the labour movement of today. Suspicion is its besetting devil.

I am anxious about the future of the Fabian Society and the Research Department. We do not seem to be securing competent successors to take over the leadership. In the L.S.E. Sidney was able to gather together a body of teachers and students and to create an organization which became self-sufficient both in brains and money. The *New Statesman* has attracted a group of able young men, and if once it can be put on a safe financial basis we shall be able to retire quietly from it. The same is true of all Sidney's work on the L.C.C. – in every case he created something that superseded him. But hitherto we have failed with the Fabian Society. The successive groups of individuals, who have aimed at taking over the leadership, have not had the combined conduct, brains and faith to enable them to do it. Each in turn, J.R. MacDonald, H.G. Wells, S.G. Hobson, Schloesser and Co., has attacked the Old Gang without being willing to do the work. I am wondering whether this new lot of rebellious spirits (Cole, Gillespie and Mellor) will prove any more capable. Cole is the ablest newcomer since H.G. Wells. But he is intolerant, impatient and not, at present, very practical. I am not certain whether the present rebel mood is in good faith or whether it is just experimental, seeing how it will go down. The root of the difficulty may be that the Fabian Society has very little to offer to an ambitious young man except unpaid work and a humble type of leadership; there is no career that would be considered a career. To the isolated lower middle-class man of humble faculties and modest needs it offers companionship and intellectual stimulus and a certain contact with men and women whose names are known. But work for it brings neither money nor fame – not even the barest livelihood. . . .

Walter Lippmann (1889–1974), assistant editor of the weekly *New Republic*, a liberal magazine published in New York, later became the most respected of American political commentators. Sir Maurice Amos (1872–1940) was a distinguished judge and adviser to the Egyptian government whom the Webbs had met in Cairo. Joseph Chamberlain had died on 2 July but Beatrice made no reference to his death. Barrow House, near Keswick, had been rented by the Fabians as a conference centre.

31 July. Barrow House

A fortnight here with two weeks' Research Department conference, the first week on the Control of Industry and the second on Insurance.

We travelled down in a large party – Harben, Cole, Gillespie, Mellor and some dozen Oxford and Cambridge undergraduates, with others joining in from Birmingham, Glasgow, Manchester and Liverpool, mostly university Fabians. During the week about eight Americans joined us: Walter Lippmann (political science lecturer), Professor Barrett and his wife and two single ladies. GBS and Sydney Olivier stayed at the hotel close by, and George Trevelyan and Maurice Amos and his wife looked in.

We began in turmoil. We went to bed on Saturday evening, tired out with our long journey, with the incessant talk and the inevitable scrimmage in settling in a party of sixty persons in a ramshackle establishment. When I came down on Sunday morning to take up my duties as Director I found the admirable 'Hanky' [Miss Hankinson] in a state of exasperation, and the Oxford men in an attitude of heroic defiance. There had taken place, after our retirement, a concerted strike against the 'eleven o'clock' rule. The Oxford group had refused to go to bed and Miss Hankinson had felt it her duty to stay up with them. As she had had a hard week with the I.L.P. her temper was short: she told me that unless the rules were obeyed, she would leave on Monday and that the servants would go with her.

We parleyed with both sides. In the afternoon I cut the gordian knot of rebellion by quietly informing the rebels that I should sit up with them every night, for as many hours as they had the heart to keep an old woman out of her bed. Guided by the beneficent Harben, the group, after sticking up a manifesto denouncing all rules in general and the school rules in particular, gave way and announced their intention of agreeing to the rules (which they had signed before being accepted as guests) rather than break up the conference.

But the atmosphere remained hostile to the management, and the eight Oxford boys, with Cole and Mellor, sat at a separate table, drank copiously and defiantly of the beer they ordered in, hoisted the Red Flag in front of the house and brought the police inspector to remonstrate with us for the uproarious singing of revolutionary songs at the station and in the market place, at the exact time when the great Keswick Evangelical Convention was arriving for the week of Religious Experiences. At our daily discussions they sat in a corner of the room, a solid Guild Socialist phalanx, and walked out of the room when any of their number were called to order; refused in the intervals between the meetings to speak to any one but each other, and generally misbehaved themselves.

GBS was rather attracted by their rebellious attitude, and in his summing-up address, mingled flattery and good advice. But it was all very exhausting to me, as I had to take the chair every day and stand between them and the hardworked establishment. I don't know why they adopted such defiant bad manners. G.D.H. Cole told me that they intended to use us 'as a platform', but the platform will give way if they stamp on it too heavily. They are obsessed with Guild Socialism and no other subject seems to them worth thinking about. They, and Harben with them, apparently believe that the 'General Expropriatory Strike' is a working policy. It is all very surprising, as Cole is a really able man, with much concentrated energy. Fortunately they do not tamper with sex conventions – they seem to dislike women. But all other conventions they break or ignore.

The second week was much pleasanter; some fifty quiet folk, half men, half women, a general atmosphere of good comradeship and useful discussion among actuaries and secretaries of Approved Societies. . . .

Meanwhile, Europe has flamed up. All the great powers may be at war in a few days, perhaps in a few hours. A hideous business. Ulsterites, Suffragettes, Guild Socialists and rebels of all sorts and degrees may be swept out of mind and sight in national defence and national subsistence.

[*Beatrice inserted this additional note in August 1918.* All through the last week of the Barrow conferences there had been the rumblings of the approaching earthquake without our awakening to the meaning of it. Sidney had refused to believe in the probability of war among the great European powers: 'It would be too insane.' We had never interested ourselves in European politics and had known nothing of the diplomatic world. The only Ambassadors who had come to Grosvenor Road were two successive Japanese Ambassadors, the Minister (Nansen) of Norway. I cannot remember any minor member of a foreign embassy visiting us. We had not seen Grey since he had been Foreign Secretary, it being assumed that he knew we were no longer interested in each other's subjects. On our few European travels we had gone merely as tourists seeking recreation. So far as foreign affairs were concerned our investigations had been directed, in our two long journeys, to (a) developments in democratic institutions in the U.S.A. and the self-governing dominions, and (b) to the relations between the white and the coloured races. But we were just beginning to be interested in Continental affairs: we were on the eve of leaving England for the International Socialist Congress at Vienna, and we had a plan of a six months' sojourn in Germany in order to study developments in state action and in German co-operation, trade unionism and professional organization. . . . In the third and fourth year of the war, Sidney, being the only member of the Labour Party Executive who knew French and German sufficiently to talk to and translate the foreign delegates, or who had even an elementary knowledge of European history and geography, had, perforce, to become the Labour Party's draftsman and adviser on all foreign questions.]

PART IV

The Earthquake
August 1914–November 1918

Introduction to Part IV

ON 28 JUNE 1914 the Archduke Franz-Ferdinand, heir to the Austrian throne, was assassinated by a Serbian nationalist in Sarajevo. To most people, including the Webbs, the ensuing war came as a great and wholly unexpected natural catastrophe.

During the first two years of the conflict Beatrice had very little to engage her energies to take her mind off the nightmare of suffering across the Channel. The Webbs were still politically unpopular and their isolation meant that in the call-up of talent for public service they were almost completely neglected. Beatrice began to feel that she was 'packing up', and that even if she recovered from the serious breakdown which afflicted her in late 1916 she could expect nothing but retirement and a chance to complete the great work on local government.

Beatrice's changing moods throughout the war were much in tune with events. For the first two years, after the initial shock and confusion, and up to the disaster of the Somme offensive in July 1916, there was the slow adjustment to the prospect of a long and bloody war, in the course of which there would be a steady extension of compulsion over persons, property and production, growing shortages and increasing hardship. It looked as though nothing could end the war but the collapse of one side or the exhaustion of both. But 1917 brought decisive changes that broke the stalemate. The entry of the United States into the war immediately eased the strain on Atlantic shipping and provided a flow of armaments that was soon followed by large and fresh drafts of men; the February revolution in Russia raised the hopes of the liberals and socialists who had long hated Tsarist despotism; the attempt to organize a meeting of socialist parties from both sides in neutral Stockholm seemed to open up the prospect of a negotiated peace.

Among the many changes which the war brought about was the

new strength of the labour movement. It enormously increased the working-man's belief in his own power and the Labour Party itself achieved a new significance, despite its internal divisions. One group, led by MacDonald and Snowden, opposed the war, and the rest, led by Henderson and Clynes, supported it and took part in the Coalition government. This division was healed in August 1917, when Arthur Henderson resigned from the Cabinet and set the Labour Party on an independent and more self-confident course.

Released from.Cabinet responsibility and free to concentrate on post-war policy and organization, Henderson and MacDonald brought Sidney Webb in to their collaboration, their aim being to change Labour from an interest group into a national party. One result was a new initiative in foreign policy. A statement of *Labour's War Aims*, largely drafted by Sidney, was overwhelmingly endorsed by a special conference of the T.U.C. and the Labour Party on 28 December 1917. In February 1918 a deputation consisting of Henderson, MacDonald, Webb and four trade unionists went to Paris to persuade French socialists to accept the British memorandum, and this visit was followed by an Allied socialist conference in London at the end of February 1918, when the Labour Party's brief was adopted. In the event, these peace moves proved ineffective, undermined on the right by the greater impact of President Wilson's fourteen points, and on the left by the defeat of moderate socialism in Russia when the Bolsheviks took over in November 1917 and made a separate peace with Germany. This new initiative within the Labour Party was, however, matched by important changes in its internal organization.

A new constitution, for the most part the work of Henderson and Webb, was adopted at a special conference in February 1918. It turned the loosely-knit Labour alliance into a national party with a mass membership and a network of local branches: previously individuals could only join through membership of the I.L.P., the Fabians, or a trade union. It also consolidated the political power of the trade unions, for their block votes at party conferences greatly outnumbered those of socialist societies and local parties. At the same time the I.L.P. was weakened. Separate I.L.P. representation on the National Executive disappeared, and the local branches had to compete with the newly-formed divisional Labour parties. Although at the time this arrangement seemed practical in view of the financial power of the unions, it created a built-in tension between the local parties – who did the day-to-day work of propaganda – and the trade unions, who paid the bills and controlled most of the votes at the annual conference. The new constitution also produced another long-term source of contention. It included what became known as 'Clause IV', which committed the party to 'the common ownership of the means of production and the best obtainable system of popular administration and control of each industry and service' – ambiguous phrases which left the municipal socialists, Co-operators, state collectivists and Guild Socialists to argue indefinitely as to what the clause meant.

Along with the new constitution there was a new programme written by Sidney, *Labour and the New Social Order*, which provided the framework of Labour policy between the First and Second world wars.

These developments, decisive for the Labour Party, also had a profound effect on the Webb partnership. From now on Sidney was to be an active and significant leader of the Labour Party, a novel position for a man who had often opposed it and played no direct part in it before he replaced Sanders on the Labour Party Executive in 1916. By the time the war ended the Webbs were entering into a new and surprisingly vigorous phase of life.

∽ 1914 ∾

The anti-war demonstration in Trafalgar Square on Sunday 2 August was originally called by George Lansbury and the *Daily Herald*, but Keir Hardie persuaded the Labour Party to support it. The sequence of events leading to the British declaration of war were as follows. On 1 August, Germany declared war on Russia. On 2 August, Germany entered Luxembourg and presented a twelve-hour ultimatum to Belgium. The Cabinet decided that evening that the invasion of Belgium would be decisive. On 3 August, Germany declared war on France and, after Belgium had rejected the German ultimatum, Grey spoke to the House of Commons in favour of intervention. On 4 August Asquith announced to Parliament that the Germans had invaded Belgium. The Germans appealed to Britain to allow this violation of an international treaty. The British replied with an ultimatum expiring at midnight. The Bank Holiday was prolonged for three days and the government took over the railways. J. L. Hammond (1872–1949), journalist and writer, was the author of several noteworthy social histories with his wife Barbara.

5 August. [41 Grosvenor Road]
It was a strange London on Sunday: crowded with excursionists to London and balked would-be travellers to the Continent, all in a state of suppressed uneasiness and excitement. We sauntered through the crowd to Trafalgar Square, where Labour, socialist and pacifist demonstrators, with a few trade union flags, were gesticulating from the steps of the monument to a mixed crowd of admirers, hooligan warmongers and merely curious holiday-makers. It was an undignified and futile exhibition, this singing of the 'Red Flag' and passing of well-worn radical resolutions in favour of universal peace. We turned into the National Liberal Club: the lobby was crowded with men, all silent and perturbed. Sidney went up into the smoking-room and brought down Massingham and Hammond. Both these men were bitter and depressed. We argued with them that if Belgian neutrality was defied we had to go to war – they vehemently denied it. On Monday the public mind was cleared and solidified by Grey's speech. Even staunch Liberals agree that we had to stand by Belgium. But there is no enthusiasm about the war: at present it is, on the part of England, a passionless war, a terrible nightmare sweeping over all classes, no one able to realize how the disaster came about.

212

The closing of the Bank [of England] for four days and the paralysis of business (no one seems to know whether the closing is limited to banks, and many businesses have stopped because there is no money to pay wages) gives the business quarters of London a dispirited air. Every train that steams out of London, every cart in the street, is assumed to be commandeered by the government for the purposes of war. Omnibuses and taxi-cabs are getting sparse. There is strained solemnity on every face – no one has the remotest idea of what is going to happen now that we are actually at war with Germany. Personally I have an uncomfortable conviction that Germany is terribly efficient, overpoweringly efficient in its army. As for its navy, who knows what will prove to be the winning factor in strategy or arms? And there is complete uncertainty as to what is the ultimate issue before the civilized world. To the Englishman of today it seems the survival of France, Belgium and Holland. To the Englishman of tomorrow it may seem a mistaken backing-up of the Slav against the Teuton. Even if we realize that the mistake was due to the unbearable insolence of the Prussian autocracy, we may live to regret it. If we are beaten at sea as well as the French on land, it will mean compulsory military service and a long submission to discipline. The 'servile state' will be on us as vengeance for our past disorder – 'the Webbs' won't be in it – figuratively, I mean; actually they may be helping to run it. There never has been a war in which the issues are so blurred and indistinct. We English, at any rate, are quite uncertain who ought to win from the standpoint of the world's freedom and man's spiritual development. The best result would be that every nation should be soundly beaten and no one victorious. That might bring us all to reason.

A significant group of Liberal M.P.s had opposed Grey's foreign policy and the increasing expenditure on armaments; a number were as anti-war or pacifist as the I.L.P. But the 'peace party' in the Cabinet proved to be smaller than expected. Only the ageing John Morley and John Burns resigned, and neither played any further role in politics. Ramsay MacDonald, less a pacifist than a man who thought both sides had committed unforgivable blunders, resigned as chairman of the Parliamentary Labour Party and on 5 August, when it decided to vote for war credits, Henderson replaced him. The immediate effect of the war was a sharp increase in unemployment, though Beatrice was later to note how jobs were eventually found for those dismissed as 'unemployable' at the time of the Poor Law Commission. A conference supported by the Labour Party, the Trades Union Congress and the Co-operative movement had been called to protest against the drift to war. By the time it met on 5 August the situation had so changed that it set up the War Emergency Workers' National Committee. This body, on which Sidney sat, did excellent work on rents, prices, allowances for the families of enlisted men and pensions to war casualties. It also helped to secure representation of the workers on a whole range of government committees. Sidney drafted many of its documents, and through his membership began to build a new relationship with Labour politicians and trade union officials.

6 August. [41 Grosvenor Road]
It is difficult not to feel distracted with depression and anxiety. There is still no enthusiasm for the war but a good deal of quiet determination, even such pacifists as the Courtneys agreeing that we had to stand by Belgium. If this little race had not been attacked the war would have been positively unpopular – it could hardly have taken place. The government have played a bold hand, far more radically collectivist than we could have hoped for. The retirement of John Burns (no one noticed Lord Morley's resignation) from the government, and of J.R. MacDonald from the chairmanship of the Labour Party, are both desirable events. Sidney is busy devising plans for increasing employment during the war. If only we could hear of a decisive naval victory, we could settle back to our work . . . .

10 August. [41 Grosvenor Road]
. . . . We shall do very little the next months but sit on committees – government committees and labour committees. I attended one at the Local Government Board with Burns in the chair, and Sidney went off to another. Every one is excited and perturbed; and most of us are haunted by the horrors that we know are taking place a few hundred miles away.

[*Beatrice added this additional note in August 1918.* 'We shall see the unemployed marching down Whitehall to destroy the House of Commons,' said John Burns a few days after the declaration of war. Confronted with the collapse of credit and the probable difficulty of getting supplies of raw material, and without the slightest expectation of a large army, leave alone compulsory military service, the dread of all of us was a period of acute unemployment. And if there had not started up an immediate demand for half a million soldiers, to be followed by an unprecedented expenditure on munitions, we should have had serious unemployment. The mistaken Prince of

Wales Fund, and the ubiquitous Local Representative Committees to administer relief 'to distress arising out of the war' took up the energies of all social reformers for the first three months of the war. It is possible that we learnt how not to do it. I was on the central London Committee, Sidney on the Intelligence Committee which prepared the statistics upon which we proceeded and which proved that no action was required. The real remedy for unemployment was, however, demonstrated to be that proposed by the Minority Report – maintenance under training (in this case in the army) with the organization of production and the state of the labour market by the government, according to national needs.]

MacDonald wrote a powerful article on the causes of the war in the *Labour Leader* of 12 August. Shaw was to write a scandalizing attack on the government in 'Commonsense about the War', which was published as a special supplement in the *New Statesman* on 14 November. The article to which Beatrice was referring was published in the *Daily News* on 11 August, and Shaw sent it enclosed in a letter denouncing the 'imbecility' of the Entente.

12 August. [41 Grosvenor Road]
Here are J.R.M.'s and GBS's declarations of faith: we are unable to accept either one or the other. I don't believe that alliances or ententes make all that difference; the root of evil is the spirit which has manifested itself in alliances or the absence of alliances. Germany was determined to push her claims by the sword, we fortified our *status quo* (which gave us a quarter of the world's surface), the French armed for a war revenge. Sooner or later the conflict would have come, in detail or in wholesale. I am inclined to think that the wholesale conflict will be shorter and more terrible, a dramatic lesson to all nations. It may end in revolution in Germany – and that will spread to Russia in time. We have not the knowledge to decide on the details of diplomacy: it is the spirit that is wrong and that will only be altered by world suffering and world conversion. When and where will arise the spirit of love?

Field-Marshal Lord Kitchener (1850–1916) had made his reputation at Khartoum in 1896 and in the Boer War. He was appointed Secretary of State for War on 5 August and raised a volunteer army of three million men. He was drowned on the way to Russia when the *Hampshire* sank in 1916. The Germans occupied Brussels on 21 August and Namur fell on 24 August.

215

25 August. [41 Grosvenor Road]
Capacity for work destroyed by anxiety and restless searching for more news. We in England are probably the least concerned of all the principal combatants, but even to us the outlook is gloomy and terribly tragic. All those who know the forces engaged believe that the war will last months, perhaps years: that both sides are desperate – the French will fight to a finish and we and the Russians are bound to see them through. . . .

Haldane dined with us last night: serious with the first bad news of the war – the fall of Namur. He was full of his past participation in diplomacy and military organization. He was greatly admiring of Kitchener, and anxious to tell us that it was he who insisted on 'K' going to the War Office. 'K' says we must prepare for a three years' war and is expecting initial disasters. The Germans expect to walk through the French Army 'like butter' and our own Expeditionary Force they consider a mere 'demonstration'. . . .

We are going away for ten days' or a fortnight's holiday to walk ourselves into a quieter state of mind. Sidney has been drafting memoranda for government departments and resolutions for Labour meetings. I have been drifting between letter-writing and reading successive editions of papers. It is almost impossible to keep one's mind off that horrible hell a few hundred miles away.

Rufus Isaacs, formerly Attorney-General in Asquith's Cabinet, was appointed Lord Chief Justice in 1913. He spent much of the war as a financial envoy and then Ambassador in Washington. A number of anti-war Liberals now began to associate with the I.L.P., and later moved into the Labour Party. Among them were Charles Trevelyan, the Liberal M.P.s Charles Roden Buxton (1875–1942) and Arthur Ponsonby (1871–1946) and the publicist Norman Angell (1874–1947). With the journalist E.D. Morel (1873–1924), Ramsay Mac-Donald and Philip Snowden, this group now formed the Union of Democratic Control to campaign for greater accountability in foreign policy and open instead of secret diplomacy. Sidney wrote a Fabian tract, *The War and the Workers*, dealing with social problems caused by the sudden fall in trade and the enlistment of tens of thousands of men. The *Labour Leader* was the weekly journal of the I.L.P.

28 August. [Seaford, Sussex]
Before we left London we dined with Haldane to meet Grey, Lloyd George, Isaacs and Montagu. These men are changed. Grey has lost his conventional aloofness: he was intensely 'human', eager for intimate discussion of practical difficulties and terribly concerned

that he had not been able to prevent the war – suffering, I think, from an over-sensitive consciousness of personal responsibility. Haldane has lost his bland self-sufficiency. Lloyd George showed at his best in his lack of self-consciousness, his freedom from pedantry, his alert open-mindedness and his calm cheeriness. Montagu and Isaacs were eager to be helpful. They were all working at their highest efficiency, no dinners and week-ends. At dinner we talked finance and unemployment. Lloyd George was convinced that the Germans had methodically prepared for war in the financial as well as in the military sphere, and had succeeded in getting comfortably into debt for some £800 million. Consequently her merchants were flush of money. He was equally certain that Holland was, at present, aiding and abetting Germany with all sort of accommodations.

All the Ministers grave and fully aware that we were in for the supreme struggle for the life of the British Empire, and that the war would be waged along all frontiers and in every department of life. Whatever else might be the outcome, the war would mean political ruin to one side and financial disaster to all. 'We well-to-do,' said Haldane, 'will have in the future to live on half our incomes.' Grey thought that the war would mean the advent of labour parties to power. Lloyd George is prepared for the boldest measures to re-establish credit and keep the population employed. There was, according to him, a great feeling of confidence in the temper of the United Kingdom and of the Empire: there was no friction, all were working with a quite amazing unanimity. Of course the Cabinet are wise to emphasize and even exaggerate the gravity of the struggle; and the Germans, by their brutalities, burnings and wanton destruction, are helping us mightily: they may cow the combatants they can get at, but they increase the anger of the combatants they cannot get at – and these happen at present to be the stronger and more formidable. . . .

There are two perturbing moral paradoxes in this war. There has been a disgusting misuse of religious emotion in the assumption of the Almighty's approval of the aims of each of the conflicting group of combatants. France, it is true, has kept herself free from this loathsome cant, and our 'religiosity' has been tactfully limited to formal medieval phrases and to an Erastian prayer for the use of the established Church. But the Kaiser and the Tsar have outdone each other in fervent appeals to their tribal Gods: the German vulgar and familiar, the Russian dignified and barbaric. The theologians

217

of Europe have disgraced themselves. No Eastern mystic would be guilty of such vulgar blasphemy. To those who aspire to faith and holiness and love as the end or purpose of the evolution of life – this horrible caricature of religion is depressing.

The other disturbing reflection is that war is a stimulus to service, heroism and all forms of self-devotion. Hosts of men and women are willing to serve the community under this coarse stimulus who, in ordinary times, are dully immune to any other motive but self-interest qualified by self-indulgence. War, in fact, means an increase of corporate feeling and collective action in all directions. An unholy alliance, disconcerting to the collectivist who is also a believer in love as the bond between races as well as between individuals. I am beginning to loathe the newspapers – with their bombast and lies about atrocities, or their delighted gossip about the famine and disease in 'enemy' countries.

With one tiny exception, the whole nation is unanimous for the war. The tiny minority is the I.L.P., with its Executive, and its few admirers among disgruntled Whigs who have quarrelled with the government. The *Labour Leader* is the only anti-war organ; but it has attracted first-rate literary talent to controvert or support the I.L.P. manifesto. The brutal invasion of Belgium has compelled the anti-war propagandists to come out in favour of non-resistance, pure and undefiled: if we are not to defend Belgium, why defend ourselves? There is no morality in watching a child being murdered, refusing to interfere until you, yourself, are attacked, and then fighting for your own life – there may be morality in refraining from any physical force whatsoever, whatever the provocation. I don't believe in non-resistance. Physical force does not differ in morality from mental force: both alike are dependent, for their rightness, on the purpose for which they are exercised – is the purpose consistent with love or not? The act of killing may be a manifestation of love. It is only right to add that it usually is not.

There are no entries in the diary between 28 August and 21 October. The fall of Antwerp on 9 October resulted in a new flood of Belgian refugees. Georgina's youngest daughter was Mary Amelia (1889–1943). Barbara Meinertzhagen (1876–1963), known as 'Bardie', was Beatrice's favourite niece. Married to the solicitor Bernard Drake, she became an active Fabian. Margaret (1880–1959) married George Macaulay Booth in 1906. Their fifth child Paulina, was born in 1915. Katharine Beatrice (1885–1977), known as 'Bobo', married in 1912 Robert (Robin) Mayor (1869–1947].

21 October. [41 Grosvenor Road]

We are in the depths of gloom. Germany is not winning, but Belgium has been martyred and millions of her population have sought refuge in Holland, England and France. The streets of London are crowded with disconsolate Belgian families, walking hand in hand, trying to be cheerful in sightseeing. Meanwhile, a mass of our own youth have taken to soldiering: indeed the recruits are the only light-hearted ones. But we know the casualties to be awful and there is the continuous consciousness of the mad horror of these battlefields, where the quick and the dead rot together. To me it is no consolation that the sixty millions of Germans are also feeling the sorrow and bitter disillusionment. By this time there must be a million of their own dead and wounded, in most cases the husbands, brothers and sons of as kindly a people as our own.

The gloom is intensified by the slow dying of one of our sisters: Georgie Meinertzhagen, who, only a fortnight ago, seemed a vigorous elderly woman, full of vitality, is now dying of cancer of the liver, accelerated by an operation for gall-stones. I saw her yesterday, in the nursing home, surrounded by her daughters, the younger ones scared and miserable, Barbara calm but tragically sorrowful, Margaret with a baby coming, Bobo with one just come. We old people ought not to regret leaving life, but it saddens those of us who live on. And Sidney and I know that even we two must be parted: we cannot hope to go together. I am haunted by the dread of that parting. . . .

The dim-out of London was for reasons of security and energy-saving, though there were no air raids until the Zeppelin airship attacks later in the war. The constraints of a Defence of the Realm Act – 'Dora' – were to be intensified by a temperance campaign led by Lloyd George to restrict the sales of liquor.

3 November. [41 Grosvenor Road]

Georgie Meinertzhagen died after a fortnight's suffering – not acute pain but the slow ebbing of strength and great discomfort.

I was never intimate with this sister: she married when I was still a school-girl. When, in after years, I was struggling into an intellectual career, she was unsympathetic and somewhat contemptuous. 'All vanity', I remember her remarking, with a tolerant laugh, as she watched me at my somewhat futile attempt to master mathematics. The little intimacy I had with her was over her unhappy relations with her husband. But she was a favourite sister with others of the sisterhood: she had wit, and personal charm, a charm that increased with age. Since her widowhood she had been singularly happy and well; full of new-found enthusiasm for the women's cause, making new friends by her warmth, her humour and her attractive person – tall and straight, white-haired and dark-eyed, with singular grace of bearing and friendliness of manner. She hated authority, accuracy, expertness, general principles and toil. She believed in impulse, generosity, courage, mother-wit, and treating every case as an exception to the rule. It was her misfortune to marry a man of narrow sympathies, of many conventions and more prejudices and with no sense of humour. Her children are devoted to her – but they have lived apart from her and have been little influenced by her, largely because she never tried to influence them. Her eldest, Dan, was an indolent genius, scientific and artistic, who died in the first promise of his manhood – the great sorrow of her life. Barbara Drake is an intellectual and attractive woman, following in my footsteps as an economic writer and a Fabian. The eight other children I barely know. . . .

Work this autumn has gone badly. I have been idle and distracted, mooning over an extravagant expenditure on newspapers for hours during the day, trying to find my bearings in a mass of detail, the technique of which I do not know; puzzling over the paradoxical morality of war, and suffering from mental and physical depression. And though Georgie's death leaves no gap in my life, it is yet another break with the past – a past which is rapidly becoming the greater part of my personal life. One wonders, which one next? The great war will raise issues which I have no longer the strength and elasticity to understand. The root of my trouble is, of course, a bad conscience: I am neither doing my share of emergency work nor yet carrying forward, with sufficient steadfastness, my own work. Now and again I bolster up my conscience with the plea that I am elderly and past work – the very way to become so.

The darkening of London, now the days are short, adds to the national sobriety but also to the national gloom. It is reported that Berlin and its suburbs are blazing with light so as to produce optimism. Our government seems to think that what our people want is increased anxiety and seriousness: they certainly have helped to create a consciousness of personal peril by absence of light and absence of liquor. . . .

ᘉ 1915 ᘇ

3 January. [41 Grosvenor Road?]
Ten days' walking and motoring with GBS — tempestuous weather and heated argument. The terms of settlement [of the war] and his proposals for bringing about equality were the subjects discussed. Sex questions were off, he having put Mrs Pat out of his head. He has been firing off brilliant but ill-digested stuff at the newspapers and in lectures. Yet his aims are straight. He has kept the crucial purpose of socialism before us as distinguished from the machinery for getting it. And his protest against the self-righteousness of British public opinion about the causes of the war is, in my humble opinion, justified. We were all three of us gloomy as to the results on the socialist and labour movement. It rids us of the rebels — Feminist and Guild Socialist. The danger ahead is that the country may slip into a subtle form of reaction, lose faith in democracy and gain enjoyment from the mere display of power. We shall almost certainly have some form of conscription. Whether it be military service or physical training, class-ridden or democratic, depends on the vitality of the socialist movement. The terms of peace may be oppressive, leading to a war of revenge, or conciliatory, leading to supernational law. I still think that the only safeguard against future wars is a long continued war almost equally disastrous to all the races and governments concerned. If we are triumphant we shall be demoralized.

Robin Page Arnot (b. 1890), close associate of Cole and Mellor in the Guild Socialist movement and the Fabian Research Department, became one of the founders of the Communist Party in 1920 and remained a lifelong member. J.S. Middleton (1878–1962), assistant secretary of the Labour Party since 1903, became its general secretary 1935–45. Joseph Rowntree (1836–1925), a director of the confectionery firm, founded the Joseph Rowntree Trust and was an active philanthropist and temperance advocate. Leonard Woolf (1880–1969), who had retired from a civil service post in Ceylon on his marriage in 1912 to Virginia Stephen (1882–1941), was an active Fabian. The work which he began on the initiative of the Webbs became the influential book *International Government*, published in 1916. When Woolf was drafting a *New Statesman* supplement on the Prevention of War, Sidney's letter of comment anticipated the movement to regulate international affairs which led to the Hague Court and the League of Nations.

14 February. [41 Grosvenor Road]

Hard at work on professional organizations for the fourth part of our report on the Control of Industry. It is most exhilarating to get back to research, and research into a quite new subject. In our work on trade unionism we omitted the professional organization of brainworkers and only referred to it in a note as requiring investigation. It was only when the syndicalists and Guild Socialists claimed (for the manual working trade unions) complete control over the organization of industry, that we insisted that we must enquire into the self-government claimed and exercised by organizations of brainworkers, such as the lawyers, the medical men, the teachers and the civil engineers. The Guild Socialists were not sympathetic and took no part in the enquiry. . . .

The Fabian Society and Research Department show signs of healthy development. This autumn I have tried to inspire new work without controlling the direction of it. Cole is now vice-president, with GBS as nominal head. He and Arnot and Sanders have arranged with Henderson and Middleton to issue a Labour Yearbook. Owing to the generosity of Joseph Rowntree we have started L.S. Woolf on an enquiry into possible developments of supernational law. Cole and Mellor are writing elaborate descriptions of British trade unionism which the Department is going to publish in a series. Sidney and I want to start the F.R.D. as we started the London School of Economics and the *New Statesman*, and then leave it in younger hands. We should be only too glad to retire into the life of research and pleasant social companionship that I, at any rate, enjoyed before I joined the Poor Law Commission. Since then I have been the servant of successive organizations.

I often speculate about G.D.H. Cole's future. He interests me because he shows remarkable intensity of purpose. Is he as persistent as intense? He has a clear-cutting and somewhat subtle intellect. But he lacks humour and the *bonhomie* which springs from it, and he has an absurd habit of ruling out everybody and everything that he does not happen to like or find convenient. Since the outbreak of war he has modified this attitude, and is now willing to work with the Labour Party in order to get into closer touch with the trade unions. He and Sidney irritate each other. Cole indulges in a long list of personal hatreds. The weak point of his outlook is that there is no one that he does like except as a temporary tool; he resents anyone who is not a follower and has a contempt for all leaders other than himself. With his keen intelligence and aristocratic temperament it is hard to believe that he will remain enamoured with the cruder forms of democracy embodied in the Guild Socialist idealization of the manual working class.

18 April. [41 Grosvenor Road]
For unknown reasons the governing cliques are far more hopeful than heretofore of eventual victory. We dined with Haldane alone the other day: his state of mind was one of quiet confidence, more concerned to curb anti-German unreasonableness and hostility to any machinery for preventing future wars than anxious about the military situation. By next Xmas he expects to have peace. The basis of this optimism is the exhaustion of German manpower. There is still very little hatred of Germany among the people we see – far more fear of the growth of bureaucratic and militarist tendencies in our own country. . . . Sidney remains stolidly patriotic; I am still a depressed agnostic. One continues one's work – and I am enjoying the enquiry into professional associations – with a background of exasperated misery. Does one over-rate the horror and insanity of the killing and maiming of millions of the best of the human race? I cannot bear to look at the fresh young faces in each week's 'Roll of Honour'. And yet there is moral magnificence in the unsensational dutifulness unto death of the millions now enlisting. The common youth, workman, clerk, or shop assistant, squares his shoulders, spits out his ugly joke; he is obsessed by his thoughts of food, drink and women, but dies game without any particular consciousness of being a hero or a patriot. And the young intellectual, with a privileged life before him, accepts risks and discipline with equal equanimity.

The professional rebel does not enlist, he dislikes discipline and personal inconvenience too fiercely. But he has become chronically downhearted. The little group of Guild Socialists are anti-war, but in a faint-hearted way, as if they felt ashamed of refusing their share of danger and hardship. . . .

26 April. [41 Grosvenor Road]
The war hurricane that is sweeping round our lives is going to uproot many things, great and small, public institutions and private hopes and interests. Among the small things that I am going to lose is the recent friendship with Betty Balfour. Before it is

given up I want to add it to my inventory of past and lost possessions.

With all the others of the Balfour clan, including its greatest representative, I have never had more than a friendly acquaintance, the sort of acquaintance that is made, suspended or completely dropped without remotest feeling, on either side, of constraint or pain. Our visits to Whittingehame and Arthur Balfour's occasional presence here were like attractive scenes of foreign travel, obviously mere flying pleasures – here today and gone tomorrow. But Lady Betty, the wife of Gerald, had insisted on a warm personal friendship and had followed me about with manifestations of almost reverential affection. As she is the most charming of women, quite the most fascinating woman I have ever known, I acquiesced and let my elderly heart be captivated. So we wrote long letters to each other, she came here and I (and sometimes Sidney) went to Fisher's Hill. This spring there has been dead silence on her part. Probably she is absorbed in other interests and attracted to other personalities. Just now I feel sore and hurt. Presently she will fall into her place in the attractive scene of Arthur Balfour and his family which we passed through and enjoyed without claiming or even desiring that it should become part of our world.

There can be no real friendship between persons inspired by radically different social ideals and whose daily life is rooted in altogether different traditions and circumstances. There may be friendly relations either because you are temporarily working together, or because you are mutually attracted. But sooner or later the difference in standards of personal or public conduct grates on nerves and rouses dislike and distaste on one side or the other – usually on the side where manners count more than morals. I think I understand the meaning of what seems strangely capricious behaviour. The whole life of this charming woman is centred in admiration for her famous brother-in-law. She is a devoted mother, a considerate and affectionate wife, an attractive friend. Yet all these feelings are subordinate to a worship of the great relative. Arthur Balfour is as much to the centre of the thought and feeling of his large family as Joseph Chamberlain was at Highbury, and of all his family, Betty is the most devout worshipper. For a few years he had a liking for me – a 'curiosity infatuation', a state of mind which is one of the marks of the sensitive indolent intellectual whose recreation is intercourse with attractive persons. Persons interest

Arthur Balfour because causes bore him: he is too sceptical to believe in them, too aloof from the common man to be moved by the needs and desires of the multitude. There could be no real friendship between us, since friendship with men based on mutual attraction, even if I had not been too elderly for it, is barred to me by my perfect marriage: the only friendships I have had with men are as fellow workers, mere comradeship in fact. Betty Balfour, I think, thought that there would be a lasting friendship between her great man and the Webbs. Directly it became clear that A.J.B. had ceased to be interested in us, she also had a revulsion of feeling. She had no more use for me. She became aware of all my defects, and as she had never cared for me for myself, the disillusionment was complete. There remained the task of getting out of a personal intimacy which she had initiated and fostered. That task I have made easy by my silent consent. I doubt whether we shall meet again.

[*Beatrice later wrote three footnotes to this entry. The first was in December 1915.* I add to this entry before putting away this volume the last scene of my friendship with Betty Balfour. She called here in October by appointment and stayed some time talking to Sidney and myself. The poor lady was evidently constrained and perturbed. In fact she was so agitated and unhappy in expression that I thought she had had some mysterious illness. A critical glance at me – a look of unmistakable hostility in her eyes – convinced me that it was not illness but a sort of unpleasant consciousness that she felt herself under some obligation to a person whom she now disliked. I met her the next day, accidentally, at a conference of the National Union of Women Workers. She had recovered her self-possession and lost her look of constraint. Her mind was made up and she greeted me with cold politeness. No suggestion of future meetings – in fact a tentative suggestion by me was decidedly rejected. Since then there has been silence on both sides.

The second note was added in August 1918. To finish the story. I met Betty Balfour again this spring, walking with her sister in St James's Park. She accosted me, as if she felt compelled to do so. But when in answer to her remark, 'When shall we meet again, I wonder?' I smilingly invited her to 'come and see us', she unmistakably refused to do so. In fact if she had stopped to speak to me in order to show a defiant unfriendliness, she could hardly have managed better. I was so taken aback that when the two sisters had passed out of sight I sat down on a bench to recover from my disconcerted surprise at the unnecessary rudeness of the proceeding. And yet I am convinced that the rudeness was not deliberate but merely the result of a conflict in her mind between two inconsistent impulses, an old affection and a new dislike.

The third note was written at the same time in 1918. The friendliness between Arthur Balfour and the Webbs died a slow and natural death. The last time he dined with us was in the spring of 1914 to meet the eminent Hindu scientist Dr Bose [Sir Jogadish Chandra Bose, F.R.S. (1858–1937)]. I met him once again walking in St James's Park just after the outbreak of war, and tried to interest him in the gross mismanagement of the Prince of Wales Fund [to relieve distress caused by the war]. But it was clear that neither the person approaching him nor the subject interested him, and that his expression of personal but acute boredom – an expression I had noticed before when he was addressed by a Conservative member whom he did not happen to like – was not wholly undeliberate. So I ceased to trouble him.]

R.C.K. Ensor (1877–1958), prominent journalist and historian, was an active Fabian in the first years of the century.

3 May. [41 Grosvenor Road]
The inner circle of the Fabian Society is distinguished for the intensity of the difference of opinion with regard to the cause of the war and the right way of ending it. Clifford Allen, the youngest member of the Executive, is a fanatical anti-war pro-German advocate who distorts every fact to prove his country wrong. Ensor, one of the most accomplished of the middle-aged members, is complacently convinced of the imperative need not only of beating Germany but of dismembering the German empire, of setting up Hungary and the Slav provinces of Austria as independent states, whilst adding south Germany to a Germanized Austria! Prussian Germany is to be stripped of her colonies and compelled to disarm. Sidney is just the sane British patriot repudiating any attempt to dismember or humiliate the German people and intent on a brave attempt, engineered by Great Britain and the U.S.A., to establish a supernational control over all states alike. Sanders agrees, but is more distinctly anti-German. The bulk of the

226

members follow Sidney, but there is a small but intense section of pacifists. The Guild Socialists would be pro-war if they were not in rebellion against the government on principle, and if they did not hate the thought of fighting themselves, being hedonists. The junta that control the I.L.P. are vehement pacifists, the leading men of the British Socialist Party violent anti-German patriots. The ruck of the trade union officials are just sane and commonplace supporters of the British government against its enemies.

The war has developed the antagonism between the Parliamentary Labour Party and the I.L.P. almost to a breaking point, the latter being now in close communion with the sentimental Whigs of the Arthur Ponsonby–C.P. Trevelyan–Courtney type, whilst there is a distinct increase of friendliness between the 'Front Bench' of the Fabian Society and the Parliamentary Labour Party. Perhaps the most noted result is the consciousness of world failure on the part of the international labour and socialist movement, a consciousness of a certain self-deception – all our fine talk, all our glowing shibboleths are proved to be mere surface froth. . . . And oddly enough, there is, at present, no anger with them. There is no jingo mob. There is a section of the working class who are slacking and drinking, who, like the army contractors, are making the country's need the opportunity for exactions, but there is no popular anti-pacifist feeling. . . . The criminal classes are the only ones to visibly improve in character. They have given up crime and enlisted in large numbers. The women of all classes have emerged into public life – industrial, social and militarist. . . .

Martha Jackson, affectionately known as 'Dada', who was the Potter nurse for many years, was in fact one of their poorer relations.

10 May. [41 Grosvenor Road]
Last night I lay awake thinking over the absence of any recognized ethic of friendship. To most men, friendship does not entail the continuance of the feeling of friendship when the intimacy has ceased to be a pleasure to both sides. Successive friendships seem, on this assumption, to have each one its natural life; to be born, to grow, to decay and finally to die. Sometimes the friendship will die a violent death, but among well-bred persons death by senile decay is preferred. 'We have ceased to be friends' is a no more tragic phrase than 'we have ceased to be neighbours'. . . . A friend is a

book which you read and when you have satisfied your curiosity the thing is put on the shelf, in the waste-paper basket or sold. This assumption of lack of permanence, is, to me, tragic – and the few troubles of my life have arisen from broken friendships. But if all friendships are to be permanent then it is unwise to enter into personal intimacy and mutual affection unless you are certain of your own and the other person's faithfulness. . . . Some of the pleasantest and most hopeful of human relations are discontinuous because they have never reached that degree of mutual affection which leads to their being carried on when the occasion for personal comradeship ceases. The test of a closer relation than mere friendliness is, I think, intimate written correspondence. One does not correspond for the joy of it with a friendly acquaintance, a colleague on a committee, a neighbour or the most faithful of servants, unless you have permitted the relationship to become a friendship with some obligation of permanence. As one gets aged, one is less inclined to take this step forward from human friendliness to personal friendship.

There are, indeed, some persons, some of the holiest and most loving, who preserve this equable relationship of friendliness with all their fellow beings. . . . Towards all men they are pitiful, helpful and calmly and wisely sympathetic. They are never hurt or wounded by neglect because their love transcends any personal aspect. Such are the saints of the world. . . . They measure their intimacy and their warmth of expression, the carefulness of their thought, not according to the attractiveness of the person concerned, but according to the person's need. Such a one was our old nurse Dada, whose memory is the shining light of the childhood of the Potter girls. She had no friends because all who needed friendship were her friends. . . . But the saint has no need of recognized conventions, since the saint's morality absorbs and transcends these conventions. It is the fellowship of ordinary sensual men that needs an agreed mode of conduct. I know of no rule but the ungracious doctrine of restricted liabilities: do not agree to become an intimate friend unless you are prepared to carry out the obligations of friendship to the bitter end. And if others refuse to meet their liabilities, turn your thoughts away, try to forget their indebtedness, imagine that the relation has been no more than human kindliness and that it has ceased because the occasion for it has passed away. . . .

228

The 'Basis' was the statement of principles governing Fabian policy. Stephen Hobhouse (1881–1964) was the eldest child of Maggie and Henry Hobhouse. After a brief career in the Board of Education he was influenced by the work of Leo Tolstoy; he resigned his appointment, became a Quaker, was imprisoned as a conscientious objector, and took up benevolent work in the East End. He also disinherited himself from the family property, finally accepting a settlement of £260 a year. Rosa Waugh (1891–1970), the daughter of Benjamin Waugh (1839–1908), founder and secretary of the Society for the Prevention of Cruelty to Children, shared his pacifist opinions.

15 May. [41 Grosvenor Road]
At the annual meeting of the Fabian Society yesterday evening, the 'rebels' made their great attack on the Executive of the Fabian Society. They had started the attack by a cleverly written manifesto in the April *Fabian News*, signed by the new Guild Socialist clique and the old pro-Labour Party set (led by Schloesser) in favour of a revision of the Basis restricting the Society to the work of research and ousting all Liberals or supporters of Liberals from the Society. Upon this manifesto, nine of this new opposition stood for election to the Executive. Of course, they were heavily beaten – they were, in fact, at the bottom of the poll. Cole and Clifford Allen just retained their seats, whilst Mellor and Arnot found themselves last of the list of defeated candidates. But they persisted in their attempt to carry the annual meeting. Clifford Allen made a dignified speech, Mellor was frank and good-humoured – half buffoon, half bully. Cole disgraced himself and ruined his cause: first by an ill-tempered and tactless argument and then, when the vote went against him, by a silly display of temper. When the show of hands was decisively against the rebel resolution, someone suggested that there was no need to count. 'Let us know how many fools there are in the world,' he spat out. When called to order, he sprang to his feet: 'I withdraw the word fools, I say "bloody fools".' Then, white with rage, he sprang from the platform and marched dramatically out of the hall, a few minutes later sending in a letter to Sanders, resigning his membership of the Society in terms which were meant to be insolent but were merely childish. Mellor followed suit today, and I assume most of the Oxford Fabians will follow their leader. So there ends my amicable attempts to work peacefully with the rebels.

The truth is that Cole, having conquered the tiny world of the Oxford Fabians, thought he could dominate the slightly bigger world of the London Fabian Society. But the members of the parent society are a stodgy body, accustomed to their old leaders and by no means impressed with the would-be new ones, who insult them on every occasion. And Cole and Co., instead of biding their time and meanwhile using the Society as a platform, had determined to prove their power by forcibly ousting the old folk from their leadership. It is the old story of H.G. Wells and J.R. MacDonald. It is all the more annoying to us as we are honestly anxious to find successors, and if these rebellious youths and maidens had only refrained from asking for a public execution of the old people, we would have gladly stepped down from our position directly they had secured some sort of respect from the members at large. But these young people delight in 'frightfulness' for its own sake. . . . The labour and socialist movement is not a pleasant atmosphere to live in, and sometimes I think it would be well to wind up the Fabian Society and retire definitely into our researches. But that would be a mean proceeding. One ought to take one's share of the rough and tumble of life: the labour movement is not rich in intellect and experience. The implication is conceited but I think true – even old folk like we would be missed.

Another scene this afternoon ought to have been restful and inspiring. I found it depressing and almost repulsive. Stephen Hobhouse was married to Rosa Waugh, at the Friends Meeting House, St Martin's Lane. I have always been attracted by the Friends: I respect Stephen, and I thought I should find 'a meeting for worship with family affection added to it' a rest to my soul, fretted by the petty quarrels of the Fabians and gloomy with the tragedy of the war. Perhaps my nerves were ragged. But the artificiality of this social assembly obviously not for worship, the ugliness and coldness of the building, the self-consciousness of Stephen and Rosa – Stephen the worked-up mystic, Rosa the dramatic missionary – sitting, in studied silence, to be gazed on by the congregation, was not a pleasing sight. The melodramatic declaration of mutual love, the commonplace utterances of the Elders, familiarly addressing their God, the stilted reading of the Registrar's formulae of civil marriage, were not inspiring sounds. The ceremony offended one's sense of decorum and beauty. . . . It may be that the spirit of love was lacking in me and not in them. But I shall not return to the Friends Meeting House. I prefer St Paul's.

[*Beatrice added this note in August 1918*. Stephen Hobhouse . . . is my most distinguished nephew — if by distinguished is meant certain good qualities in such excess as to excite the attention of the world he lives in. . . . It is difficult to summarize Stephen's characteristics or to estimate his influence. Superficially he is not to my mind an attractive personality. His lugubrious manner and long doleful face, the absence of spontaneity and joy in everything he does, and a marked strain of self-conscious morality mars his very substantial gifts of character and intellect. Those who have actually worked with him report real self-effacement and a solidly wise judgement. . . . His marriage, though a happy one, has, I think, been unfortunate in emphasizing all the weak points of his personal temperament and theological creed. Rosa is a warm-hearted little soul, but she has not the semblance of an intellect and is vain and egotistical. . . . she goes about falsifying facts and censuring persons and institutions without either knowledge or the desire for it, and with a total lack of sympathy for sins she has no mind to or virtues she does not possess. Hence they find themselves with little influence among the poor, but imperfect folk among whom they live, and with less public influence than is warranted by Stephen's sterling qualities. The career of both Stephen and Rosa shows the weak strand in the Quaker faith — the tendency to spiritual pride and the anarchy of the doctrine of the 'inner light', so difficult to distinguish from sanctimonious self-will. The desire 'to testify' on all occasions seems sometimes not to differ from a desire to annoy persons with whom they are at variance. . . . Stephen, having determined to spend the income from the settlement on good works, announces the fact to his father in terms which are quite unnecessarily provocative.]

The meeting at Barrow House brought together a group of Fabians and some members of the 'Bryce Committee', nominally chaired by Lord Bryce but actually started by the Cambridge historian Goldsworthy Lowes Dickinson (1862–1932) in the first weeks of the war to study problems of international organization. Philip Guedalla (1889–1944) was a Liberal barrister and popular historian. R.E. Cross was the Rowntree family solicitor. William Brace (1865–1948), a leader of the South Wales miners, held a minor government post 1917–18. George Roberts (1869–1928), secretary of a printing union in Norwich and M.P. for that town, also entered the wartime coalition and remained in it when the Labour Party withdrew in 1918. The Coalition government was announced on 19 May. Failures on the Western Front and in

231

the Dardanelles, together with insufficient ammunition for the troops in France, had led to a political crisis.

5 June. [41 Grosvenor Road]
Back from a delightful holiday and a five days' conference at Barrow House on the machinery for preventing war, and an eight days' walk across the mountains with GBS, J.C. Squire and Guedalla.

The conference was a complete success. Besides the bevy of Fabians, there came the little group of able men, who have been working, under the chairmanship of Bryce, on the same subject – J.A. Hobson, Graham Wallas, R.E. Cross and Lowes Dickinson, also a shrewd American lawyer and odds and ends of ex-Fabians and university men. Sidney conducted the proceedings with marked lucidity and urbanity, explaining L.S. Woolf's memorandum and the scheme worked out by the Committee of the Research Department. GBS scintillated perversely brilliant criticism and paradoxical proposals, Graham Wallas enthused us with his philosophy; Hobson, Cross and Lowes Dickinson controverted details by the light of the vaguer conclusions of the Bryce committee, and Squire, Shove and Guedalla exercised their young wits at the expense of the rival contentions of their elders. The weather was glorious and the view from the terrace was melodramatic in its beauty. One result was that the Bryce group joined the Fabian Research Committee as consultative members. Moreover, we had pleasant and helpful private talks with Wallas, Hobson and Lowes Dickinson, combining the wisdom of the Fabians with that of the *Nation* group of writers. The Woolf memorandum is to be developed into a big work on International Relations, past, present and future. The absence of a clique bent on hostilities, like the Cole-Mellor group at the last conference, added much to the efficiency and amenity of the gathering.

Meanwhile, the coalition government threatens to break the Labour Party into warring sections. Rumours as to the meaning of this sudden and unexpected change fly hither and thither. Some say that it has been engineered by Lloyd George and Balfour: others declare that it is the only way round the administrative incompetence of Kitchener; others again hint that the government is expecting a big disaster at the Dardanelles and the breakdown of the Russian defence and want to silence criticism; whilst the knowing ones whisper that it means compulsory military service. The Parliamentary Labour Party eventually decided to let Henderson take Cabinet office with two under-secretaries – Brace and Roberts. Personally I think they would have been better advised to keep out of it. But without knowing the seriousness of the situation one is no judge. In fact in almost every department of war politics, one can have no opinion because all the essential facts are hidden from one. The misery of acute restlessness is due to the combination of mortal concern and complete ignorance: we are a prey to rumour, both as to what is happening at the front and what the government intends to do. Add to this that the whole range of questions raised by the war stand outside one's experience and culture, and it is easy to explain the deep depression and restlessness that has spread throughout the labour and socialist world. Let us hope the soldiers are enjoying it – those who are not at the front!

The novelist Arnold Bennett (1867–1931) had become a director of the *New Statesman* in March 1915. He gave the paper financial support and in 1916 began to write articles under the name of Sardonyx. Vaughan Nash (1861–1932), journalist and civil servant, was interested in social questions. Reginald McKenna, the Liberal Home Secretary from 1911, had become Chancellor of the Exchequer when Asquith formed the Coalition government. Though the Conservatives were admitted the Liberals retained the key posts in the Cabinet; even Bonar Law, their leader, had to be content with the Colonial Office. The Labour Party hesitated about an invitation to join, and then empowered Arthur Henderson to enter the Cabinet as President of the Board of Education. Haldane, who became Lord Chancellor in 1912, had been attacked as 'pro-German' because he had written sympathetically about German philosophy.

14 June. [41 Grosvenor Road]
We had heard much gossip as to the cause of Haldane's enforced retirement. Arnold Bennett reported, on McKenna's authority, that Haldane was a wreck; Vaughan Nash, who is helping at 10 Downing Street, told Sidney that Asquith and other members of the Cabinet found Haldane woolly-headed and troublesome; sound radicals regard him as sacrificed to the Northcliffe Press. Hence it was interesting to hear his own version. In response to an affectionate letter from me, he dined with us last night and seemed glad to unburden his mind. Asquith had not consulted him about the reconstruction – the first he heard of it was the statement circulated in the Cabinet box that the government was dissolved and that all

Ministers were to send in their resignations. He, of course, told Asquith to feel free to dispense with his services, and his old friend accepted his resignation with the excuse that the Unionists demanded it. Churchill fought hard and succeeded in imposing himself and is working with Balfour at the Admiralty. Haldane professed to us to be relieved: except that he regretted not being in with Grey at any peace negotiations. . . . He says that he had reported to the Cabinet in 1911 that Germany was preparing for war. His advice was to prepare secretly for war whilst doing all that could be done to keep on friendly relations with Germany. He believed at that time that there was a chance of avoiding war; now he realized that, given the continuance of the German military caste in power, war had been inevitable. On the whole he was glad that it had come now. Looking back on the ten years of Liberal administration he thought that the Cabinet ought to have delayed old age pensions and national insurance and pushed forward public expenditure on infants and children and on industrial and physical training. . . . He did not look a physical wreck, but perpetual over-eating and over-smoking has no doubt dulled his intellect. He was far more friendly than he has been for many a long year, more friendly than he has been since he became a Cabinet Minister. He states that Grey is seriously incapacitated and very depressed; he is suffering from pigmentation of the eyes – a disease which cannot get better but may get worse. Lloyd George is the one Minister who has scored a popular success (with emphasis on *popular*). He is the 'man of the hour' with the Tories; he is still trusted by large sections of the Radicals and Labour men.

Jane Addams (1860–1935), the social worker who founded Hull House in Chicago in 1889, had been visited there soon afterwards by the Webbs on their first visit to the United States. She was an active suffragist and pacifist who was awarded the Nobel Peace Prize in 1931. She was one of a number of American peace workers who visited Europe in 1915 in a vain effort to stop the war.

22 June. [41 Grosvenor Road]
Jane Addams, with whom we stayed at Hull House, Chicago, on our first world tour, dined with us last night. Since we knew her seventeen years ago she has become a world celebrity – the most famous woman of the U.S.A., representing the best aspects of the feminist movement and the most distinguished elements in the

social reform movement. Some say that she has been too much in the limelight of late, and that she is no longer either so sane or so subtle in her public utterances. But to us she seemed the same gentle, dignified, sympathetic woman, though like the rest of us she has lost in brilliancy and personal charm – the inevitable result of age, personal notoriety and much business. Her late mission to the governments of the world, as the leading representative of the neutral women at the Hague Conference of Women, has brought her into still greater prominence. She and one or two other women of neutral countries were charged with the 'Peace Mission' to the governments of Germany, Austria, Hungary, Italy, France, Belgium and England. She had found Sir Edward Grey politely encouraging, expressing his own personal pacific sentiments, but saying nothing about his government. . . .

Jane Addams herself thinks it inconceivable that the U.S.A. should come into the war and she clearly sees little or no difference between British and German policy, either before or during the war – at least that is the impression she leaves on our minds. Her great thesis to us was 'the neutrality of the seas'.

The Munitions Act was passed in July; it prohibited strikes by men employed on 'war work' and tied them to their jobs. Though Lloyd George, appointed Minister of Munitions in May, obtained the consent of the union leaders, the Act caused much resentment in the industrial areas.

8 July. [41 Grosvenor Road]
From all one hears Lloyd George is going the way of Chamberlain, exchanging the leadership of the Radicals for the leadership of an imperialist nationalist party. He is said to be gradually discarding his old followers and accreting a circle of admiring Tories. The temptation to become the Prime Minister to a go-ahead Tory-Democratic Imperial-Federation Party will be irresistible – he, certainly, is not the man to resist it. Even tariff reform, in the guise of a commercial boycott of Germany after the war, is just the quackery to attract him. His present subservience to the Tories is pitiable; in politics the greatest enemies, once they get over their enmity, become the closest of conspirators.

There had been talk of prohibiting intoxicating liquor – in the end the government appealed for voluntary restraint. In April the King had ordered that no intoxicants were to be served in the Royal palaces – as an example to the nation. Balfour was now First Lord of the Admiralty.

22 July. [41 Grosvenor Road]
We dined alone with Haldane – a luxurious dinner. He had taken the [temperance] pledge at the same time as the King and Kitchener: it was a consolation for loss of office that he chose to think that it was the Lord Chancellor that was bound, not Lord Haldane. So we enjoyed his dry champagne and his super-excellent liqueurs. He was very genial, anxious that we and the *New Statesman* should start a campaign for the reconstruction of our social life after the war. Sidney got angry with him because he evaded the issue of increased taxation of the rich; tried to counter Sidney's plea of immediate and drastic taxation by the stale objection of the commitments of the wealthy and the throwing out of employment of their dependants and retainers. The flare-up passed over and he subsequently agreed that the rich would have to pay more and said that he was doing his level best to prevent the government from cutting down the grants for education. He wanted to think out the demobilization of the army after the war and we suggested that he should engage a clever young man to work under a committee to prepare a scheme. In all this talk we could not discover what conclusion he desired, except that he wanted 'intelligent criticism of the government'. He seemed to be ploughing a lonely furrow. 'The country is being governed by three men: Balfour, Kitchener and Lloyd George, and Balfour is the real Prime Minister.' From which remark we gathered that he had broken with Asquith. I doubt whether our old friend has much initiative left over from his free use of alcohol, tobacco and all delectable food. The same complaint lies at the root of Asquith's slackness. He has become senile from self-indulgence. The breakdown of British war administration is due to Kitchener's ignorance of civil life and to Asquith's apathy and rooted disinclination to trouble about anything until it becomes a public scandal. Slackness has become a national vice. The Englishman is as able as the German, but he has a shockingly low standard of work.

VOLUME 33

The Webbs had been staying at Penalt Vicarage, near Beatrice's old Wye Valley home at The Argoed. Ben Tillett (1860–1943), one of the leaders of the 1889 dock strike, was general secretary of the Dockers' Union from 1887 to 1922. Havelock Wilson (1859–1929) was president of the Seamen's Union. He had been a Liberal M.P. and never joined the Labour Party. John Hodges (1855–1937), president of the Iron and Steel Trades Confederation, became Minister of Labour 1916–17. Robert Smillie (1857–1940), the popular leader of the Miners' Federation, was a pacifist and one of the leaders on the left of the I.L.P. All through the autumn, the debate on conscription dragged on in the Cabinet and in the country. The Derby Scheme, named after Lord Derby (1865–1948), the director of recruiting, was a voluntary prelude to compulsory registration. Introduced in October, it had barely time to be tested before Asquith was obliged to introduce the Military Service Act of January 1916 conscripting single men between 18 and 41. As a concession to liberal principles, conscientious objectors were allowed to appeal. *John Bull*, the jingoistic weekly owned by Horatio Bottomley (1860–1933), had capped a series of attacks on the 'traitor and coward' MacDonald by publishing on 4 September the birth certificate which showed he was 'the illegitimate son of a Scotch servant girl' and that his true surname was Ramsay. It was a personal shock to MacDonald who had never seen the details.

9 September. Bristol, Trades Union Congress
Sidney and I came here from Penalt on our way to London, to refresh our impression of current trade unionism and to ascertain the labour feeling about conscription and the war. The Parliamentary Committee is conventionally warlike and most of the elder trade union officials agree with it. A tiny fraction of the congress accept the I.L.P. and U.D.C. [Union of Democratic Control] standpoint. Indeed, the working-class assembly showed itself this morning quite primitive in its racial emotion. Tillett, Roberts, Havelock Wilson and Hodges made the usual patriotic speeches of the savage and uncompromising type, accusing the anti-war party of being 'cowards and traitors'. The bulk of the delegates were more good-tempered and tolerant: but they were out to win the war, and only seven out of three hundred held up their hands against the Parliamentary Committee's patriotic resolution. Very different was the reception of the Parliamentary Committee's mild and inconclusive resolution against conscription, supported by tame

237

Front Bench speeches. Smillie's vigorous denunciation of 'the accursed thing' and his threatening words that 'if the government attempted to introduce conscription it would be the duty of organized labour to prevent its enforcement' were enthusiastically cheered. This enthusiasm was so distasteful to the P.C. that they hastily invited Lloyd George to come down from London to address the congress (a fact they announced after he had accepted the invitation), nominally to explain his munitions programme, but really to neutralize the anti-conscription fervour. So we shall watch the brilliant Tory demagogue (reported to be madly in favour of conscription) twisting the congress back to unconditional support of the government. . . .

Lloyd George appeared on Thursday afternoon: the floor, the galleries and the platform were packed and the heat was suffocating. We were close behind the great man and could watch every gesture and every expression of his mobile face. He looked exactly like a conjurer and one expected him to say, 'No deception, gentlemen, there is nothing up my sleeve, you can see for yourself.' The audience, after giving him a great reception, settled down to be amused and flattered. But his speech left a bad impression, it lacked sincerity: he told obvious little lies, and his tale of working-class slackness and drink was much resented. There was a curious strain of contempt underlying his pleasant banter and specious statement. The Parliamentary Committee was obsequious; the delegates were flattered by his presence and showed it. But here and there men were boiling over with anger at his prevarications. . . .

J.R. MacDonald spoke the next day. His speech was a far more accomplished performance than that of the Cabinet Minister. He carefully avoided the pacifist issue on the ground that he was there not to express his own views but to represent the Labour Party Executive. But he made a dignified and impassioned appeal for unity on all labour and economic questions and hinted darkly at the evil time in store for the workers. He had a magnificent reception, warmer than that given to Lloyd George, partly due, no doubt, to *John Bull*'s scurrilous publication of his birth certificate showing that he was illegitimate. His oration was, perhaps, a little too clever, but it was exquisitely phrased and finely delivered and on the whole it rang true. We were on friendly terms with J.R. MacDonald for the first time for twenty years. . . .

Whittinghame House in East Lothian, home of the Balfour family

Below: Lord George Hamilton. *Below right:* Lady Elcho, in court dress
Below left: Sketch of Mrs Patrick Campbell in *Pygmalion*, 1914

Above: View of Hadspen House c. 1910

Left: Family group at Hadspen c. 1911. Standing left to right: Stephen, Arthur, Paul and Eleanor Hobhouse. Seated: Henry and Margaret Hobhouse, Felix Clay, Jack Hobhouse. Foreground: Rachel Clay with her children, Janet, Henry and Margaret

Left: Arthur Hobhouse with Barbara Meinertzhagen *Right:* Georgie Meinertzhagen, 1910

Right: William Pember Reeves

Below: Maud Pember Reeves, photograph dated 13 May 1914

Above: Rivers Blanco White

Right: Amber Pember Reeves, with her daughter Jane c. 1913

Left: Fabian Summer School group in Wales, July 1913. Beatrice and Sidney Webb seated second and third from left

Right: Beatrice and Sidney Webb in India, February 1912. She wrote 'At Lakmansjula Bridge we embarked on *sahnais* to float downstream for five hours shooting innumerable rapids'

Left: Photograph of Beatrice and Sidney Webb taken by Bernard Shaw and pasted into the diary for April 1914. 'A delightful ten days walking and talking with GBS'

Hugh Dalton   George Cole

Fabian Summer School, Llanbedr, 1909. Left to right: James Strachey, unknown, Margery Olivier, unknown, Rupert Brooke, Arthur Colegate, unknown, Rivers Blanco White, Amber Reeves, Clifford Sharp

Above left: 'The Wire Puller', a cartoon published in the *Manchester Evening Chronicle*, 11 March 1908. Described by Beatrice in her diary as 'a disagreeable infringement of our anonymity'

Above right: 'The Inevitability of Gradualness', a cartoon by Frank Reynolds published in *Punch*, 4 July 1923

Below: Beatrice and Sidney Webb at the 1923 Labour Party Conference

Above: Women members of the Labour Party, including Marion Phillips, seated front row left, and Beatrice Webb, seated second from right

Right: Bernard Shaw at the Labour Party Conference, Portsmouth 1909

Below: Labour Party group at Easton Lodge, 1923. Standing left to right: Otto Wells, Canon Adderley, Mr and Mrs Shinwell, Will Thorne. Seated: Arthur Henderson, Countess of Warwick, Ramsay MacDonald, Rudolph Breitscheid

Above left: George Lansbury

Above right: Philip Snowden

Left: Arthur Henderson addressing Labour Party Conference delegates, June 1923

Labour Party M.P.s outside the House of Commons in 1906. Front row left to right: Arthur Henderson, Ramsay MacDonald, Keir Hardy, David Shackleton. Back row: George Barnes, Philip Snowden, John Hodges, Will Crooks, Joe O'Grady

The special feature on the teaching profession was published in the *New Statesman* on 2 October 1915.

25 September. [41 Grosvenor Road]
Finished the final revise of the supplement to the *New Statesman* on teachers' professional organizations. It is an elaborate piece of research costing me, from start to finish, six solid months, with a good deal of casual help from Sidney. It ought, of course, to have been published under the joint name. . . . We had not realized how much work he would do on it, and once it had been announced, he would not let me change the ostensible authorship. Sidney has no vanity or personal ambition, he never feels that he is not getting his deserts: his reward is perfect peace of mind and always-present consciousness of 'good fortune'; he sits at his work, day in, day out, doing every job as it comes along, leaving the result, as he often says, 'in the lap of the gods'. He is far more philosophical about the war than I am. 'It is a sag back, but presently there will be a sag forward, and humanity will move forward to greater knowledge and greater goodwill: the Great War will seem to future generations a landmark of progress.'
I wonder: the evil let loose seems too stupendous.

In October, the Bulgarians came in on the German side; the Austrians, relieved of the Russian pressure, attacked Belgrade. By mid-October, Germans, Austrians and Bulgarians were sweeping over Serbia. A British and French force was landed at Salonica.

[?] *October.* [41 Grosvenor Road]
. . . the war itself has become almost suddenly far more serious. If Germany breaks through and connects with Turkey, the British Empire is threatened for the first time: the battleground shifts from Europe, where we are impregnable, to Asia, where we have great dependencies to lose. It may be that we cannot effectively protect our Empire without putting in all our resources. But the property-owners refuse to pool their incomes and the wage-earners refuse to pool their labour. . . . What England lacks today is not patriotism or courage, but the capacity to use her brains and muscles to the best advantage. We have become deplorably slack and our brain-workers are even slacker than our manual workers. . . . Meanwhile, the horror and terror of the war eats into one's vitality, and I exist

in a state of chronic weakness brought about by continuous sleep-lessness. Perhaps I shall feel better when the two lectures are off my mind and I can get back to research. Research is restful to the mind and calming to the temper. . . .

Zeppelin raids became regular on moonlight nights in the summer of 1915, and some reached the Midlands and the East coast. They were generally more frightening than damaging: only 200 tons of bombs were dropped in the whole course of the war by the airships. This raid in early October killed forty people in London. The attacks by Gotha aeroplanes in the summer of 1917 caused more panic and casualties with a total bomb load of 73 tons.

8 October. [41 Grosvenor Road]
The window rattled behind me: then all the windows rattled and we became conscious of the booming of guns getting nearer. 'At last the Zeppelins', Sidney said, with almost boyish glee. From the balcony we could see shrapnel bursting over the river and beyond, somewhat aimlessly. In another few minutes a long sinuous airship appeared high up in the blue black sky, lit up faintly by the searchlights. It seemed to come from over the houses just behind us, we thought along Victoria Street, but it was actually passing along the Strand. It moved slowly, seemingly across the river, the shells bursting far below it. Then there were two bursts that seemed to nearly hit it and it disappeared. I imagine it bounded upwards. The show was over. It was a gruesome reflection afterwards that while we were being pleasantly excited men, women and children were being killed and maimed. At the time it was impossible not to take it as a 'Sight'. . . .

There was apparently no panic, even in the crowded Strand. The Londoner persists in taking Zeppelin raids as an entertainment – a risky entertainment, but no more risky than some forms of sport. . . .

Pessimism about the war is becoming more pronounced: the optimists are silent, mere passive resisters to the panic-mongers. Even Sidney is getting alarmed about the financial position, and many of us feel doubtful whether our working class would endure any considerable hardships without breaking into industrial disorder. Germany and France ruthlessly suppress their pessimists; our government dare not do so, because, like the Ulster rebels of eighteen months ago, they are in high places. Our newspapers are amazingly free with their exasperated criticism, and certain notables, like poor Haldane, are pursued with venom.

There is a chronic conspiracy to get rid of Asquith and Grey. There is a great deal of screaming, 'You see, I was right,' a great many cries for 'someone's head'. GBS is angry with the *New Statesman* because Sharp refuses to join in the abuse and the demand for resignations. Shaw's theory is that you have got to get rid of one set of Ministers after another until you find a group who will 'sit up'. It is a foolish theory arising from impatience and hurt egotism. He hates Grey, and has a contempt for Asquith; and a strange unfounded assumption that, somewhere or other, there is a strong man − and a strong man who will carry out GBS's policy. . . .

The Fabian Society organized a series of autumn lectures by Shaw and the Webbs at the King's Hall. Beatrice's first lecture on 2 November, 'The War and the Spirit of Revolt', reflected on the 'discreditable' state of the country in the months before the war. The second lecture, 'The War and the Demand for "The Servile State"', was given on 16 November. Sidney's talk on 'The Internationalist Organization which will prevent War' showed how the Webbs pressed this theme throughout the conflict.

14 November. [41 Grosvenor Road]
In my last lecture on 'The War and the Spirit of Revolt' I had to define my position towards metaphysics. My thesis was that the Spirit of Revolt − the Revolt that looks to violence as its method − was identical with the Spirit of War. Revolutionary violence within a state and national wars on other states were both manifestations of the impulse to impose your will on other human beings. The soul of England, reflected in the rebel movements prior to the war, was not dissimilar from the soul of Germany reflected in her desire for world power. In both cases there was the excuse that the existing distribution of the good things of life was unfair, the exception being the Ulster rebels, who proposed to use violence to prevent a majority altering the existing distribution of power by constitutional means. What was the remedy for this lunatic desire to impose your policy or your culture on unwilling peoples? . . . I criticized the use of the creed of Intellectualism as suitable only to discover the right method of reaching the desired ends; I criticized the creed of Impulse, as ignoring the sphere of the Intellect and also of refusing to select any one among the emotions or Impulses, regarding all as equally valid. There was only one desirable emotion, but that one emotion should be held to be not the means, but the one and only end of human life. That emotion was the state of mind, which for

lack of a better word, we call love – some call it heavenly love, to distinguish it from animal love. To my dismay, I found myself hailed by some religious papers as a convert to religion, even to Christianity. That makes me feel a hypocrite, gaining the confidence and the admiration of persons with whose metaphysic I do not agree. . . .

I deceive others unintentionally because most of the devout assume that [my] metaphysic must be bound up with the Christian religion. It is true that I take part in the rites of the Christian Church, when these rites are beautifully and sympathetically rendered, as in the services of St Paul's. But exactly the same rites are repellent, even offensive to me, if they take place in an ugly building, without music, or are performed by a mediocre man. As a matter of fact the Christian religion, as set forth in the Bible or as developed in the dogmas of the Churches, attracts neither my heart nor my intellect. The character of Jesus of Nazareth has never appealed to me. The vision of Buddha, the personality of St Francis, the thought of Plato and of Goethe, even the writings of many minor moderns, have helped me far more to realize the purpose of love and the way it may be fulfilled by the use of the intellect, than all the books of the *New Testament*. As for the *Old Testament*, it is intellectually and ethically repulsive to me.

Sometimes I try to discover what is the Ideal that moves me. It is not a conception of a rightly organized society; it is not a vision of a perfect man – a Saviour or a Superman. It is far nearer the thought of an Abstract Being divested of all human appetite but combining the quality of an always working intellect with an impersonal love. And when I do think of the future man as I strive to make him in myself and in others, I forecast an Impersonality – if I may so express it – perpetually disentangling the material circumstances of the universe by intellectual processes, and, by his emotional will, casting out all other feelings, all other sensations other than that of an all-embracing beneficence. Physical appetites are to me the devil: they are signs of the disease that ends in death, the root of the hatred, malice and greed that make the life of man a futility.

But it would not be true to say that this faith in love with its attendant practice of prayer is a continuous state of mind. If it were, I should be a consistently happy person, which I am not. I enjoy life after a manner – I seldom want to leave it. Human nature and its problems interest me, research excites me, companionship delights me. But I am haunted with the fear that all my struggles may be in vain; that disease and death are the ends towards which the individual, the race and the whole conceivable universe are moving with relentless certainty. . . .

The Webbs eventually worked up their *New Statesman* articles into *A Constitution for the Socialist Commonwealth of Great Britain* (1920) and *The Decay of Capitalist Civilization* (1923).

13 December. [41 Grosvenor Road]
I have been working well these last weeks, collecting material for an essay on the professional organization of medical men. It is a long task and sometimes I get impatient. We want to come to an end of this report on the Control of Industry. When that is finished, we must set to work on the book *What is Socialism?* That work will be a summary of our knowledge and of our faith, our last Testament. It will follow the lines – better thought out and more comprehensively illustrated – of our articles in the *New Statesman*. Equality of circumstance, as essential to public welfare and private manners, will be the keynote of the book. A change of heart and the application of the scientific method will be the essential conditions of success in reconstruction; democracy, in all its forms, the necessary machinery, at any rate until common consent can be attained in some more perfect way. . . .

∽ 1916 ∾

The links between the trade union leaders and the government, and the ban on official strikes in war industry, left the workshop initiative to the unofficial shop stewards' movement. The Clyde Workers' Committee, set up in 1915, combined industrial militancy with left-wing and anti-war politics, and after a great strike early in 1916 a number of its members were arrested and deported from Scotland. The threat of industrial and military conscription had undoubtedly stimulated much opposition. On 30 December, the Labour Executive decided to call a representative conference on 6 January, when a resolution was carried which called for the withdrawal of the new Military Service Bill. The Executive then decided by a small majority that the Labour Ministers must resign. On 12 January a meeting of the Labour Party and the Parliamentary Labour Party was given assurances by Asquith and agreed that the Ministers should continue in office pending the annual party conference at Bristol later in the month. 'A clear and notable victory for the patriots', Beatrice noted on 18 January.

243

2 January. [41 Grosvenor Road]
The year opens badly for labour. The Munitions Act and the Defence of the Realm Act, together with the suppression of a free press, has been followed by the Cabinet's decision in favour of compulsory military service. This decision is the last of a series of cleverly devised steps, each step seeming at once harmless and inevitable, even to the opponents of compulsion, but in fact necessitating the next step forward to a system of military and industrial conscription. . . . But it is obvious that if the war continues, the married men will have to go into the trenches, and directly the Minister of Munitions *dares to do it*, industrial conscription will be introduced into the whole of industry. The 'servile state' will have been established.

Sidney, who is now on the Executive of the Labour Party, in place of Sanders who has taken a commission, attended the meeting of the three executives to decide on the policy of the Labour Party and the trade union movement. He says that though the question of conscription was not discussed (the meeting decided to call an immediate national conference), it was clear that nearly all the Labour M.P.s and a majority of the other leaders were converted to a minimum measure of conscription. Henderson told them that the alternative was a general election and that if that took place every Labour M.P. would lose his seat – certainly every member who was against military service. The extinction of the Labour Party in the House of Commons seemed to these men a catastrophe far greater than the extinction of the Labour faith in the country. They did not realize that Labour might be far stronger for the passing of its parliamentary representatives. And not one of them suggested that there ought to be some *quid pro quo* if they decided to support the Cabinet proposal.

Meanwhile the rank and file, especially on the Clyde, are getting more and more discontented and revolutionary. Unfortunately the Labour conference that will come together on Thursday will be made up of the executives and their nominees, not of delegates from the branches and districts. Sidney has scant hope that it will have more backbone than the Parliamentary Labour Party. The one hope is the miners, the railwaymen and the engineers. If compulsion comes and is extended, we shall witness the disruption of the labour and socialist movement and an era of disorder and suppression.

We are not intervening with our counsel. The workmen's

organizations must decide for themselves. We can only stand by and answer such questions as are asked by those who consult us privately.

J.H. Thomas (1874–1949) was general secretary of the National Union of Railwaymen, and Labour M.P. who became Colonial Secretary in 1924. Albert Bellamy (1871–1931) was president of the National Union of Railwaymen and a Labour M.P. 1928–31.

6 January. [41 Grosvenor Road]
The Labour conference today, representing about three million workers, decided by a majority of three to one against any form of compulsion and recommended the Labour M.P.s to oppose the present Bill in all its stages.

At the meeting of the three executives yesterday afternoon, the sub-committee proposed a wordy resolution against the principle of compulsion, but ending in a definite acceptance of the Bill on the ground of the Prime Minister's pledge against 'military necessity'. Sidney proposed an amendment definitely declining to support the Bill on the ground that the case for even limited compulsion had not been made out. Much to his surprise this was accepted, and ordered to be printed for the conference, as the agreed resolution of the three committees.

But the conference would have no compromise with the accursed thing. The delegates were quite good-humoured about it, and except for a sinister threat of industrial disturbance from the railwaymen and from the Yorkshire textiles, the speeches were as cool as they were determined. Henderson, after beginning well by asserting that he should resign from the government if the Labour Party decided against the Bill, lost his temper, owing to unmannerly interruptions, and challenged the I.L.P. M.P.s to resign their seats as he intended to, so as to test the wishes of the constituencies. Snowden could not resist taking up the challenge, and was understood to say that he would resign his seat at Blackburn if Henderson would fight him. J.R. MacDonald swept these challenges and counter-challenges on one side as inconsistent with our parliamentary institutions, and proceeded, with eloquence, to state the case against the Bill. The most weighty speeches were from Thomas and Bellamy of the N.U.R., who dilated on the trickery of the whole proceedings and refused to acquiesce in conscription whatever the

245

military experts might say about the 'military necessity'. Bellamy threatened, if the government carried conscription, industrial disorder on such a scale that we should lose the war, assuming that success depended on Great Britain. The dominant impression left by the conference was one of extreme suspicion and distrust of the government. . . .

Sidney has just returned from the meeting of the executives: after desultory talk they decided by 13 to 11 to ask Henderson, Roberts and Brace to retire from the government. The Labour members decided that the party will oppose the Bill though individual members will be free to vote for it. The decision of the conference has given the pacifist M.P.s a mandate, and it is quite clear that there will not be that 'general consent' that Asquith postulated as essential to the introduction of the principle of compulsion. . . .

Henry Gosling (1861–1930), secretary of the Watermen's Union and president of the Transport Workers' Federation, became Minister of Transport in 1924. George Barnes was to take Henderson's place in the War Cabinet in the summer of 1917.

20 January. [41 Grosvenor Road]
Again on a government committee, the Statutory Pensions Committee, set up to grant supplementary pensions to discharged and disabled men. The Parliamentary Labour Party asked me to be one of their three nominees and I felt obliged to accept. It is neither an agreeable nor an interesting job, and my colleagues – Conservative politicians, army and navy representatives and philanthropic ladies and lawyers – are not sympathetic. The one and only advantage is that it gives me an inside position from which to watch the demobilization of the army. My Labour colleagues are Gosling and Barnes, neither of them strong men. It is pathetic to watch the 'Labour man' struggling with an environment that he cannot master. However, he is a portent, foreshadowing the coming of social equality: his presence compels the governing class to realize that they exist on sufferance, that they have 'to make good' and that all their assumptions as to social right will be challenged.

31 January. [41 Grosvenor Road]
The cause of national unity and the continued existence in this Parliament of a Labour Party have been furthered by the equivocal

resolutions of the Bristol conference. The 900 delegates, representing from two to three million manual workers, administered a good-tempered but effective snub to the I.L.P. pacifists. The leaders, MacDonald, Snowden and Anderson, were given warm ovations, but all their resolutions were rejected by great majorities. The resolution against the Military Service Act was nullified by the refusal to agitate for its repeal, whilst Henderson and his two attendant Ministers were authorized to remain in the government. The plain truth is that three out of every four delegates wanted no trouble either about the Military Service Act or about the Munitions Act. They wanted to assure their pacifist leaders that they admired their pugnacious idealism, but did not want it to interfere with the winning of the war. There was no bitterness among the delegates. Even the I.L.P. leaders were glad that there was to be no split, as there undoubtedly would have been if Henderson and Co. had been ordered out of the government. The British workman, his wife and daughters, are making good money, more than ever before, and they are working long hours and have no time to be discontented. So long as full employment and the bigger income continues there will be nothing more serious than revolutionary talk, and occasional local outbreaks of disorder. And as no one is allowed to report either the talk or the disorder, the world will be assured that there is industrial peace in Great Britain.

22 February. [41 Grosvenor Road]
C.M. Lloyd is back on leave; he is very pessimistic. He does not believe that there is much chance of the British breaking through. He is disgusted with the drinking habits, slackness and want of intelligence of the British officer. The ordinary officer, whether he be a professional or a 'Kitchener Army' man, has no notion of accurate orders or of seeing that these orders are executed, exactly and punctually. He muddles everything, and consequently muddles away many lives in every attack. The common soldier obeys orders but with very little intelligence or zeal. His strength lies in his lack of imagination: if he is well led 'he sticks it'. . . .

Cole, who was a fellow of Magdalen College, was given total exemption by the Oxford tribunal on condition that he continued working for the Amalgamated Society of Engineers. Mellor and Arnot had their appeals dismissed.

9 March. [41 Grosvenor Road]

We are watching with amusement the three young men, who are the kernel of the Fabian Research Department, struggling to escape the net of conscription. Cole, Mellor and Arnot are pleading 'conscientious objection', also work of national importance. Disapproval of violence is certainly no part of their creed – they were always preaching violent action on the part of the manual workers, before the war, at least Cole and Mellor were; Arnot has, I think, certain qualms about the use of force. What they all detest is being forced to do anything they don't like, especially being forced to do it by a government they abhor. They are not conscientious objectors: they are professional rebels. Not one of the three is really entitled to exemption under the Act, unless every one who objects is to be exempted; in which case there would be no conscription. Hence they have provided themselves with the other plea – 'work of national importance'. With ingenious audacity, Cole and Mellor have installed themselves in the office of the A.S.E., their friends on the Executive having applied to have them 'badged' as necessary officials, especially engaged to collate all the wage-agreements in munition areas. Certainly this is the first time a trade union has engaged a university man as an official, and I very much doubt whether the engagement of any officials by the Executive, without the consent of the members, is permissible under the rules. To help Arnot, Sidney and Henderson have testified that the *Labour Yearbook* is a work of national importance, and Sidney has stated that he knows that Arnot has a conscientious objection to fighting. We want all of them to get off; we hate compulsion to kill; and we realize that these ardent young men are getting right into the heart of the trade union movement and are creating an intellectual centre for trade unionism. They, and we, are becoming the constant advisers of the labour movement; and the young and the old counsellors do not differ in the advice they give as much as the young ones imagine. There is no friction between us today. . . .

Emile Vandervelde (1866–1938), a professor of economics at the University of Brussels, had been chairman of the socialist group in the Belgian parliament. In the autumn of 1915 the I.L.P. delegates had been refused permission to attend a meeting at Zimmerwald in Switzerland, where the anti-war socialists (including Lenin) took the first steps towards a new and revolutionary International.

31 March. [41 Grosvenor Road]

Huysmans, the secretary of the International Socialist Bureau, is in London interviewing the executives represented in the British Section – the three socialist societies and the Parliamentary Labour Party and the Labour Party Executive. He and Vandervelde spent over an hour with the Fabian Executive on Tuesday, and he came on here to dinner and a quiet talk. He is an accomplished Belgian, belonging to the highly educated Continental middle class, a fluent speaker in three or four languages and with an unrivalled knowledge of the personalities of the socialist movements of all countries. Since the outbreak of the war he has, at the Hague headquarters of the International Socialist Bureau, talked with deputations of socialists from all the belligerent countries. The official delegates of the German socialists, it seems, are anxious to meet the representatives of the labour and socialist movements of the Allied countries; they believe that their action has been wholly misunderstood. They assert that they had as much right to support their country in its defensive war as the French, Belgian and British socialists, that the Allied socialists have gone further in this direction as they have been represented in Coalition Cabinets. The French socialists, by a 60 per cent majority, are against any meeting of the I.S.B., and Vandervelde agrees with this decision. 'How could men who were voting credits to destroy each other in the trenches, consult together: it would revolt the conscience of Europe.' ('Platform oratory', whispered Huysmans to us.) The French socialists, have, however, prepared resolutions embodying terms of peace to which all socialists could agree.

Huysmans pleaded for a like statement from the British Labour Party. If all the socialist parties were to set down what they considered a righteous peace, it might be found that there was common agreement on certain points, i.e. 'no annexations, the rehabilitation of Belgium, the autonomy of Poland, arbitration and disarmament'. This common measure of agreement might be published to the world as the 'Voice of Labour'. We tried to convince him that, as far as Great Britain was concerned, no such statement could be hoped for. The British trade unions who dominate the Labour Party know nothing about foreign policy. Moreover, they dislike general propositions and they would not desire to hamper their own government. . . .

He was pessimistic about the future of the socialist movement:

the bubble of 'Workers of the World Unite' was smashed for the next generation. Personally, he was most concerned to prevent the rise of a new International of the extreme pacifist revolutionary type, made up of *émigré* socialists from all countries, as the rival of the officially recognized body. It was for this purpose that he wanted some sort of declaration, whether or not this declaration had any influence on the terms of peace, for the express object of making it appear that there was some solidarity among socialists of all countries.

He did not convince us. It was the old game of shibboleths, acclaimed by all with fervour, without making the remotest difference to men's real thoughts or feelings, inside or outside the socialist movement. Confronted with millions killed and maimed on the battlefields, women and children massacred and whole countries devastated, 'International Socialist Brotherhood' had a hollow sound, like a mocking laugh at a funeral. . . .

A British garrison at Kut in Mesopotamia fell to the Turks on 29 April after three months of severe fighting. The French were desperately trying to halt the massive German attacks on Verdun which had begun in February. The Clyde Workers' Committee was now the effective though unofficial spokesman for the Clydeside engineering workers.

4 April. [41 Grosvenor Road]
Alternate waves of optimism and pessimism, originating in one or other official of the W.O. or Admiralty, beat upon the mind of the outer circle of journalists and politicians. A few weeks ago the rumour was that the W.O. thought that the war would be over in August owing to the exhaustion of Germany attacked on all fronts; that the Admiralty had the submarines well in hand, etc. etc. But today there are new elements of anxiety: the almost certain surrender of the Kut force, diminishing our prestige in the East; the success of the submarine campaign in reducing our already narrow margin of mercantile marine; the belief that the German lines are impregnable, and the fear that France will not hold out during the winter. There is also the steady depreciation, by the war press, of our organizing capacity and technical skill. Whatever else the war is doing, it is not increasing our self-conceit. . . .

The state of my own and other people's mind surprises me. We are becoming callous to the horrors of the war. At first it was a continuous waking nightmare. But with a few months of it one ceases to feel about it. Today one goes on with one's researches, enjoys one's comforts and pleasures and even reads the daily war news with mild interest, exactly as if slaughter and devastation, on a colossal scale, were part of the expected routine of life. This callousness to the horrors of war explains the way in which the wealthy governing class have tolerated the horrors of peace due to the existing social order. Is there no depth of misery and degradation, endured by other persons, which will not be accepted as normal and inevitable? The horrors of peace are as dependent for their existence on the human will, are as much the deliberate choice of those who govern as the horrors of war. Both are the results of lack of imagination, moral as well as intellectual imagination. . . .

Sidney reports that the trade union M.P.s are doing their worst to prevent the War Emergency Committee getting to work on an After the War programme, largely from jealousy but also because they don't want to be compelled to think, to the extent of accepting or refusing the proposals. They are as 'mulish' about an After the War programme as they were about the National Minimum campaign of 1912—13. And the fact that Henderson, Roberts and Brace are ministers does not help towards independent thought. Obviously these Ministers do not want to embarrass a government to which they now belong and may continue to belong after the war is over. The other trade union members are either expecting or hoping for office or are merely apathetic.

Three of the Clyde Workers' Committee came down to London about the strike. They were 'rebels' holding fast to the illusion of revolution. But they felt that on this occasion they were beaten. The young men of the Fabian Research Department arranged a meeting between them and the A.S.E. Executive and persuaded them to put themselves in the hands of the District Committee of the A.S.E. What with the apathy of the governing cliques and the revolutionary myths of little knots of local leaders, the influence of trade unionism has, for the time being, almost ceased to exist. One wonders when the National Guildsmen will realize the weakness of their chosen instrument. The creed is still the moving force among the young generation of intellectuals; it occupies, in fact, much the same position as municipal socialism did with the Fabians and their followers in the 90s. The new generation dreams on and works as hard for the organization of the manual workers as the Fabians did for that of the citizen consumer.

The No-Conscription Fellowship was founded by Fenner Brockway (b. 1888), an I.L.P. journalist then editing the *Labour Leader*. He later wrote a book on prison reform, collaborating with Stephen Hobhouse in using reports made by imprisoned conscientious objectors. He became general secretary of the I.L.P., and in later life a Labour politician specializing in colonial policy. Robert Trevelyan (1872–1951), poet and brother of Charles and George Trevelyan, had been a helper in the Poor Law campaign. Olive Schreiner (1862–1920) was the South African feminist and author of *The Story of an African Farm* (1883). Arnold Lupton (1847–1930), professor of mining at Leeds University, was a Liberal M.P. 1906–10. Dr John Clifford (1836–1921) was a famous Nonconformist preacher and the leader of resistance to the 1902 Education Act. C.H. Norman (b. 1886) was a Fabian who held several offices in the anti-war movement. Margaret Llewelyn Davies (1861–1944) was the secretary of the Women's Co-operative Guild, which did much to educate and represent working-class women.

8 April. [41 Grosvenor Road]
The Friends Meeting House in Devonshire House Hotel, a large ugly circular hall with a big gallery running round it, was packed with some 2,000 young men – the National Convention of the No-Conscription Fellowship. . . . Among the 2,000 were many diverse types. The intellectual pietist, slender in figure, delicate in feature and complexion, benevolent in expression, was the dominant type. These youths were saliently conscious of their own righteousness. That they are superior alike in heart and intelligence to the 'average sensual man' is an undoubted fact: ought one to quarrel with them for being aware of it? And yet the constant expression, in word and manner, of the sentiment avowed by one of them: 'We are the people whose eyes are open,' was unpleasing. There were not a few professional rebels, out to smash the Military Service Act, because it was the latest and biggest embodiment of authority hostile to the conduct of their own lives according to their own desires. Here and there were misguided youths who had been swept into the movement because 'conscientious objection' had served to excuse their refusal to enlist and possibly might save them from the terrors and discomforts of fighting – pasty-faced furtive boys, who looked dazed at the amount of heroism that was being expected from them. They were obviously scared by the unanimity with which it was decided 'to refuse alternative service', and they will certainly take advantage of the resolution declaring that every member of the Fellowship must follow his own conscience in this matter. On the platform were the sympathizers with the movement – exactly the

persons you would expect to find at such a meeting, older pacifists and older rebels – Bertrand Russell, Robert Trevelyan, George Lansbury, Olive Schreiner, Lupton, Stephen and Rosa Hobhouse, Dr Clifford, C.H. Norman, Miss Llewelyn Davies and the Snowdens: the pacifist predominating over the rebel element. . . .

The muddled mixture of motives – the claim to be exempt from a given legal obligation, and the use of this privilege as a weapon against the carrying out of the will of the majority – marred the persuasive effect of this demonstration of the No-Conscription Fellowship. The first argument advanced by all the speakers was: 'I believe war to be an evil thing: killing our fellow men is expressly forbidden by my religion, and by the religion, by law established, of my country. Under the Military Service Act *bona fide* conscientious objectors are granted unconditional exemption: I claim this exemption.'

But this plea did not satisfy the militant majority. They declared their intention to defy the Act, so that the Act should become inoperative, even if all the conscientious objectors, on religious grounds, should be relieved from service. They *want* to be martyrs, so as to bring about a revulsion of feeling against any prosecution of the war. They are as hostile to voluntary recruiting as they are to conscription. If the government decided to rely on the recruiting sergeant, they would send a missionary down to oppose him. These men are not so much conscientious objectors as a militant minority of elects, intent on thwarting the will of the majority of ordinary citizens expressed in a national policy.

Now it seems clear that organized society could not continue to be organized, if every citizen had the right to be a conscientious objector to some part of our social order and insisted that he should be permitted not only to break the law himself but to persuade other citizens to break it. Moreover, when the conscientious objection is to carrying out an unpleasant social obligation like defending your country or paying taxes, conscience may become the cover for cowardice, greed or any other form of selfishness. Hence the state, in defence, must make the alternative to fulfilling the common obligation sufficiently irksome to test the conscience of the objectors. . . . The social salvation of the twentieth century is not coming by the dissidence of dissent. Democracy means either discipline or anarchy. The problem is how can we combine the disciplined acceptance of the decisions of the community with the determination to get those decisions altered by the conversion of our fellow citizens to the faith that is in us.

The government had long been divided on the question of compulsory military service. Early in May the Cabinet agreed on a Bill extending compulsion to all male subjects to the age of forty-one, married or single, but Asquith feared Labour opposition and did not enforce it resolutely. Alfred Harmsworth, Lord Northcliffe, founder of the *Daily Mail* and owner of *The Times*, was the most powerful of all the 'press lords' and the most vehement for efficient prosecution of the war. He did much to bring down Asquith and promote Lloyd George as war leader. On Easter Day, 25 April 1916, a small band of Irish patriots seized the centre of Dublin as part of an aborted scheme for a nationwide rising. The rebellion was quickly crushed and seventeen of its leaders executed.

1 May. [41 Grosvenor Road]
A series of political crises: the newspapers excited, everyone else indifferent. Ten days ago it looked as if the government would break up on compulsion, and the withdrawal of more men from the army. Asquith was confronted with the pledge he gave to the Labour Party that if the H. of C. determined on extending the principle of conscription to married men, 'someone else would have to take my place.' But as one might have expected, he has broken his pledge. The actual proposal eventually agreed to was the silly and dishonest one of pretending to try voluntary recruiting again for married men, with the proviso that if they did not come in within a month, they were to be conscripted, whilst extending compulsion immediately to all youths reaching eighteen years of age and also to time-expired men. This compromise was accepted by the Labour Party, in spite of Sidney's appeal to stand firm. When the Bill was introduced, everyone saw the absurdity and unfairness of it: so now we have compulsion, *sans phrase*. What with irritation and boredom with pledges which are always broken, and anxiety about the military position, nearly everyone was glad to have the controversy closed. The Northcliffe Press has won hands down. It is humiliating that the Labour Party has shown, if anything, less resistance than the Liberal Party. On the top of this defeat we have the criminal lunacy of the Irish rebellion, playing into the hands of the reactionaries.

Alice Stopford Green (1847–1929), author and widow of the historian J.R. Green, was a radical and Irish nationalist who had been friendly with Beatrice before her marriage to Sidney. She had also been a near neighbour at Millbank.

She settled in Dublin and later became a senator in the Free State. Sir Roger Casement (1846–1916), a former British consul who exposed the cruel treatment of Africans in the Belgian Congo, was an Ulster Protestant and Irish nationalist. He sought help for his cause in Germany and on Good Friday, on the eve of the rising, was landed in Ireland from a German submarine. He was captured, convicted and hanged for treason. Intelligence sources circulated his 'Black Diaries' which purported to reveal his homosexuality and may have been forged: they certainly helped to prejudice informed persons against him. Shaw published a letter – 'Shall Roger Casement Hang?' – on 22 July 1916. The *Manchester Guardian* printed it after *The Times*, the *Daily News* and the *Nation* had rejected it. Shaw did draft a defence speech for Casement, – most of which Casement discarded in his last remarks – and drew up a petition to Asquith. He made a final plea for Casement in the *Daily News* of 2 August, the day before the Irishman was hanged. Sir Charles Russell (1863–1928) was a prominent solicitor who held several government appointments. George Gavan Duffy (1881–1951) was an Irish barrister who eventually became president of the High Court of Ireland. Timothy Healy (1855–1931), Irish lawyer, politician and nationalist, became the first governor-general of the Irish Free State in 1922.

21 May. [41 Grosvenor Road]
A painful luncheon party: Mrs Green and the Bernard Shaws to consult about the tragic plight of Roger Casement. Alice Green has made herself responsible for the defence of her old friend. He has no money and only two relatives in England – cousins who are school-teachers. On reaching London, with his Scotland Yard escort, he appealed to the only solicitor he knew, Charles Russell (the son of the late Russell of Killowen), who has a large Irish Catholic connection. Russell refused to defend him and sent his clerk to the Tower to tell him so. Meanwhile, Mrs Green had got Gavan Duffy to write and offer to conduct the defence. The letter was not delivered for a fortnight, the unhappy rebel being in solitary confinement with the consciousness of being deserted. Alice declares that throughout this time he was harassed by visits from detectives, examining and cross-examining him. At last Gavan Duffy was permitted to see him and counsel was briefed only four and twenty hours before he had to be defended in the police court. To enable this to be done Mrs Green had to put down £300. But where is the money to come from for the trial in the High Court? Gavan Duffy has already injured himself by taking up the rebels' cause: his partners are said to have repudiated him. It is difficult to get a first-rate lawyer to look at the case, even with a fee. Healey has refused. [Sir John] Simon will not touch it; the best that his

friends can do is to offer a big fee to a second-rate K.C., who might hope to make a name for himself. But where was the money to come from?

So I asked the Bernard Shaws to meet her. Charlotte is a wealthy Irish rebel, and I had noticed that when Casement's 'treason' was mentioned, her eyes had flashed defiance and she had defended his action. And GBS had publicly urged clemency and had also defended Casement's action. But GBS as usual had his own plan. Casement was to defend his own case, he was to make a great oration of defiance which would 'bring down the house'. To this Mrs Green retorted tearfully that the man was desperately ill, that he was quite incapable of handling a court full of lawyers, that the most he could do was the final speech after the verdict. 'Then we had better get our suit of mourning,' Shaw remarked with an almost gay laugh. 'I will write him a speech which will thunder down the ages.' 'But his friends want to get him reprieved,' indignantly replied the distracted woman friend.

The meeting turned out to be a useless and painful proceeding. The Shaws were determined not to pay up — not 'to waste our money on lawyers'. GBS went off to write the speech which was 'to thunder down the ages'. Alice Green retired in dismay, and I felt a fool for having intervened to bring Irish together in a common cause. Alice has been heroic: her house has been searched, she herself has been up before Scotland Yard, she is spending her strength and her means in trying to save the life of her unfortunate friend. The Shaws don't care enough about it to spend money; and Shaw wants to compel Casement and Casement's friends to 'produce' the defence as a national dramatic event. 'I know how to do it,' was GBS's one contribution to the tragedy-laden dispute between the weeping woman friend and the intellectual sprite at play with the life and death of a poor human. The man is both kindly and tolerant, but his conceit is monstrous, and he is wholly unaware of the pain he gives by his jeering words and laughing gestures — especially to romantics like Alice Green. He never hurts my feelings because I am as intellectually detached as he is. He sometimes irritates Sidney with his argumentative perversities, but there is an old comradeship between them, and GBS's admiration for Sidney's ability has become part of his own *amour propre*. And there is this to be said: if everyone were as intellectual and unemotional as he is, as free from conventions in thought and feeling, his flashes might alter the direction of opinion. There would remain his instability of purpose. He is himself always in a state of reaction from his last state of mind or generalizing from his most recent experience. A world made up of Bernard Shaws would be a world in moral dissolution.

1 June. [41 Grosvenor Road]
. . . . Except for the nightmare of the war, which fades with familiarity, we have had an unusually peaceful time of leisurely but persistent work of one kind or another. Sometimes I have felt hurt that Sidney has not been called upon by the government to do work of national importance. He has been curiously ignored by the rulers of the world, though constantly consulted by the underlings of government departments and the lesser lights of the Labour movement. Within the Labour Party he has a certain influence and is allowed to draft manifestoes, Bills, questions in Parliament, resolutions for conferences and meetings for other people to gather – like Anderson's Conscription of Wealth Bill and all the reports and circulars of the War Emergency Committee. But the inner ring of pro-war Labour men exclude him from their counsels, whilst his pro-war opinions exclude him from the pacifist movement. He has been exceptionally well and happy, directing the work of the Research Department and writing a book on *How to Pay for the War* and helping with anything I have in hand.

I have been at work on three different jobs. Research for the monograph on the professional organizations of medical men has been my main occupation; but I have attended twice a week at the organizing committee of the Statutory Pensions Committee, and I have been laying the foundation of a new organization, developed out of the Fabian Research Department: the proposed Labour Research Society. . . . This proposed organization is a device to connect in one working fellowship the Fabian Society, the National Guildsmen and the trade union movement. Cole and Mellor stuck to the Research Department in spite of their break with the Fabian Society. These young men were, it was clear, real enthusiasts, inspired by the ideal of industrial democracy, and intent on getting it translated into fact by persistent work.

I still think that their plan of carrying on the nation's industries by huge associations of producers an impossible one, and undesirable if it were possible. But the trend of events is so unfavourable to freedom for the producer that their ideal is valuable as a corrective. The political state is getting far too much power and this power is far too much in the hands of the capitalist brainworker. Any addition to the efficiency and influence of the manual workers' organizations, any increase of the workman's collective control over the conditions of employment, any raising of his status and standard of life, is all to the good. On the other hand, Cole and Mellor have realized some of the immediate difficulties of their task, the colossal stupidity of the trade union rank and file and the timidity and 'smugness' of the trade union leaders. So our points of view are slowly converging. We let them make every possible use of the F.R.D. and they cease to attack us. And as they dislike the predominance of the Fabian Society in the Department and as I want an organization on a more catholic basis, I have proposed to gradually alter both the name and the constitution of the Department into a Labour Research Society, to include members of all recognized socialist and labour organizations so long as they are in favour of research for the advancement of the manual workers. A technical or scientific society for the labour movement as a whole is what we are after. . . .

On 2 June the Webbs took up residence for six weeks at Wyndham Croft, a substantial house at Turner's Hill, Sussex, with a fine view of the South Downs. They had exchanged houses with the owner, Mrs Alfred Willet – 'an instance of mutual trust between two strangers brought about by war economy'. Bernard Shaw stayed at Wyndham Croft from 6–20 June: he was writing *Heartbreak House*; Shaw faithfully reflects its setting in the last scene of the play. Harley Granville-Barker and Lillah McCarthy left for America soon after the war began: they were divorced in June 1918 and he married the wealthy Helen Huntingdon.

6 June. [Wyndham Croft]
Walking with GBS before settling down at Wyndham Croft. He is a delightful companion for an outing, always amusing and good-tempered, sufficiently exasperating in argument to avoid tameness in companionship – the curse of the comradeship of the old. He is a delightful raconteur – a perfect gossip, elaborating by witty exaggerations the life-stories of his friends into human comedies, and sometimes into inhuman tragedies. The last of these is the disaster to the Granville-Barker marriage – Harley having become infatuated with the wife of an American millionaire.

The marriage was predestined to a bad end: each one of them is an egoist and there is and has never been any intellectual sympathy between them. She is a finely built woman of statuesque beauty and great personal dignity, a good craftswoman in acting, but without the temperament of an artist, and with no intellect and not much intelligence. He is intellectual to the last degree, fastidious in taste and unscrupulous in minor morals, sacrificing all things to the development of his talent or the satisfaction of some artistic or intellectual whim. Both have been distracted from their professional partnership by the flattering camaraderie of the Asquith set. I doubt whether Granville-Barker will ever do work equal to his talents; he has no persistency of purpose; he is carried away from his more serious aims by enjoyment of social life and by intellectual and artistic fashions. He is an imitator not an originator, a first-rate 'producer' of anything he understands but incapable, through lack of personal experience, of expressing in his art the deepest feelings or wisest thoughts of his contemporaries. Men and women are to him animals first and intellectuals afterwards, they are never saints or heroes. Religious exaltation, heroic effort, persistent faithfulness to an individual or a cause are qualities unknown to him. Hence his wayward egotism, amounting almost to dishonesty in money matters and to cruelty in his relation to his wife.

Are 'charmers' always wayward and do they always lack the quality of faithfulness? Is good faith a radically ungracious characteristic? In order to be faithful in all things must you necessarily be unpleasant in many things? Or could absolute faithfulness and perfect courtesy be combined? All the faithful I have known have been rough and unsympathetic at times, all the charming persons I have known have been faithless in some of the relations of life.

Leonard and Virginia Woolf were also guests of the Webbs for the week-end, though Beatrice makes no comment on their visit. 'We talked quite incessantly,' Virginia wrote to Vanessa Bell. 'We were taken for brisk walks, still talking hard. Mrs Webb pounces on one, rather like a moulting eagle, with a bald neck and a bloodstained beak. However, I got on with her better than I expected.'

17 June. [Wyndham Croft]
Charlotte Shaw joined us for the last few days of GBS's visit. Except for the details of daily life, these two have not much common interest. Charlotte detests the stage and is no longer interested in socialism. Pacifist she is — because she is a rebel.

Christian Science (or is it Higher Thought?) is her main preoccupation. One good result is that her temper has become excellent; and she looks happy and healthy. She is still very proud of her famous man and angry with any criticism of his work. But her thoughts centre in the crude reasoning of the male and female preachers of the new American mysticism. She has in fact become '*dévote*' — the modern *dévote*, who combines a love of personal luxury with intense interest and the happy peacefulness of her own soul. I am, perhaps unjustifiably, irritated at the selfishness of her expenditure. I have never known her ask an overworked person to Ayot. She has never lent the house, in her absence, to poorer friends who need rest and change. Once we took it off her hands because she wanted to take all her servants away (not because we wanted it) and, of course, we can always get a holiday. In old days she was generous, out of her superfluity, to the London School of Economics and the Fabian Society. But she has lost the last remnant of conscience about property. These new cults do not lead to self-sacrifice, they concentrate attention on your own state of mind: you must be kindly and happy, you need not do anything for others or for the community. Faith and not works is the purpose — faith in your own happiness. (I doubt whether I am fair to Charlotte: she and I are not sympathetic.)

24 June. [Wyndham Croft]
I have had, in the last few days, a deplorable proof of the lack of Christian Science in myself. Owing to certain physical symptoms showing a steady decline in energy and weight for some months past, I became obsessed by the conviction that I had an internal growth, that this would necessitate an operation and that I should die under it. Each link in the chain of proof was unsound, but to my distempered imagination, each supposition seemed an uncontrovertible fact. And I even infected poor Sidney with my fear. So we journeyed up to London with melancholy expectation, to see a specialist. He dispelled my fears, telling me there was no sign of any organic trouble. I was to eat more and, if sleeplessness continued, I was to take a sleeping draught. I feel humiliated — humiliated alike by my absurd obsession and by the absence of courage, even if it had been justified, in meeting physical pain and death. With millions of young men facing death and dying on the battlefields of Europe, it seems contemptible for an old woman,

who has had a full and happy life, to blink miserably at the inevitable end. But I have always been the prey to fear. As a child I would suffer mental agony over some trifling incident: fear of physical pain, fear of the exposure of some wretched little delinquency, or a state of emotional misery arising out of the presumed dislike of someone I cared for. Oddly enough I never feared death as a child: I sometimes longed for it and even contemplated suicide.

These occasional and temporary obsessions or panics are my 'Mr Hyde'. To many of the untoward incidents of life I am wholly indifferent – quite exceptionally indifferent. To most persons, even to those who think they know me well, like my sisters, I think I present an even surface of impersonal attitude and equable temperament. It is due to my will-power, which in spite of mental agony, remains supreme, so far as outward behaviour is concerned. That does not prevent the mean misery of these obsessions. And they sometimes hamper my work for days or weeks together. Sidney is an ideal companion for me: *he is always sane.*

Why does one fear death? One does not fear sleep; one is always glad to sink into sleep. Some part of the fear is for Sidney: leaving him alone in the world; those long hours of agony he would have to endure; the thought that there would be no one to cherish him as he sank into the weakness of old age. But he is brave and has still sufficient vitality to enjoy work and human companionship. His very love for me would help his natural humanity: he would become absorbed in finishing the work we had planned together. And with the wearing out of his energies there would come the wearing out of his sorrow. I should become a holy memory to him, and old people live in their memories. . . .

[*Beatrice added this additional note in 1919.* This illness was the opening phase of a breakdown, which lasted in an acute form for six months and from which I did not recover for over two years. Partly war neurosis, partly too persistent work to keep myself from brooding over the horrors of the war, partly I think general discouragement arising out of our unpopularity with all sections of the political and official world. Sidney, with his sublime unselfconsciousness, was wholly unaffected by the coldness with which we were regarded. But the hostile atmosphere undoubtedly lowered my resistance to neurasthenia. Oddly enough, the first push upwards came from an article in the *Lancet* which I read at Margate in October, describing all the symptoms of neurasthenia, which I promptly recognized as my own. Once aware that my disorder was more mental than physical I took myself in hand, did short intervals of regular work and physical exercise, and gradually pulled myself into the normal routine of a working life. But the breakdown proved to be the turning-point from middle to old age. I now feel that I am packing up so that I may be ready to depart when the day comes.]

The great and bloody offensive on the Somme was launched on 1 July. The British casualties on the first day alone were over 57,000, of whom 19,240 were killed.

2 July. [Wyndham Croft]
We hear from overseas the dull noiseless thud beating on the drum of the ear, hour after hour, day by day, telling of the cancelling out of whole populations on the vast battlefield. One sometimes wonders how one can go on, eating and drinking, walking and sleeping, reading and dictating, apparently unmoved by the world's misery.

6 July. [Wyndham Croft]
Graham Wallas has been staying here. The oddly slovenly young man of a quarter of a century ago, who stayed with me, before my marriage at Box House, and after my marriage at The Argoed, with his incapacity for steady work, his large appetite and delightful but alarming disinterested devotion to unpaying and unpopular causes, is now a leader of thought, with a settled and sufficient livelihood and a body of devoted disciples. He is an encouraging example of the markedly good man who is also, according to his own desires, a markedly successful man, with a fully satisfied conscience combined with a pleasant consciousness of public appreciation. His books are widely read in the U.S.A., his lectures are well attended, he sits on royal commissions, and is often referred to and consulted. He has many friends among leading publicists and minor cabinet ministers. He, Audrey, and a learned and dutiful daughter [May Wallas, later a language teacher at the L.S.E.] are all devoted to one another, and they are surrounded by students and other persons to whom they are generous and helpful. He has no use for the Fabian Society or the Labour Party or the trade union movement: he dislikes all vocational organizations: they are all conspiracies against the public. He is a convinced cosmopolitan,

an accomplished critic of democracy, a good hater of all forms of supernaturalism: his fear of the Church really amounts to an obsession. He is in favour of most of our proposals but is too sceptical about popular government to want democratic government generally extended to industry. He bores Sidney, he interests me passably. His wide and conversational speculations about man in society do not impress us; our concrete studies do not interest him. . . . One thing is clear. Graham Wallas has a greater consciousness of success than we have. He does not feel as I certainly do, beaten by events. The war is a world catastrophe beyond the control of his philosophy. Such social philosophy as I possess does not provide any remedies for racial wars. Today I feel like the fly, not on but under the wheel. . . .

The Reconstruction Committee, of which Vaughan Nash was secretary, was a small group of civil servants. Early in 1917 it was reorganized into a larger and more representative body.

8 July. [Wyndham Croft]
Vaughan Nash came down yesterday for the afternoon to consult Sidney about his Reconstruction Committee. This Committee has been set up by the Prime Minister with V.N. as trusted organizer and conciliator between the several government departments. He is perhaps the best person for the task; he is not only a democratic collectivist but also a charming personality, without conceit or personal ambition. . . . He and we have had a long continued relationship of mutual respect and liking without any personal intimacy or working comradeship. . . .

V.N. suggested that Sidney should come on the sub-committee on the Relations between Capital and Labour, which Sidney accepted, and that I should be on the Committee on Maternity Provision, which I refused, feeling that I have only just enough strength for the work I have in hand.

The History of Germany by Heinrich von Treitschke had just begun to appear in translation. Arnold Freeman (1885–1972), Fabian and Warden of Sheffield Educational Settlement, was joint author, with Sidney Webb, of *Great Britain after the War*.

15 July. [Wyndham Croft]
Our six weeks in the country has been a good time for Sidney and a

263

bad time for me. A delightful countryside, comfortable house, lovely garden with wide views towards the sea, absolute quiet and bracing air – it might well have been a perfect holiday. But I have been sick in body and mind. Constant discomfort, sleeplessness, incapacity either to walk or to work, culminating in the panic about an internal growth, that nightmare of the middle-aged. No progress with the report on Professional Organization, not more than a week's work in the six spent here. I have read three volumes of Treitschke and one volume of Disraeli's Life with interest, and made extracts. But the worst is that I do not know whether I shall be fit for work when I get back to London. I had hoped to come back completely rested. I do not know whether I ought to eat less or more, whether I ought to force myself to exercise my body and mind or to take a rest cure. No medical man seems able to tell you what to do, his advice is guess-work: the best he can do is to test certain organs for organic disease. We have no science of health, no one is observed unless he is diseased or under the fear of disease. We ought to be examined once a year by a health expert who knows us and who would warn us about unhygienic habits of mind or body and watch the results of the regime he recommended.

For Sidney the time has been healthy and happy . . . He has enjoyed the comfort and beauty of the place and the walks with GBS, Sharp, Squire and Graham Wallas. He has done a lot of miscellaneous work for the School of Economics, for the Research Department, for Vaughan Nash's Committee, for the W.E.A. [Workers' Educational Association] handbook that he and Arnold Freeman are preparing. He has written, with some help from me, the opening pages of the Report on Professional Organizations, and he has finished the separate section on the Legal Profession. In the intervals he has read some twenty or thirty books. It has set him up in health and he goes back to London completely rested and refreshed.

The notes Beatrice made on techniques of social investigation were eventually published as an appendix to *My Apprenticeship* in 1926.

18 July. [Wyndham Croft]
Our last day is dark and gloomy, almost dank. I feel ill and depressed at the end of my holiday. Sidney cheers me by reminding me that I have felt like that before. Anyhow, the perpetual dwelling

on one's state of body, even if it is approaching dissolution, is a poor business. But I do want to finish three books, or make Sidney finish them: the *Report on the Control of Industry, What is Socialism?* and *Methods of Investigation.* The historical work which is unfinished can be done by other persons from our material and MSS. Also, I should like to start the Labour Research Department well on its way. With these jobs done, I think I should go willingly, even with a certain satisfaction. The new problems must be solved by younger minds. God bless them. . . .

The Fabian summer gathering, held at Baliol School in the Yorkshire village of Sedbergh, included talks by Rebecca West (1892–1983) on 'Feminism' and, on 5 September, Beatrice on 'Professional Organization'.

13 September. [? Sedbergh]
A fortnight away from London to give our two servants the necessary holidays – a week at the Fabian school and a week with GBS at the hotel near by. The time has been painful for me, because I have suffered from perpetual head trouble; throbbing and dizziness during the night destroying sleep, and dizziness and pain during the day – a nervous breakdown as disheartening as it has been disagreeable. Clearly I am in a rotten state, and something must be done before I can get to work again. . . . GBS was at his best, witty, wise and outstandingly good-natured. He is remarkably virile just now – bathes or works all day – and he is really stupendous in the output of letters and articles. *O'Flaherty V.C.* is a brilliant but serious piece of work, a jewel of a one-act play. *The Inca of Perusalem* is poor in comparison. I note that Charlotte having retired from the Fabian Society, GBS is far more oncoming! . . .

Beatrice Ross (known as 'Bichy' or 'Bice') was Mary Playne's secretary-companion for many years.

18 October. Longfords
Here trying to recover strength for work, in this peaceful and comfortable home – an attempt not hitherto successful, in spite of dear sister Mary's overwhelming kindness and consideration. I spend my days in elaborate idleness, sauntering in the garden, learning to knit, reading newspapers and driving with Mary in the pony-cart. I should enjoy it if it were not for the perpetual dizziness

and the long restless nights. With Sidney away they become painfully fearsome. I have discovered from the second medical man that I have consulted that it is the muscle of the heart, that shows slight weakness, which seems to account for some of the symptoms. It may mean that any kind of work is out of the question for weeks, perhaps months, and that I shall have to readjust my life to a low level of effort.

The Playne household is transformed by the war. The majority of the rooms are dismantled, the bedrooms locked up, the hall and drawing-room bare for working parties. [There are] only the new sitting-room for the family and Arthur's little office and one spare bedroom and dressing-room. The meals are of the simplest. Mary and Bichy are at work most of the day. Large working parties of neighbours gather at Longfords to turn out hospital necessaries and comforts for the troops twice or three times a week. Longfords has become a veritable house of industry, with Bichy as organizer and Mary to preside, saint-like, over the whole family life, a frail but happy old woman, whilst Arthur, a pleasant healthy old man, busies himself with magistrate's work and with attending county council committee meetings, without apparently taking any part in the discussions or decisions. . . .

Shaw wrote to the Webbs on 5 October and again on 13 October to explain why he was resigning his directorship of the *New Statesman*. He complained that Clifford Sharp, who supinely followed Asquith, would never attack the 'social prestige of the country house and plutocrat professionals'; and he added that a journal which was so prudent that it would not print his provocative articles no longer interested him. By the end of November British casualties on the Somme were over 400,000, with little gained and the 'volunteer' army destroyed in the process.

3 November. Fort Paragon Hotel, Margate
One of the highest privileges of the well-to-do is to be able to live in comfort and perfect health conditions when they are ill. Shall we have the wit to communalize this advantage? It would mean not only the necessary national expenditure but also all sorts of precautions against malingering. How do I know that I am not malingering?

GBS has definitely severed his connection with the *New Statesman*. . . . The immediate and real reason, not mentioned to the press, is an adequate one – Sharp's refusal to insert his articles, signed or unsigned. Clifford is a hard-minded conservative collectivist, who obstinately refuses to condemn either measures or men unless he has an alternative plan or an alternative government to propose. He is also a materialist, a despiser of all ideals which cannot be embodied, in the near future, in social machinery to improve the conditions of life. Sentimentality is said to be the emotion of the unimaginative, but Sharp has neither imagination nor emotion. Unless he can see through a question and all round it with his intellect, he refuses to admit that the question exists. Above all he loathes the professional rebel. When he does not see the collectivist solution he remains stolidly conservative. Possibly Shaw's prophecy that Sharp will presently dispense with Sidney may be fulfilled. Arnold Bennett is the one director with whom he seems in complete sympathy, and A.B. is just starting a weekly article of the hard pro–Liberal–Minister type. But if the paper succeeds, we do not grudge Sharp his independence. The new generation must take its own line. It is useless for the older generation 'to cut up rough'. We shall watch the *New Statesman* cutting itself loose from us as we watched the London School of Economics going its own way – with placid content.

The gloom of the war deepens. Both sides seem to be hardening; the greater the losses, the more determined are each set of belligerents to get some sort of equivalent gain out of it. This is certainly the state of mind of the English governing class, and it looks as if it were so in Germany. If the price of food goes up and all the belligerents find themselves on diminishing rations, the mass of the people may revolt. At present the rebels, in England, are more unpopular than they were at the beginning of the war. The change might be sudden but at present there is no sign of it.

Beatrice does not mention the death, in November, of her relative-in-law Charles Booth, with whom she had once been closely associated in social research.

17 November. Margate
The last days at Margate alone, feeling none too well to begin London life again next Saturday. These last days have been saddened by hearing that our dear sister Mary is again to be operated on for cancer of the breast. She came here out of kindness to me and left last week, alarmed by some symptoms, an alarm which has been justified by the surgeon's diagnosis. She has been very sweet.

Sometimes she has irritated me with her fussiness about my health, but I have been lost in wonder at her saintliness. There is no other word for her attitude towards life. She has continuously grown in grace with advancing old age. The mechanism of her mind is failing: she has lost her memory and her power of understanding many things and she has a strange restlessness, due, I suppose, to weakness. If it were not for Arthur and for the loss of her gracious influence at Longfords, I should wish her not to live much longer, especially if she has to face pain and weariness. 'I should like to see the end of the war and then I would gladly go,' she said to me in our last walk together. All the remaining sisters are saddened old women, except Rosy, still in middle life, but who is, poor woman, much troubled by her sick child. What has saddened us all is the war, and the terror of the world catastrophe.

2 December. Grosvenor Road

At work again. The neurasthenia has apparently cleared away, the month's dullness at Margate having sufficiently strengthened my nerves to make mental work a stimulus to bodily health. I find myself returning to the report on Vocational Organization with positive zest – a relief from the depression of the war, the only relief possible. One tries to remind oneself that peace will come and that the world will need all the thought of young and old to reconstruct the social and industrial order. . . .

I find my mind gradually crystalizing as to my own secret desires, though I attach no importance to these desires, as I have no knowledge. I want a peace in which none of the great belligerents gain anything whatsoever. I want all of them to feel that the war has been a hideous calamity without any compensating advantages – a gigantic and wicked folly from which no good can come. I should hate Germany to win or to gain the least of her ends. I should deplore the strengthening of British prestige and power, and I should be sorry to see Alsace returned to France. I should like the propertied classes of all the belligerents to be mulcted, and the working classes to suffer sufficiently to make them wisely revolutionary. The only indemnity should be paid to Belgium and the only state I would sweep away would be Turkey, and that, if possible, without giving anything to Russia. On this basis of universal loss and humiliation I would build the new League of Nations with the U.S.A. as one of the guarantors.

Rumania declared war on Austro-Hungary on 27 August 1916 but the Allies failed to provide any effective assistance and her army was defeated in the course of the autumn. In Salonica, the Anglo-French forces had encouraged the reformist and pro-Allied politician Eleutherios Venizelos (1864–1936) to form a provisional government in defiance of the pro-German King Constantine and to declare war on Germany and Bulgaria. But all these depressing events were overshadowed by the domestic political crisis at the beginning of December. The widespread anxiety about the direction of the war by Asquith and the generals resulted in the collapse of the government, but Asquith's resignation on 5 December was only brought about by backstairs intrigue. Lloyd George, who had taken over the War Office after Kitchener's death on 6 June, now became the leader of a new 'win-the-war' Coalition of 15 Conservatives, 12 Liberals and 6 Labour. Arthur Henderson became a member of the inner War Cabinet. Sir Edward Carson (1854–1935), the leader of the defiant Ulster Unionists in 1914, who was Attorney General in 1915, became First Lord of the Admiralty 1916–17, when he joined the War Cabinet.

7 December. [41 Grosvenor Road]
The turmoil of the political world of the last few days has been brought about by a series of disasters – the collapse of Rumania, the trouble in Greece, the cessation of the Somme offensive, the revival of the submarine menace, and most important of all the prospect of an actual shortage of food in the U.K. But this turmoil has been sedulously fostered by the Tory press, restive under the presumed pacific tendencies of Grey and the incapacity of the other Ministers to take energetic action. We have expressed our view of the cleavage of policy in an article in the coming issue of the *New Statesman*. Asquith and his lieutenants are mildly against any interference with anyone or anything: the Lloyd George–Curzon group want to mobilize labour whilst retaining for the ruling class property intact and the control of trade and industry. Lloyd George is indifferent rather than hostile to democracy. He wants to win the war; and as he finds more effective resistance to any interference from the capitalists than he does from the ranks of labour, he limits his demands to the enslavement of the working class.

A servile state, as Germany has proved recently, is an efficient instrument for waging war: an equalitarian democratic state might be more efficient, but it would entail upsetting the existing social order – at any rate for the period of the war. A Lloyd George–Curzon–Carson administration will not promote an equalitarian regime! The conclusion is obvious. As we personally belong to the ruling class, the outlook is not detrimental to the comfort and freedom of our lives. But it is ruinous to the cause that we have at heart: it means death and disease to millions of our fellow citizens, a balking among four-fifths of the population of all impulse towards a freer and more responsible life. It means the continual suppression by an imperialist government of Ireland and India and other subject races. And it means a continuance, to the bitter end, not only of the present war, but of faith in war as the universal solvent. It means the supremacy of all I think evil and the suppression of all I think good. Lloyd George would represent Mammon, though Heaven knows that Asquith and Co. do not represent God. God is unrepresented in the effective political world of today.

J.R. Clynes (1869–1949), leader of the Gasworkers' Union and M.P. for Plaistow since 1910, became Parliamentary Secretary to the Ministry of Food in 1917. William Tyson Wilson (1885–1921), M.P. for Westhoughton since 1906, was an official of the Amalgamated Society of Carpenters. Stephen Walsh (1859–1929), a miner and M.P. for Ince, became Parliamentary Secretary of the Ministry of National Service in 1917, and Secretary of State for War in 1924.

8 December. [41 Grosvenor Road]
. . . There had been a joint meeting of the Executive of the Labour Party and the Labour M.P.s to discuss Lloyd George's offer of places in the government – a meeting which came to no decision. Unfortunately the meeting decided to hear Lloyd George, and Henderson arranged that they should meet him immediately (12 o'clock) at the War Office. Thither they went, a private gathering not supposed to be reported. Sidney states that Lloyd George was at his worst, evasive in his statement of policy and cynical in his offer of places in the government. The pro-war Labour members drank in his sweet words; the pacifists maintained a stony silence, whilst Sidney and one or two of the waverers asked questions to which Lloyd George gave non-committal answers. All he definitely promised was a Ministry of Labour and a Food Controller – whilst he clearly intimated compulsory mobilization of labour. The joint meeting discussed these proposals at 8.30 at the House of Commons. The pacifists again laid low – Sidney thought they were playing for the disgracing of the pro-war Labour members by acceptance of Lloyd George's bait of office. The three office-holders in the Asquith administration, together with Barnes and Clynes, all of whom had been against joining Lloyd George, veered round. The miners'

270

members, true to their idiotic rule of never voting without instructions, expressed no opinion and took no part in the decision. After speeches against taking office, from Sidney, Tyson, Wilson and Walsh, the meeting decided by eighteen votes to twelve in favour of accepting office. There was no display of temper, the most fervent objectors voting silently against it, not really wishing to prevent it. From the narrow standpoint of the pacifist movement, as a sect, the inclusion of pro-war Labour members in the Lloyd George government may be a fortunate circumstance, a discredit to their warlike opinions. Sidney came back glad that he had done his best to prevent a decision disastrous to the Labour Party but inclined to be philosophical. He has long ceased to care about getting his own way and he is always interested, as a student, in watching these breakdowns in Labour democracy.

It is very difficult to analyse the state of mind of these men. The prospect of six offices with an aggregate income of some £15,000 a year, to be distributed among eighteen persons, is a big temptation. To enjoy an income of £4,000 a year, or even of £1,000, for a year or two, means to any trade union official personal independence for the rest of his life. But I don't believe that this pecuniary motive was dominant in the minds of the eighteen who voted for accepting office. A thorough beating of the Germans may have passed through their minds. But their main motive, at any rate the motive of which they are individually and collectively most conscious, is the illusion that the mere presence of labour men in the government, apart from anything they may do or prevent being done, is in itself a sign of democratic progress. It was this illusion that was responsible for the fanatical fervour with which the I.L.P. started twenty years ago to get labour representatives, whatever their personal character or capacity, on to representative authorities, central or local, from a parish council to the House of Commons. And naturally enough, each individual labour man thinks that he, at any rate, knows his own mind and will get his own way. Neither as individuals nor as a class do labour men realize that they are mere office-mongers when they serve with men of trained intelligence or even with experienced middle-class administrators.

It was this illusion that brought Clynes round; he argued that Labour must have some say in the terms of peace. Poor labour men, they will not get much say in the terms of industrial peace at home, leave alone those of the peace of the world!

VOLUME 34

The title of the Sharp editorial published on 9 December referred to 2 Kings 9:31, and the full quotation reads 'Had Zimri peace, who slew his master?' – the article in effect comparing Lloyd George's overthrow of the Asquith–Grey regime to the Israelite general's murder of his king. Sharp was an avid supporter of Asquith, and though he conceded that 'in the matter of sheer energy and initiative' Lloyd George was 'head and shoulders above everybody else in the upper political world – excepting possibly Mr Churchill', he doubted the Welshman's organizing ability and questioned his character. For a man lacking in 'high moral purpose' to become 'the spokesman and representative of England at one of the greatest moments in her history would be not only a profound humiliation but a disaster'. Beatrice included the missing and emptily rhetorical paragraphs. Two days later, on 11 December, Shaw (who consistently opposed Asquith and Grey) wrote to Beatrice complaining that Sharp had made 'a ghastly mess of this job. . . . I wish you would drop the paper as I did; it will end by disgracing you.'

9 December. [41 Grosvenor Road]
Here is the end of Sharp's article in the current issue of the *New Statesman*, 'Had Zimri Peace?' The printer refused to set it up unless the unfavourable criticism of Lloyd George was omitted. The first part of Sharp's article, taken with Sidney's, is sufficiently defiant to be unpleasant reading for the new dictator. I doubt whether Sharp will get his exemption extended, and the *New Statesman* may find itself, in company with the *Labour Leader* and the *Herald*, suppressed.

12 December. [41 Grosvenor Road]
The Lloyd George government, announced today, is a brilliant improvisation, reactionary in composition and undemocratic in form. For the first time (since Cromwell) we have a dictatorship by one, or possibly by three, men; for the first time we see called to high office distinguished experts not in Parliament; for the first time we behold Labour leaders in open alliance with Tory chieftains; for the first time a Cabinet has been created, not by a party political organization or by any combination of party organizations, nor by the will of the House of Commons, but by a powerful combination of newspaper proprietors. The House of Commons in fact almost disappears as the originator and controller of the Cabinet. . . .

There are some counterbalancing advantages in the fall of the Asquith government. It was an intensely Whig government. Asquith and his favourite colleagues hated state intervention, either in its regulative or its administrative aspect. This government will be boldly and even brutally interventionist – it will break all conventions and even control inconvenient vested interests. The British ruling class is really far more concerned for their prestige as the leading members of a ruling race than for their interests as property-owners within their own country. . . .

Germany and Austria made a peace offer on 12 December. The French had recovered their position at Verdun in October and November.

18 December. [41 Grosvenor Road]
The peace overtures of Germany find the country (except for the little sect of pacifists) curiously united in favour of carrying on the war without an attempt to negotiate. Difference of opinion shows itself only as to what sort of answer shall be given – how far the answer ought to be explanatory or a mere *non possumus*. Either our public men are perfect masters of bluff or the governing clique believe that the country can and will hold out, that there is no substantial danger of famine in food or material for munitions. The depression caused by Rumania's defeat has worn off, whilst all eyes are turned to the French success and the appearance of demoralization of the German army on the Western Front. The proposals believed to have been put forward by the Germans make it more than ever clear that the real issue of this war is Teuton v. Slav.

⮌ 1917 ⮎

Beatrice worked on and off for the next six years on the manuscript combining memoirs and diary extracts that was published in *My Apprenticeship* in 1926. From this point onwards, either she or a secretary made a fair typed copy of her handwritten diary.

3 January. [41 Grosvenor Road]
I have bought a small cheap typewriter and I am using up some of my spare hours in the afternoon in copying out and editing my

manuscript diaries so as to make a book of my life. It is no more tiring than endless reading, hardly more so than my desperate attempt at Longfords to knit soldiers' socks. And it is more interesting to me than either, and perhaps more useful. Why should I burden a literary executor with this task of selection? Also I shall add notes about persons and events whilst I have still memory and judgement. . . .

I have recovered my health except that I am no longer able to walk long distances. We lead a secluded life. We are both too indolent to see anyone who does not insist on seeing us. . . the dark background of the war, the consciousness of a sort of end of our life, disinclines us for society. We have our work, a few friends, a few strangers in search of information, my sisters and our deep and enduring comradeship to keep us occupied, as interested and happy as one can be in these times. . . .

On 17 February 1917 the Reconstruction Committee was enlarged with wide-ranging terms of reference; its working vice-chairman, E.S. Montagu, was told to co-ordinate official and informed thinking about post-war social problems. Vaughan Nash remained secretary of the new body. The other members included W.G.S. Adams (1874–1966), recently appointed Gladstone professor of politics at Oxford, who served as Lloyd George's private secretary until 1927; the Tory M.P. John Hills (1867–1938), who had supported Beatrice's Poor Law campaign and had been wounded in 1916; Thomas Jones (1870–1955), a Fabian and professor of economics who was a close friend of the Webbs, and had now become Lloyd George's go-between in discreet policy negotiations; Philip Kerr, later Marquess of Lothian (1882–1940), who was the founder and editor of the *Round Table*; B. Seebohm Rowntree, the social investigator; Lord Salisbury and Leslie Scott (1869–1950), a Conservative M.P. who later became Solicitor-General and a Lord Justice of Appeal. On the Labour side, apart from Beatrice Webb, there were J.R. Clynes and J.H. Thomas, while Arthur Greenwood (1880–1954), a Fabian school-teacher who went on to become a prominent Labour politician, served as one of the assistant secretaries. He was later joined by Marion Phillips, who had served the Poor Law Commission in a similar capacity. She went on to organize the women's sections of the Labour Party. Frank Goldstone (1870–1955), who afterwards became general secretary of the National Union of Teachers, also worked as an official of the Committee. On 25 February 1917, after Jones had lunched with the Webbs at Grosvenor Road, he noted in his diary that 'Mrs Webb is full of interest in Reconstruction and eager to begin devouring reports.'

19 February. [41 Grosvenor Road]
Enter the Reconstruction Committee. Routed out of my secret and

pleasurable occupation of typing and editing the 'book of my life' by an invitation to join the new Reconstruction Committee set up by the Prime Minister. I had successfully reduced my work on the Statutory Pensions Committee to a perfunctory attendance, having finished my self-appointed task, as a representative of the Labour Party, of getting labour representatives on all the local pension committees. I am not interested in the pensioning of soldiers and their dependants. Except for the relation of the treatment of disabled soldiers to a reorganized medical service, all the details of the work bored me. I don't want the ex-soldier to be treated better than the civilian population; and the function of the Statutory Committee seemed to be just this differentiation. Petting the ex-soldier on the cheap is the note of all its activities.

But this new task, the task of surveying and unravelling the whole tangle of governmental activities introduced by the war, of reconsidering the relation of the state to industry, of central to local government – relations disordered by war activities – all with a view to practical schemes of reform, is an attractive one. It means the sort of work that Sidney and I are skilled in, if only I have the strength to perform it. Moreover, the Reconstruction Committee is not made up, like the Statutory Committee, of retired officials, retired admirals and generals with a couple of countesses and a few philanthropists thrown in, but of young and vigorous persons with the Prime Minister as chairman and the youngest and ablest of the ex-Cabinet Ministers as vice-chairman. Out of the fifteen members there are three Fabians, as well as two Labour men, and one of the two assistant secretaries is a Fabian. . . . Altogether, if I keep my health and mind my manners, I shall find the work far more stimulating than that of the two government committees I have served on since the war. . . .

Lord Devonport (1856–1934), head of the grocery firm of Kearley and Tonge, was Food Controller 1916–17. R.E. Prothero (1851–1937), land agent for the Duke of Bedford, was Minister of Agriculture. John Hodges was Minister of Labour. H.A.L. Fisher, the historian, was at the Board of Education.

22 February. [41 Grosvenor Road]
Tom Jones, one of my fellow Fabians on the Committee and a member of the new secretariat of the War Cabinet, came to lunch here today to talk over the work of the Committee. He gave a most

amusing account of the improvisation of the Committee by the Prime Minister. The Reconstruction Committee of the Asquith government had consisted of Cabinet Ministers, with an ex-private secretary and an acting private secretary of Asquith's as joint secretaries. The present P.M. had asked one of the retiring Cabinet Ministers (Montagu) to undertake the vice-chairmanship and reorganize the Reconstruction Committee for the new government. Montagu proposed a central committee of three – himself with Vaughan Nash and Bonham Carter (the secretaries of the late Reconstruction Committee) as assistants. This Junta was to revise the reports of the litter of sub-committees and advise the War Cabinet as to their value. But this was too much for the Prime Minister. 'This is a mere shadow of Asquith,' he remarked to the young men of his secretariat. 'Bring me a list of persons with ideas.' Such a list being hastily furnished, he spent a spare ten minutes in considering it. He struck out some of the names – H.G. Wells and GBS, for instance – and added some others, among them Jack Hills and Seebohm Rowntree. Then he proceeded to pick out fourteen. He came to the Webbs and pondered: 'Yes, we will have one of the Webbs. . . .Mrs Webb I think. . . . Webb will be angry, Mrs Webb won't.' Then, apparently, without consulting Montagu or Vaughan Nash, he ordered a letter to be written to each of the selected ones inviting them, in the name of the War Cabinet, to serve on the new Reconstruction Committee. . . . It is the maddest bit of machinery, and if there be neither open revolt or silent obstruction in Whitehall, I shall be agreeably surprised. . . .

The swollen world of Whitehall is seething, conflicting elements warring against each other. The permanent officials, who in pre-war times lived demure and dignified lives, mildly excited here and there by inter-departmental jealousies, are now fighting desperately for the control of their departments, against invading 'interests' and interloping amateurs. Under the Lloyd George regimen, each department has been handed over to the 'interest' with which it is concerned. In that way, our little Welsh attorney thinks, you combine the least political opposition with the maximum technical knowledge.

The Insurance Commission . . . is controlled by the great industrial [insurance] companies; the Board of Trade is controlled by the shipowners; the Food Controller is a wholesale grocer; the Ministry of Munitions is largely managed by the representatives of the manufacturers of munitions, whilst a duke's land agent has been placed at the head of the Board of Agriculture. Finally, a trade union official is Minister of Labour and has been given, as the permanent head of his department, an ex-trade union official. The one shining example of this 'vested interest-cum-expert' government is the distinguished university professor, H.A.L. Fisher, now president of the Board of Education. And round about, and in and out, of this government by 'interested parties' there are streams of amateurs as private secretaries to ministers or grouped in advisory committees. . . . In this welter of official life it is doubtful how far our Committee will be permitted to function. The ferment may produce new ideas but the prospect is not encouraging.

The collapse of the Tsarist regime in February 1917 (Russian old-style date for March) was greeted with joy by progressives everywhere, and the advent of a people's government raised hopes of a negotiated and reasonable peace. Woodrow Wilson (1856–1924), the liberal professor of politics who had been elected President of the United States in 1916, had made several attempts to promote such a peace, but the deteriorating American relations with Germany were brought to breaking-point by the resumption of unrestricted submarine warfare at the beginning of February. On 2 April, Wilson made a speech promising to 'make the world safe for democracy' by a combination of self-determination and international law, and on 6 April the United States formally declared war on Germany.

18 March. [41 Grosvenor Road]
I was not able to attend the first meeting of the Reconstruction Committee, addressed by the Prime Minister. The summons came after we had left London for the week-end. I feel old and weak, and if I had not Sidney to inspire and help me I should think I had made a mistake in joining the Committee. The life I should enjoy, at present, would be a comfortable small country house, noiseless, except for birds and the rustling of water and wind, with my diaries to type. Sidney, meanwhile, might complete those endless volumes of historical material which are almost finished; and the two of us together might write the two books we want to bring out before we die – *What is Socialism?* and *Methods of Investigation.* But the *New Statesman* and this new Reconstruction Committee are going to keep us in London, with its noise and its dirt and its constant overstrain of nervous strength and consequent sleeplessness. What troubles me is the doubt whether my feelings of old age and

weariness are justified physiologically or whether I am giving way to an obsession. I am in my sixtieth year; if it were not for the war I have a right to retire. Until the war is over I suppose that Sidney and I ought to render national service. . . .

The Russian revolution and the entry of the U.S.A. into the war completely alter the situation. The Entente does now represent democracy at war with autocracy. If the Russian revolution succeeds democracy has won. With a democratic Russia it is inconceivable that there should not be a revolution in Germany and Austria, even if it were delayed until after peace.

Arthur McManus (1889–1927) was a Clydeside engineer and leader of the strike movement who later became general secretary of the Communist Party. Frederick Huth Jackson (1863–1921) was a banker and supporter of progressive causes whose daughter Konradin (1896–1964) married Arthur Hobhouse (1886–1965) in 1919. J.J. Mallon (1875–1961), who became Warden of Toynbee Hall 1919–54, was a Fabian and member of many official wartime committees. Clifford Sharp, temporarily replaced as editor of the *New Statesman* by J.C. Squire, maintained links with the Intelligence Service for some time after he returned to his editorial chair.

15 May. [41 Grosvenor Road]
. . . Tom Jones, who walked away with me from the last meeting of the Reconstruction Committee, told me that the Prime Minister was entirely absorbed in the war and could take little interest in anything else. Milner and the British Junker party are seriously alarmed at the revolutionary tendencies in the U.K. and in the Empire, heightened by the Russian revolution. They would gladly have peace with the Hohenzollerns if they could get good terms for Great Britain, France and Belgium, leaving the Slavs to stew in their own juice, as mixed for them by Germany. The U.S.A., on the other hand, is bent on destroying the Hohenzollerns and has no fear of revolution in European countries – rather welcomes it.

'Society' is in strange condition today. In spite of the deep cleavages of opinion on crucial issues – militarist autocracy v. revolutionary democracy, 'the knock-out blow' v. 'peace at any price', there is no cessation of social intercourse or even of co-operation between persons holding conflicting views. We, for instance, find ourselves one day planning reconstruction with Lord Salisbury, another day with the Glasgow deportee McManus. Cole meets Huth Jackson at dinner, Mallon seems to be the secret agent of the War Office and also the confidant of the organizers of the Leeds conference, who claim to be ready to bring about a revolution of the Russian type. The Fabian Society and the Fabian Research Department are peculiarly middle ground, the Society being predominantly pro-war but including among its members 'absolutist' C.O.s.

Among the curious episodes of this chaos of opinion is the use made of Clifford Sharp by a government to which he has been hostile. Called up from the editorship of the *New Statesman*, against our pleading, he was, within a few weeks, withdrawn from his training as an artillery officer and sent by the War Office to Stockholm — nominally as an independent journalist but really as an agent . . . to fathom Swedish opinion and to pick up information from foreign socialists. . . .

Logan Pearsall Smith (1865–1946), brother of Alys Russell (now separated from Bertrand Russell) and an old acquaintance of the Webbs', owned a charming house in Hampshire, near the Solent.

3 June. [Chilling]
A delightful holiday at Logan Smith's Elizabethan manor house set in cornfields, five minutes from the sea, with GBS as companion and our host as week-end guest. I was much exhausted with two months' hard work on the Reconstruction Committee, suffering again from dizziness and general incapacity, especially for physical exercise. I feel too old and frail for the work of the Committee, though it interests and amuses me and I do it with zest and even with unnecessary energy.

The Committee is not a satisfactory creation and I think it is bound to be superseded. The vice-chairman, Edwin Montagu, is a great disappointment. We had always heard that he was one of the best-informed and hardest-working of the Asquith crew. As acting chairman of our Committee he has been, during the first months, a dead failure. . . . He is wholly inexperienced in committee work and incapable of formulating a consistent procedure. Unfortunately, he has an incompetent staff. Vaughan Nash, the chief official, a gentle refined man of the 'domestic-secretary' type, is woollyheaded, easily frightened off any decisive step and, like most weak men in responsible positions, suspicious and secretive. He has accreted, as staff, a set of dreamy cultivated amateurs, preachers of ideals rather than practical administrators or trained secretarial officers. Montagu, in the few hours he gives to the Committee, sits smoking a huge cigar, with Vaughan Nash talking to him. Indeed, the whole of the staff seem to spend most of a very short working day talking together over cigarettes or tea, or listening to committees talking. No one seems to read the papers that pour into the office from government departments and from the litter of sub-committees of the late Reconstruction Committee. When the vice-chairman or the secretary submit memoranda it is quite evident that they have not taken the trouble to read even the office papers relating to the subject matter. . . .

What is needed for the task of reconstruction is a powerful brain as Minister of Reconstruction with a first-rate staff of civil servants and an advisory committee of picked amateurs to start ideas and represent the Ministers on sub-committees. The present sub-committees should be required to report or should be superseded by others. The essential requirement is one big brain at the top. Sidney and I think the best man available is Winston Churchill. . . .

Robert Smillie was the chairman of the conference called by the I.L.P. and the B.S.P. to welcome the Russian revolution, to demand a peace without annexations and indemnities, to resist wartime incursions on civil liberty, and to establish (on the Russian model) Councils of Workmen's and Soldiers' Deputies to rally popular support for these aims. It was a gathering swept by euphoria. The Petrograd Soviet had meanwhile invited the Labour Party, the I.L.P. and the B.S.P. to send representatives to Russia to discuss the war and the prospects of peace. All three parties accepted, and the government agreed to issue passports. The Labour Party nominated Henderson (who had already left on an official mission to Russia in the last week of May), G.H. Roberts and a minor union official named Carter. The I.L.P. chose MacDonald and Jowett, and the B.S.P. sent E.C. Fairchild. These delegates were followed on to the Aberdeen train by Emmeline Pankhurst, now a militant patriot, and 'Captain' Tupper, an equally jingo official of the Seamen's Union, who persuaded his members to refuse to sail with the anti-war delegates on board. Roberts and Carter, in turn, would not sail without the left-wingers, and nothing came of the proposed mission.

7 June. [41 Grosvenor Road]
The Leeds conference, welcomed by Massingham in the *Nation* as the 'birth of a new party', is significant as proving the existence of a powerful ferment in the labour movement which may either lead to new growth or to progressive disintegration. We fear that it is only

one among many signs that the labour movement after the war will break into internecine struggles which will eliminate it as a force in national politics. The thousand or more delegates to the Leeds conference were, so one of them declared, 'mentally drunk', and quite incapable of coherent thinking. They were swayed by emotions: an emotion towards peace and an emotion towards workers' control. It is an odd irony that the concrete example of 'workers' control' arising out of the Leeds conference was the seamen's refusal to permit MacDonald and Roberts to proceed to Petrograd to forward the propaganda for a negotiated peace! The very 'bourgeois' leaders on the platform talked grandiloquently about 'revolution'. To read the speeches one would think that they shared the thoughts and feelings of the Petrograd extremists. But who can imagine MacDonald or the Andersons or even the Snowdens leading a revolution of the Russian type — even if there existed the material for such a revolution in the British working class.

Sir Eric Geddes (1875–1937), a former executive of the North-Eastern Railway, had been in charge of military transportation in France. After the war he became Minister of Transport and the wielder of the 'Geddes Axe', which drastically cut spending on public services. Beatrice had been fidgety about the powerlessness of the Reconstruction Committee and had suggested action by like-minded members to overcome the passivity of E.S. Montagu. Though the main committee was disbanded, the specialist panels continued. One gave Beatrice the chance to revive the issue of Poor Law reform. Another, chaired by Haldane, reviewed the structure of the civil service.

18 July. [41 Grosvenor Road]
Exit the Reconstruction Committee. The last meeting of the autonomous Reconstruction Committee with Montagu in the chair. As I predicted, the machine was too rickety to survive. This morning's papers tell us that Montagu has been appointed Secretary for India; Winston Churchill Minister of Munitions, and Addison (who failed at the Munitions) Minister of Reconstruction. Carson's inclusion in the Cabinet and the translation of Geddes, one of the temporary bureaucrats, to be First Lord of the Admiralty, are the most sensational of the changes, but they do not affect my world of internal affairs. A Minister of Reconstruction clearly means that the Reconstruction Committee either ceases to exist or becomes a mere advisory committee or panel of advisors to the Minister of Reconstruction. The specially appointed sub-committees will, I

assume, continue to function, and I shall have enough to do on the Local Government Committee and the Machinery of Government Committee. . . . I feel too old and tired for the immense changes that lie in front of us. To Sidney they are exhilarating, they stimulate him – he is perpetually thinking of how to mould them in his own dear disinterested way. He refuses to dwell on the horrors of the war and he believes that through the war will come the changes he believes in.

In May, Arthur Henderson went to Petrograd on behalf of the War Cabinet. He returned convinced that the Labour Party should support the call for an international socialist conference in Stockholm, made by the neutral Scandinavian and Dutch parties and supported by the new Russian government led by the moderate socialist lawyer Alexander Kerensky (1881–1970). But the Labour Party was deeply divided. The pro-war leaders were unwilling to meet German and Austrian delegates, or do anything that might encourage demands for a negotiated peace. There were moderates, such as Henderson, who had come to fear the consequences if an exhausted Russia tried to continue fighting – the situation in Petrograd, Beatrice noted, was 'tragic disorder drifting into anarchy'. And there was strong support from the left and the pacifists for such a meeting. The trade unions were divided; opposition came from the Sailors' and Firemen's Union, because their members had suffered from U–boat warfare. The Labour Party convened a special conference on 10 August to discuss the Stockholm meeting. Before it met, however, a serious rift had developed between Lloyd George and Henderson. The Premier had at first seemed to encourage a Labour decision to go to Stockholm but under pressure from the recalcitrants in his Cabinet and from the French government, Lloyd George declined to say whether he would issue the necessary passports. When the Labour conference voted three to one to participate in the Stockholm meeting, Lloyd George denounced it as 'a fraternizing conference with the enemy'. This rallied support for his policy when the Labour conference was recalled on 21 August: the miners reversed their vote, leaving only a narrow majority in favour of Stockholm. Lloyd George then withheld the passports. Henderson had already resigned on 11 August. 'We none of us realized the enormous importance of Henderson's ejection from the Cabinet,' Beatrice wrote in May 1918. 'He came out of the Cabinet with a veritable hatred of Lloyd George, who insulted him at their last interview immediately after the Labour conference. . . . From that day Henderson determined to create an independent political party, capable of becoming His Majesty's Government, and he turned to Sidney to help him.'

5 August. [41 Grosvenor Road]
Sidney has been unusually busy with the Labour Party, owing to the crisis over the Stockholm meeting of the International, and he

spent yesterday drafting the resolutions for the Labour Party conference on the 10th and the Allied Conference on the 28th and 29th. Whether the Labour Party will accept his draft we doubt: it is an anti-German but not a British imperialist peace that he suggests – couched in the phraseology of international socialism. No one knows whether the British government desires the Stockholm conference or not. We believe that the German government does and that the French and Italian governments are against it. The pacifist M.P.s. believe that it will happen, we think it will not happen. But if it does take place, we two go to Stockholm – if a British delegation representing all parties is decided on by the Labour Party Executive and is permitted by the British government and the Seamen's Union. The Labour Party conference will show us what are the sentiments of the world of labour after three years' war.

12 August. [41 Grosvenor Road]
The Labour Party conference surprised itself, the Labour Party Executive and the political world, by deciding by a three to one majority in favour of going to Stockholm. This decision, which depended on the vote of the miners and the railwaymen, given *en bloc* after hearing Henderson's speech, has led to a Cabinet crisis. Henderson has been dismissed by the Prime Minister; not only dismissed, but dismissed with a public charge of having deceived the War Cabinet and misled his own party. But all the evidence, documentary and circumstantial, which is before us points to the fact that it is the Prime Minister and War Cabinet who have been caught out in an unsuccessful gamble. All published documents prove that Henderson, since his return from Petrograd via Stockholm, has been consistently in favour of the British Labour Party being represented at the Stockholm International conference: all published documents show that he was left a free hand by the War Cabinet to recommend this course to the Labour Party. And so far as his colleagues on the Labour Party Executive know, he has been equally straight in his private utterances. His counsel and his votes in committee have all been in strict accordance with his public words. Moreover, all the Labour Ministers (all of whom were against going to Stockholm) *knew that he was privately advising the Labour Party to go to Stockholm.* Now Lloyd George declares that Henderson, in spite of his public utterances, assured the War

Cabinet that he was going to recommend the Labour Party conference not to send delegates to Stockholm. How he could take this course, even if he agreed to do so, it is difficult to understand since he was party to the resolution of the Executive in favour of Stockholm and as secretary of the party he was obliged to carry it out or to resign his office.

The plain truth is that the War Cabinet, on the information given them by their tame Labour men, believed that the Labour conference would either negative the Stockholm delegation or would agree to it by so small a vote that it would be easy for the Cabinet to arrange with the French government to veto it or with the seamen to make it impossible. Henderson himself thought that he would be defeated and that Stockholm would be rejected. He signified as much to Sidney on Thursday, and he may have said as much to one or other of his Cabinet colleagues. The War Cabinet counted on this rejection: they wanted to appear ready to leave Labour freedom to decide while secretly intending to stop any international gathering. It was only another gamble made safer by duplicity – a way of behaving for which the Prime Minister has become notorious. . . .

22 August. [41 Grosvenor Road]
The net result of the episode is that Henderson emerges as the one and only leader to the exclusion of the Labour Ministers on the one hand, and, on the other, of MacDonald and the pacifists. But the movement itself shows signs of serious disintegration. Henderson's dismissal and the refusal of passports after the big majority of the first conference is a direct challenge to organized labour: the acquiescence of the Labour Ministers in this high-handed act and the refusal of the second conference to condemn their acquiescence places organized labour in a humiliating and servile position. The trade union movement, with its careless drift first in one direction then in another, looks to the outsider like armies of children led by servants – with groups of heady rebels mouthing phrases the meaning of which they cannot explain. It is not an inspiring spectacle.

The meeting of Allied socialists voted in favour of Stockholm but failed to agree on a statement of war aims. When the Stockholm movement collapsed, the possibilities of a democratic peace and a democratic Russia collapsed with it.

284

Albert Thomas (1878–1932), one of the leading French socialists, was currently Minister of Munitions. Pierre Renaudel (1871–1934) was on the right of the French socialist movement: he edited the party newspaper *L'Humanité*.

1 September. [41 Grosvenor Road]

The Inter-Allied Socialist conference was a fiasco. The French delegation was made up of equal numbers of the 'majority pro-war' and 'minority stop-the-war' parties. The majority, led by Thomas and Renaudel, had come to obstruct and prevent a pro-Stockholm decision, and they used every device of delay and denial they could invent. The Russian delegates were tiresome and childish in their insistence on their own importance and their long-winded revolutionary pedantry; the Italians were 'impossibilist', the Belgians were hostile in a dignified and eloquent manner; the Greeks were represented by an absurd and fussy little English spinster; the Portuguese, thanks to the fact that they could speak neither French nor English, were silent. The British, made up of four mutually contemptuous sections, all alike contemptuous of the foreigners, were well-behaved but divided in opinion. The foreigners wrangled for two days with each other and the conference finally broke up into two separate and informal meetings – the British and French majority parties and the Belgian delegation at the Waldorf Hotel, and the British and French minorities and the Russian and Italian delegations at the Fabian Hall. From these meetings will issue, I assume, separate reports. One wonders what Stockholm would have been like! . . .

Leonard Courtney maintained his links with his native Cornwall all his life. Hadspen House, near Castle Cary in Somerset, was the Hobhouse family home. At the end of 1916 Stephen Hobhouse had been sentenced to six months' hard labour in solitary confinement at Wormwood Scrubs prison. In April 1917 he was sentenced to another two years' hard labour at Exeter prison after a second court martial. In protest Margaret Hobhouse wrote *I Appeal Unto Caesar* in July 1917, in which she put the case of the conscientious objector. It sold 20,000 copies and Stephen Hobhouse was released in December 1917.

22 September. [41 Grosvenor Road]

A fortnight with the Courtneys at Bude and a week-end with the Hobhouses at Hadspen has proved the most restful holiday we have had for years. The sisters, as they grow old, are more than ever dependent on each other's affection, and the remaining brothers-in-law are more completely included in the strong family feeling.

Dear old Leonard, the patriarch of the family and acknowledged as its central figure by the second and third generation, is a marvellous old man, striding over cliffs and downs, scrambling over walls and through hedges in search of camps and tumuli, twelve or fifteen miles a day at a rate of four miles an hour. He keeps his interest keen in the war and foreign affairs generally; all home questions except proportional representation he is indifferent to. But in spite of his anti-war bias he remains cheerful, serenely contemptuous of his country's leaders and hopeful that a 'bad peace' will bring the British people to its senses. Kate remains morbidly obsessed with her country's wrongdoing and aggressively disputatious in her reiteration of the pacifist ethical stereos. She is a dear kind honest soul, but her sentimentality on all issues is a veritable vice. Her servants cheat and oppress her, and if she governed a state she would be defied by her subjects and cheated and oppressed by all other states. All sentimentalists or seemingly sentimentalists are good, all stern persons are bad. Anyone can take her in if only they profess the right sentiments. However, her own fundamental kindness, generosity and truth radiate and bring warmth and light wherever these qualities meet with the faintest response from other beings. . . .

Margaret Hobhouse is elated over the success of her little book on the woes of the conscientious objectors, and has thoroughly enjoyed pushing it. The war activity of her four sons (three in the army and one in prison for refusing service) has given her a public interest. She retains the qualities she had as a girl: high spirits, restless energy with a background of cynical melancholy. I doubt whether the admirable Henry has had the remotest influence on her; her quixotic son Stephen has had considerable influence on her, though she is in perpetual revolt against his uncompromising virtue. . . .

One of the amusements of life is watching the 'careering' of the young men who have grown up under the shadow of the Fabian Society and some of whom have come under our direct personal influence for years together. . . .

Clifford Sharp has developed in the last few years into a considerable personage. He is the son of a solicitor – comes of good professional stock: he has not climbed out of his class nor does he show the slightest desire to do so. He married a charming little person [Rosamund Bland], a fellow Fabian, without money

286

or influence, but with literary tastes and housewifely talents. To this day they do without a servant. He loitered through the university course and never took a degree, spending his time in reading literature and discussing socialism. When I first met him, he struck me as a singularly lethargic, awkward-mannered youth, but able and responsible in his opinions, and with the power of accurate yet literary language. When we started the little monthly *The Crusade* in connection with the National Committee, Sharp became editor . . . and carried forward the propaganda whilst we were abroad. When, on our return, we decided to start a weekly, Sharp slipped into the editorship. He has made a notable success and shown a fine steadfastness and good judgement in the conduct of this journalistic adventure. He has remained a bureaucratic collectivist: he is a conventional patriot, holding the National Guildsmen and C.O.s in contempt, conservative in his heart and instincts, cold and reasonable in his methods of approach and disinterested and public-spirited in the main objects of his life. He has not a sympathetic or attractive personality, he has little emotional imagination, he is quite oddly ungracious in his manner. . . . But he gives you confidence, you feel him to be absolutely trustworthy as a colleague. It was a blow to us when he was called up and became a cadet artillery man. . . . Meanwhile, J.C. Squire is carrying on the *New Statesman* successfully in Sharp's absence.

[*Beatrice added the following note in May 1918.* A notable society dame is reported to have exclaimed, 'Jack Collins Squire will be the most distinguished literary man of the twentieth century.' She was referring to him as poet and parodist. I am blind to poetry, a great grief to me. I positively dislike the form of the verse – to me it merely darkens understanding: I long to see the thought translated into prose, musical prose, but unmistakably prose. But I realize the distinction of some of J.C.S.'s poems, the melancholy mysticism of his philosophy, the rare beauty of some of his word pictures of nature. His more popular gift is the grace and ease with which he uses the rapier of parody. . . . As temporary editor in Sharp's absence, J.C.S. has tried loyally to keep true to the Sharp tradition, but the paper has almost inevitably become more literary in content, much to E.D. Simon's disgust, who has even threatened to withdraw his financial support if this dilution of an essentially political economic paper with the inferior element of pure literature is not effectually checked! The plain truth is that J.C.S., though a good collectivist because he loathes the motive of profit-making and is emotionally on the side of all 'underdogs', is not interested in political democracy or in administrative science. He hates the destruction of anything which has charm or fine tradition; he is in fact a conservative of all that is distinguished because it is old: old faiths, old customs, old universities, old houses and, last but not least, old books. He is a picturesque figure, with his warm Italian colouring, his slight well-knit and active form, his low but broad forehead set in masses of curly dark hair. He pretends to be a bohemian, he imbibes alcohol and tobacco, defiantly, when he wills to, making up his credit for physical fastidiousness by refusing to eat meat because of his horror of a butcher's shop. But he is a bourgeois born in his devotion to wife and children, his loyalty to friends, and his persistent industry. He has always been delightfully kind to the Webbs, but I fear he regards us as sadly limited in our interests and utilitarian in our tastes.]

3 October. [41 Grosvenor Road]
J.H. Thomas, the general secretary of the Railwaymen, dined here last night to talk over the policy to be pursued on the Local Government Committee of the Ministry of Reconstruction. He is one of the ablest of the trade union leaders and one of the most statesmanlike of their parliamentary representatives. He and Henderson are running the new party. It is interesting to note that, for the first time, he told Sidney that the responsible T.U. officials would like him to stand for Parliament, and Henderson repeated this request yesterday. But I gather that this desire is due, in the main, to their feeling that the Labour Party ought not to continue to make use of Sidney without giving him the opportunity of making use of the Labour Party! As Sidney has not the remotest wish to go into Parliament, and much prefers to remain in the background, I hardly think the request will be pressed. We should hate to be forced into political life in our old age. Sidney would not refuse if the Labour Party appealed to him – he is strong enough for it, but he personally feels he can be more use as a confidential counsellor than as a competitor for ostensible leadership. The position of parliamentary leadership is so little coveted! And in the Labour Party the . . . leaders are conscious of their incapacity for constructive thought. Sidney delights in it – it is his peculiar craft.

The big British offensive in Flanders had begun on 31 July and continued through the autumn with very heavy casualties. Rain and mud made the fighting conditions in Passchendaele appalling. The French army had been in a mutinous state since the spring. In Russia, the people had lost the wish to continue fighting and the collapse of the army enabled the Bolsheviks to carry out a second revolution in November (called the 'October Revolution' in the Russian calendar).

5 October. [41 Grosvenor Road]
Six successive air raids have wrecked the nerves of Londoners, with the result of a good deal of discreditable panic even among the well-to-do and the educated. The first two nights I felt myself under the sway of foolish fear. My feet were cold and my heart pattered its protest against physical danger. But the fear wore off, and by Monday night's raid, the nearest to us, I had recovered self-possession and read through the noise of the barrage with the help of an additional cigarette. . . .

I am perpetually asking myself how the war is affecting the mind of the Englishman? The sustained horror of it is depressing. Friends lose husbands and sons; promising men, on whose career one had counted, are swept away. One realizes that an indescribable torrent of misery and bestiality has overwhelmed millions of men on the battlefields and desolated cities and countrysides in the occupied districts. This war seems a universal bankruptcy of human intelligence and human goodwill. It adds to my depression that the problems involved in its settlement are wholly outside my grasp. I have come to no conclusions as to the fundamental cause of it, or as to the right end of it. But there is one consolation. The catastrophe is so huge and so discreditable to the governments of the world that it must lead to big changes. Never again will the manual workers accept the position of outcasts from all that makes for civilization; never again will they agree to a position of social servility; never again will they trust the representatives of the ruling class to dictate foreign and colonial policy without even deigning to discuss it. Their leaders will fall into all sorts of traps, but the great multitude behind will press forward, stumbling slowly over innumerable obstacles to a world based on social equality. . . .

Meanwhile revolutionary ideas, more especially of the syndicalist type, are being discredited by the collapse of Russia. The folly of the I.L.P. in acclaiming the Russian Soviet government of 'Workmen and Soldiers' representatives' as the 'new model' is becoming every day more obvious. The success of the Labour Party depends largely on how far its leaders can free themselves of the old assumptions of the capitalist state whilst keeping themselves free from the cant of anarchic rebellion against any form of deliberately ordered social action.

In November 1916 Lord Lansdowne had urged the Cabinet to make peace. A year later, on 29 November, after the Russian collapse, the *Daily Telegraph* published his proposals for a compromise peace. The Local Government Committee was one of the specialist bodies set up by the Reconstruction Committee, and Beatrice persuaded it to adopt some of her Poor Law proposals. The lobbying through of these Minority Report policies, she wrote in 1918, 'was, I think, my masterpiece'. But no more came of this report and a thoroughgoing reform of the Poor Law was not completed until after the election of the 1945 Labour Government.

11 December. [41 Grosvenor Road]
It is a year since the Lloyd George government came in and we seem further off than ever from the end of the war. The collapse of Russia, the invasion of Italy, the checkmate on the French front and the continued menace of the submarine have placed the Central Powers in the ascendant. There seems some justification for the Lansdowne cry: 'The war has lasted long enough, leave the Slav to his fate as a subjugated race, and make peace with the Mammon of Unrighteousness – he is ready to settle on terms of equality with the Anglo-Saxon with the Latin thrown in.' The U.S.A. answers that it is bent on beating German militarism, i.e. Germany. Wilson is an ideologue fighting a creed war, supremely conscious of America's mission to make the world Safe for Democracy – the very last thing that the German government will agree to. So the war must go on, a hideous background to the lives of the non-combatants and hell to the combatants. Sidney still retains his equanimity if not his optimism. I am still a melancholy agnostic.

There are two consolations. The insanity of war is being proved even to the most imperialist state. The approaching world famine is making the equalitarian state not only conceivable but probable. Inequality of circumstance is becoming an open and acknowledged scandal, the machinery for bringing about equality of distribution is being rapidly created. . . . Unless the mass of men and women fail utterly in steadfastness and intelligence, a greater measure of equality is almost bound to come. The state of things brought about by the war is, in fact, the greatest opportunity for a big step forward that the world has ever seen – indeed, a radical revolution is the only alternative to ruin. We are at the end of one civilization: the question is, are we at the beginning of another?

This autumn's work has been exhilarating. I have piloted the Minority Report proposals through the Local Government Committee and unless some unforeseen obstacle arises we shall get a unanimous report before Xmas. This is the crown of those three years' hard propaganda after the three years' hard grind on the Poor Law Commission. My success was mainly due to Lord George Hamilton's generous help, coupled with innumerable argumentative memoranda with which I plied both the members of the Committee and persons having influence with one or other of them. Also, I have learnt committee manners – an art in itself.

Meanwhile Sidney has become the intellectual leader of the Labour Party and he is also happy and contented with his work. The time is ripe for bold constructive leadership. It may be that this last decade of our working life is to prove the most operative.

Anyway, I have put my diaries away again, partly because I felt my attempt to compose 'The Book of my Life' was not successful, but mainly because there is sterner work to do, and work for which I am peculiarly fitted by long experience and training.

[*Beatrice added this additional note in May 1918.* I sent all my past diaries back to the bank. But as my work on the government committees slackened, I reverted to the idea of copying and editing these untidy MSS, taking my current diary first and working backwards. If, as we are told, the memory of old persons becomes progressively clearer for distant as compared to recent times, this is clearly the right procedure, so that when one has become a patriarch one will be writing notes about one's infancy! This May, during a delightful holiday in a cottage in Radnorshire, I have spent many happy hours at my typewriter copying and note-writing, whilst Sidney writes articles and reviews for the *New Statesman* or drafts documents for the Labour Party.]

291

∽ 1918 ∾

Maxim Litvinov (1876–1952), married to the English novelist Ivy Low (1889–1977), was the first Soviet plenipotentiary in Britain. From 1927 to 1939 he was Commissar of Foreign Affairs. Bill Playne (1870–1935) was the only child of Arthur and Mary Playne. He was married to Manuella Meinertzhagen.

10 January. [41 Grosvenor Road]
Five days of complete rest at Longfords. Arthur and Mary Playne and their companian Bichy Ross lead a sheltered and secluded life, in two or three rooms of their charming home in the midst of delightful gardens and grounds. Arthur is a lithe and happy old man, doing little or nothing of any importance, but occupying himself with mechanical magistrate's work and silent attendance on county council committees. . . . Mary is a benign old woman, somewhat restless in body and forgetful in mind – she knits endlessly and smokes at intervals. Bichy Ross, a buxom middle-aged woman, energetic and amazingly pleasant-tempered and dutiful, superintends the communal kitchen and working parties. Bill and his wife live 1½ miles away from the family home – we never see them, as he apparently dislikes Sidney and loathes me. The mill at the bottom of the garden grinds out cloth; there is no connection at all between the house of the leading capitalist and the hands who toil a few yards off: neither good feeling nor bad – mere indifference. . . .

The new year opens in gloom. Germany is stronger and more successful relatively to the Allies than she has ever been since the first rush to Paris. The governing class of Great Britain is no longer certain of ultimate victory – all the prophecies of failure of manpower or financial inability on the part of Germany have been falsified. The submarine peril is not lessening and confidence in the capacity of the U.S.A. to relieve the situation is, to say the least, not increasing. The mass of the population is irritated by the scarcity of food in the shops; the propertied class is getting more and more frightened at the coming taxation in redemption of war debt, and the always swelling demands of the manual workers for equality of circumstances. Both sides are preparing for class war.

Sidney and I have plenty of work before us – Sidney in the

292

Labour Party and I on government committees. The Labour Party is bounding forward into public notice and Henderson becomes every day more audacious in his programme. The party itself is tumultuous in its cross-currents. Its apparent unanimity arose from its being, for the first time, in open opposition to the government on all economic issues and insisting on independence in the statement of war aims. It is the 'new thing' round which all who are discontented with the old order forgather.

I feel old, very old and sometimes stale and tired. I no longer feel certain that the right will prevail. Sometimes I think that Germany will win the war and damn democracy. Now and again I regain the wider vision, but on the whole, gloom predominates. . . .

Litvinov, the Bolshevik 'ambassador', lunched with us on Wednesday; he is an anglicized Russian Jew of unprepossessing appearance, but with a certain honest sturdiness. He has lived nine years in London, married an English wife and earned a humble livelihood as clerk in a publisher's office. He is not a bad sort – a crude Marxist in his views, without experience of administration or knowledge of political or economic facts. He believes in government by the 'proletariat' and he does not believe the English race capable of it. He is pessimistic about the Russian revolution. Unless capitalism is overthrown in other countries the Russian revolution will not survive. If European militarism does not destroy it, economic pressure will. When we asked him what was the alternative to the success of the Bolshevik revolution, he replied: 'We shall become a colony of the German empire.'

W.P. Purdy (1872–1929) was an official of the Shipwrights' Union. Tom Shaw (1872–1938), secretary of the International Federation of Textile Workers and M.P. for Preston, became Minister of Labour in 1924. The new Labour Party constitution opened the organization to individual membership and established local branches.

21 January. Nottingham
Two days awaiting the Labour Party conference and chatting with the members of the Executive. There are about forty of the leading Labour men in this hotel. But this crowd is sharply divided into members of the Executive of the Labour Party and those who are primarily members of the National Administrative Committee of the I.L.P., each section having its own private sitting-room. There

293

is no overt hostility: they all greet each other with good-mannered intimacy, cloaking their differences in banter and chaff. There are some who belong to both camps. Sidney and I are on friendly terms with all, though we belong to the Labour Party group. We have had much talk with Henderson and Purdy, and other trade unionists who are on the Labour Party Executive. Henderson is nervous about the rejection of his new constitution by the block vote of the big unions. Cotton has a majority against, and the miners, who decide today, are still uncertain on which side they will cast their vote. The opposition of the cotton delegates is led by Tom Shaw, a pro-war socialist. He wants the Labour Party to remain a close preserve of the officials of the great unions, acting as a select group in the House of Commons, making terms with either of the principal parties and securing places for leading trade union officials either as Ministers or as permanent officials. He dislikes the advent of the ambitious middle-class politician or the intrusion of the missionary intellectual. This conservative section is, to some extent, backed up by the revolutionary syndicalist who is against 'parliamentarianism'. But Shaw's main strength lies in the jealous exclusiveness of the trade union bureaucracy. . . . The I.L.P. opposition to the new constitution is from an exactly contrary standpoint. The leaders of the I.L.P. want to construct a 'People's Party' in which the trade unions would take their place in the constituency organization, either as local bodies or as individuals. Henderson wants to make the best of both worlds. By the new constitution he aims at combining the mass vote and financial support of the big battalions incorporated in the national unions with the initiative and enthusiasm of the brainworking individual members of the local Labour parties. He is ambitious: he sees a chance of a Labour Party government, or a predominantly Labour government, with himself as Premier. I was amused to find that he looks forward to having Sidney either as secretary to the Labour Premier or to the Labour Cabinet.

Meanwhile the leaders of the labour movement are distinctly uneasy about the spirit of revolt among the rank and file, which openly proclaims its sympathy with the lurid doings in Petrograd. . . . The I.L.P. leaders do not know whether they want a revolutionary movement or not. . . . J.R. MacDonald tries hard to sit on the fence and bewilders his admirers by his agility in saving himself from tumbling over on one side or the other. He is playing a waiting game, helping neither side, doing nothing either to foment or to prevent trouble.

24 January. [Nottingham]
The usual good-humoured tone in the conference, in spite of contentious business and underlying unrest. . . . The new constitution was adjourned for one month for consideration by the affiliated bodies. It would have been rejected altogether if it had not been for a powerful speech by Henderson, appealing to the great working-class organizations not to miss becoming a great national party through petty jealousy of trades councils and outside middle-class members. . . .

31 January. [41 Grosvenor Road]
I was rung up this morning by Mrs Asquith's secretary. 'Mrs Asquith wanted to see Mrs Webb. Would Mrs Webb come to Cavendish Square or should Mrs Asquith go to Grosvenor Road?' I replied that I should be most happy to see Mrs Asquith here. So the little lady appeared, after an interval of twelve years or more since we last met. She greeted me effusively. 'You are more beautiful than ever – let me come where I can look at you.' And then followed two hours of rapid and somewhat incoherent talk about 'Henry' and his political concerns, vivid and entertaining abuse of Lloyd George, Bonar Law, Arthur Balfour, and Winston Churchill – all the great ones who had deserted her husband. . . . Her object in coming was quite clearly to tout for the support of Sidney for a coalition between the Liberal leaders and the Labour Party. 'Would Mr Webb come and see my husband?' 'I am afraid Mr Henderson would not like that, Mrs Asquith,' I replied, in as pleasant a tone as I could muster. 'My husband is merely a friendly outside helper to Mr Henderson and the Labour members, and he would not like to interfere in an essentially parliamentary question.' 'Oh, Mr Henderson was lunching with us yesterday, hasn't he a swelled head,' she added, and proceeded to mimic Henderson's self-conscious entrance into her drawing-room. . . . 'I am glad Mr Henderson has been to see Mr Asquith. That makes me more certain that it would be undesirable for my husband to intervene.' And then we began to discuss the possibility of a Labour government, she maintaining that it was impossible because they had not the men, whilst I tried to explain that until they had a majority in the House of Commons

and had qualified men to take office, it was undesirable that the Labour Party should form a government or part of a government. . . . She ended by embracing me most affectionately. So we parted. She impressed me as she has always impressed me: a scatter-brained and somewhat vulgar but vital little woman acquainted with the mentality of great personages but wholly unversed in great affairs, and with the social creed of the commonplace plutocrat. . . . I think she left feeling that the Webbs were as usual obdurate and that nothing was to be gained by trying to deal with them. When I told Sidney that I had saved him from seeing Asquith he was decidedly content. The Liberal leaders have always taken us up when they are in opposition and have always dropped us when they are in office. The policy of permeation is played out and labour and socialism must either be in control or in whole-hearted opposition. . . .

Lord Howard de Walden (1880–1946) wrote operas and plays; his wife was called Margherita. Cynthia Asquith (1887–1960) was the daughter of Lady Elcho (now Lady Wemyss), and the wife of Asquith's son, Herbert. She wrote two volumes of autobiography and a biography of Countess Tolstoy. She wrote in her diary after this lunch party that Mrs Sidney Webb 'froze me with her grim talk about the "classes"'. Joseph Caillaux (1863–1944), a pre-war French Prime Minister, was one of several prominent Frenchmen recently indicted for defeatism and treason: he was sentenced to three years' imprisonment but later amnestied. Georges Clemenceau (1841–1929), known as 'the Tiger', was the war-winning Premier of France.

7 February. [41 Grosvenor Road]
This interview was followed up by another overture. A few days later I was again rung up, this time by Mrs Asquith herself. When would I lunch with her? She knew that Mr Webb would not come, but I had promised to. Would I lunch with her that very day? 'Certainly,' I replied, 'I shall be most happy to do so.' Without positive rudeness I could hardly refuse to go some time or other. There were two couples of fashionables when I arrived – the de Waldens and another (whose name I did not catch). Lady Howard de Walden had brought her hostess a gold chain bag with priceless jewels hanging from it – a birthday gift, I gathered. Mrs Asquith seemed to refuse it as too luxurious for wartime and unsuited to her puritanical simplicity. We were joined at lunch by 'Henry', Massingham and Cynthia Asquith. I was placed next to 'Henry'. He was elaborately polite and friendly to me and we talked Russia

and Caillaux and everything else except the Labour Party. He struck me as an old man whose keenness of intellect had been undermined by trivial intercourse and high living. He was clearly inclined to peace – he praised Caillaux – said he would come out top and might easily be the next Prime Minister. 'Clemenceau is a passing phase.' I have never liked Asquith personally, and all I could do was to respond to his cordiality by mere pleasantness. . . .

14 February. [41 Grosvenor Road]
Saw Sidney off to Paris with the rest of the Labour delegation. Sidney is very happy in his new role of adviser-in-chief to the Labour Party, and Henderson, Middleton and the trade union leaders quite clearly are grateful to him. His old enemy MacDonald is friendly in manner to him, and if he is not liked by the I.L.P., they have confidence in his essential friendliness. And he is too old to excite jealousy in the young men.

Will Thorne (1857–1946), a gasworker who was taught to read by Eleanor Marx, was one of the leaders of the New Unionism; he had been M.P. for Plaistow since 1906. John McGurk (1874–1944) was a Lancashire miner who sat on the Labour Party Executive. C.W. Bowerman, M.P. for Deptford, was currently secretary to the T.U.C.

19 February. [41 Grosvenor Road]
Sidney, back from Paris, reports that the unpunctuality and indecision of the French socialists in all arrangements was distracting. . . . But a fair measure of unanimity was reached, which it is to be hoped will be further defined and affirmed at the London conference. Henderson and MacDonald were the only operative members of the British delegation – both of them made admirable speeches. But not even MacDonald could talk French, and Henderson could not even understand it. Sidney had not only to act as one of the responsible delegates but also as interpreter and general courier to the whole party. Huysmans was invaluable. The three trade unionists – Thorne, McGurk and Bowerman – were 'cripples' and spent most of their time in eating and drinking, enjoying the luxurious plenty of Paris. The position of privilege, irrespective of capacity – a position occupied by many trade union officials – is becoming the most scandalous circumstance of the labour movement. It makes one despair of the Labour Party as an organ of government. These

men are not only incapable of doing the work themselves, they are not fit judges of other men's capacity. It is a mere lucky chance that they have Sidney at their disposal, and it is only his long service to labour and socialism that makes them trust him sufficiently to enable him to do their work. The cleavage between the somewhat neurotic intellectuals of the I.L.P. and the trade union leaders is becoming more marked.

Leo Kamenev (1883–1936), former exile in Paris and one of the leaders of the Bolshevik revolution in 1917, was executed as a Trotskyist during the great purges of 1936–37. Leon Trotsky (1879–1940), the War Commissar, was the most brilliant of the colleagues of V.I. Lenin (1870–1924), but was driven into exile and later murdered. After prolonged negotiations, the Bolsheviks signed a Treaty with the Germans at Brest-Litovsk on 3 March, in which the Russians had to give way to their territorial claims.

27 February. [41 Grosvenor Road]
Litvinov brought to see us yesterday evening Kamenev, who with another comrade has come to enlighten the Western democracies on Bolshevik foreign and home policy. These two have been accredited as 'ambassadors' to the French and Swiss people respectively. Litvinov, who a month ago was feeling himself a great personage, is now quivering with mortified racial and personal vanity. He has not only been ignored by the British government, but he has been referred to contemptuously in the House of Commons as a man of many aliases and even as an undesirable, if not criminal, alien. The 'ambassadors' to France and Switzerland, when they landed at Aberdeen, were searched and had all their belongings, including a cheque for £5,000 and their 'diplomatic valise' taken from them and sent to Scotland Yard to be examined – they being instructed to call there on their arrival in London. Our Russian comrade threatened us with reprisals on the English in Petrograd. Litvinov said that he had, some days ago, wired to Trotsky that he would prefer to return to Russia, as his position was humiliating – and that he had only delayed his departure in order to help the Bolshevik emissaries to bring their case before the democracies of England and France. . . .
I asked them whether the Bolshevik government wished us to accept the terms of their peace with Germany as a settled fact. They both replied that we should be compelled to do so because we could not beat Germany. They did not seem to care for the lost provinces

– nor did the Russian proletariat, they said. All they wanted was to be let alone to complete the social transformation they had begun. 'We have given the factories to the workers and the land to the peasants. Was that not a sufficiently glorious achievement to make up for all their other failures?' I asked whether the Germans might not establish themselves in Petrograd and disestablish the revolutionary government. 'Take a city with three million starving inhabitants mostly with rifles?", they jeeringly replied. 'What good would that do them?'

We were courteous to them, but so far as we could make out, they did not want us to help them in any way but only to listen to their story. They were clearly conscious that the Bolsheviks were discredited and the only answer they had to make was threats on the British in Petrograd. 'I have means of letting Trotsky know and he will be without conventional scruples,' asserted Litvinov. It did not seem to occur to these simple-minded advocates of physical force that being without scruples was hardly a recommendation for supreme power in Russia, from the standpoint of the Allies. Poor fools! . . .

Lord Milner joined the War Cabinet in December 1916 and became Lloyd George's stalwart supporter. His views on peace were loosely considered pro-German.

1 March. [41 Grosvenor Road]
We dined yesterday with Haldane to meet one other guest, at his own request – the Prime Minister. Haldane asked me some weeks ago whether we would spend an evening alone with him and the P.M. to discuss the memorandum which I had circulated to the Machinery of Government Committee on the reorganization of government departments. It is needless to say that there was no such discussion, neither the P.M. nor our host showing any inclination for it.

Prime Ministers usually excite, in all but the most sophisticated minds, a measure of awe and instinctive deference. No such feeling is possible with Lloyd George. The low standard of intellect and conduct of the little Welsh conjurer is so obvious, and withal he is so pleasant and lively, that official deference and personal respect fades into an atmosphere of agreeable low company – but low company of a most stimulating kind, intimate camaraderie with a fellow adventurer. We talked about reconstruction, current politics, the late crisis, the personal traits of generals and Ministers, the Russian revolution, the terms of peace and the prospects of the next election. His object in meeting us was, I think, to find out whether any co-operation with the Labour Party was practicable – or at any rate how the land lay with regard to the Labour Party and the Asquithian Liberals. It was, in fact, a counter-thrust to the Asquith touting for coalition with the Labour Party. He could not approach Henderson, so he approached Sidney. Like many other persons who have known Henderson as a Cabinet Minister, he thinks that all the recent success of the Labour Party must be due to someone else – who else is there but Webb? 'I know Henderson,' he laughingly remarked. 'It is not Henderson who has made the *réclame* – all the distinction comes from' . . . and he waved his hand towards Sidney. He made distinct advances, pressed us repeatedly to come and dine with him and meet Milner, apparently to discuss the terms of peace. But I was not responsive. I don't want to go to Downing Street. In fact, I had told Haldane when I accepted the invitation to meet the P.M. that we would not go to 10 Downing Street. But we parted with cordiality.

The P.M. re-seen (we have not met him for three or four years) did not impress me favourably, in spite of his flattering friendliness. He is a blatant intriguer, and every word he says is of the nature of an offer 'to do a deal'! He neither likes nor dislikes you: you are a mere instrument, one among many, sometimes of value, sometimes not worth picking up. He bears no malice for past opposition, he has no gratitude for past services. He is no doubt genuinely patriotic and public-spirited, but all his ways are crooked and he is obsessed by the craving for power. His one serviceable gift is executive energy. He sees that things are done and not merely talked about. Unfortunately, he does not care whether or not they are thought about. He is the best of boon companions: witty, sympathetic, capable of superficial argument and quick retort, and brilliant in his observations on men and things.

What was clear from our talk is that the P.M. and Milner are thinking of a peace at the expense of Russia. He repeated with more frankness and emphasis what he has said publicly – that the Russians must lie in the bed made by the Bolsheviks, that neither France nor England would fight on to restore Courland and Lithuania, leave alone to restore the lost Poland. I interposed:

'Would Wilson and U.S.A. agree?' 'The U.S.A.', he almost snapped out, 'could not go on with the war if England and France refused to do so.'

I am not at all sure whether his desire to meet us and his desire that we should meet Milner is not connected with this possible sacrifice of Russia and her revolution. He wants to know how the Labour Party would take such a peace – whether it would be considered a betrayal of the cause of democracy. I gather that Haldane is also looking forward to a reconciliation between the Junkers of Germany and those of England over an agreed extension of both empires. With Russia to cut up, the map of the world is capable of all sorts of rearrangements which would give all the more powerful and ambitious belligerents an opportunity to expand their jurisdiction over the more helpless races – not only the German empire but the empires of Great Britain, of France, of Italy and of Japan. But would the one disinterested power, the U.S.A., agree to such a peace, and would the democracies of the powers look benignantly on the victory of the Junkers of all countries?

F.W. Hirst (1873–1953) was editor of the *Economist* 1907–16 and a governor of the L.S.E.

7 *March*. [41 Grosvenor Road]
On reflection, I think it is unfair to blame Milner and Haldane for wishing to make peace with the German Junkers. Haldane has always believed in the German governing class, or rather in the financial and industrial and professorial sections of it. He has always been an admirer of the Prussian state and of German mentality. Milner too, by birth, by training, and by temperament has an almost identical 'make-up' with that of the German imperialist. He admires and hates the same characteristics in men and states. It is the same reason that makes Parmoor a pacifist, and it is a rare joke to see our dear brother-in-law posing to himself and to the revolutionaries of the Labour movement as a believer in democratic liberties. All these public-spirited and highly gifted men honestly believe in German civilization. And obviously there are magnificent elements in the German state, and in many Germans it is these elements that are predominant. But neither Haldane nor Milner have the moral fastidiousness necessary to realize the sheer brutal

devilry of the German world purpose. With the P.M. it is different. By birth and training he is a pacifist rebel against authority, and he is totally unaware of and unsympathetic to the finer elements in the German character. If he desires peace at the expense of democracy to the glorification of German autocratic efficiency and militarism throughout the world, it is mere cynical ·opportunism.

What will the professional pacifists say to a cynical peace? All the pacifists who are pacifists on account of the injury to property by war (and every day the number of these increases – the Lansdownes, Parmoors, Hirsts and Dick Holts) will be made keener in their demand for peace by immediate negotiation with Germany, the consequent defeat of the Russian revolution adding an agreeable zest to the endeavour to come to terms. The Tolstoyans will blindly and fanatically continue their cry for peace at any price. But the men and women who are believers in democratic equality between man and man and race and race will become more in favour of continuing the war. This is largely the state of mind of Huysmans, Henderson and ourselves. . . .

William Gillies (1885–1958) was for many years head of the international department of the Labour Party. Herbert Tracey (1884–1955) became its chief publicity officer. Marion Phillips, Beatrice wrote, had succeeded in 'wrenching the secretaryship of the Women's Labour League from Margaret Bondfield'. 'Handsome in a coarse and sumptuous way, with plenty of brain of a common sort and a sharp satirical tongue,' Beatrice observed in May 1918, 'she is much disliked by the other leading women of the labour movement. . . . On the whole I rather like her. . . . Her worst defect is her insolently critical attitude towards all persons and institutions.' She was for years the head of the women's section of the Labour Party. The national agent in charge of the party's electoral arrangements 1908–19 was Arthur Peters, a former hairdresser. A number of Fabian intellectuals moved into the party offices to set up advisory committees for policy and propaganda. Beatrice had also completed the translation of the Fabian Research Department into the Labour Research Department, which moved into Victoria Street to provide the party with research support in return for a payment of £150 a year. R.H. Tawney (1880–1962) was a W.E.A. lecturer and strong Christian Socialist who had been invalided out of the war. He was to become one of the most influential Labour intellectuals and a distinguished history professor at the L.S.E. C. Delisle Burns (1879–1942), author and historian, was currently a civil servant in the Ministry of Reconstruction. Arnold Toynbee (1888–1975) was to become one of the best-known historians of his time.

20 March. [41 Grosvenor Road]
The Labour Party is the most ramshackle institution in its topmost storey. Henderson sits alone in the untidy office at 1 Victoria Street: no member of the Executive or of the Parliamentary Party ever comes near him except Sidney. J.R. MacDonald, the treasurer, supposed to be his fellow Executive officer, is conspicuous by his absence. Neither the pacifist nor the pro-war M.P.s trouble him with their advice or take counsel with him as to their own action. Snowden, the chairman of the I.L.P., the leading socialist organization within the Labour Party, never loses an opportunity of sneering at Henderson or denouncing the 'official Labour Party'. The fair-minded and gentle-natured Middleton, the assistant secretary, sits in another tiny room and supervises two seedy male clerks (ex-trade union workmen) and as many somewhat inferior female typists. There is the little dwarf-like Gillies – an honest, over-sensitive and obstinate-minded but well-informed little Glasgow Fabian – as intelligence officer, and a certain journalist, Tracey, a pleasant and, I think, competent young man, as publicity officer. Upstairs, superintending the women's section, sits the redoubtable Marion Phillips – hardly an element of solidarity in an office. There are some one hundred parliamentary agents, most of whom I saw yesterday at a Fabian Research Department reception – old men, unkempt men, half-educated men, an inferior brand of the trade union branch official – with no alertness and little organizing capacity. The chief parliamentary agent, Peters, is of the Sunday School type, who trudges through his work with a sort of mechanical persistence, carrying out Henderson's orders. And added to this decrepit staff is the circle of rebellious spirits and idealist intellectuals who have gathered round G.D.H. Cole and ourselves – Tawney, J.J. Mallon, Delisle Burns, Arthur Greenwood, Arnold Toynbee and H.J. Gillespie. These young men have formed themselves into a sort of informal advisory committee, sometimes presided over by Sidney as Henderson's representative, sometimes left to their own devices. This morning I found them forgathered in the Fabian Common Room engaged in constituting a series of advisory committees to the Labour Party on some half-dozen subjects, whilst two of them – Tawney and Arnold Toynbee – were drafting a leaflet against the intervention of Japan in Russia. Cole, in fact, regards himself as Sidney's successor, if not his supersessor, as chief intellectual adviser to Henderson. The I.L.P. leaders seem altogether

out of it. I suggested, when called in to advise as to the membership of the advisory committees, that J.R. MacDonald and W.C. Anderson should be asked to be chairman of the two principal committees. The suggestion was accepted, but without enthusiasm. Unless the two old parties have completely lost their cunning, it is difficult to imagine that such a crazy piece of machinery as the existing Labour Party will play a big part in the reconstruction of· the United Kingdom and the British Empire after the war. All one can say is that the very formation of such a party, and the gathering round it of distinguished intellectuals, represents a sort of subconscious determination of the politically conscious minority of the working class and its intellectual adherents, to get a radically different state of society after the war. Always, the old, old question repeats itself – is there sufficient public spirit and sufficient knowledge and reasoning power to make the change from the capitalist to the equalitarian state practicable? . . .

On 21 March the Germans launched a massive attack on the British Fifth Army south of Arras in the hope of forcing a decision before the flowing tide of fresh American troops could sweep them out of France. They broke through in many places, threatening to separate the British and French armies and roll the British away from the vital Channel ports. The desperate fighting continued until the end of April, when the Germans launched a final and unsuccessful offensive against the French.

31 March. [41 Grosvenor Road]
A week of miserable anxiety. We first realized the seriousness of the German onslaught last Sunday – a realization further intensified by Tom Jones, who came straight from the Cabinet to supper with us. Not one minute did I sleep that night, and even Sidney has been disturbed in his usual equanimity, though he does not let his anxiety have any influence on his output of work. The success of the Germans when all the authorities thought the Western Front secure is only another instance of their superiority in forethought, in technique and in concentration of purpose. What is the explanation of the paralysis of British brains which shows itself in the War Office, in the Admiralty, in Parliament, and in private enterprise?

The answer is a complicated one. The British governing class, whether aristocratic or bourgeois, has no abiding faith in the concentrated and disinterested intellectual toil involved in the scientific method. Science to them is a sort of intellectual adventure to be undertaken by a rare type of man. The adventure may or may not turn out worth while, but in any case it is silly to expect this adventurous spirit from ordinary men in the conduct of daily life. Indeed, applied to social, economic and political questions the scientific method is to be shunned as likely to lead to experiments dangerous to liberty and property and the existing order of society. Also, science means measurement; it means the objective testing of persons and policies, and this measurement and testing is against all good comradeship in common undertakings. For the Englishman of all classes – peer, shopkeeper and workman – is a kindly creature who hates the thought that anyone who is related to him, who belongs to his own set or class, or with whom he usually consorts, should be made uncomfortable or dispossessed of that to which he is accustomed, however inefficient he may be. The perpetual emphasis on rights as against obligations is part of this preference for the comfort of the individual over the welfare of the whole community. The Englishman, though he has a talent for impromptu organization – for the organization that introduces order or good manners into a meeting or a society – dislikes and suspects any more deliberation and self-control than is necessary for this imperfect purpose. Finally he is a protestant and delights in sectarianism, in little cliques of fellow thinkers who regard their thoughts as religious exercises. The Englishman hates the impersonality of science.

1 April. [41 Grosvenor Road]
I can see Sidney sitting down early last July to draft the memorandum on *War Aims*, and early in October to draft *Labour and the New Social Order* – exactly as he sits down morning after morning to draft memoranda, articles, reports and chapters of books, or corrects the MS of some humble author, quite oblivious of the fact that he was a man of destiny creating 'the most powerful organized political force in the U.K. excepting only the state.' [*New Republic*, 16 February 1918.]

   For assuredly this new and, I fear, wholly undeserved reputation of the Labour Party is based on little more than these two publications. He made the reputation of the Progressive Party of the L.C.C. by his ideas and intellectual propaganda. Is he going to do likewise for the Labour Party? The analogy is not comforting. The Progressive Party went to pieces after the leaders of the Progressives quarrelled with and denounced Sidney over the Edu-

305

cation Bill of 1902–03. Now he is an elderly man and the Labour Party cannot reckon to have him for more than a few years, even if the leaders are wise enough to continue to make use of him.

Paul Hobhouse (b. 1894), a captain in the Somerset Light Infantry, was the youngest son of Margaret Hobhouse. There were rumours that he might have been taken prisoner, but he was killed in the fighting near St Quentin on 21 March.

16 April. [41 Grosvenor Road]

A fortnight of gloom and anxiety. The absence of any counter-offensive, even in the pauses of the German advance, has made us all sceptical of any power to resist the German army. . . . One goes about the daily task in a sort of dream, exactly as if one had suffered some dreadful personal bereavement. And a great personal sorrow has come to our family. Paul Hobhouse, last seen to fall fighting desperately on the first day of the great battle in the first trench of the ill-fated 14th Division of the 5th Army, has not since been heard of. All sorts of rumours are flying around about as to the state of mind of our soldiers, and we none of us know what the country is thinking about it. The mass of people are probably as bewildered as one is oneself.

The Irish problem had rumbled on through the war. The government now put forward proposals which gave up the idea of a separate Ulster and proposed extending conscription to Ireland.

25 April. [41 Grosvenor Road]

We had the first of a series of meetings of Labour leaders at dinner last night to discuss some kind of common policy. The loneliness of Henderson in his tiny office, and his consciousness of isolation, led me to suggest that our house might be used as a meeting-place. He responded gladly, and at his request I asked him to meet the Andersons, J.H. Thomas, George Lansbury – the latter regarded as important as editor of the *Herald*. The meeting went off unexpectedly well, and they all agreed to meet here again at lunch on Monday. Sidney and I did little more than promote an exchange of views. The main question raised was what should the Labour Party do if the Lloyd George combination collapsed over Ireland or over the ill success of the war. Henderson put forward the view that if Asquith were asked to form a government and stated that he could not do so without the participation of the Labour Party, the leaders would be obliged to take office 'on terms'. Henderson declared that he would ask that the Liberal leaders accept the *War Aims* of the Labour Party and give a guarantee of good faith by offering a sufficient number of places to the Labour Party to be filled by the party itself. He intimated that leaders not in Parliament would have to be taken in — Webb and Lansbury, he suggested half-jocularly. Thomas supported him. Lansbury said he would support any government prepared to end the war, and would judge any offer from the Liberals exclusively from that standpoint. Sidney laid down quite other conditions — half the candidatures for the general election and the acceptance of the Reconstruction proposals. . . . The discussion was on a high level of ability and the temper was admirable.

Leonard Courtney died on 10 May. The Webbs took their holiday at a cottage in Radnorshire belonging to two of Beatrice's nieces in the Holt family — Elizabeth Russell (1875–1947) whose husband E.S. Russell, a Unitarian minister, had been killed in 1917; and Mary (1880–1955), who married J.H. Russell, a sheep farmer in Montana.

[?] *13 May. Bryan's Ground* [near Presteigne, Radnorshire]
Leonard Courtney passed away after a short illness, the day after we left London for our Whitsun holiday. I saw him on Wednesday, weak from one of his recurring attacks of internal haemorrhage, but still vigorous in intellect and emotion. He denounced Wilson, his eyes flashing under his heavy eyebrows as he beat the bed with his closed fist. He had just dictated a letter and sent Kate off with it to *The Times* (*The Times* refused it and it appeared next day in the *Manchester Guardian*) — the plea of a noble old man for readiness to negotiate with the Germans when they were so minded.

He and Kate had become not only the central figures of two families to the third generation, but also of a distinguished group of Liberal journalists and publicists. He was one of those rare natures that grow in breadth of vision and warmth of sympathy with old age. He was a noble old man. When I first remember him, as Kate's fiancé, he was distinctly unpleasing, at any rate to his lively sister-in-law. He wore his personal distinction badly. Our family life did not suit him. He and Father disliked each other. Father thought him an intolerable doctrinaire prig with little knowledge of human nature or of practical affairs; he thought Father a somewhat loose commercial man of limited culture and reactionary views. As years went on Father became proud of his son-in-law, and when Leonard refused to support Gladstonian Home Rule in 1886, Father's respect became admiration. . . .

Leonard combined moral genius and a good mechanical intellect with considerable artistic faculties. . . . What he lacked was any distinction in the quality of his intellect. He had no subtlety, no originality – he thought in the grooves made by other minds and by minds of the plainer sort. . . . He was, to all who disagreed with him, an impossible person to talk to except on the trivialities of daily life. Unless you agreed, he refused to discuss, for the sufficient reason that he had not the mental equipment to carry on an argument on any other premises but his own. Sidney and I, for instance, in spite of our affection and admiration for him, never succeeded in doing more than 'make conversation' – never once did we find ourselves in communion with him on an intellectual issue, even where our views did not clash. . . . Kate has lost her other and most loved self, but her devotion to his memory and her amazing kindliness will cover her loneliness, and her old age will, I think, be a happy one.

The militant campaign for women's suffrage had been called off during the war, but in June 1918 the vote was given to women over thirty, and the same Act established complete male suffrage. A small number of seats in the House of Commons were still reserved for M.P.s elected by graduates of Oxford, Cambridge, London and provincial universities: Sidney was to be nominated for the University of London seat. A further Act passed in November made women eligible to stand for Parliament.

16 June. [41 Grosvenor Road]
I note with interest that not once in this diary have I mentioned the outstanding event of the year's home affairs – the passage of the Representation of the People Act, extending the suffrage from eight to about eighteen millions and admitting women to citizenship. This revolution has been on my consciousness the whole time, but it has not risen into expression because I have been a mere spectator. It is only the events that are vital to one's own life that get into so personal a record. I have always assumed political democracy as a necessary part of the machinery of government; I have never exerted myself to get it. It has no glamour for me. I have been, for

instance, wholly indifferent to my own political disfranchisement. But I do not ignore the fact that the coming of the Labour Party as a political force has been largely occasioned by this year's extension of the franchise.

Almost accidentally, this great revolution has forced Sidney to enter the political arena for a few months, as part of the stage army of the Labour Party. Sidney from the first decided that the Labour Party must contest the university seats as part of its pretensions to be a national party, and if these seats were to be contested, he had to stand for London. We are spending money and time on the election — more as a great propagandist attack on the conscience and intelligence of 10,000 graduates than as a serious attempt to win a seat. Sidney does not want to be in Parliament unless there proves to be a real 'change of heart', and a change of heart common to brainworkers as well as manual workers. If there is not this revolution in public purpose we are better outside, trying to make it by writing and speaking and researching. . . . My daily work is divided into three parts: government committees, Labour advisory committees and London University election. About once a week we have some Labour men to meet Henderson. We had all the chairmen of the Advisory Committees — MacDonald, Anderson, Jowett, Tawney and J.A. Hobson to meet Henderson, and all the secretaries came in afterwards. I get on very well with MacDonald and he and I generally find ourselves in agreement against the wilder spirits.

E.S. Talbot (1844–1934) had been Bishop of Southwark 1905–11 and of Winchester 1911–23. He was a High Churchman sympathetic to the Webbs' social policies. His wife was the Hon. Lavinia Lyttelton. William Temple (1881–1944) was rector of St. James's, Piccadilly, in 1918 when he joined the Labour Party. He later became Archbishop of Canterbury. His wife was Frances Anson.

23 June. [41 Grosvenor Road]
. . . Our old friends the Talbots and our new friends the William Temples dined here last night to meet Henderson and discuss the future of the Church. William Temple was a Fabian for many years and he has recently joined the Labour Party. He is the leader of the 'Life and Liberty' movement, a movement for the self-determination of the Anglican Church, even at the cost of disestablishment. . . . Henderson was, of course, for disestablishment but

inclined to be generous about endowments. . . . He sat and listened to Temple, Talbot and ourselves: he shows to much better advantage with outsiders than with his labour colleagues, with whom he lacks graciousness and is apt to be sullen and rude. . . . Temple is a vigorous democratic priest. He is too fat and too exuberant a talker for an ideal Man of God – his phrases run away with him but he is sincere, courageous and disinterested.

J.R. Clynes became Food Controller in June on the resignation of Lord Rhondda.

30 June. [41 Grosvenor Road]
The Labour conference has come and gone in the full limelight. It must be an odd sensation for the wire-pullers of the two old parties to watch this young rival take the platform with self-assurance, not only in social reconstruction, but also in world politics. It is the only national non-governmental gathering the incidents of which are flashed to the Foreign Offices of the world. The dramatic appearance of Kerensky – the noisy protest of the little knot of British Bolsheviks, the overwhelming reception accorded to him, the great oration in Russian watched and heard in dead silence, the kiss on the cheek of the blushing Henderson – the whole scene a magnificent staging of the new people's party claiming its right to control international affairs. Instead of the split in the Labour Party prophesied by the Tory press, the leaders stood solidly together, and whilst Henderson carried the breaking of the party truce, Clynes, the Minister, was elected at the head of the poll for the Executive. It is not logical but it is war on the old social order. The three great successes of the conference were Henderson's management of the Kerensky episode, which really amounted to genius, the Clynes speech justifying acceptance of office, and, I venture to add, the Webb programme. . . .

I watched and talked to Kerensky in the ante-chamber whilst he was awaiting the decision of the conference. He is singularly like Massingham in appearance and expression, only that he has the flash of genius in eye and gesture. He is a great orator – that fact shone through the strange but musical language which not a single man among the delegates understood. But he seems, as one watches his expression, to lack executive will and intellectual stability – he gave you no confidence that he knew what he wanted done. One can

310

see him dominating masses of Russians by the nervous magnetism of his personality and then, when they crowd behind him, hesitating which way to lead them. He is a creature and a creator of impulse: is he not an originator and executor of a possible plan of campaign? He appealed passionately for help, but he gave no indication as to the character of the help he demanded. There was, at the end, a disappointing sense of vagueness and futility. . . .

The American novelist Upton Sinclair, who ran a reformist magazine under his own name, had published a letter from H.G. Wells attacking Lenin as a power-hungry 'little beast' and adding: 'He's just a Russian Sidney Webb, a rotten little incessant egotistical intriguer.' Wells had published an emotional religious tract in 1917.

12 July. [41 Grosvenor Road]
Here is H.G. Wells's latest attempt to injure us which is, I assume at his request, being distributed broadcast among journalists and our common acquaintances. It interests me as a strange display of his morbid obsession about us. Donald of the *Daily Chronicle* told me that he spent a whole morning abusing us. From his *God the Invisible King* I thought he had cured himself of these disreputable feelings, but it seems not. The abuse of Sidney is not clever and neither he nor I feel any anger at it.

Lloyd George announced in July that 305,000 American troops were now in France.

23 July. [41 Grosvenor Road]
The U.S.A. is today in the ascendant. Delegations of Americans, socialist, labour, university or directly governmental (they are all indirectly governmental – no anti's being allowed across the water) look us up in order to assure us in modest, but determined, tones that America means to continue the war until Germany, or rather Germany's lords, own themselves beaten and ready to accept the dictates of the triumphant democracy. . . . Frenchmen who come over here tell us that the Americans are now the rage in France – they have captured the French imagination by their clean mental and physical strength, the simple dogmatism of their faith and the largeness and lavishness of their preparations. . . .

Both Oliver Lodge and Eleanor Sidgwick were active members of the Society for Psychical Research. Richard Atkin (1867–1944) was a distinguished judge. The Committee of Women in Industry, which he chaired, had been set up to determine whether the government had honoured its pledge that women 'dilutees' would be paid men's wages when they did men's work. Beatrice concluded that the pledge had not been implemented, and when she failed to convince her colleagues she prepared a minority report which went on to consider the general case for equal pay. The Fabian Society published it as *The Wages of Men and Women – Should they be Equal?*

1 September. [41 Grosvenor Road]
A month's holiday at Presteigne with GBS and Maggie Hobhouse as successive visitors. Long walks over the hills enlivened by discussions with GBS: mornings spent typing the diary of 1912–16, with Sidney writing articles for the *New Statesman*, pamphlets for the Labour Party and his own election literature – a right happy time. Variety was added to our life by observing the spiritualistic obsession of our two nieces – Betty Russell, a war widow, and her unmarried sister, Molly Holt. These two are kindly, comely women, in the prime of life with one little boy of four years old to dote on, a score of acres to farm and many humble neighbours to be kind to. But with untrained and idle minds and Betty's man 'on the other side' as the occasion, they have fallen a natural prey to the professional medium. Voight Peters, recommended by Oliver Lodge and Mrs Sidgwick as the most trustworthy broker of the Spirit world, is an unsavoury mortal . . . a veritable 'Mr Sludge the Medium'. . . .
I attended one seance. We sat round a table with hands touching in the gloaming. With shiverings and contortions he came under 'direct control'. He spoke baby English interlarded with a few familiar French terms in a squeaky voice with eyes screwed up and fingers twirled and twisted. He was apparently set on converting me. But all the spirits who claimed to be present in my honour – Father, Mother and others of vague identity – failed to present characteristics which I could recognize. In fact, if they had deliberately tried to make themselves unrecognizable they could hardly have been more successful. . . . The unhappy spirit-monger became impatient and suggested that I was 'resisting' – 'there is too much dust around you through which the spirits cannot penetrate.' With signs of mental exhaustion he broke up the sitting. This man struck me as half dupe of his own hysteria, half deliberately fraudulent. . . . But he made a bad mistake when he described my mother as 'the most lovable of women'!

The day before I left Presteigne I had a telegram from the Prime Minister asking me, in no uncertain language, to be chairman of a committee on the relation of men's and women's wages. The subject did not attract me, but I was flattered and excited at being offered the chairmanship and forthwith wired a gracious acceptance. Great was my discountenance when the following day I received an apologetic telegram announcing that Mr Justice Atkin was to be chairman and that I had only been invited to be a common or garden member of yet another committee. It appears that an incompetent typist had repeated the message to the selected chairman to all the members of the committee, and that they each and all accepted the chairmanship. It remains to be added that we all accepted the position with dignified good humour.

Sir William Tyrell (1866–1947), a senior Foreign Office official, was at this time head of its political intelligence department, and a member of the Phillimore Committee set up to study the possibility of a League of Nations.

26 September. [41 Grosvenor Road]
. . . Kerensky dined with us the other night and is lunching with us on Wednesday to meet Sir William Tyrell. He has lost the nervous tension so noticeable in his appearance two months ago. He has an impressive personality, a broad and cultured outlook on men and affairs, a fine and fastidious political morality. Clearly he has neither experience nor knowledge of administration; the technical problems of democratic government do not interest him. But compared to the American or British trade unionists, he belongs to the aristocracy of intellect in an old civilization and regards, with dreamy philosophy, the social organization of the European continent in dissolution. He has not, and has never had, any sympathy with the 'dictatorship of the proletariat'. He is trying to engineer from his position as an *émigré*, a reconciliation of classes in Russia.

'Æ' was the pen-name of George William Russell (1867–1935), Irish poet and nationalist. He was much concerned about the possible extension of conscription to Ireland and the violent response it might evoke.

11 October. [41 Grosvenor Road]
Our own preoccupations have been broken into by the arrival of Æ and his colleagues to address a joint meeting of the Labour Party

313

Executive and the Parliamentary Committee of the Trades Union Congress. (Æ is staying with us.) Poet, artist, saint and propagandist, George Russell is a sensationally delightful person and many are those who glow about his personal charm. He bores Sidney; I enjoy his wonderful talk. He is vain but modest, somewhat too concerned with his own intervention and with the effect of his own personality in the troublous Irish world; yet fully, almost self-consciously, aware of the limitations in his mental life. He believes in the undifferentiated man, doing some simple individual job with dutiful care but with his heart in pleasant comely things, and developing, here and there, into the mystic and the saint. The less organization and government the better, and only just enough science to add intellectual curiosity in the processes of nature in the life of the agriculturist. He hates cities, railways, machinery, division of labour, rule, method and specialized science or logical reasoning. . . . After listening to one of his tirades I fired up: 'So far as Anglo-Saxons are concerned, you are stabbing democracy in the back by your perpetual derision of parliamentary institutions and all that these involved. You are not only mischievous, you are grossly ignorant.' He laughed at my railing and reverted to Ireland. . . .

VOLUME 35

On 4 October the German government began negotiations for an armistice and a peace settlement based upon the 'Fourteen Points' which President Wilson had set out in a speech on 8 January 1918. The apparent acceptance of Wilson's terms on 12 October was premature. After the torpedoeing of the Irish mailboat *Leinster* on the same day, with great loss of life, Wilson's terms stiffened and the German government had to give much more ground before asking for a cease-fire on 7 November and capitulating four days later.

13 October. [41 Grosvenor Road]
The acceptance by Germany of President Wilson's terms will be welcomed by all the good and cursed by all the bad men among the Allies. The struggle of the next few days will test the relative power of the saints and the sinners among the Allied nations. The fact that the U.S.A. controls the situation is some guarantee of the victory of the saints. If it were not for that supremely important fact, I should

fear the defeat of virtue. Revenge and greed die hard when satisfaction seems at hand.

28 October. [41 Grosvenor Road]
Apparently the sinners have prevailed, even over President Wilson. There is an unnecessary hardness in his subsequent communication. It may be that the German government will surrender unconditionally; but in that case the terms Germany will have to accept will be past endurance: they will break her or turn her into a secret rebel against the world.

On 4 November the crews of the German fleet mutinied and raised the red flag. Two days later the revolution spread to Munich. The Austro-Hungarian regime had also collapsed into revolution.

4 November. [41 Grosvenor Road]
There is little or no elation among the general body of citizens about the coming peace. We are magnificently successful in the completeness of our victory over the Central Powers, a miracle when we remember the spring German offensive. But are we confronted with another Russia in Austria, possibly even in Germany, a continent in rampant revolution over which there will be no government to which we can dictate our terms? Great Britain and France are themselves exhausted, living on their own vitals, whilst they smash German civilization. For whose benefit? Will Wilson be able to resist the brutality of his own philistines flushed with victory?

The absence of public rejoicing and sombre looks of private persons arises, I think, from preoccupation as to the kind of world we shall all live in when peace has come. Burdened with a huge public debt, living under the shadow of swollen government departments, with a working class seething with discontent, and a ruling class with all its traditions and standards topsy-turvy, with civil servants suspecting businessmen and businessmen conspiring to protect their profits, and all alike abusing the politician, no citizen knows what is going to happen to himself or his children, or to his own social circle, or to the state or to the Empire. All that he does know is that the old order is seriously threatened with dissolution without any new order being in sight. What are the social ideals germinating in the minds of the five millions who will presently return from the battlefields and battle seas? What is the outlook of the millions of men and women who have been earning high wages and working long hours at the war trades and will presently find themselves seeking work? What are the sympathies of the eight millions of new women voters? The Bolsheviks grin at us from a ruined Russia and their creed, like the plague of influenza, seems to be spreading westwards from one country to another. Will famine become chronic over whole stretches of Europe, and will some deadly pestilence be generated out of famine to scourge even those races who have a sufficiency of food? Will western Europe flare up in the flames of anarchic revolution? Individuals brood over these questions and wonder what will have happened this time next year. Hence the depressed and distracted air of the strange medley of soldiers and civilians who throng the thoroughfares of the capital of the victorious Empire.

Sidney reports that Henderson is in the depths of depression, doubtful whether he will win his seat, or if he does so, whether he will have any party to lead. The Prime Minister is said to be assured that an election on 7 December will return him to power as 'the man who won the war', and who alone can be trusted with reconstruction. The Labour Ministers, including Clynes, are pressing the Labour Party Executive for a continuance of the Coalition during the period of reconstruction, and it is quite uncertain whether the labour movement, as a whole, will be prepared to assert itself at the polls in opposition to the present government. Most of the glamour around the Labour Party during the spring due to its international and national programme has faded away, personal jealousies and internecine strife having dissipated it from below, whilst the near prospect of a brilliant peace has dissolved it from above. Sidney, of course, remains unmoved in his determination that the Labour Party shall become H.M. Opposition, but his expectation of being elected by the London graduates has considerably lessened. We are not personally depressed because we have the patience of lifelong propagandists who have watched their ideas taking root in the minds of the former opponents. But we are contemplating retirement from active political life after the elections, to finish our books and watch the young folk work for the success of social democracy at some future election.

J.A. Kaye (1895–1919), the assistant secretary of the Fabian Research

Department, committed suicide. G.D.H. Cole married Margaret Postgate (1893–1980) in August 1918, and set up house in Chelsea.

7 November. [41 Grosvenor Road]
Sidney reports a vehement discussion at the Labour Party Executive as to whether they should recommend the conference on Thursday to decide to break away from the Coalition and call upon the Labour Ministers either to leave the government or leave the Labour Party. The Parliamentary Labour Party, under pressure from the Labour Ministers, decided to wait until peace was actually signed between the belligerents. That would mean accepting office in the new government and continuing in office, at any rate for the many months that will elapse prior to signing the treaty of peace. If this policy be pursued it seems extremely unlikely that the Labour Ministers would carry out their present intention, which could always be reversed, of resigning from the government on the formal conclusion of peace. . . . Clynes threatened that all candidates who did not get the Lloyd George letter would be swept into oblivion and that the Labour Party would be finally smashed. By twelve to four, the Executive insisted on its former policy, that at this election they must be in opposition to the present government whatever fate were in store for them in the ballot boxes. The Labour members have no nerve, or perhaps they lack personal disinterestedness; they hate being out of Parliament, still more losing office. What with placemen on the one hand, and professional rebels on the other, the Labour Party goes into the electoral battle a distracted, divided and depressed rabble of some three hundred nondescript candidates. Sidney thinks that the party will be fortunate if it comes back sixty strong, and all the successful ones will be for massed trade union constituencies. He has now no hope of winning London university or any other middle-class constituency.

We visited the G.D.H. Coles this afternoon in the first abode of their married life. I forget whether I have before described this promising union of two devoted fellow workers. Margaret Postgate, familiarly known as 'Mopps' because of the mop of short thick black wavy hair in which is set swarthy complexion, mobile mouth, sharp nose and chin and most brilliantly defiant eyes, is the daughter of a professor of classics, one of a typical university family. She is herself a distinguished Cambridge graduate. She succeeded Arnot as paid secretary to the Research Department and shocked us old folk with her daringly unconventional ways and rebellious attitude. She kept what hours she chose, smoked the masculine pipe, was on affectionate terms first with Arnot then with Cole, receiving meanwhile the adoration of Kaye, the obedient servitor of the group. But though her manners have been disorderly, her ways have been straight: she has wit and reasoning power of an unusual quality, and she is fundamentally sweet-tempered and kind. Courtship and marriage have increased her womanliness and self-restraint. She and Cole seem perfect intellectual comrades. On both sides the marriage is an unworldly one. . . . These two are now friendly with us, convinced that, however we may differ from their vision of the future, we mean to help, not to hinder, their career in the labour movement.

The war at last came to an end at 11 a.m. on 11 November. The celebrations in London were rowdier than in the rest of the country.

11 November. [41 Grosvenor Road]
Peace!
  London today is a pandemonium of noise and revelry, soldiers and flappers being most in evidence. Multitudes are making all the row they can, and in spite of depressing fog and steady rain, discords of sound and struggling, rushing beings and vehicles fill the streets. Paris, I imagine, will be more spontaneous and magnificent in its rejoicing. Berlin, also, is reported to be elated having got rid, not only of the war, but also of its oppressors. The people are everywhere rejoicing. Thrones are everywhere crashing and the men of property are everywhere secretly trembling. 'A biting wind is blowing for the cause of property,' writes an Austrian journalist. How soon will the tide of revolution catch up the tide of victory? That is a question which is exercising Whitehall and Buckingham Palace and which is causing anxiety even among the more thoughtful democrats. Will it be six months or a year?

PART V

A Distinct Dash of Adventure

November 1918–January 1924

Introduction to Part V

To POPULAR CRIES OF 'Hang the Kaiser!' and 'Vote for the Man who won the War', Lloyd George romped home in the election held on 14 December 1918. He had appealed to the country as the leader of the Coalition government, endorsing candidates of all parties who continued to support it – the 'coupon' election, Asquith contemptuously called it. The new electorate, three times as big as it was in 1910, returned Lloyd George and his Coalition, largely made up of businessmen and opportunists, with a huge majority of 340. The Asquithian Liberals were reduced to a tiny band of thirty. The only effective opposition came from the Labour Party. Apart from ten Labour M.P.s who supported Lloyd George, the party as a whole had opted out of the Coalition and they returned sixty members to Parliament. Ironically, just when the party was emerging as a possible alternative government, its ablest leaders – Henderson, MacDonald and Snowden – lost their seats, largely due to their opposition to the war.

Although the election result was essentially a great personal victory for Lloyd George, he found himself increasingly a prisoner of the Tories who had elected him – Stanley Baldwin (1867–1947) described them to John Maynard Keynes (1883–1946) as 'a lot of hard-faced men who look as if they have done very well out of the war'. For the next four years, the Coalition struggled in vain to cope with the intractable problems of a world ruined by war and revolution. There was a treaty to draft at Versailles and, for all Lloyd George's assertions that 'we must not allow any sense of revenge, any spirit of greed,' the final settlement was a punitive one. The victorious allies had barely done their work before Keynes denounced the treaty-making in *The Economic Consequences of the Peace*. There was the bill for the war, and all the ensuing arguments about reparations, debts, tariffs, taxes and wages, which turned on

321

the need for someone to pay for it – economic issues which lay behind the wave of industrial unrest which was to sweep to a climax in the General Strike of 1926. The working people were becoming increasingly aware of their industrial strength. Trade union membership had gone up from two and a half million in 1910 to over eight million in 1920. In the immediate post-war years, more working days were lost in disputes than in the comparably troubled period before the war. Increasing unemployment only added to the sense of disillusionment. Surprisingly, the slump in British industry in the winter of 1920 was unexpected, and by June 1921 unemployment had risen to two million.

The repeated strikes intensified the fear of revolution. Lloyd George's government had given armed support to the Russian counter-revolution, and in 1920 it came close to a second round of military intervention in Russia: the 'Red Peril' was a potent threat in the first years of the new Communist International, when the old Socialist International split and almost collapsed, and Communist parties were set up to defend and imitate the Soviet example. Even in favourable conditions, as wages fell and unemployment rose, the Communists were too sectarian and incompetent to make much headway in Britain, and the Labour Party repeatedly rebuffed their attempts at infiltration. It was the Irish who in fact took the gun in hand. After the Easter rising in 1916 there was no longer hope of a peaceful Home Rule settlement. At the end of the war a guerrilla campaign eventually forced Lloyd George to sign a treaty setting up the Irish Free State in the twenty-six counties of the south and partitioning the north to preserve a Protestant enclave in Ulster. The Free State was given Dominion status on 6 December 1921 but there was much opposition to such a settlement and by April 1922 an Irish republic had been proclaimed by the extremists. A new party, the Republican Party, was formed under Eamon De Valera (1882–1975) and civil war broke out, with the Irish Republican Army continuing the struggle for an independent Ireland.

These events played a large part in lowering the prestige of the government. There was also a scandal over the selling of titles and other honours, which gravely undermined Lloyd George's standing, while his adventurous foreign policy alienated the French and threw Germany and Russia together. By 1922 it was clear that the Coalition was disintegrating. Dissident Tories began to assert themselves and seek an independent role. At a historic meeting at the Carlton Club on 19 October 1922 the Conservatives decided, by 187 votes to 87, to leave the Coalition. An election followed on 15 November in which the Conservatives won a majority of 88 over the other parties. The Liberals were still split – Lloyd George and his followers secured 57 seats and the Asquith group 60 seats. The Labour Party again increased its strength, returning 142 M.P.s. One of these was Sidney Webb, who had been selected as the Labour candidate by the miners of Seaham in Durham in gratitude for the work he had done on the Sankey Commission to secure a better deal for the miners.

A. Bonar Law was now Prime Minister, but he was a sick man and he was replaced by Stanley Baldwin on 20 May 1923. Baldwin was more anxious to heal the wounds of dissension within his own party than to give a lead to the nation, and though his forthright declaration in favour of Protection united the Tories, it also succeeded in healing the breach among the Liberals. By December the country was plunged yet again into an election. It gave the Conservatives 258 seats, the Liberals 158 and the Labour Party 191. The Conservatives could not form a government against the combined Opposition parties, and despite misgivings and alarm, the new Parliament agreed that Labour should take office. Neville Chamberlain (1869–1940) voiced the reassuring feeling that they were 'too weak to do much harm', and after Baldwin resigned on 22 January 1924 the first Labour government took office with Liberal toleration and support.

During these years Beatrice was much more closely involved with the Labour Party, but its steady advance gave her little satisfaction. While Sidney calculated the party's electoral gains, she was noting the bickering strife between its complacent leaders and its dissatisfied left, and asking whether the party was really fit to govern. She gave Sidney comradely support when he became the intellectual workhorse of the party, the counsellor of the turbulent miners and, most demanding of all, the president of the Board of Trade – a post to which MacDonald appointed him in the new government. But her heart was not completely in such a subordinate role in their partnership. It was not possible to get back to research on the massive history of local government; instead she reworked her early diaries into the autobiography which appeared as *My Apprenticeship*. The demands of Sidney's political career left her little room for her own interests, but she increasingly enjoyed the country life at Liphook in Hampshire where in 1923 they bought a cottage for their retirement.

Noel Williams was killed at Tournai in Belgium nineteen days before the Armistice.

17 November. [41 Grosvenor Road]
The emergency Labour conference yesterday decided, by a large majority, to withdraw its representatives from the Coalition, the miners, the railwaymen and the engineers carrying it against the cotton weavers and labourers and sundry smaller unions. Clynes was the protagonist of the Labour Ministers; Smillie, Thomas and Henderson, with GBS as Fabian delegate, intervening brilliantly, championing what was a foregone conclusion. In the evening there was a tumultuous mass meeting at the Albert Hall, with dense crowds outside. The hugeness of the gathering did not redeem it from the political, intellectual and spiritual failure. The platform was weak and divided in aim, every speech was interrupted by irreverent and spiteful remarks, by rowdy singing and red-flag waving. Indeed the more popular speakers spent most of their words in remonstrating with the audience about their levity and insolence. Even the rebels of the Research Department who forgathered in our box were disheartened.

The two great parties are gathering up their forces, coalescing on the boom of victory and the fear of revolution – the two most potent emotions of today. . . . All that can be said is that the governing class is willing to promise anything that is unanimously demanded by the labour movement rather than endanger their hold on the seat of power. Whether after they have won the election they will be equally complacent is not so certain. . . .

The toll of the war for our family is three killed and four others wounded, two seriously injured, out of a total of seventeen nephews and nephews-in-law in khaki. Betty Russell has lost her husband, Maggie Hobhouse has lost her Paul, and now, three weeks before the signing of the Armistice, the dead body of Noel Williams is reported found. Paul and Noel were among our favourite nephews, clean-living gallant youths of intellectual promise. Rosy Dobbs, who loved Noel better and trusted him more than she did all her Dobbs children, is terribly grieved. Margaret, with her exuberant energy, has rallied. Every day one meets saddened women, with haggard faces and lethargic movements, and one dare not ask after husband or son. The revelry of the streets and the flying flags seem a flippant mockery of the desolation caused by the slaughter of tens of millions of the best of the white race.

G.H. Wardle, a right-wing trade unionist, had been acting chairman of the Labour Party in 1917. Sir Philip Magnus (1842–1933) was a Conservative who sat for London University 1906–22.

21 November. [41 Grosvenor Road]
Conditions are improving for the Labour Party. Clynes and three colleagues have resigned from the government; Barnes and Roberts have left the Labour Party and futile Wardle is miserable in mid-air. Liberals all over the country, denounced by Lloyd George and apparently deserted by Asquith, are cursing their fate; and the more virile are joining the Labour Party; the weak ones are slinking into the back lines of the Coalition. The Northcliffe press is showing its teeth to the government – the *Daily Mail* has offered the Labour Party a full column of space every day until the election, without editing, to advertise its policy and its candidates. (This led to the *Daily News* doing likewise.) Apparently Northcliffe has not been invited to the peace conference. He is also said to be seriously frightened at the growing revolutionary feeling and prophesies that the Labour Party will win more seats than it thinks. Sidney is working hard, writing innumerable letters to enquiring graduates, and it looks like being a close contest between him and Magnus, the medical man and the teacher, both Conservatives, being far behind. But Sidney is severely handicapped by his now notorious connection with the Labour Party, and his assumed comradeship with J.R. MacDonald and Snowden. On his own record he could have won the seat, but he would have lost the educational campaign. My estimate of the poll is Magnus [Unionist] 2,900, Webb 2,300, Somerville [National Union of Teachers] 1,200, Herringham [Independent] 800, Norden [Independent] 300.

[On 31 December Beatrice gave the actual figures: Magnus 2,800, Webb 2,100, Somerville 800, Herringham 700, Nordon 200. She thought Sidney's vote was 'a brilliant testimony to his personal popularity'.]

8 December. [41 Grosvenor Road]
The War Cabinet committee on Women in Industry bores me. I am not in the least interested in the relation of men's and women's wages. My colleagues do not attract me. And it looks like my being forced to have a minority report, all by myself. . . . Moreover we all feel that the committee's report will be stillborn. . . . Alterations of the wage system will depend on the relative political and

industrial forces and neither the government nor the trade unions, certainly not the employers, will proceed on the lines of ideal principle.

We are watching with painful anxiety the tragedy of Continental Europe . . . The struggle is between political democracy, based on geographical constituencies with majority rule, and the dictatorship, not of the proletariat, as some say, but of the militant minor ties of the proletariat – soldiers, sailors, and revolutionary workers, in public meeting assembled. . . . In the dark hours of sleepless nights I wonder whether it is the end of western civilization. Sidney comforts me by his stolid faith in human sanity and human kindliness. He sees no reason to believe that the great German people will not pass through the ordeal of defeat and the ordeal of revolution towards an ordered freedom. He is not so optimistic towards Russia: he has no liking for what he imagines to be the Russian temperament. He hates what is called 'temperament'.

12 December. [41 Grosvenor Road]
I feel physically sick when I read the frenzied appeals of the Coalition leaders – the Prime Minister, Winston Churchill and Geddes, to hang the Kaiser, ruin and humiliate the German people, even to deprive Germany of her art treasures and libraries. These preliminaries of peace have become almost as disgusting as the war itself. It may be all election talk, but it is mean and brutal talk, degrading to the electorate. It is the nemesis of having, as Premier, a man of low moral and intellectual values. The one outstanding virtue of the Labour Party, a virtue which is its very own, not imposed upon it by its intellectuals, is its high sense of international morality. Alone among British politicians, the leaders of the Labour Party do honestly believe in the brotherhood of man.

There were substantial British forces at Archangel and Murmansk. They had been originally sent to guard the Allied munition dumps there against the Germans, but were now used for intervention against the Bolsheviks. Robert Bruce-Lockhart (1887–1970) was a British diplomat and intelligence agent in revolutionary Russia. At this time Britain had no official relations with the Bolsheviks but at Lloyd George's request, Lockhart was soon to head a mission to establish unofficial relations. He lunched with the Webbs on 20 November. 'Sidney is rather like a Russian Socialist with straggling beard and unkempt hair,' he wrote in his diary. 'She is very charming but a little dogmatic.'

22 December. [41 Grosvenor Road]
We leave tomorrow for a fortnight's country holiday. It is the end
of a period. For the last three years, such energies as I have had,
poor in quantity and quality, have been absorbed in government
committees. . . . This coming year I shall devote myself to three
tasks: getting our own publications forward, helping with the
advisory committees of the Labour Party, and in holiday intervals,
typing out the back volumes of my diary. This latter occupation – I
can hardly call it work – pleases me most. I am tired of investigating
new subjects. I want to brood over the past and reflect on men and
their affairs. It amuses me to watch, in these jottings of my diary,
the development of my own thought and of Sidney's activities. I
want to summarize my life and see what it all amounts to. For long
years I have constrained my intellect, forced it to concentrate on one
subject-matter after another, in some of the dullest and least
illuminating details of social organization. . . . And I want, before
I cease to have any faculty of expressing myself, to add to my past
diaries, in the form of notes, descriptions of persons and reflections
arising from being 'wise after the event'.

Sidney is disappointed that he has not won the university seat. I
think he had been looking forward to a spell in Parliament, wanted
to test his powers as a parliamentarian. And yet he does not want it
sufficiently to get himself adopted for a constituency which he could
win, he wants to be pushed into Parliament, he does not want to
push himself in. . . . He fought the university seat because no
other member of the Labour Party would dream of doing it. He
cannot bring himself even to hint that he has a claim to a winnable
constituency.

The Labour Party Executive and its attendant intellectuals are
concerned with our war on Russia, or rather on Bolshevik Russia.
Squire [*New Statesman*] handed on to the Labour Party
Advisory Committee on Foreign Affairs a letter from Sharp from
Stockholm – a remarkable indictment of our armed intervention.
As Sharp's temperamental sympathies are dead against the Bolshevik
spirit and his intellect condemns the Bolshevik conception of social
order, he is a notable witness against the policy of intervention. The
root of our anxiety is distrust of the military and naval authorities
who are masters of the situation at Murmansk and Archangel. We
know these men: they are wholly ignorant of the art of government,
angrily contemptuous of any form of democracy. All their sympathies

are with the old regime of Tsar and military bureaucracy with the attendant opportunities for foreign capitalist exploitation. They would unhesitatingly shoot down every nationalist in Ireland, every striker in Great Britain, and blow from the cannon mouth every Indian rebel. . . . But one would think that even our War Office would hesitate before committing itself to maintaining order in Russia against the will of the mass of Russian peasants and town workmen.

It seems extraordinarily difficult to get at the truth about Russia. Lockhart, the British consul at Moscow who, after being imprisoned by the Bolsheviks, was allowed to get back to England, could give us no clear account of what was being actually done or even any decided impression for or against the Bolshevik government. He tells us that Lenin is a great man – 'the greatest man thrown up by the war' – fanatically disinterested, with an immense will-power and organizing capacity of unusual quality. But it seems that Lenin himself despairs of establishing his system in Russia: 'the material is too inferior', he is reported to have said. He desires to transfer his services and his creed to Germany, which he believes is fit to accept and make use of him. Lockhart is disillusioned with the social organization of the Soviets and 'workers control', and declares that Lenin has stopped all management by the workers concerned and instituted a simple bureaucracy deriving its authority from the central Soviet with more or less shadowy advisory committees of the different grades of workers. About the reality and extent of the 'terror' Lockhart is equally vague.

▴

∽ 1919 ∽

James Sexton (1856–1938) was a leader of the Seamen's Union and a Labour M.P. William Adamson (1863–1936) was a Scottish miners' official and chairman of the Parliamentary Labour Party 1917–21.

10 January. [41 Grosvenor Road]
The British general election of 1918 seems to be curiously analogous to the German general election of 1871. Lloyd George, like Bismarck, appealed to an enormously enlarged electorate after a dramatic national victory for unconditional support – for a parlia-

328

ment without an organized opposition. In both cases the most powerful party prior to the war had been a liberal party which during the war had patriotically supported the war. In both cases there had been a small socialist minority that had opposed the war. Bismarck's election swept away the national liberal party and started a social democratic party on a career which ended in its becoming, in the course of thirty or forty years, the most powerful political party in the German empire.

The parliamentary revolution in Great Britain has been far more complete. The Liberal Party, which has for years governed the Empire, has been reduced to an insignificant fraction, with all its leaders without exception at the bottom of the poll. The Labour Party has doubled its numbers and polled one-fourth of the entire voting electorate. It is now 'His Majesty's Opposition', or claims to be in that position. Lloyd George, with his Conservative phalanx, is apparently in complete command of the situation; as the only alternative government there stands the Labour Party, with its completely socialist programme and its utopia of the equalitarian state. But the Parliamentary Labour Party is a very tame lion. All the militants (because they happen to be also pacifists) have been ousted from Parliament. Out of the fifty-nine Labour members twenty-five are miners – for general political purposes dead stuff. Among the others are such fat-heads as Bowerman and such buffoons, simpletons and corrupt persons as Sexton, Thorne and Tillett. The party is led by the respectable but dull-witted Adamson, elected chairman because he is a miner. Clynes and Thomas are the only good speakers and such intellectuals as have survived the election are very inferior.

Sidney reports that at the joint meeting of the Labour Party and the Parliamentary Party it was decided with only one dissentient – O'Grady – to claim the position of His Majesty's Opposition. Whereupon Sidney, in the absence of Henderson (laid up with influenza) offered the services of the Labour Party staff as well as his own to help the Parliamentary Party to carry out its new and difficult duties. The offer was received with friendly appreciation, but no suggestions were made by the M.P.s of how it could be carried out. There is, in fact, some sign that the group of pro-war trade union officials wish to sever their connection with the political organization of the Labour Party and to attempt to run the Parliamentary Party from the offices of the Trades Union Congress.

Whether when they are actually on the Front Opposition Bench they will realize their incapacity, or whether they will slip complacently into the position of tame subservience to the government, time will show. . . .

14 January. [41 Grosvenor Road]
I have never seen Adamson, the chairman of the Parliamentary Labour Party, before he lunched with us yesterday, except as a squat figure on the platform of the Albert Hall mass meeting just prior to the election. . . . He is a middle-aged Scottish miner, typical British proletarian in body and mind, with an instinctive suspicion of all intellectuals or enthusiasts. . . . He came to us straight from his interview with the Speaker on the all-important question of the claim of the Parliamentary Labour Party to be His Majesty's Opposition. I think he had hesitated before accepting our invitation and he was more at home with me than with Sidney. But we soon got on friendly terms and a good lunch relaxed his cautious temperament.

He repeated slowly and mechanically the Speaker's evasive answer to his claim to be the Leader of His Majesty's Opposition: he was clearly pleased and self-complacent with the vision of himself as the principal figure on the Front Opposition Bench, and only dimly conscious that he would need help to fill the position. He had brought with him a typewritten paper and read from it the requirements which he and his pals among the Labour members had decided were necessary to enable the fifty-eight to tackle Lloyd George and his immense following. 'Two clerks, three typists – we cannot do with less,' he deprecatingly insisted. But what exercised his mind most were the messengers. The Liberals, in the last Parliament, he said, had had three messengers; *he thought* and it was clear from his wrinkled forehead and slowly emphatic tone that he had thought strenuously on this question – *he thought* that the Parliamentary Labour Party might take over one of these messengers to fetch members to important divisions. He waited anxiously for Sidney's reply. 'There is always the telephone,' I said, to relieve the intense gravity of his suggestion, but he shook his head. No, the messenger was all important. Sidney cheerfully agreed but gently implied that the Parliamentary Labour Party would require something more than three clerks, two typists and one messenger. Could not the Labour Party Executive, advisory committees and staff

330

supply them with information on foreign affairs, finance and other technical questions not connected with trade unionism? Sidney asked. 'Ye-es' (this dubiously), 'concise notes, statistics, facts, that is what we want.' But he would be frank with us, he added with some energy. At their meeting yesterday they had discussed their relations with the Labour Party at Eccleston Square – in the past it had not been satisfactory. The Labour Party Executive, he complained, had during the last two years taken the initiative in deciding policy without consulting the Labour M.P.s – the Labour members had found themselves committed to programmes (Sidney looked like a guilty little boy) with which they might not agree. This must be remedied by joint meetings (Sidney looked relieved) of the M.P.s and the Labour Party Executive, a sort of joint committee. They were willing to co-opt experts from the Executive to sit on their standing committees.

After this Sidney discussed with sympathetic attention all his requirements, made a few additional notes and took him off to Eccleston Square to the meeting which had already been arranged. 'You must make use of my husband for all he is worth,' I laughingly said as I stood in the hall. 'We mean to make use of your husband,' he retorted, with a broad indulgent smile and beneficent wink at the fond woman; but the sing-song voice was decidedly non-committal as regards the man. 'Poor old Sidney,' I said to myself as the front door slammed, 'trying to direct political affairs with that bent stick.' Adamson fumbles in political life as we should fumble with a pickaxe in the dark recesses of a mine, and gets about the same output as we should do. The thought of him as the leader of His Majesty's Opposition is even more strangely absurd than Barnes in the War Cabinet or at the peace conference. . . .

In the months following the Armistice there was an alarming number of strikes – among shipwrights, engineers, gas and electricity workers. The catchword was 'direct action', and there was rioting in Glasgow. Threat of imprisonment under the Defence of the Realm Act calmed the situation.

8 February. [41 Grosvenor Road]
Sidney and I watch the chaotic strikes – the most melodramatic being the strike of the London electricians – with complete calm. The men will be beaten, but in being beaten they will undermine this government by unwittingly convincing organized labour that

the British citizen will not tolerate the direct action of a minority as a means of gaining its public ends. In order to win, constitutional methods will have to be adopted. The first effect, however, is to disintegrate the trade union movement and to damage the Labour Party in the eyes of the common run of men and women, especially women electors.

The miners were demanding a 30 per cent increase in wages, a six-hour instead of an eight-hour day and nationalization of the mines. The government offered an immediate advance of a shilling a day on wages and proposed a Royal Commission under the chairmanship of Mr Justice Sankey (1866–1948) – who became a judge in 1914, later joined the Labour Party and became Lord Chancellor in 1929 – with the promise of a prompt report to be delivered by 20 March. On these terms the miners postponed strike notices until 22 March. William Hughes (1864–1952) was Prime Minister of Australia 1915–23. Joseph Cross (1870–1925) was secretary of the Amalgamated Weavers' Association. G.H. Stuart-Bunning (1870–1951) was general secretary of the Postmen's Federation and chairman of the T.U.C. 1919. Sir Richard Redmayne (1865–1955) was Chief Inspector of Mines 1908–20. Mrs Pankhurst had become a fervent patriot but her daughter Sylvia Pankhurst (1882–1960) had moved from being a militant suffragette to an equally militant socialist. Maurice Hankey (1877–1963) was secretary to the Cabinet 1919–38. Arthur Shaw (1880–1939) was general secretary of the Bleachers, Dyers and Textile Workers. Leo Chiozza Money (1870–1944) was an economist and Liberal M.P. from 1906 to 1918, when he was defeated as a Labour candidate. Frank Hodges (1887–1947) was secretary of the miners' union 1918–24, and a member of the Sankey Commission.

22 February. [41 Grosvenor Road]
A curious episode and difficult to explain. A week today Haldane called here; he had been summoned to Downing Street the evening before and asked by the P.M. to arrange 'another dinner with the Webbs'. He had given a non-committal answer – would we come? 'Certainly we will meet the P.M. at your house. We should not care to go to Downing Street but we have not the remotest objection to being his fellow guests. In fact we should enjoy it,' I answered. 'We are quite ready to discuss any subject with Mr Lloyd George and to give him our most considered advice if he wants it,' said Sidney. 'At any rate he always entertains us,' I added. Haldane and we agreed on a date ten days off, but next morning Haldane's butler telephoned that the P.M. had fixed the coming Thursday and that 'his Lordship had put off an engagement and hoped we should do likewise.' So we went. Three and a half solid hours of lively and interesting talk with the P.M., with Haldane occasionally

intervening, left us completely puzzled. Why was it worth while for a great man, burdened with the world's destiny at the Paris conference and coming straight from an exhausting conference with the miners that very afternoon, to spend a long evening alone with us? As it afterwards turned out, we learnt a good deal from this meeting and made ample use of it. But what did *he* get or expect to get from it?

He and we talked with the freedom and intimacy of old friends – it is impossible to do otherwise with Lloyd George. He is so easy in manner, so amusing, so direct and apparently spontaneous in his observations and retorts, and he enjoys like qualities in others. He opened the evening by telling us about the Paris conference – the antagonistic temperaments of Wilson and Clemenceau – how he interpreted the doctrinaire puritan to the autocratic and emotional Celt. He scoffed at Hughes of Australia and at Clemenceau's admiration for this blatant British imperialist. But directly we sat down to Haldane's excellent dinner, he begged permission to 'talk shop'. He wanted to consult us about the personnel of the Royal Commission on the miners' claims and on the larger question of nationalization. He explained that he had offered this commission to the miners and gave us the gist of his address that afternoon. He felt in his coat pocket. 'I meant to have brought the list of names that has been suggested to me, but I find I have not. Perhaps your butler would telephone to Downing Street and ask my secretary (he spoke directly to Haldane's discreet body servant) for the list of names of the Royal Commission on the Mines.' (There proved to be no response to the telephone at Downing Street – an odd incident in a Prime Minister's abode.)

He expected, he continued to explain, that the miners would refuse to be represented, might even refuse to give evidence. But the commission would be set up, whether they agreed to it or not, and would report on wages and hours by the 30th, and on nationalization later on. If the miners carried out their threat of a strike, the government would fight. 'We shall beat them – we control the food.' But he wanted our advice as to the personnel of the commission. He must have trade unionists. Clynes had been suggested as the obvious person, and a man named Cross connected with the textiles. Sidney acclaimed Clynes, but if it was Cross of the Cotton Weavers he was an unfit man; he mentioned instead Purdy and Stuart-Bunning. The P.M. mentioned other names as the representatives of the community – Redmayne of the Home Office. 'A paid official,' retorted Sidney. 'He could hardly be considered impartial.' And then Sidney explained with decisive firmness and lucidity that if such a commission were set up there would have to be four sets of representatives: trade unionists, employers, and two kinds of outsiders holding the rival assumptions of the parties concerned. This seemed a novel idea to Lloyd George. He insisted that he wanted 'impartial persons'. No such persons exist, we assured him, and in this assertion Haldane supported us. 'Who would you suggest as outsiders?' he asked. Here we were in a difficulty as we could hardly give Sidney's name. We proposed Cole: the P.M. had never heard of him. We described him but the P.M. was not convinced. Other names were mentioned, among them Tawney and Greenwood. All through this drawn-out conversation we were wondering, since he wanted to see us, why he did not ask Sidney to serve. Haldane intervened: 'Appoint Webb and Cole as the miners' experts.' Still the P.M. did not respond. 'Who wants the commission and what is the conclusion you want it to come out at?' I asked innocently. 'The membership must depend on the report you wish it to make,' Sidney said with impatient bluntness. More fencing. 'I have no prejudices against nationalization,' suavely intoned the P.M., then, with a burst of confidence – 'This morning I persuaded the Cabinet, but with difficulty, to accept a Bill for nationalization of the railways and power stations.'

From this and other calculated indiscretions we gathered that the P.M. meant the commission to report in favour of nationalizing the mines, though the omission from the proposed membership of any convinced nationalizers roused my suspicion. 'Tom Jones – you know Tom Jones – he has the matter in hand. See Tom Jones about it. Tell him I told you to see him.' 'I will telephone him tomorrow to come to lunch,' I agreed, and the discussion on the proposed commission petered out. After dinner the P.M. and Haldane settled down to their luxurious cigars and we to our cigarettes, chatting over many things with no apparent intent on his side. . . . The prestige of a lonely dinner with the P.M., at his own request, is considerable, and the amusement of watching this remarkable political performer is great. But as we walked away at midnight, through the drifting rain, we felt that the evening had been empty of meaning. The account of the transaction is an interesting entry in my diary, I reflected. But it proved otherwise.

I telephoned the next morning to Tom Jones to lunch with us 'at the request of the P.M.'! Tom Jones, who is now acting secretary of the War Cabinet in the absence of Hankey, is a simple-minded, true-hearted man whose peace of mind is perpetually destroyed by the conflict of his personal devotion to Lloyd George with his sense of truth and fair play between individuals and loyalty to the principles of democracy. He let the cat out of the bag, and a very ugly cat it was. The persons in the list of names which could not be got from Downing Street were all hostile to nationalization. The mysterious Shaw was not the egregious Tom of the Cotton Weavers but a far abler man — the trade union secretary of the Woollen Trade Board, known to the Research Department as the most astute of the supporters of joint control with a capitalist trust. The 'impartial persons' designated were of the capitalist-cum-Guild-Socialist school who dislike the least government control, leave alone government ownership and management. Jones felt compelled to consult us about the membership, but he would not hear of Cole or Chiozza Money and he sat glum when I suggested, in friendly intimacy, that he might consider Sidney. And from other things he said or did not say we gathered that Lloyd George had been converted, possibly in the last few days or hours before he met us, to the plan of the coal-owners published this morning. (He denied, by the way, that the P.M. had got the Cabinet to accept railway nationalization. 'State ownership of power stations, yes,' he explained, 'but the Cabinet was wholly unaware that the Bill the P.M. described to them had anything to do with nationalizing the railways.') That little game of appointing a committee to report against nationalization must be stopped, we said directly the door closed on him.

Sidney thereupon sat down and wrote a long letter to Smillie explaining the exact meaning of the coal-owners' proposals and telling him what he believed were the government's intentions with regard to the membership and therefore the report of the Coal Commission and the risk of a [*illegible*] defeat of the strike. This morning he wrote off to Cole and Chiozza Money, and Money arranged by telephone a meeting between him and Sidney and Smillie and Hodges at the Russell Hotel for this very afternoon.

Sidney found Smillie depressed with a cold and the feeling of responsibility. The four sat for a couple of hours discussing every aspect of the question. Money was boiling over with lively wrath, said the coal-owners' proposals were infamous; he wanted the miners to go straight into the fight and win. Sidney reasoned in favour of accepting the commission on terms: it must be a court to investigate, not a tribunal to determine; it must report by the 14th; it must be composed of equal numbers, employers and their outside experts, and the outsiders on the men's side must be selected by the miners. If the government refused this offer, the miners would have put themselves right with public opinion in refusing to take part in a commission packed against them, and would go into a pitched battle with a better chance of success. (Sidney believes that they would be badly beaten if they held out for nationalization, the bulk of the miners caring for nothing but hours and earnings.) If the government accepted, there could not be a unanimous report against them − they would either get a majority report in favour of their claims or two reports of equal authority. The miners must have as their representatives two of the only three men who could argue their case − Cole, Chiozza Money and himself. He thinks he persuaded the other three as to the wisdom of accepting the commission on these terms, but Smillie doubted whether he could get his delegates' meeting to go that far in meeting the government. The miners were out for a fight.

We await the events with some anxiety. We believe that such a commission would mean substantial victory for the miners' case. If the government, confident of their power to beat the miners, goes into battle − theirs is the responsibility. 'Blockading the miners' will be a difficult and dangerous task. The railwaymen and the transport workers might be drawn in; the army might refuse to act. And then?

The miners insisted on an equal share in the Coal Commission, telling Lloyd George that they would postpone their strike for three weeks if he agreed, allowing him ten minutes to decide before their meeting dissolved and their delegates went back to the coalfields. Lloyd George was angry but agreed. He appointed three colliery-owners, three industrialists, three union representatives and Tawney, Money and Sidney Webb as experts acceptable to the miners. The industrialists were Sir Arthur Balfour (1873−1957), a Sheffield steel magnate; Sir Arthur Duckham (1879−1932), a consulting engineer who had served with Beatrice on the Reconstruction Committee; and Sir Thomas Royden (1871−1950), M.P. for Bootle and president of the Liverpool Chamber of Shipping. Herbert Smith (1863−1938) was a Yorkshire miner who succeeded Smillie as president of the Miners' Federation in 1921.

12 March. [41 Grosvenor Road]
I looked in at the Coal Commission this afternoon. It was a scene of strange contrasts. The robing room of the House of Lords is appropriately decorated with highly ornate frescoes of faded and sentimental pomp. But today it is serving as the crowded stage – crowded by an audience of all the interests in a mood of exasperated anxiety – for a body calling itself a royal commission on the mining industry, but in its proceedings far more like a revolutionary tribunal sitting in judgement on the capitalist owners and organizers of the nation's industries until the 20th March.

The ostensible business of the Commission is to examine and report on the miners' claim for a rise of wages and a reduction of hours; but owing to the superior skill of the miners' representatives it has become a state trial of the coal-owners and royalty owners conducted on behalf of the producers and consumers of the product, culminating in the question – why not nationalize the industry? Mr Justice Sankey is an urbane lawyer, who treats every commissioner, in turn, as the most distinguished of the lot and gives almost unlimited licence to questions and answers, interruptions and retorts. On his right sit the representatives of capital: three inferior businessmen who are coal-owners and three superior businessmen representing other interests. On his left sit Smillie, Hodges and Smith, three miners' officials, then Sidney, Tawney and Chiozza Money – typical intellectuals of the Labour Party. Smillie is the protagonist of the miners' cause, Chiozza Money is the most aggressive and self-assertive of the miners' advocates, Sidney draws out damaging admissions and claps on the right conclusion to every line of argument, whilst Tawney raises the whole discussion to the highest planes of moral rectitude and sweet reasonableness. The other side are absurdly outclassed. The three mine-owners are narrow-minded profit-makers with less technical knowledge than the miners' officials, or, at any rate, less power of displaying it, with not the remotest inkling of the wider political and economic issues which are always being raised by the miners' advocates. Balfour of Sheffield is a heavy reactionary with a quite undeserved reputation, Sidney thinks. My old friend of the Reconstruction Committee, Arthur Duckham, is undoubtedly able and he gives the impression of being indifferent to the result, or uncertain as to what he wants it to be. He sits mostly silent, holding a watching brief not for the employers but for the present government.

Royden, M.P., a well-bred and accomplished capitalist at large, is looking to politics as a career and is not over-anxious to offend the coming democracy. The official evidence against the coal-owners' administration of the mines has been overwhelming, and the public opinion, which was hostile a week ago to the miners, is now indignant with the coal-owners' profits at the consumers' expense. But the significance of the proceedings is the precedent set for similar state trials of the organization of each industry – by a court made up half of the prosecuting proletariat, half of the capitalist defendants, with power to call for all accounts and all documents and to search out the most secret ways of the profit-making craft. Sidney is enjoying himself hugely. I have never seen him so keen on any task since the halcyon days of the L.C.C.

The Sankey Commission, eager to avert a strike, rushed out an interim report on 20 March. Each faction made its own proposals. The chairman and the independent members reported in favour of a wage advance of two shillings a day, establishment of the six-hour day after July 1921 and immediate reduction of hours to seven, and a levy of one penny a ton to raise a fund for better housing. The mine-owners proposed a wage advance of 1s 6d for a seven-hour day. The miner members reiterated their demand for a 30 per cent wage increase, six-hour day and nationalization. The government endorsed Sankey's proposals with a promise of a progressive reorganization of the whole industry, and the miners accepted after a ballot of the members. The larger question of nationalization was to be further considered by the Commission.

20 March. [41 Grosvenor Road]
This afternoon, while Sidney, Tawney and I were having a cup of tea, Tom Jones broke in upon us in a great state of excitement. He had seen the three reports. The War Cabinet was meeting at six o'clock to consider what they would do. They were determined not to be bullied into conceding the miners' demands – especially nationalization. He was hot about the miners' representatives having included nationalization as one of their recommendations. 'The Commission has been instructed to report on wages and hours only.' 'Not in the reference,' interrupted Sidney. 'And Smillie at the recent conference with the P.M. did not take up the attitude that nationalization was a *sine qua non*; he had implied that if the wages and hours were granted, nationalization could wait.' Sidney explained that the wages and hours could not be granted without raising the price of coal unless unification were carried out, and

unification meant nationalization. Jones agreed, and admitted that nationalization was implied in the chairman's report. But the Cabinet was obdurate. Churchill and Curzon were intent on a battle with the miners – all the arrangements had been made -- tanks were ready, the army could be depended on, food would be withdrawn and so on. What could be done? asked Jones in genuine concern. Could anything be done to bring pressure to bear on the Cabinet, this evening, to alter their decision? . . . Jones said that the Cabinet would prefer to grant all the other demands rather than promise nationalization. 'The government is prepared to give away the whole annual product of the nation in advance and more than the whole annual product rather than tamper with property,' I interjected. 'The Exchequer could subsidize the bad mines so that the price of coals should not be raised – the Cabinet would be willing to do that. They would do anything from shooting the miners or starving their wives and children to subsidizing profits or wages out of taxes to avoid nationalization,' Jones answered.

Alys Russell now lived in Hampshire with her brother Logan Pearsall Smith. A successful edition of his *Trivia* was published in 1917. Sir Ernest Cassel (1852–1921) was a German-born financier and philanthropist. His gift to the London School of Economics led to the establishment of a Faculty of Commerce. Arthur Steel-Maitland (1876–1935), chairman of the L.S.E. governors, had been a special commissioner to the Poor Law Commission and was a Tory M.P. from 1910–35. Professor W.G.S. Adams, currently serving as Lloyd George's private secretary, was to become Warden of All Souls, Oxford. Miss MacTaggart was a very competent administrative secretary to the L.S.E. George Santayana (1863–1952), the American philosopher, lived in seclusion, a reflection of his philosophy of moral detachment, qualified hedonism, and aesthetic pleasure.

29 April. [41 Grosvenor Road]
A delightful twelve days with Logan Pearsall Smith and Alys Russell at Big Chilling. During the eight days that Sidney was there – he had to go up for three days to the Coal Commission – we wrote Part I (five chapters) of our new book on British Socialism from the draft that I had prepared in the last two months. The walks by the sea in mid-springtide in brilliant sunshine – waves, birds and buds – were healthful and happy. We enjoyed the companionship of our hosts. Logan spent his time in cross-examining us about our experience, thoughts and feelings. He is an observant and subtle psychologist. The publication of his *Trivia* has brought

339

him literary fame through his invention of a novel literary form. His particular speciality is to represent, with scientific accuracy and literary charm, the actual content of his own mind as an example of the mind of most intellectuals. He exercises this new craft with consummate skill and with ruthless and cynical frankness, revealing how much of the stream of thoughts and feelings, even of the enlightened and moral man, is pathologically trivial in their vanity and egotism. The evenings of Sidney's absence he read us extracts from his selections from Santayana's works, an author who, he thinks, combines the most perfect style with the truest philosophy of life. Anyway this poetical prose, intoned in Logan's pleasant voice, was a recreation after the day's work on the prosaic facts of British Socialism.

In the intervals of other business Sidney has been busy with his old love – the School of Economics. His position as one of the Cassel Trustees, dispensing the seven thousand a year to be devoted to a faculty of Commerce, has given him a position of vantage for the reorganization of the work of the School after the arid period of the war. For this purpose he had to undertake the unpleasant task of telling an old friend, W. Pember Reeves, that the time had come for him to resign the directorship. Though there was great discontent with Reeves's directorship on the part of the staff of lecturers and an open breach between Reeves and Miss MacTaggart, the real administrator of the School no one volunteered to say the decisive word. Sidney, feeling that he was responsible ten years ago for getting Reeves appointed, on the express understanding that Reeves should retire after seven years' service, felt he must bring the resignation about. It was a painful interview. Reeves clung to the directorship and argued his fitness. Sidney was firm and Reeves eventually agreed to resign, remarking, somewhat bitterly, that Sidney 'was ruthless in the pursuit of his causes and allowed no personal considerations, either on his own behalf or on that of his friends, to stand in the way of the success of an institution or a movement he believed in'. Which is of course true! The last few days Sidney has been colloguing with Steel-Maitland as to the choice of a new Director. Professor Adams of Oxford refused the position and there is no member of the existing staff who is fit for the job.

The terms of the Treaty of Versailles were known after 7 May when they were presented to the Germans and it was signed on 28 June – 'in many respects terrible terms to impose upon a country', said Lloyd George.

10 May. [41 Grosvenor Road]
A hard and brutal peace, made more intolerable by the contumely of circumstances deliberately devised, in the method of its delivery to the representatives of the German people. What disgusts me most is the fact that Great Britain gets the cleanest cut of all out of the possessions of the fallen enemy. France has hurt Germany most, Italy has been the most unreasonable. But it is Great Britain who adds most to her territory, prestige and power. The German colonies, Mesopotamia, the acknowledgement of Egyptian sovereignty, the destruction of the German navy and mercantile marine, the undisputed dominion over the ocean highways – all this without further effort or risk – are a greater and better secured asset than extensions of frontiers which have to be fortified, huge indemnities which cannot be paid, and the right to continue in costly and hazardous occupation of enemy country. Moreover, France has suffered, relatively to her strength, incomparably more than Great Britain, alike in men and material. Meanwhile Germany has gained little or nothing from her abandonment of autocracy and militarism; and Wilson's Fourteen Points, upon which Germany surrendered, have been, in the spirit and in the letter, repudiated. That is my verdict. . . .

Austen Chamberlain was Chancellor of the Exchequer 1919–21.

20 May. [41 Grosvenor Road]
Victorious troops, British, Dominion and American, march through London, day by day, with bands playing and colours flying, to be reviewed by the King. What with brilliant sunshine and the consciousness of being a victorious race, the crowds in the streets have lost the look of strain and anxiety and have become smiling and buoyant. The war profiteers with their gains and the officers and men with their 'bonuses' vie with each other in extravagant eating and drinking, extravagant shopping and 'all-night' dancing, with all that that means. Chamberlain's 'carrying over' Budget relieves the propertied classes from immediate fear of an increased income tax and a capital levy, and the prodigally administered unemployment benefit gives the workers unaccustomed leisure with maintenance.

341

But those who realize the financial position have little peace of mind. No political party is prepared for the stern measures of equalization and discipline necessary if we are to avoid embittered class war. . . . The present Cabinet has no policy but to hold on desperately to the present distribution of wealth and to bolster up the financial interest of favoured cliques by administrative protection. The Liberal leaders out of Parliament go on repeating the old shibboleths of free trade and retrenchment – they have no longer the category of political reform. The Labour M.P.s show no sign of becoming a political party, leave alone His Majesty's Opposition. Our mild attempt to bring them together failed absurdly. We invited forty-five of them to a series of little dinners. Thirty-five accepted but only seventeen turned up on the appointed nights, and these faithful ones were new members. The joint committee of the Labour Party Executive and the Parliamentary Party has collapsed, and there is little or no communication between Westminster and Eccleston Square. . . .

2 June. [41 Grosvenor Road]
We spent the week-end with our old friend Harben and his wife. He has inherited an elaborate establishment, a dignified mansion in a beautifully timbered park with many acres of woodland and a model farm. They live in great luxury – too delectable food and wine for our ascetic digestion, so that we both came back more fatigued than we went. . . . His socialist opinions seem oddly out of place, unless we regard them, like the pledge of the drunkard, as a hope of some way of curbing from outside his self-indulgent propensities. His children will inherit what is left of the fortune, they will not inherit the socialist faith, and they will not be fitted for the equalitarian state. And the life is clearly not a happy one for the wife, at least not peacefully and securely happy. . . .

The second report of the Sankey Commission dealing with nationalization appeared on 20 June. There were in fact four documents, three of which recommended some measure of nationalization. As there was no clear majority the government evaded the issue. The miners felt tricked and the coal-owners hardened their attitude. All that came of the high hopes of the Sankey Commission was the Coal Mines Act of 1919 which enacted the seven-hour day. An emergency Act in 1920 limited profits temporarily and extended the duration of government control. Sir Adam Nimmo (d. 1939) was president of the Mining Association and director of a number of companies. He replaced

R.W. Cooper as a mine-owners' representative. Sir Allan Macgregor Smith, chairman of the Engineering and Allied Employers' Federation, replaced Sir Thomas Royden. Sir Theodore Morison (1863–1936) was an educationalist and writer. At this time he was principal of Armstrong College, Newcastle. A.L. Bowley (1869–1957), a specialist in income distribution, had joined the staff of the L.S.E. in 1895 and had been professor of statistics since 1915.

23 June. [41 Grosvenor Road]
The second and final stage of the Coal Commission has not been so exciting as the first, but it has been an equally strenuous time for the commissioners. One of the coal-owners and the agreeable but futile Royden retired in favour of Nimmo (the ablest of the coal-owners) and Allan Smith (the notorious official of the engineering employers), who is considered the star among the professional representatives of capitalism. These two militants carried the war into the enemies' camp, but in such an objectionable way that at the end of the sittings they were no longer on speaking terms with the chairman and did not appear themselves or permit the other two coal-owners to appear at the final meeting for signing the four reports. Sankey's temper gave way at the end: he became intolerant of Nimmo and Allan Smith, neglectful of Chiozza Money, relying exclusively on Tawney and Sidney as counsellors and also as intermediaries with the miners' three officials. Smillie's melodramatic cross-examination of the [mine-owning] dukes and his fanatical and unintelligent obstinacy about 'no compensation' to the royalty-owners injured the miners' case in the country. But after wrestling with Smillie and co-operating with the Judge, Sidney and Tawney, supported by Chiozza Money, Smith and Hodges, brought about a satisfactory conclusion to the whole business – a chairman's report in favour of nationalization and a separate but short endorsement of this report, with one or two demurrers on particular proposals, by the six miners' representatives, thus securing a majority of the Commission for nationalization. Sidney gathered from Sankey that in reporting in favour of nationalization he had the P.M.'s approval. Sankey added that there would be a general election – not before July and not later than November – and that nationalization of the coalmines would be in the Lloyd George programme. What is absurdly clear is that Lloyd George is busily putting about that a general election is imminent and that it will be precipitated by a breach between him and the reactionaries in the Cabinet. Whether this is merely

part of the process of bluffing the Conservatives into accepting his policy or whether it is a feeler for Radical and Labour support, none of us know – perhaps he does not know himself. If the first policy fails, he may fall back on the second.

Sidney has come out of the Commission with a great admiration for Tawney, for his personal charm, his quiet wisdom, and his rapier-like intellect. Tawney has, in fact, been the great success of the Commission. For Chiozza Money, Sidney has a somewhat contemptuous liking – contemptuous is too strong a word – for his cleverness and untiring industry he certainly respects him. Smillie, the protagonist of revolutionary labour, the outstanding personality of the Commission from the standpoint of the newspapers, has been a trying colleague, with his fanatical unreason, always acting and speaking as if the day of judgement on capitalism was coming within a week. . . . Sidney has thoroughly enjoyed service on the Commission and says that he has had a rollicking good time. He believes that the Coal Commission will be the beginning of a landslide into the communal control of industries and services.

Sidney has also been busy with the affairs of the London School of Economics. Steel-Maitland, after resigning from the government to go into the City, went off to Italy for a holiday and left it to Sidney to decide who should be Director. Eventually the choice was narrowed down to Beveridge, Theodore Morison and Bowley – and Beveridge was Sidney's choice and has been accepted by the governors. He has his defects – he is not the sweetest-tempered of men and has a certain narrowness of outlook. But he is a good administrator, an initiator of both ideas and plans, and a man who will concentrate his energies on the School. Our relations with him are pleasant and friendly. His views are slightly anti-Labour but pro-collectivist, and he is an innovator, not a conventional-minded man. He is also 'well seen' by the government departments, and the School is being used more and more for the training of public servants. Moreover, there was really no alternative. . . .

On 23 June the Germans scuttled their surrendered ships anchored in Scapa Flow.

24 June. Longfords
We are all so disgusted with the Peace that we have ceased to discuss it – one tries to banish it from one's mind as an unclean thing that will

be swept away by common consent when the world is once again sane. Two years ago I was angry with GBS when he said that if the Allies won, 'they would skin Germany alive.' He made, of course, a small verbal error: he ought to have said, 'they would *try* to skin Germany alive.' As it is necessary that Germany should keep alive, if only in order to fulfil the right conditions of the Peace, and as, in any case, sixty million persons cannot be compelled to die, the Allies will fail. The dramatic sinking of the German fleet by the German sailors in British waters is to my mind the most fitting celebration of this Peace by Violence. The Germans will sink other things besides their fleet before the Allies repent this use of victory: the capitalist system for instance. The Germans have a great game to play with Western civilization if they choose to play it, if they have the originality and the collective determination to carry it through. They can compel their victors to accept the new order which they devise to heal the sorrow and the misery of their own people. . . .

5 July. [41 Grosvenor Road]
Completed Part I of our new book on Socialism – the indictment of profit-making capitalism. I started at the end of February after finishing the Minority Report on Women in Industry. It has entailed a lot of reading and considerable toil of thought. But I have worked well at it and we are back in our old style of partnership, I designing the separate chapters and dictating a rough draft and re-dictating until it expresses my mind, and then Sidney correcting all of it, and rewriting and adding sections to it after discussion with me – the finished product representing the combined thought of 'the Webbs'. In the end we never disagree! . . .

Alfred Cripps, Lord Parmoor, was vicar-general (appointments made by Anglican bishops to assist them especially in legal and administrative matters) at Canterbury 1902–24 and at York 1900–14. Herbert Murray Burge (1862–1925) was Bishop of Southwark 1911–19 and of Oxford 1919–25.

14 July. [41 Grosvenor Road]
The three old wives – Kate, Mary and Beatrice – watched this morning with gladness, tinged with sorrowful memories of our sister Theresa, our dear brother-in-law Alfred married to Marion Ellis, daughter of the late Liberal statesman John Ellis. Alfred has excellent taste in women. He chose the most charming of the Potter

sisters; he wanted, as a widower, to marry the saint-like Beatrice Creighton, and he has now won an exceptionally attractive woman, good as gold, able, and most pleasant to look at. All his children and their mates were there beaming their goodwill. The two were reverently ecstatic. Southwark Cathedral and Bishop Burge added a gracious solemnity to the marriage of the vicar-general of York and Canterbury.

During the war Parmoor has developed into a political idealist. Whatever may have been his reasons for being against the war at the beginning, the horrors of it, and the revengeful spirit of the peace, have turned him into something very like an international socialist. So does evil company corrupt good manners! All the men who held fast by the capitalist creed that he used to believe in have been eager to crush Germany and impose their countries' material power on the world; all those who have believed in the coming of a brotherhood of individuals and races, based on equality in material circumstances, have hated the rule of force and spoils of the victors. The Church has bitterly disappointed him in its casuistical support of the peace-that-be. . . . *determination of right and wrong*

We spent the week-end at Lion Phillimore's with Edward Grey, whom we had not seen since August 1914 – when he told us, at a dinner at Haldane's, that this war would bring into being labour governments all over the world. When I reminded him of his prophecy, he said: 'I thought that the crust of the present social order had worn very thin and that a great war would break it down. I did not believe that the war could last for more than a year. But now after four years I believe that we shall see a world revolution comparable to the break-up of the Roman Empire.' He is far more convinced of the imminence of revolution here in England than we are. 'Any day Downing Street may find that they have behind them neither the police nor the army, and that some other body, not sitting at Westminster, is exercising the executive authority based on the People's will.' He awaits calmly, through his physical blindness and curious intellectual aloofness and personal disinterestedness, the coming changes. It is difficult to discover whether his attitude is one of hope and faith or lack of hope and faith in the new social order. He is uncertain whether it will be order or anarchy. For the rest, he is the same true-hearted, public-spirited and fair-minded English gentleman that he has always been; without originality, without any specific intellectual gifts, without the desire for social change, and without any prejudices against it, without evil instincts and without heroic passion — an incarnation of negative goodness. . . .

Pat Dobbs (1900–81) was the eldest son of Rosy and George Dobbs. Arthur Henderson had done well in a by-election at Widnes, Lancashire and was back in the House of Commons. In the by-election at Rusholme, Manchester, Dr R. Dunstan stood as a socialist against a left-wing Liberal; the Tory was returned. This contest raised the question of the relationship between the Liberals and the Labour Party. Ivy Schmidt was Beatrice's secretary. After her marriage she became more widely known as Molly Bolton, an active Labour member of the L.C.C.

24 September. [41 Grosvenor Road]
A healthful and happy time — two months' stay at the cottage at Bryan's Ground, rented from the Russell-Holt sisters — Arnot, Pat Dobbs, Ivy Schmidt, Tawney and GBS to stay with us successively. Sidney drafted the three final chapters for the new edition of *The History of Trade Unionism* and laboriously revised the text of the old edition in its earlier chapters, whilst I drafted the section on trade unionism for our big work on socialism for Sidney's revision and final drafting. . . .

Henderson dined with us yesterday and reported progress. He is naturally enough self-complacent about his great victory at Widnes, but considerably disconcerted at being asked by the Labour Party Executive (at which Sidney was not present) to go down and speak for Dunstan at Rusholme so soon after he had received the active support of the Liberals at Widnes. Sidney was in favour of fighting Rusholme — partly because the Labour Party Executive could not have prevented it, and partly because he thinks it is better to sacrifice some seats now and build up a Labour Party rather than split the Labour Party by an alliance with Asquithian Liberals. The Labour Party has to go through much tribulation before it is sufficiently sound to exercise any real influence: with its present leaderlessness it can exercise no effective control over the government. Henderson is inclined to shirk House of Commons work, hating to find himself subordinate to Adamson and in competition with Clynes and Thomas for the chairmanship of the party — if the party succeeds in displacing Adamson, which I rather doubt if Henderson sulks. . . .

He wanted Sidney to draft a complete scheme for 'socializing industry' – the whole of industry. Said that 'we must come down to bedrock and show that the principle of socialization was applicable today to all industries.' Why should the miners and the railwaymen have the privilege of being socialized? The engineers and other operatives resented this partiality. It would be far better electioneering to have a complete scheme for all industry and get it accepted by the Labour Party conference. We pointed out the difficulties – the demarcation between one industry and another, the absence of brain-power and goodwill in the government service, the peculiar technical requirements in each industry, the universal alarm that any such scheme would arouse, and rightly arouse, considering the incapacity of the Labour Party for the every-day work of their own organizations. At the same time he had a vague idea of making each industry bear the whole cost of its unemployment by a reserve fund from the profits of good years.

Altogether he was in a state of complete puzzledom about the meaning of nationalization, and even suggested that when the mine-owners and railways shareholders were bought out, they should still continue to receive part of the 'profits' whilst the remainder should be divided between the producers and the state. All this confusion I trace to Cole's attempt to make Henderson understand his subtle schemes for manipulating the Labour Party Executive so as to secure the issue of some startling manifesto in favour of revolutionary Guild Socialism. Cole working through Henderson is almost as amusing as Sidney working through Adamson.

'Back to our books' is the moral. Until the intellectuals are really scientific there is not much hope for the Labour movement. The brainworking capitalists will be secure as the rulers of industry. All that we have hitherto done is to change them from dictators into constitutional monarchs – about the stage in political democracy reached by William of Orange.

Industrial unrest and dissatisfaction continued throughout the autumn. The railway strike, begun on 26 September, brought all the railways to a standstill. It was provoked by the high-handed attitude of Sir Auckland Geddes (1879–1945), currently president of the Board of Trade, with whom the railwaymen had been negotiating since February for an increase in wages. Troops were called out and wartime emergency regulations were brought into force. His brother, Sir Eric Geddes, was Minister of Transport. A settlement was made on 5 October providing for the maintenance of wage levels for a year. The government policy of intervention against Russia was vigorously opposed by the labour movement and the Labour Party conference in June voted for direct action to oppose it.

28 September. [41 Grosvenor Road]
The Great Strike – which has been brewing since the close of the war – has happened. Not of the engineers as was expected, nor of the miners as the public has long expected, but of the railwaymen. Never has there been a strike of anything like this in magnitude or social significance which has burst on the world so suddenly; the parliamentary committee, of which Thomas is chairman, knew nothing about it, the Labour Party office and Labour Research Department were equally ignorant – even the Triple Alliance, to which the railwaymen belong, was uninformed. As for the general public, they knew nothing of it before the day when all the trains stopped running.

In our view it has been desired, if not engineered, by the government, engineered by the Geddes brothers, and subconsciously desired by the P.M. The Geddes brothers represent the universal determination of the capitalists to reduce wages to pre-war level – if possible, pre-war-money level, but in any case pre-war-commodity-value level. The P.M. has let the strike happen because he sees in it a good stunt for the next election – he may even think of an immediate election on the issue of Bolshevism and the dictatorship of the extremists of the manual working class. Such an issue would effectively submerge the failure in Russia and all the scandals of his government. It would strike a big blow at the Labour Party and side-track the Asquithian Liberals. It might be the making of a centre party publicly pledged to uphold the condition of political democracy and secretly intent on fastening profit-making capitalism more firmly on the community. We think that the railwaymen were justified in making the continuance of the war wage a test question, though the manner of the strike is not easy to justify. It is exactly one of those occasions when 'direct action' is justified by its success, and condemned by its failure. The purpose of the strike, to stop a reduction of the wages of the lowest grade of labour, is the most commendable of all strikes. Whether the means taken are right depends on the event.

We are all at sea as to what will happen in the next few days. There are rumours that the government are preparing heroic measures – for confiscating the railwaymen's funds, for starving the railwaymen's families, for running the railways with soldiers: there are equally rumours that the trade unions are preparing for Soviets to take over the government of the country. We tend to believe that these suppositions are baseless and that in a week or so there will be a compromise arranged between Thomas and Downing Street – the difference between the terms offered by the government and those stated to be acceptable to the men is really very small, much smaller than seemed to be the case when Geddes hurled his ultimatum at the N.U.R. Executive and the N.U.R. Executive hurled back its proclamation for a strike. But we may be wrong: the situation may develop into a political battle between organized labour and the government backed up, not only by the whole propertied class, but by the great mass of apathetic men and women of the wage-earning class. In that case we think that labour will lose this particular battle. But this defeat will drive the organized workers into political action and probably strengthen the Labour Party of five years hence. . ..

In 1914, at the climax of the syndicalist agitation, the railwaymen, miners and transport workers formed the 'Triple Alliance' for joint action; but owing to the war it was never called into action. The rail strike was settled within a few days by a compromise.

2 October. [41 Grosvenor Road]
The strike has developed unfavourably for the men. The government organization of the food supply is perfect, and there has been a great response to the call for patriotic volunteers. As the facts appear, the railwaymen seem to have been tricked into a false position which no sane person can defend. Lloyd George's offer made on Friday completely transformed Geddes's ultimatum and does not differ substantially from the men's demand. But the offer was made in vague terms across the table and not one of the N.U.R. Executive – all men working at their trade – understood it; they refused to follow Thomas's advice to put off the strike and take time to reconsider the whole business. Now it appears that the strike was a breach of contract, and the government has used this to enable them to confiscate the week's wage which is owing to the men. Now, after the event, the railwaymen call on the Triple Alliance and all the other trade unions to help them out of this hopelessly rotten situation. . . .

The Webbs always made their own printing and publishing arrangements; though they distributed their books to the trade through Longman's, they usually prepared cheap editions for Fabians, trade union members and similar groups. T. Fisher Unwin (1848–1935), founder of the publishing firm which became Allen and Unwin, was married to Jane Cobden, the first woman to be a member of the L.C.C. and the daughter of the great Liberal leader Richard Cobden. They gave his old home, Dunford House, near Midhurst, Sussex, as a country retreat for staff and students of the London School of Economics. The gift led to recurring problems, for Mrs Unwin remained possessively fretful about the house, and it was eventually given up in favour of a financial gift to the L.S.E.

18 November. [41 Grosvenor Road]
For the last six weeks I have been helping Sidney with the three final chapters of *The History of Trade Unionism* – adding sections to each, more especially to the second one, on the status of trade unions within the state. . . . We have arranged to print off a special edition at low price of 5s for the trade unions and other working-class organizations, and have sent out, in conjunction with the Labour Research Department, 60,000 circulars asking for orders prior to December 11th and for new affiliations to the Department . . . Sidney spends most afternoons on the government's profiteering committees and in helping Beveridge organize new developments of the London School of Economics. He is in fact acting very much as if he was chairman of the School and has secured from the Fisher Unwins the gift of a country hostel for students and professors – the old home of Cobden.

Meanwhile, the Labour Party has had two notable successes: great victories in the municipal elections throughout the country, especially in London, and the adoption by the Cabinet of the non-interventionist policy towards Russia. The disasters to the anti-Bolshevik forces are doubtless the immediate cause of the Cabinet's somewhat ignominious confession of the failure of its policy of subsidizing civil war in Russia. But the excellent news service of the *Daily Herald* and the repeated and angry protests from the labour and socialist world has made it impossible for the government to hide its head in the sand. Even the middle class would not stand further expenditure in Russia, with prices steadily rising and the national debt increasing, a debt which sooner or later must be paid by the property-owners.

The dark place in all our thoughts at present is the condition of Central Europe. . . . There is always the question of questions: is

Europe going to recover, or are we on the eve of the first stage in the decline of the white race?

The divisions in the Second International caused by the Russian revolution meant that several socialist parties refused to attend the Geneva conference, put off until August 1920. German Social Democrats and the Labour Party dominated the rump of the organization – the French, the Americans, the left of the German socialists and the I.L.P. all abstained. W.W. Hutchinson (1878–1965), pattern-maker and Guild Socialist, was on the Executive of the Amalgamated Society of Engineers. Benjamin Spoor (1878–1928), who had succeeded to Henderson's seat at Bishop Auckland, became Chief Whip in the 1924 Labour Government. Neal McLean (1875–1953) was elected for Govan in 1918. Arthur Ponsonby was the son of Sir Henry Ponsonby, who was Queen Victoria's private secretary. He had been a Liberal M.P. and was one of the pacifically-minded Liberals who went over to the Labour Party during and just after the war.

1 December. [41 Grosvenor Road]
Again distracted from work on the book by a small but difficult task. The twenty or thirty delegates from the British section of the International Congress met the other day at the House of Commons preparatory to the meeting at Geneva in February or July, and appointed a committee of eight to draw up memoranda on the political system of socialism and on socialization respectively. . . . The meeting of these twenty delegates was significant as typical of the different elements in the fast-developing Labour Party. Henderson was there, dominating the gathering with his ponderous and somewhat pompous common sense, Hutchinson of the Parliamentary Committee acting as a mild-mannered chairman. The I.L.P. contingent was the strongest faction, among them J.R. MacDonald and both the Snowdens, Ben Spoor and Neal McLean (I.L.P. M.P.s) and C.P. Trevelyan and Arthur Ponsonby – typical aristocratic recruits to the most popular of the socialist societies. Adamson came in, invited as chairman of the Parliamentary Labour Party, and sat himself down at the extreme corner of the long table, solitary and ignored, ugly, ineffective, almost mentally deficient relatively to his position as leader of His Majesty's Opposition. . . . But what amused me was to see those ultra Whigs, by condition and temperament – Trevelyan and Ponsonby – sitting among the left wing of the Labour Party, whilst Sidney and I sat as supporters of Henderson and the trade union movement. . . .

There had been sporadic outbreaks of violence in Ireland throughout the year, largely organized by the group called Sinn Fein which had emerged in the 1916 rising. Ambushes and killings culminated in an attack on Field Marshal French, the Viceroy. To counteract the growing disaffection Lloyd George produced one more scheme for Home Rule – two separate parliaments with a single federal council for the whole of Ireland. The Republican Congress in America refused to ratify the Peace Treaty and Woodrow Wilson refused to compromise over the League of Nations. On 2 October he had suffered a stroke and he never recovered his political influence.

25 December. [41 Grosvenor Road]
We have had a happy, healthy, hard-working time since we returned from our country recess the end of September. But I have been haunted, almost more than during the war, with the horrors that are going on in Austria and other Continental countries and with the fact that Europe is on the eve of worse catastrophies than she has yet lived through. The big events of the year: the evil peace, the moral, political and physical fall of Wilson, the savage suppression of Ireland and the success of Bolsheviks – four world tragedies – are horribly perturbing to a benevolent British bourgeois progressive. Where is the freedom broadening down 'from precedent to precedent', either within the British Empire or in the world outside? Before the war we had come to assume that this desired process, combining progress with order, had become the normal way of the world, and a way that was peculiarly Anglo-Saxon. Today we are confronted with Europe in social chaos, Great Britain oppressing subject races, and the U.S.A. folding herself in her self-righteous prosperity, refusing to take part in the settlement of Europe, and leading within her own boundaries an enraged crusade against the new industrial democracy. Even the unprecedented successes of British Labour at the by-elections and for local authorities does not fill us with confidence. We are not convinced that there is in the newcomers sufficient character and intelligence to lead the people in the direction of social democracy.

A great bookselling adventure – selling 19,000 copies of the new edition of our *History of Trade Unionism* to the trade unions prior to publication at the absurd low price of five shillings post free with one in thirteen copies thrown in. We expect to take in sufficient money to pay our whole printers' bill for the three thousand public edition at £1 1s 0d as well as the 19,000 cheap edition. But even if we do not quite manage this, we shall be rewarded by being read by the right people.

∽ 1920 ∾

5 February. [41 Grosvenor Road]
Tom Jones sent a note yesterday, saying that political affairs were critical: might he come to lunch the following day? 'By all means,' I replied, and he came. He wanted to tell us that the P.M. was in trouble about his Cabinet and about his seat, immediately about the miners' demand for nationalization, and generally because he had not made up his mind whether he would continue to manipulate the Coalition or come out into opposition. The P.M. feels there is a set against him in the labour movement, Jones told us with a note of interrogation in his voice. He reported that Cabinet meetings had been continuously stormy. Most of the Ministers (and Jones expressly mentioned Fisher by name) were dead against nationalization, the capital levy, and dny generous dealing with Ireland. They were sullen about Russia and unwilling, if not actually hostile, to any recognition of the Bolshevik government. The King's speech had been under discussion, and nearly all the positive proposals – he mentioned the abolition of the Poor Law – had been struck out by the Cabinet. . . .

We told Jones that whether Lloyd George would be accepted by the Labour Party in the House of Commons *after the next election* we did not know: the 'Bolshevik' speech before the last election stuck in the throat of every Labour man. But one thing was clear: if he wanted the chance of leading or even of co-operating with the Labour Party at some future time, *he had to take his decision now.* The parting of the ways had come, and no one who was not prepared to go the whole way towards the socialist equalitarian state *as his goal* would be accepted even as a colleague. . . . Lloyd George's present colleagues had not the remotest intention of changing the existing order. . . .

18 February. [41 Grosvenor Road]
In the last few months Sidney has been the central figure in an internal struggle among the miners in the Seaham division of

Durham. In August, he had pathetic requests from various miners' lodges and I.L.P. branches within this division that he should allow himself to be nominated as candidate for adoption by the divisional Labour Party, made up almost exclusively of miners' lodges. He wanted to refuse straight away, but I begged him to pause, because I thought he ought to respond to any request by organized labour to have him as their parliamentary candidate in the coming crucial contest. So he temporized and tried meanwhile to find out what were the wishes of the Central Executive of the Durham Miners' Association. For five months they maintained dead silence on the matter. At last, about a week ago, having received more requests – in all from twelve separate organizations – he provisionally accepted nomination. Yesterday he got a courteously but formally worded letter from the political secretary of the Durham Miners' Association to say that the matter had been considered by the Executive, and that they had decided that as Seaham had been 'endorsed as a miners' constituency', and as they had candidates who had been selected by ballot as parliamentary candidates and who had not yet been placed, they had informed the Seaham Labour Party that they ought to select a miner to fight the seat. Sidney wrote immediately to all his supporters withdrawing his name and sent a copy of his letter to the political secretary with the assurance that he only desired to be of service to the Association and would abide by the decision.

Now this dispute raises in an acute form the question whether or not the trade unions are going to limit the candidates to members of their respective organizations. Sidney stated that he would be financially responsible for the election and would neither ask nor accept the trade union funds in payment of his expenses. Further, the Durham miners have excluded the officials from being M.P.s, so that the miners are limited to checkweighmen and working miners, who would in any case have to give up their work and their pay if elected. What is interesting is that, according to some Durham miners who came up to London, Sidney's selection by some of the lodges was only a sign of a growing distrust of the competence of the present miners' members for parliamentary careers and a desire to make use of sympathetic intellectuals. So far as Sidney is concerned, the matter is closed, but it may lead to a reversal of the present rule or custom of limiting the choice of trade unionists to their own membership. If so, it will be immensely significant.

355

George Lansbury made a six-week visit to Russia in February and his wireless message was the first to be made to Britain by any newspaperman since the revolution.

25 February. [41 Grosvenor Road]
I have been working in the mornings at the report on Socialization and the Constitution of the State of Tomorrow, and spending spare hours in the late afternoon and evening typing out my diary, a task which amuses and interests me vastly. I find all sorts of interesting facts and impressions, not to mention the development of my own inner emotional and intellectual life, which I had completely forgotten. I am, in fact, on one of the water-sheds of life. Behind me is the long record of each stage of my journey, a record which excites my curiosity, in piecing it together into a connected whole and describing the successive environments of men and things that I have passed through. In front of me, the last stage of our working comradeship and probably a short stage, completing as far as strength permits all our unfinished work. . . .

Meanwhile the big public event is the victory of Soviet Russia over all her enemies and the transformation of the Bolshevik government into a bureaucratic administration exercising far-reaching coercive power over the life and liberty of the individual citizen. George Lansbury's spectacular visit to Russia and his wireless message to the *Daily Herald* have certainly raised his prestige and that of his paper. Lansbury has, in fact, become the 'chartered revolutionary of the world'. He has achieved a position from which he can collogue with the Coalition government and get all sorts of permits denied to the authorized representatives of organized labour, and yet preach revolution from the platform of the Albert Hall and be accepted as a leader by the most *enragé* of British Bolshevists. He has gained his position not only because of his many talents, but also because he is known to be a fervent and pious Christian and a model domestic man. He is one of the most significant men of today, ranking in his unique position above either the leading trade unionists or the leaders of the I.L.P. He has no constructive capacity – he cannot, in fact, distinguish between one type of society and another. But as a ferment for dissolving the present order of things by a strange combination of mystical love for men and an impatient iconoclastic fervour against all existing institutions, he is certainly most uniquely effective.

356

In 1911 Lloyd George had asked Robert Morant to supervise the new National Insurance Act. Morant was at this time First Secretary at the Ministry of Health, which had been set up in 1919 largely on his initiative. He died on 13 March after a few days' illness.

18 March. [41 Grosvenor Road]
Robert Morant gone, died suddenly of septic pneumonia at the zenith of his powers and in the place in which his talent was of most service. With all his faults – and he had some grave ones – he remains one of the biggest minds and one of the most attractive personalities I have known. Looking over five and twenty years of friendship and common work, he has been a stalwart, alike as a brilliant and devoted public servant and also as a true friend. His loss is like the loss of Creighton or of W.C. Anderson – irreparable. He will not be replaced by some other man. . . . He had some of the enigmatical quality of Creighton, a strange complex of mysticism and cynicism, of principle and opportunism, of quixotic affection and swift calculation. . . . At the service this afternoon there was a great gathering of civil servants – a fine body of men – I think the most upright and intelligent class in the community. Far from the civil service being over-staffed, it is under-staffed and underpaid. The silly cry of a 'swollen bureaucracy' is perhaps the meanest ingratitude of political parties and of the political press. . . .

11 May. [41 Grosvenor Road]
The last six weeks has been strenuous work, day after day, finishing our book on *A Constitution for the Socialist Commonwealth of Great Britain*. It has been a great lark writing it: I have never enjoyed writing a book so much. . . . Neither of us would have written the book alone – it is the jointest of our joint efforts. No one will like our constitution: we shall offend all sides and sections with some of our proposals. But someone must begin to think things out, and our task in life is to be pioneers in social engineering.

The sitting member for Seaham was a solicitor, Major Evan Hayward, a Coalition Liberal elected in 1918 with Lloyd George's 'coupon'. Just before the Webbs left for Durham they were at a dinner to celebrate the departure of W. Sanders and the appointment of F.W. Galton, their first research secretary, as general secretary of the Fabian Society.

357

8 June. [? Roker Hotel, Sunderland]

On 18 February I entered in this diary the first act of our connection with the Seaham division of Durham. The Seaham miners persisted in their demand for Sidney as candidate in spite of the opposition of the Executive of the Durham Miners' Association, who had scheduled the seat for a miner and had some half-a-dozen official candidates to provide for. So Sidney consented to come here for a fortnight's tour of the constituency and then to abide by the decision of the local Labour Party, and promised to stand if the selection conference were practically unanimous. So here we are, speaking in all the miners' villages 'on approval'. There seems little doubt that he will be selected as their candidate so we are in for the job of winning the constituency.

The division is a long narrow belt of coast with some eighteen pit villages at about two-mile intervals, and the port of Seaham as the centre. The miners themselves are a mixed lot, drawn to new mines from all parts of the United Kingdom – Staffordshire, Lancashire, Scotland and Ireland. They are very well off in the way of wages; their houses are substantially built but terribly overcrowded; their hours short, and they enjoy the priceless advantage of field and wood and coast wherein to roam about in their spare time and as a playground for their children. But there is no centre of intellectual or spiritual life; a mechanically black-leg-proof union is the only corporate life. [Apart from] a dingy and commercialized Co-operative and a vigorous Club movement for the purpose of drinking 'out of hours' [there is] little or no social life, nothing but the 'pictures' in the larger villages or the same pictures on a more sumptuous scale in Sunderland. The women have no leisure and not much sleep with the three, sometimes four, shift system and the perpetual coal-dust to grapple with. Consequence, every woman is short and pale. There is a lot of money flying about and much spent in alcohol and betting. The life seems, in fact, to be completely materialist, though fairly respectable.

There are groups of fervent chapel folk. Here and there is a bookish miner, usually a secularist with quite a large bookcase filled with the well-known poets and classics, a little philosophy and more economics. It is to these 'bookish miners' that is due the pertinacity with which Sidney's candidature has been pursued. How far they represent their rough and stupid fellow miners is doubtful, though probably these will vote in herds when the day comes. But the present member is a Liberal who stood with uncertain colours as the Coalition. He is an astute wire-puller and is reported to have suborned the old officials of some of the principal lodges. He was returned with a three thousand majority over the miners' candidate at the last election. There is little or no organization in the constituency and a quarrel with the Executive at Durham over the prospective candidate. The bookish miners are not good organizers or leaders, and there is no one of light and leading in the constituency. Against this is the fact that it is virgin soil. These miners are not blasé. They are children in politics; they are not critical and they are solid trade unionists. And the climate is invigorating and the coast beautiful and we have discovered a pleasant little hotel to live at with a private sitting room at 7s 6d a day, overlooking the sea. So on the whole we are content to proceed with this adventure. But it will mean six weeks' work in the year, organizing and lecturing – £300 a year expenditure or more prior to the election, and probably £800 or £1,000 for the election, whenever it comes. And we are both over sixty! And it is I who am responsible for persuading Sidney to undertake it with the risk, if not the certainty, of getting into Parliament and all the disturbance of our daily life that this would involve. . . .

The Webbs had attended the Labour Party conference at Scarborough 18–25 June. Edward Mandell House (1858–1938), known as Colonel House, was Woodrow Wilson's closest adviser, particularly in foreign affairs. He was a member of the U.S. peace commission and helped draft the Treaty of Versailles and the covenant of the League of Nations. His friendship with Wilson ended in 1919 because of differences on the conduct of the peace negotiations. A delegation of representatives of the Labour Party, the T.U.C. and the I.L.P. visited the Soviet Union in May 1920, and the visit convinced them that the new Russia was under a dictatorship. It had a particularly profound effect on the I.L.P., which now shed its Communist sympathizers to the Communist Party of Great Britain, formed on 31 July as an affiliate of the new Third or Communist International.

1 July. [41 Grosvenor Road]
We were well satisfied with the Labour Party conference. Hutchinson of the Amalgamated Society of Engineers (a quiet, progressive-minded trade unionist) made an admirable chairman. Over the great assembly of twelve hundred delegates (including many extremists, with a crowded strangers' gallery) he kept perfect order

by tapping the glass of water in front of him with his pencil. The conference discussed with admirable temper and intelligence foreign and imperial affairs – Russia, Hungary, India, Ireland – together with the internal organization of the Labour Party and its relation to the Parliamentary Labour Party. The speaking was excellent and there was a unity of sentiment and a considerateness of statement that was beyond praise. The weak side of the Labour movement showed itself behind the scenes, i.e. the utter lack of any desire for mutual consultation among the leading men. We were staying in the big hotel at which the Labour Party Executive, the principal miners' delegates and the leading men of the other unions, as well as practically all the intellectuals, were quartered. Never once did I see MacDonald, Thomas, Clynes, Smillie, Hodges, Shaw, talk to one another . . . each leader, whilst scrupulously polite to all the others, sat apart with his wife and admirers, or fellow delegates of the same industry. MacDonald wandered about, a restless and uneasy spirit, generally in company with the ex-Liberal M.P.s who have joined the Labour Party and who are now posing as left-wing. . . .

Colonel House and his wife spent an evening with us last week. Mrs House is a typical American society woman, eager to be in the centre of the picture, with an ugly voice and fussy egotistical intelligence, who resented the fact that House wanted to talk and we wanted to talk to him. Having to deal with three persons who knew their own mind she collapsed into silence (for which I was remorseful afterwards) and hurried House away as soon as she decently could. But we were interested in our interview. He is a plain, homely American gentleman without egotism but not unaware of his own importance. He talked with apparent intimacy about Wilson's failure owing to his contempt for the Senate and his refusal to take with him to Paris trusted Republican leaders or any representative men who were not his sworn liegemen, but who would have helped him afterwards to carry his fellow countrymen. . . .

The Labour-Socialist delegates from Russia have brought over many diverse impressions of Russia. All agreed on the wicked policy of intervention. By a large majority they condemn the Soviet form of government for Great Britain. Some of them have seen a horrible spectre of socialism in the Soviet despotism – a new creed autocracy more terrible than any theocracy. The conclusion to which Sidney and I had come from a distance – that the Soviet government had changed its basic ideal from workers' control and general anarchic freedom to the rigid consumers' collectivism – seems to be true. The Soviet government is the 'servile state' in being – the very thought of which was denounced by the rebels of 1910–14. But it is a servile state run by fanatics who refuse any compromise with the 'bourgeois fetish' of personal freedom. It is only fair to add that the fanaticism in question is the faith in the common good as interpreted by the Communists.

11 July. [41 Grosvenor Road]
Sidney was unanimously chosen yesterday by the Seaham divisional Labour Party to fight the next general election. There is a strange irony in these simple-minded miners, living in a remote backwater, seeking out and persistently pressing into their service the most astute and subtle – and, be it added, the least popular leader of the labour and socialist movement. The explanation is that these leading men in these isolated pit villages are readers of books and not hearers of revivalist speeches and propagandist lectures. . . .

Rabindranath Tagore (1861–1941), Indian poet, novelist and mystical philosopher who enjoyed an international reputation as a spiritual leader, was also a social reformer and internationalist.

20 July. [41 Grosvenor Road]
Tagore, whom we met at lunch yesterday at Kate Courtney's, is in no doubt about the purpose of life: it is divine love working through the direct communion of individual minds with God – the imminence of God, as he terms it. But he ignores science, or the knowledge of God working through nature, ascertained by the physical senses, and he unhesitatingly condemns any application of science to human relations, any deliberate ordering of these relations by the light of knowledge of results. Hence, whilst he resents any criticism of Hindu tradition or of Hindu rites, still more of Hindu mysticism, he is a bitter and uninformed critic of Western government, of Western industrial organization and of Western nationalism, of Western science. 'All governments are evil,' he dogmatically asserts. 'The intellect solves no problems,' is his constant implication. But he is not content to be the seer and the poet – the man who attains wisdom through contemplation – he must needs condemn the man of action, the lawyer, the administrator and the politician

and even the scientific worker. This quite unconscious and spiritual insolence, this all-embracing consciousness of his own supreme righteousness (compared to men of action) is due, I think, to the atmosphere of adulation in which the mystic genius lives and has his being. . . .

The practical man is always being opposed and criticized, and he has to live with his critics and often actually to work with them. This tends to make him humble and tolerant, especially in a democratic country in which he cannot use force to compel his fellows to agree with him in word and act. The man of action may become cynical; he may become pessimistic; he may even take to violent courses. But he seldom becomes, at least within a Western democracy, insolently contemptuous of all other types of men. He may dislike the artist, the poet and the mystic. But he does not condemn them; he often values and adores them.

In this digression – a digression due to a latent feeling of anger at Tagore's quite obvious dislike of all that the Webbs stand for – I fail to do justice to Tagore as a unique person. He has perfect manners and he is a person of great intellect, distinction, and outstanding personal charm. He is beautiful to look at; he clothes himself exquisitely; the rich, soft grey-ribbed silk wrap, in which his tall and graceful figure is enveloped, tones into his iron-grey hair and beard. A finely-wrought thick gold chain, winding in and out of the grey garment, tones into the rich brown hue of his skin. His speech has the perfect intonation and slow chant-like moderation of the dramatic saint. He is indeed an almost too perfect personification of his part in the world's history. . . . He is not the perfect saint. He is far too conscious of his own personality. Perhaps one likes him the better when one discovers that after all he is an imperfect and limited human being and, like the rest of us, far too conscious of his own excellence and of other men's failings.

Charles Roden Buxton was one of the Liberal pacifists who had joined the Labour Party. His brother, Noel Buxton (1869–1948), had been a Liberal M.P. intermittently since 1905 and was returned as a Labour member in 1922. In the spring of 1920 the Poles, encouraged by the French, invaded Russia and supported a nationalist government in the Ukraine as a buffer between themselves and the Bolsheviks. When the Bolsheviks counter-attacked by invading Poland in July, the Poles sought Allied help. On 14 August, Warsaw was saved by a Polish victory at the battle of the Vistula and an agreement was reached between the Poles and the Russians at the Treaty of Riga. The Bolshevik scare now began to die down. Ernest Bevin (1881–1951), who became the general secretary of the Transport Workers' Union in 1921, was the dominating trade union leader between the wars. In 1945, after being wartime Minister of Labour, he became Foreign Secretary.

20 August. [41 Grosvenor Road]
Our week at the Second International in Geneva, in brilliant sun and seething heat, left on my mind a mixed impression of apparent futility and real usefulness. 'All that is senile in the labour and socialist movements,' was the verdict of the rebels, at home and abroad. 'A first-rate conference – one of the most practically useful we have ever had,' asserted the accomplished Camille Huysmans. 'Dull and depressing,' remarked the admirable C.R. Buxton, fresh from investigating Soviet Russia. 'It thrills me,' whispered his no less admirable brother Noel, 'makes me more convinced than ever that I was right to leave the Liberals and come over to Labour'. . . .

Beneath the surface of the conference was a half-recognized anxiety among all who had been Ministers (e.g. the Germans) or who were Ministers (the Danes and the Swedes) or who expected to be Ministers (the British and Belgians) as to whether they themselves, as leaders, had the knowledge or their fellow countrymen had the public spirit and solidarity to bring about the socialist state? To all the delegates, even to the one or two British who felt obliged to oppose, because according to English ideas there must be a recognized opposition in every well-conducted assembly, the Russian Communist dictatorship seemed a huge and disastrous failure. To the Germans it is more than a failure; it is a menace that might destroy the chances of any socialist government, that might even destroy the socialist faith among all sections of the German people. Without science, without goodwill, without tolerance, all of us feel that no social democracy is possible. . . .

Our sojourn for ten days' rest in the High Alps at Argentière led to our being absent from London in the critical days when Henderson and Bowerman, instigated by Bevin, called together the great conference of trade union executives and formed the Council of Action against War with Russia on behalf of Poland. . . . Without doubt many non-Labour elements – all the middle-class pacifists and many middle-class tax-payers – were grateful for the Labour Party's intervention, believing that, whatever Lloyd George might say, it did stem the British government drift towards war with

Russia. But threats are one thing, performance is another. And I very much doubt whether 'direct action', unless it proved to be a symptom of public opinion among all classes, would have been sufficiently universal to be effective. Now that Poland seems to be beating Russia, the British government has reacted and is backing France in her subsidies to Polish militarism. Never has the European outlook been so gloomy as it is now – it is almost worse than in August 1914. Then we were threatened by a flood of violence, which, whatever its results, could, by its very nature, only be temporary. Now we seem [to be] sinking into a morass of violence out of which we are not climbing and, maybe, cannot climb. It is like a nightmare which one dreams is not a nightmare but an awakened state of mind.

On the top of this colossal foreign turmoil comes the ballot for the miners' strike. The miners have a strong case, but it is not a case that justifies, from a national point of view, direct action of the magnitude intended. The miners are among the best paid of manual workers. They are earning, as a matter of fact, as much money as they can spend in their comparatively low state of civilization. Their contention that the price of coal ought to be lowered is a matter for the organization of the citizen consumers in Parliament, and, though here they are on stronger ground, so is the separate question of nationalization. On the other hand, the Miners' Federation, as a legal contracting body, have been swindled by the government. The Cabinet promised to carry out the first Sankey Report and have failed to do so, and it was on that promise that the miners gave up the strike when all circumstances were in their favour. Further, if the country is to be run on the basis of the scramble for the product, direct action is always legitimate. . . .

L.B. Krassin (1870–1926) was an engineering specialist who became a Bolshevik in 1903. He was in London in 1920 to conclude a commercial treaty with Britain. Leslie Haden Guest (1877–1960) was a doctor, journalist and active Fabian who became a Labour M.P. Aylmer Maude (1858–1938) was a follower of Tolstoy and a translator of his work. Many of the fifty-odd foreign socialists invited were, for one reason or another, unable to attend. The Europeans who did attend thought the impromptu invitation to the Russians 'an amazing example of an almost anarchic tolerance on the part of the Fabians' and were afraid of being compromised.

4 September. [41 Grosvenor Road]
A week at the Fabian summer school, Priorsfield, Godalming. Last spring the Fabian Executive determined to set apart a week for the entertainment of foreign socialists in order to promote reconciliation and mutual consultation. . . . When we arrived as joint Directors of the school on Saturday 28th [August], I felt that our plan had failed and that the failure would be a disappointment to all the English and American frequenters of the school who had come specially to meet the continental foreigners. But the week turned out to be a brilliant success . . . the crowning success was the lightning visit of Kamenev and Krassin on the Thursday afternoon. On the previous Sunday morning, when we were all discussing the programme for the week, I suggested that our Russian comrades should be invited to visit the school. The suggestion was received by all the English (except Haden Guest and Aylmer Maude) with the enthusiasm of a holiday party anxious for a sensation. Our foreign guests looked serious and evidently had some misgivings. . . .

Kamenev, a short thickset man with blunt features and a shifty eye, has changed considerably in appearance and manner since the evening, three years ago, when he was brought to Grosvenor Road by Litvinov. . . . Without intellectual distinction, moral refinement or personal charm, he is still a somewhat unpleasant personage.

Krassin, with his tall, lithe figure, his head perfectly set on his shoulders, with his finely chiselled features, simple manner and keen direct glance, looks every inch of him the highly-bred and highly-trained human being, a veritable aristocrat of intellect and bearing. So far as one can gather from listening to him, he is a curious combination of the practical expert and the convinced adherent of a dogmatic creed. But one is tempted to wonder whether this creed does not consist almost entirely in an insistent demand for the subordination of each individual to the working plan of the scientifically trained mind: though, of course, the plan is assumed to be devised in the interests of the community as a whole. . . .

Sidney and I received our visitors in a private sitting-room and gave them tea and cigarettes. . . . Presently it became clear that our Russian comrades were not only willing, but anxious, to address the whole of the guests. So we ushered them into the drawing-room in which some seventy or eighty persons were closely packed on sofa, chair and floor, eager to see and listen to these mysterious visitors from the mythical Bolshevik heaven or the mythical Bolshevik hell. Sidney devoted himself to taking notes of the speeches for the translation and I acted as informal chairman of the meeting.

Kamenev spoke for an hour in ugly but fluent French, giving a journalistic account of the situation within Russia, and of her external relations, the dominant refrains being the paramount need for peace and the pacifist tendencies of the Soviet government. The address was plausible and diplomatic. It left little impression on my mind because every word of it was devised to produce a given effect, and quite obviously so devised. . . . Directly he had finished I suggested that the translation should be deferred until our Russian comrades had left us (as they had to do at nine o'clock that evening), and called on Krassin to address us. He spoke in German, with the' clear enunciation and the limited vocabulary of an accomplished linguist speaking in a foreign tongue, so that even I could understand every word of it. It was a remarkable address, admirably conceived and delivered with a cold intensity of conviction which made it extraordinarily impressive. Especially skilful was his statement of general principles combined with a wealth and variety of illustrative fact and picturesque anecdote. The greater part of the speech was a detailed account of the industrial administration he had actually set up or hoped to introduce into Russia. *Working to a plan*, elaborated by scientific experts, under the instructions of the Communist Party, was the central idea of this industrial organization. Russia's needs, external and internal, were to be discovered and measured up and everything was to be sacrificed to fulfilling them. All the workers by hand and by brain were to accept this plan, and their one obligation as members of the Soviet Republic was to carry it out with zeal and exactitude. There were, he implied, two great sources of power in Soviet Russia which would lead to its redemption and its complete independence of the hostile world by which it was surrounded: the fervour of the faithful organized in the Communist Party; and the scientific knowledge of the experts specially trained to serve that Party in all departments of social and industrial life. . . . Finally, in a splendid peroration, which excited the most enthusiastic applause from all those assembled Fabians who understood German, he asserted that Soviet Russia alone among nations had discovered the 'philosopher's stone' of increased productivity in the consciousness, on the part of each individual Communist, that he was serving the whole community of the Russian people – a consciousness which would transform toil into the only true religion – the service of mankind. . . .

In the minds of many of the audience the question arose, 'How would it be possible to depose from power these three castes – the elders, and leaders of the Communist faith, the scientific experts and the town workmen, not to mention the two castes which were not referred to, the Red Army and the Secret Police – when the need for this autocratic government had disappeared with Russia's enemies?' 'The re-establishment of a caste system – a very natural impulse in an Asiatic race,' remarked the Belgian Socialist Minister with a grin and a shrug of his broad shoulders.

VOLUME 36

Francis Meynell (1891–1975), a poet, journalist and director of the *Daily Herald*, smuggled Tsarist jewellery from Moscow to support the paper. This was done without Lansbury's knowledge but his son, Edgar, arranged a sale through a jewellery broker. When the transaction was discovered by the intelligence service, Meynell resigned from the paper. He gave the money to the Russian Trade Delegation in London.

17 September. [41 Grosvenor Road]
The fantastically silly plotting and lying by the young men of the *Daily Herald*, in order to get £75,000 out of Lenin's government for the immediate needs of their paper, has been a severe blow to the prospects of the Labour Party. . . . The British labour movement has a melancholy record of revolutionary extremists who have ended by being Tories, and there has nearly always been an unsavoury episode of surreptitious funds. One wonders when a generation of leaders of the people will arise who will have learnt that love and pity for the downtrodden cannot achieve its end unless the emotion is accompanied with honesty of reasoning, careful observation and accurate statement of facts. Religious ends and scientific methods are indivisible if mankind is to rise above the brute's battle for life. . . .

5 October. [41 Grosvenor Road]
George Lansbury lunched here yesterday. He is at present in a

chastened mood and I gather that he *did not know* of Meynell's underground dealings and is hurt at the connivance of his son. The young men were determined, he intimated to me, that the *Daily Herald* should survive as a penny paper and Meynell was willing to accept a subsidy from the Third International, virtually from Lenin's government, to keep it alive. The £75,000 was only an instalment – more would have been forthcoming if Meynell had succeeded in his plan. . . .

Mary Macarthur died on New Year's day, 1921. Her husband, W.C. Anderson, had died in the influenza epidemic in 1919. Sir John Bland-Sutton (1855–1936) became president of the Royal College of Surgeons 1923–26.

21 October. [41 Grosvenor Road]
Sidney off to Seaham to talk to miners, who have nothing to do but to listen to the Gospel.

The long-dragged-out negotiations, nearing three months from the miners' initial demand of two shillings a shift increase and a reduction of fourteen shillings on the price of coal, have at last ended in a national strike beginning last Saturday. . . . Why did Robert Smillie, who opened the campaign at the end of July by declaring that the miners were out for nationalization – and nationalization by direct action – crumble up so completely when confronted with the fact of a general strike? . . . At the very end of the negotiations he implored the miners to accept the government terms of wages determined by output rather than resort to direct action. The answer is, I think, that Smillie . . . wanted direct action for its own sake, for the self-sacrifice and solidarity it involved, quite apart from its probable success or failure. But directly this direct action was seen to involve increased hunger and cold, not only to the British workers, but also to the famine – and disease-stricken people of Central Europe, Smillie's moral emotion swung violently back against such cruel consequences. To harden your heart to all this suffering in order to get two shillings a day more became to him an intolerable callousness, degrading the miners' cause.

Of course, the massive destruction of the instrument of a miners' strike is hugely out of proportion to the occasion for its use. When Ireland is being treated with savage brutality, when central Europe is slowly dying, both catastrophes being deliberately brought about by the Lloyd George government, it is tragically absurd to be destroying the national wealth for the sake of a two shilling increase per day in the wages of one of the best-paid sections of British labour. And yet the strike is bigger than the occasion for it: the huge vote and hasty temper in the coalfields are, in a sense, a vote against the government on all issues. What is still more apparent is that if the strike spreads to the railwaymen and transport workers, it will not be in order to get the two shillings for the miners, but in order to defeat a detested government. . . .

About five o'clock Mary Macarthur came to tell me that Bland-Sutton gave her only a few months to live; but that she had determined to undergo another operation by a young woman surgeon against the advice of this elderly specialist – just on the bare chance of survival and cure. She is magnificently brave and sat on the Hendon bench of magistrates that very morning to hear a case of child murder. It is a tragedy to think of W.C. Anderson's death two years ago, and now she is leaving us in the prime of her powers. . . .

'It is curious for me to remember,' she observed as she got up to go, 'that the last time Will and I dined here we said to each other as we walked away how terrible the survivor of the Webbs would feel life to be. Little we thought that the Webbs would survive when both of us . . . had dropped out of the race for good and all.'

'I have been packing up for some time,' I replied. 'My one terror is the fear of losing my mind before I have lost my body. That fate, at any rate, you and your husband have been spared. Every hour of your life has been worth while, and the glorious courage with which you have both faced death may be the hour of your highest vitality.'

We embraced as warm friends and promised that I should come and see her after the operation – if she survived it. She has a wonderfully rich nature, exuberant in its enjoyment of personal life, and yet how persistent in its social purpose. A rare combination.

Margaret Hobhouse had an operation in February 1919 and another on 21 July 1920.

23 October. [41 Grosvenor Road]
After Mary Macarthur comes Margaret Hobhouse. She and I had spent three days at Margate a few weeks ago. She had seemed

depressed and wanted a change of air, so I agreed to go down with her. We had long talks together about life and death and our old comradeship as girls before the lines of our lives diverged – hers into the county magnate's wife and mother of six children, and I into the professional publicist with a 'socialist agitator' as husband and comrade. But throughout these intimate talks she had never hinted at the imminence of death. Yesterday she told me that she had undergone two operations for cancer of the breast – the last as recently as July, a bad operation involving the nerves of the neck. She is now suffering from a chronic cough and breathlessness, a bad symptom. She has told her husband, and after the second operation in July she told her children, but no one else knows. And she has evidently provided herself with the means of a voluntary and easy transit from this life. Her spiritualistic experiences – her certainty that, at any rate, there is proof of telepathy, of a sort of universal consciousness underlying individual life, are a great comfort to her. Poor human beings! How deep is the craving for extended personality beyond the limits of the thoughts, the feelings, the sensations of a mere lifetime on earth. . . .

Both *The Constitution for a Socialist Commonwealth* and *The Consumers' Co-operative Movement* were published in 1920. By the summer, conditions in Ireland had gravely deteriorated and the Sinn Feiners were in open rebellion. The government reinforced the Royal Irish Constabulary by enlisting demobilized men who had not settled into civilian life. They wore the black caps of the R.I.C. with their old khaki uniforms and thus acquired the name of 'Black and Tans'. As a reprisal for the violence of the Sinn Fein, the 'Black and Tans' began their own raids and ambushes. The government, engaged in its new Home Rule proposals, failed in its efforts to inhibit reprisals and during the first months of 1921 the British forces had to cope with a widespread guerrilla war. Terence MacSwiney (1880–1920) – Lord Mayor of Cork 1918–20 – died of a hunger strike in Brixton prison. Wells published *The Outline of History*, a 750,000 word project, in 1920.

29 November. [41 Grosvenor Road]
The autumn is over. Sidney left yesterday for Seaham and I follow him the end of this week, the two of us giving a course of some thirty or forty lectures in miners' villages.

For us these three months have passed away in health and personal happiness and quiet and successful work. The course of lectures at King's Hall in explanation of the proposals in our new book went off well. . . . We filled the hall with course tickets and made a profit of £180 and sold some £30 of literature on the five nights of Webb lectures. Not so bad for the poor old Fabian Society and the 'obsolescent Webbs'! GBS gives his last lecture on Friday – a criticism of the Webb constitution – and the place will be packed. . . .

But these lectures have been a diversion. Our main task has been rewriting and extending the *New Statesman* supplement on the Consumers' Co-operative movement into a book, now in the press, awaiting completion when we return from Seaham. A side-show has been starting a social club for the wives of Labour M.P.s and T.U. officials, about which more anon.

In spite of all this peaceful and successful activity I am continually oppressed by the increasing gloom of the world's affairs. . . . Our absorbing preoccupation during the last few weeks – alas! a symbol of what is happening – have been public funerals! The public pageant of the 'unknown warrior' symbolizing the ten million white men killed in the war, the funeral of the martyred Lord Mayor of Cork, and as a reprisal, the military parade through London of the corpses of the English officers murdered in Dublin. Yesterday Downing Street was barricaded lest there should be yet another and still more impressive public ceremony – the funeral of an assassinated Prime Minister! It is said that he lives in fear of the Green Terror and is looking for a compromise with Sinn Fein.

A trifle to note. We are reconciled to H.G. Wells. He sent me his *History* with an inscription. I wrote a friendly acknowledgement, which he bettered in reply. And after he returned from Russia I asked him and his wife to dinner to meet Haldane and Krassin, Cole and the Shaws. He came: Mrs Wells was otherwise engaged. He is fat and prosperous and immensely self-congratulatory; towards us he was affable, but suspicion lurked in his eye and I doubt whether he is really friendly. Nor do I desire any renewal of friendship. But I am too near to the end of life to care to keep up a vendetta with any human being. Also I have never ceased to respect his work, and his *History* is a gallant achievement. I have still the feeling that in sex relations he is unclean – I still retain the bourgeois puritan creed that faithfulness, in the supreme relation of sex, is part of the higher morality. Not, I think, for any mystical reason but because of the intrinsic value of *faithfulness in any relation of life*, however slight or intense it may be. The only real and abiding sorrows of my life have been breaches in intimate friendships – with the Charles Booths and, later in life, with Betty Balfour. . . . We were never on terms of intimate friendship with H.G. Wells and his wife and it was he who first became hostile to us, long before the Amber Reeves affair. All the same, I was glad to feel that I felt friendly to him. As a publicist he is 'on the side of the angels'.

By a curious coincidence Mrs W.P. [Maud] Reeves spent an evening with us yesterday. With her I have always been on terms of friendliness, not impaired, as was the friendship with her husband, by the curious deterioration in intellect and character of the last years of his working life (as Director of the L.S.E.), a deterioration due to his pathological vanity. She, poor woman, has led a gallant existence of public work and faithful devotion to her husband, rendered tragic by the son's death as airman over the battlefields of France. But she has been comforted by a growing faith in his survival and his constant presence by her side – comforting her and even laughing at her sorrow. Like so many others she has become, during the war, a convinced mystic – a believer in goodness, of the simple, old-fashioned sort. . . .

21 December. Roker Hotel, Sunderland

Clearing up papers, packing books and our scanty wardrobe; a last walk on the sands, Sidney off to give his last lecture. Depressed tiredness is the sensation left by my ten lectures to Durham miners. The campaign has been remarkably successful – Sidney has lectured in every pit village. . . . If an election came now Sidney would be returned with a four-figure majority. . . . But it has been an exhausting experience for me. I am not facile at lecturing – I have no natural gift for it. Giving decidedly stiff discourses on difficult subjects to little meetings from 40 to 150 miners in bitterly cold miners' halls – starting off at six o'clock and getting home at ten – is rather an ordeal for a woman over sixty. . . . Part of my nervous exhaustion was, however, due to the shock of hearing from dear sister Maggie that the radiograph showed her lungs covered with cancer spots and that the end could not long be delayed. She is brave and I try to help her by taking an equally philosophic attitude, treating death as the last adventure in life. All the same, the thought that she also will have gone in a few months, the seventh and best beloved sister, the eldest of my living friends, is gloomy for the survivor. And feeling so near the end, it seems almost absurd to be starting on the new life of having Sidney in Parliament. I console myself with the thought that if anything should happen to me I should like to leave him in a new mental environment and with engrossing calls upon his time and thought. It would be the only distraction from the first months and years of supreme loneliness. And he remains brilliantly well and happy, ridiculously young for his age. . . .

∽ 1921 ∾

1 January. 41 Grosvenor Road
The wicked 1920 dead; but judged by British doings in Ireland and French doings in Germany, the child will be as wicked as the parent.

So far as we personally are concerned, the last year has been happy and successful, with a distinct dash of adventure. The publication of the *Socialist Constitution* was an event in our lives — the summing-up of our observation and reasoning about political and industrial organization, and on the whole the book has been well, though hardly enthusiastically, received. It is far too full of new ideas and detailed application to be a popular work. . . . There has been the Seaham adventure with a new outlook for Sidney, the growing success of the London School of Economics (a solid satisfaction to us) and the progress of the Labour Party as the only possible alternative government to the Coalition. Also, all our personal relations are of the pleasantest: we are at peace with everyone we have to work with, and all the dissidence of dissent and personal jealousies with the labour movement seem to leave us comfortably on our eminence of old age and respected service. Very different from that uncomfortable unpopularity which overtook us between 1912 and 1917, when all sorts of little cliques seemed to mark us down for abuse or avoidance. Personal popularity is a strangely capricious goddess: almost occult in its changefulness. One seems to become the victim of malign influences and then, almost suddenly, the malign influence passes on to other quarry and an almost undue appreciation follows. . . .

Beatrice spent the last two weeks of January in Manchester and Leeds going over the old ground of Co-operative history. The temporary 'dole' was becoming established as part of the social insurance system.

8 February. [41 Grosvenor Road]
The growing unemployment has added to the ferment of rebellious discontent. . . . The wonder is that there is not more outward sign of angry resentment. Perhaps it is due to the fact that the first time some sort of weekly allowance is being received without the stigma of pauperism, and that even the boards of guardians dare not refuse unconditional outdoor relief to those without it. The *principle* of deterrence is completely discarded: no one suggests that unemployment is to be 'punished'; everyone accepts the 'innocence' of the unemployed person and admits that he ought to be maintained either by his own industry or by the community. But at 'what rate'? And is he to be allowed to refuse work except at the high-standard rates brought about by the rise of prices and the shortage of workers during the war? There are vague schemes, none of them immediately practicable, of industrial maintenance; there are the echoes of the Minority Report proposals to equalize employment. . . .

The London home of the Hobhouses was at 1 Airlie Gardens, Hyde Park. Standish was the Potter family home in Gloucestershire and Rusland the house in the Lake District rented by Richard Potter as a holiday home. Konradin had a daughter Elizabeth. Rachel, married to the architect Felix Clay, and the unmarried Eleanor, who was active in relief work, were the two Hobhouse daughters. In 1923 Henry Hobhouse married Anne Grant, secretary at Hadspen since 1910.

9 February. [41 Grosvenor Road]
Since I returned from Seaham during the days and weeks in London, I have walked across the parks to Airlie Gardens to be with my dear sister and old chum in her last days of life. With great courage and cheerful endurance she is experimenting in a possible cure or rather possible arrest of her fatal disease – grimly hanging on to her life, prepared to end it, if it turns out there is no hope. I am the only person with whom she talks freely and whose companionship seems to comfort and interest her. I tell her all about my work; we talk of old days at Standish and Rusland; of her children and her relations to her husband, of the symptoms of her illness, the course of the copper inoculations (the cure she is undergoing, on the

advice of a well-known specialist); we weigh up the desirability of an overdose, if life becomes too painful and dreary, whether it is worth while to hasten the end; we hazard guesses as to how long I shall survive her. She suffers from breathlessness and painful fits of coughing and she can only sleep under narcotics. Her children come and go and I think her three boys, in their different ways, are a comfort to her — her new daughter-in-law Konradin refreshes her with her warm-hearted and effusive affection, and the thought of her being with child is a delight to her. Poor little Rachel Clay feels that her mother does not really care to see her and the strange Eleanor, though she is now decently dutiful, remains detachedly unconcerned, absorbed in her Austrian children. Henry Hobhouse shows little or no emotion: he may feel tragically about his wife's mortal illness: he certainly does not show it. He and I have never been friends. All the same, when I was away at Leeds, he wrote and thanked me warmly — his wife's 'perfect intimacy with one of her sisters was a great comfort', not only to her but to him. Those two have never been one, either in thought or feeling. Their relations have been friendly and affectionate but there has been no intimacy from the first day of courtship to the last days of life. 'I wish I could do more for you, dear old chum,' I said to her yesterday as I stood by her, watching her gasping for breath, 'but all my love cannot sweep away the loneliness of death. Paul may help you but I cannot.' 'Paul, Theresa and Mother,' she answered. 'I dare not let myself think about them. I am too weak for emotion. You are awfully kind to come here, a true friend to the very end.' 'After Sidney you are the person I love most, dear one,' and we embraced, remembering the old days of our girl friendship over forty years ago. Here we are again holding each other's hands close up to the blank wall of death.

Ada Webb recovered and lived until 1940.

16 March. [41 Grosvenor Road]
Margaret Hobhouse died early this morning. I saw her every two or three days and longed that she might sink swiftly. But in spite of all the discomfort and weariness she seemed to cling to the miracle of recovery. The last time we talked together she suggested that we should go to Eastbourne when she was better, though she was quite obviously dying. How difficult is the art of dying. I often wonder

whether one will be able to 'live up' to death so that one's last act shall be good, a help and an inspiration to others. Unfortunately I am constitutionally a coward. Whether I could master cowardice by will and philosophy and a certain subconscious religious feeling, I do not know. But when the time comes I will try to. . . .

By a strange coincidence I have visited three persons dying of cancer in the last nine months: my sister-in-law Ada Webb, Mary Macarthur and Margaret Hobhouse. And Margaret is the second of my sisters to die from it and the third to be attacked. In my young days it was tuberculosis that was the fearsome thought: now it is cancer. All elderly folk live in terror of it. . . . I take up my work again sorrowing and with a strange fear of the ordeal through which I like all others must pass. A fear, not of death, but of the fear of death.

1921 saw a fundamental change in policies and attitudes. Government intervention in the economy had seemed to offer fresh prospects for the country after the war, but it was becoming increasingly clear that the projected betterment schemes were unacceptably expensive. The runaway inflation in Germany and Austria was a warning of the danger of solving problems by creating government credit. Subsidies for housing were now cut off, controls were taken off food, the mines, railways and agriculture. This change of policy meant the abandonment of election promises and a weakening of the Coalition. The anger of the miners at the abrupt change of direction resulted in yet another coalfield strike which began on 1 April, the day when government control ended: the abandonment of a national agreement had meant a reduction of wages by as much as a half in some areas. Within a week a general strike was threatened, and when negotiations broke down the strike call was renewed for midnight on Friday 15 April. A Special Defence Force was created and civil war threatened. At the last minute Lloyd George proposed a temporary settlement on wages and the other members of the Triple Alliance (railwaymen and dockers) urged the miners to negotiate. They refused and J.H. Thomas, the general secretary of the N.U.R., called off the planned sympathetic railway strike. This was known as 'Black Friday' and regarded in the labour movement as a day of betrayal and the ruin of the Triple Alliance.

14 April. Roker Hotel, Sunderland
I was exhausted with the winter's work on the book and with sorrow, and I was glad to escape with Sidney to this quiet little place with the North Sea to look at, sometimes in dead calm and sometimes surging in on a North-East gale. The sea is always to me at once a tonic and a sedative, inspiring with new energy and calming down earthly fears. . . .

The Labour storm which has been beating up for the last two years has at last burst. I do not know whether other people are as tired as I am of these storms, but though this one is catastrophic in its bigness, I am merely bored by it. We tell each other that it means a good deal: the miners have a splendid case, there was never so great a solidarity of working-class feeling and action. With so much fervour and determination, *something must happen*. And yet it all seems to be a futility which has little constructive element in it. Of course there will be another compromise: one side or the other will get scared and temporarily give way. But no progress will be made towards a better state of things. The capitalists, the government and the labour movement will all come out of this big clash of arms rather more angry and rather more obstinately set on not playing the other's game, determined to manoeuvre for a better vantage ground from which to deliver yet another battle. It brings nearer a general election on a purely class basis – that is all. And in that election the present wicked government will win the odd trick and Sidney will find himself in Parliament. The prospect is not pleasing.

Chequers was a house in Buckinghamshire given by Lord Lee during the war to be a permanent country house for Prime Ministers and it had only recently been brought into use. Robert Williams (1881–1936), former coalminer and journalist, was general secretary of the Transport Workers' Federation 1912–23.

18 April. [Roker Hotel]
'The Strike cancelled' was the staggering new line of yesterday's evening paper. A catastrophic anti-climax (if such a term be permissible). My forebodings were justified. 'A wasteful futility' has been this aspiration towards decisive solidarity. We know nothing of what has happened except what is in the newspaper. But the leaders clearly funked it: Thomas, Bevin and even Williams and a majority of the executives of the N.U.R. and Transport Workers rode off on the refusal by the miners' Executive to ratify Hodges's unauthorized offer to give up temporarily the national pool and national rate and discuss the district rates offered by the employers. Hodges is paying the penalty of his swelled-headedness of the last years, as leading tenor of the Labour chorus. . . . The manual workers, organized as producers, cannot find men of sufficient character and intellect to lead them in the higher ranges of statesmanship. That is the plain truth. The trade union officials are

not 'fit to govern': they are not even equal to their own extremely limited business of collective bargaining with the strike as the sanction. This cancelling of the strike may produce an internal turmoil that will destroy any semblance of unity in the labour movement. Of course, it will play into the hands of the Communist Party and stimulate and justify its disruptive policy. And that makes for reaction. There must be a gay party at Downing Street or Chequers tonight! . . .

The Half Circle Club, which provided a social centre for the wives of Labour politicians, is described by Beatrice in the entry on 16 July. Richard Ellis Roberts (b.1879) was briefly literary editor of the *New Statesman*. The poetry of the American poet Vachel Lindsay (1879–1931) was particularly effective when read aloud. Susan Lawrence (1871–1947) was a middle-class Labour politician and organizer of the National Federation of Women Workers. Clynes had just replaced Adamson as Labour leader in Parliament.

24 April. 41 Grosvenor Road
I came away from Roker four days before Sidney could leave in order to be present at a gathering of the Half Circle Club and their male friends. . . . Over a hundred persons turned up and we had a rollicking evening, with friendly chatter and a vivid entertainment by Ellis Roberts, recitals from Vachel Lindsay's Negro poems, the company who could not get seats squatting on the floor, all of us trying to sing the boisterous choruses. Henderson acted as chairman, introduced Ellis Roberts and was in his most beneficent mood and delighted with the entertainment. At the end of the evening he talked quite seriously with me about developing the Half Circle Club by a grant from the Labour Party Executive so that we might entertain on a bigger scale. What interests me is the unusual friendliness, the absence of any constraint between the different sections of women who have joined; the wives of the Labour M.P.s and T.U.C., the professional Labour women like Susan Lawrence and Margaret Bondfield, the wives of the well-to-do Labour candidates like Mrs Noel Buxton and Mrs Trevelyan. I am aiming at bringing into the workaday Labour world an element of intellectual distinction. We have to remodel official society on the basis of the simple hard-working life tempered by fastidiously chosen recreation and the good manners inherent in equality between man and man.

The gossip of Eccleston Square throws no further light on the great strike fiasco. Thomas and Bevin had from the first objected to the Triple Alliance strike and Thomas had been intriguing with other parties to prevent it. . . . One of the worst features of this ludicrous and tragic business has been the failure in loyalty of these men to each other; even poor Clynes, the leader of the Parliamentary Labour Party, being left to make his speech on Friday afternoon in total ignorance of the cancelling of the strike when the Front Bench had been informed of it by Thomas. I wonder when these men will learn the elements of good comradeship. According to Cole, the Cabinet had decided to climb down when they were told that the strike was cancelled.

Apart from all these petty personal jealousies it is as clear as noonday that general strike on such a narrow issue as whether you are to decrease wages is an absurdity which could not be carried through. . . . The general strike will only be successful to resist some revolutionary action on the part of the government, like an unpopular war or a change in the constitution not sanctioned by public opinion, or the imprisonment or execution of some person or persons. Intense suffering by the strikers, overwhelming loss and inconvenience to the community will never be endured in order to improve the terms of employment of some other section of the community. A general strike must, in fact, be political in the largest sense of the word: otherwise it won't happen or will peter out before its effect is felt.

Robert Cecil (1864–1958) was Lord Salisbury's third son. He was a Liberal M.P. 1906–23, when he became president of the League of Nations Union.

19 June. Brighton Labour Party conference
After a refreshing three weeks at Dunford, the country home of the London School of Economics, in glorious sunshine and without other work but a little proof-correcting, we find ourselves once again at the Labour Party conference. Clynes brought down the news, told him by Lord Robert Cecil, that Lloyd George was considering resigning, and after the King had sent for other leaders and failed to get a government, he would advise the King to dissolve Parliament. Supposing that he, Clynes, was sent for, was he to accept office, and form a government, and go to the country as a government? The little sub-committee, Henderson, MacDonald, Clynes and Sidney, decided that he must accept and go to the country as a government. However absurd and unexpected such an

acceptance would seem to all the other politicians, it would give status to the Labour Party and improve their chances at the polls. In forming such a government, outsiders will have to be invited to join; Haldane as Lord Chancellor, possibly Parmoor and some Liberals, but they were to join *not as Liberals but as 'non-party' Labour sympathizers*. It was also taken for granted that Labour Party candidates would be included in such a Cabinet, MacDonald and Sidney, for instance. From what Henderson said to me, Sidney was to be Chancellor of the Exchequer! However, I very much doubt whether anything so dramatic will come to pass. It would be a phantom Cabinet and would disappear at the election. It is inconceivable that Labour should come back a majority with only some three hundred candidates in the field. One satisfactory feature of the present situation is the completely friendly partnership between Clynes and Henderson.

The first of a series of attempts to affiliate the newly-formed Communist Party to the Labour Party was massively defeated, but individual Communists were still able to enrol; and it was some time before the Labour Party excluded Communists attending as delegates nominated by affiliated trade unions.

27 June. [41 Grosvenor Road]
The conference was a gloomy gathering with the imminence of the miners' defeat, with the funds of every trade union fast disappearing, some of the wealthiest unions, e.g. the steel-smelters, being bankrupt, not through any strike or lock-out, but merely because of unemployment benefit; whilst other unions are not only denuded of money but are engaged in or on the eve of a strike or lock-out. But though the delegates were depressed, they were not exasperated or revolutionary. Quite the contrary: the trend of opinion was towards the right, the pendulum was once more swinging to political action. It was a Clynes-Henderson conference, the I.L.P. being in abeyance and the Communists a despised minority. And outwardly there was no sign of impending disaster to the manual working class. The leading trade union officials and Labour M.P.s were there with their wives, living at expensive hotels, and enjoying the brilliant sunshine at a fashionable seaside, without any consciousness of the disparity between their lives and the circumstances of their members. It is difficult to criticize their conduct in this respect, though my instinct is against the extreme comfort, not to say luxury, in which

the Labour Party and Trade Union Congress Executive committees live and have their being at these annual conferences. *We* find ourselves, for instance, living far more sumptuously when we go on Labour Party business than we should do if we were on our own. But who would suggest that it would pay the labour world for their executives to be quartered at hotels where they could not get the necessary facilities for committee meetings? All the same, *I think the standard ought to be a simpler one.*

In the summer of 1921 the idea of keeping Ireland under the London government was finally abandoned, and the years of alternating conciliation and coercion were over without success for either tactic. A truce was declared and conversations took place between the government and the Sinn Fein leaders, now regarded as a provisional government. The former Boer leader General Jan Smuts (1876–1950), who had served in the wartime Cabinet, went to Ireland to help negotiations; it was hoped to keep the country within the Commonwealth by giving it dominion status. Sinn Fein delegates agreed to a conference in London at which dominion status was proposed, with Northern Ireland being left to decide its own relations to the new dominion. A fatal division among the Irish leaders now appeared. The hard-line Republicans, who had led the 1916 rising and carried the brunt of the guerrilla fighting, believed that the proposals did not provide for the Republic and did not promise the end of partition. Negotiations continued throughout the summer between Lloyd George and Eamon De Valera, the President of Sinn Fein, who agreed to a conference on 11 October in London. It went on until 6 December, delays being caused by frequent references back to De Valera, who had stayed in Dublin. Finally a bargain was struck. The Irish accepted Dominion status – the Free State – in return for a private undertaking that Ulster's boundaries would be so contracted by the award of a boundary commission that it would have to join Southern Ireland in order to survive. When a treaty was signed in London, however, it was rejected by the leaders in Ireland, because it retained the oath of allegiance to the King. It was eventually accepted by the Irish parliament by a narrow majority. The refusal of the dissidents to accept the treaty soon led to a civil war between the Free Staters and the Irish Republican Army. The Labour Research Department soon became a separate and long-surviving research agency, linked to the Communist Party but continuing to offer a service to many trade unions. Fred Bramley (1874–1925) became the general secretary of the T.U.C. in 1923. There was a big demonstration of the unemployed in London on 11 July.

12 July. [41 Grosvenor Road]
There is a strange feverishness in London today, a physical feverishness brought on by the amazing light and heat of the drought; a mental feverishness arising from the truce in Ireland and the peace conference at Downing Street. We are all of us restlessly hopeful

that there is to be at last an end to the infamous tragedy of a peculiarly bestial civil war, for which we, the British democracy, are responsible. It is a blow to the government of Great Britain that it is the Premier of South Africa, backed up by those of Australasia and Canada and the foreign power of the U.S.A., to whom Ireland will owe her liberty of self-government, a sign that power to rule is passing from England to other English-speaking communities.

There remains the black fever of unemployment. The Thames Embankment at night is once again the resort of tired and hopeless men and women. This rising tide of destitution is still inarticulate and orderly. But will it remain so? And if the *miserables* of Great Britain take to direct action like the *miserables* of Ireland, will there be yet another civil war, more chaotic and disastrous because it concerns a greater mass of human beings? . . .

Meanwhile, exit the Labour Research Department! Cole, Arnot and Co. have destroyed it. And my particular policy of nursing these young men into recruits to the Labour Party has proved to be futile. Perhaps by this fostering care I have prevented them from doing as much mischief as they might have done; possibly their really disinterested and clever work may have set a high standard for any future department at Eccleston Square. But by exciting antagonisms in every direction, by offending Gillies and Bramley, by rousing the malicious jealousy of MacDonald, by alienating Greenwood and Mallon, and many members of the Labour Party Executive, and nearly all the parliamentary committee of the T.U.C. and finally by Arnot and his group joining the Communist Party . . . they have made themselves quite impossible. So the Research Department has notice to quit Eccleston Square, and all that is now in question is how exactly it is to end its existence. . . .

William James (1842–1910) taught philosophy and psychology at Harvard. Egerton Wake (1871–1929) was an I.L.P. pacifist who became the Labour Party's national agent in 1919. The Fabian Research Department appointed Stephen Hobhouse secretary of an enquiry into the prison system. In 1922 he published, in collaboration with Fenner Brockway, *English Prisons Today*. The wives of the Labour leaders were Henrietta Hodges, Eleanor Henderson, Agnes Thomas, Ethel Snowden, Lucy Buxton and Mary Trevelyan.

16 July. [41 Grosvenor Road]
Whilst I was at Dunford I read with delight William James's letters giving, in an intimate and conversational manner, his

outlook on the universe. It is strange to recall that we stayed a couple of nights with him at Bryn Mawr, U.S.A., in 1898, and that he made so little impression on me that I did not even note the meeting in my elaborate traveller's notes. I remember listening to his address to the girls with full appreciation of its literary form and with amused observation of the discontent of his audience, who felt that they were being 'talked down to' (he notices this fact in a letter about this particular address and visit to Bryn Mawr — without, of course, mentioning that he had met the Webbs). Otherwise I regarded him as one American professor like another, except that I was prejudiced against him as the brother of Henry James, whom I had known in London society and heartily disliked, a dislike which was reciprocated.

Today, and ever since I first began to read William James's works, I find him the truest to me of all metaphysicians. I am exactly at his stage of thought. I doubt where he doubted, I believe where he believed. . . . And, like James, I am more deeply convinced every day of my life that human beings, whether as individuals or in relation to one another in a community, are only admirable so long as their emotions and their thoughts are suffused with faith in a spirit of righteousness, so long as their conduct is guided by the ever-present desire to become part of the manifestation of this spirit of righteousness in the world. . . .

Our personal life flows smoothly to its end with a settled conviction, on my part, that for me the end is not far off. Every night when I embrace my boy and give him my blessing before I retire to my room there is sadness in my heart at the thought that some day — and a day that cannot be far off — it will be our last embrace and that one or other of us will have to live for days, months, possibly a decade of years, alone, bereft of our comrade in work, thought and happiness. But with this sadness there is always present a warmth of gratitude for our past and present happiness. For happy our life undoubtedly is — and that is exactly why I hate the thought of leaving it! In some ways Sidney and I have never been so happy in our personal lives. Welded by common work and experience into a complete harmony of thought and action, we are also in harmony with those with whom we work and have our being. Our servants and secretary are devoted to us; with our relatives we are on the best of terms. In our inconspicuous way we are successful: our books sell better than ever before, the London

School of Economics (Sidney's favourite child) is brilliantly developing under the able direction of Beveridge, whom Sidney selected; the *New Statesman*, though still losing money, is not losing our money and is daily gaining credit. . . . And Sidney's work in the Labour Party . . . brings with it no personal friction and a good deal of pleasurable comradeship with men who respect and trust him. . . .

For myself, I have not done badly these last nine months. I have carried out all the investigation into the Consumers' Co-operative movement. I have planned the new sections of the book and helped Sidney with the actual composition of them. I have set going the Half Circle Club, helped with Stephen Hobhouse's Prison enquiry. . . . And last and least, I have revised the diary of our first tour round the world. . . . And though I suffer now and again from insomnia and indigestion and aches and pains here and there, and occasionally have a panic about a mortal complaint – usually cancer – which turns out to be wholly imaginary, I enjoy good health, if health be measured by capacity to walk eight or ten miles, to concentrate very rapidly on investigation of fresh subjects, and to do all the lecturing and entertaining that is required of me as Sidney's wife. So far, so good. . . .

One of the new interests of my life, but one that gives me some extra work, is the running of the Half Circle Club. . . . The idea arose in my mind in a long talk I had with Mrs Frank Hodges, steaming up the Lake of Geneva at the International Socialist conference last August. Mrs Hodges is an attractive, good-looking woman, with a curiously unsatisfied expression, devoted to her husband but somehow or other discontented with her position in life. After some shyness, she let herself go about the loneliness of her life in London. In Wales she and her husband had their own set, their relatives and childhood friends; they had a common life together. But since she came to London she lived in complete isolation. She knew no one in her immediate neighbourhood. Frank was always away and was making his own friends. . . . When he came home, he was too dead tired to talk about his work or about public affairs. 'I can talk politics as well as anyone else, and the wives of other Labour Party and trade union officials feel just the same as I do. Some of us are becoming hostile to the whole labour movement in consequence.' So I got hold of Mrs Henderson and Mrs Thomas who happened to be at Geneva, and opened up communication with Mrs Clynes when I got back to London, and induced them to issue a private letter asking other Labour women to meet at my house. Hence the Half Circle Club. At first the menkind were hostile. Henderson was sceptical. Egerton Wake declared, 'Not even your genius for organizing, Mrs Webb, will make the wives of Labour men come out of their homes and hob-nob with the women organizers and the well-to-do women.' Now, Henderson and Clynes are the keenest supporters of the Club, and Egerton Wake is more than satisfied, whilst most of the women members are enthusiastic and every day brings new applicants for membership. Only J.R. MacDonald remains actively hostile. George Lansbury is suspicious, and some others jeer. But Bramley told me that it had completely revolutionized the life of some of the wives; they now felt that they were for the first time part and parcel of the labour movement.

What has interested me is getting intimate with some of these women. Mrs Clynes, for instance, turns out to be a woman of strong character and good intelligence. She dresses immaculately; looks a duchess! She reads GBS with appreciation, and delights in good music. She is a gracious hostess and though she may have social ambition she is extraordinarily free from any desire to separate herself off from the other wives of the Labour men, which is Ethel Snowden's outstanding weakness. Working in a cotton factory from ten years to twenty, when she married another cotton operative in Clynes, she has adjusted her life skilfully but un-pretentiously to her new circumstances. Has she not stayed at Balmoral and Windsor – though she never mentions it, which is characteristic of her social good sense. . . . Mrs Arthur Hender-son is a weaker and more insignificant woman, but she is a real good sort and coming on nicely. Mrs Bramley, Mrs Hutchinson, as well as Mrs Frank Hodges, are just as well-bred and personally attractive as Mrs Noel Buxton or Mrs C.P. Trevelyan. . . . Altogether the 150 women of the Half Circle Club would compare well, alike in character and intelligence and even in personal charm, with the 150 principal ladies of the Coalition or free Liberals. . . . It is this group of women, if I can keep them together in the Half Circle Club, that will settle for the World of Labour all the difficult problems that will confront the Labour Party when it comes into office. What, for instance, is going to be the attitude of the Labour Party to the Court? On what terms are

the women of the labour movement going to associate with Buckingham Palace? And who is to constitute official society and what are
going to be the Labour Party's standards in expenditure on clothes
and entertainments? We don't want to find ourselves a chaotic mob
without traditions or deliberate standards of manners and morals.

24 August. [41 Grosvenor Road]
I have lectured at three summer schools this August: the Fabian at
Priorsfield, the West Riding County Council Teachers' School at
Bingley, and this morning at the summer school of the Labour
Research Department at Herne Bay. These summer schools are the
most typical development of social life of these days: a school of
manners, without class distinctions, with definite subjects to discuss, the discussions being led by experts . . . it is an invention of
the intellectual proletariat, whether these earn their livelihood by
their hands or their brains. Old and learned persons like ourselves
are treated with great kindness and with some deference, even by
rebels. But the community life, the perpetual talking, lecturing and
being lectured to, is a physical ordeal, which Sidney and I do not
care to endure for more than a night or two. GBS, in his wonderful
good nature, stays for weeks where we stay days. He certainly is a
perfect marvel of kindness, a faithful friend to his comrades in the
Labour and socialist movement, whom he perplexes and enlightens
by his perverse and stimulating genius.

28 August. [41 Grosvenor Road]
. . . For many years I have wanted to give my personal philosophy of life – the underlying intellectual principles and emotional
impulses out of which has grown the conduct of my daily life. And
so for the last fortnight or so I have been attempting to formulate
on the one hand my faith in the scientific method as applied to social
institutions, and, on the other, my realization that without the
religious impulse directing the purpose of life, science is bankrupt,
or may lead as well to the decay and death of civilization as to its life
and ennoblement. Whether I shall succeed in writing anything that
is worthy of publication remains to be seen.

Lawrence Cripps, born 1878, was the eldest son of Beatrice's sister Blanche,
who had committed suicide. Blanche's daughter, Julia, unhappily married to the
doctor Tom Faulder, had killed herself the week before this entry with an

overdose of cocaine. Standish Cripps (1881–1925), Blanche's second son, had emigrated to New Zealand and was over on a visit with his wife and children. Dr Ethel Bentham (d. 1931) was a Labour M.P. and medical practitioner.

28 September. 41 Grosvenor Road
Lawrence Cripps and his wife dined alone with me on Saturday, and poor distracted Tom Faulder came to supper on Sunday. It appears that Julia left life with the same quiet and cheerful deliberation shown by her mother. Looking back over the last months, it is now clear to Lawrence and to Tom that she had settled to go, and had been calmly making all her arrangements whilst continuing her normal life; housekeeping, nursing, entertaining the Standish Cripps. . . . She had withdrawn property from the bank and parcelled out all her little bits of jewellery among her nephews and nieces and deposited them all in a dressing-case with Lawrence, on some excuse; she had given away many of her clothes, made presents to old servants; she had, before leaving London, mended all Tom's things and put away articles not required, settled up all her accounts, and even, in the last days of her life, knitted Tom a dark mourning waistcoat. The day before she died she sent a subscription of £1 to the Fabian Society with a notice to withdraw her name so that the *Fabian News* should not be sent to her. . . . Poor Tom; he looks a complete wreck. (He says that he has never done so well in his profession as he has done this year.) I could not do otherwise than be affectionate and uncritical; it is useless to torture him by assuming that her death was brought about by his neglect. With her strange mentality and with the blight of her mother's suicide, it is impossible to say that she might not have done the same even if circumstances had been happier. . . .

Meanwhile, I notice that suicides, like divorces, are on the increase. According to Dr Ethel Bentham, mental misery and mental sickness of every kind and degree is rampant among all classes, in spite of the falling of the death-rate and the better physical health which that is supposed to indicate. The world of man is sick at heart; its old religious faith has gone, and its new science, which seemed to the pioneers of 1870 to be able to solve all problems, has been proved by the great war to be bankrupt in directive force.

The Coles were seeking money to maintain the Labour Research Department now its links with the Labour Party and the T.U.C. had been severed.

7 October. [41 Grosvenor Road]

. . . Yesterday the Coles, who had been dining here, startled me by telling us that they were ready to accept an income [for the L.R.D.] from the Russian Trade Delegation and had prepared a plan for spending £6,000 a year of Russian money on an enquiry into capitalist enterprise, as well as continuing the trade union circular and other activities. I was so taken aback that I made no immediate objection, more especially as I had refused to stand for nomination to the Executive and had therefore no *locus standi*. But after sleeping over the news I wrote to Cole begging him to reconsider the position, and pointing out that a foreign power, of any kind, is a dangerous paymaster and that the Russian government in particular is certain to be detested – now by the right of the movement, but, as likely as not, in another few years, by the left. Cole really is an idiot if he thinks he can take money from the Bolshevik government without upsetting the mind of his present supporters and ruining himself and the L.R.D. in the eyes of all outsiders. He has no sense of the relative advantage of incompatible methods of gaining his ends . . . so he defies all principles and prejudices by going over to the Communists without agreeing with the policy or the aims of the Bolshevik government, and this in spite of the example of the injury done to his own cause by the *Daily Herald* fiasco over Russian money just a year ago. It is most depressing. The Fabian Research Department, a promising child of ours, ends in a lunatic asylum. . . .

Sir Hedley Le Bas (1868–1926) was an experienced publisher who was called in to reorganize the finances of the *New Statesman*. He became a director for some years. Glynne Williams, Ernest Simon, Arnold Bennett and Edward Whitley met most of the deficits after Harben withdrew his support.

10 October. [41 Grosvenor Road]

Meanwhile another child – the *New Statesman* – is not in an altogether happy position. The loss on it was £6,000 last year; this year Clifford Sharp prophesies a £4,000 loss. The money has as yet been forthcoming, though some of the payers-up are beginning to grumble and cry off any further contribution. We ourselves do not contribute except an occasional unpaid article from Sidney – he has ceased to write regularly for it. Clifford Sharp has drifted away from us in opinion. As we have become more and more closely connected with the Labour Party, he has become more and more sucked in to the Asquith set. . . .

16 October, Roker Hotel. [Sunderland]
Before we left London Sidney, MacDonald, Henderson, representing the Labour Party and three others representing the General Council [of the T.U.C.] interviewed the Prime Minister and the Cabinet Committee on unemployment. To Sidney fell the task of dealing with foreign relations and export credits to Russia and other destitute countries – and I gather from his colleagues and also from Maurice Hankey (whom we met the next day at lunch at H.G. Wells's), that he distinguished himself in lucidity and persuasiveness of his exposition. The P.M. and his colleagues were negative, and implied that nothing could be done except keep the unemployed from starving. Their coldness about Russia was marked. We travelled up here today with Henderson and Egerton Wake on their way to Scottish conferences. They were both very severe on MacDonald and his aloofness from, almost hostility to the Labour Party. Henderson told us that MacDonald (about 1910–11) proposed to enter a Coalition Cabinet with Lloyd George and Balfour (to oust Asquith) and offered him (Henderson) an under-secretaryship! Henderson refused decisively and declared that any such action would destroy the Labour Party and that he would not consent to it. . . .

28 October, Roker Hotel. [Sunderland]
The sixteen days at Roker have passed energetically for Sidney and slackly for me. For on only two of Sidney's nineteen meetings have I accompanied him. I came here ill at ease with rheumatism and bad sleeping. I think I shall have to return to the two meals a day and no meat. Certainly some of my secretions have gone wrong. What a nuisance it is that there is no authoritative knowledge about personal hygiene. And though I have got through three heavy volumes since I have been here, I have done no more to my book. The plain truth is that I am a little depressed, wondering whether what I have to say is really worth the toil of saying it. . . .

The net impression left on my mind from all Sidney and others have told me is that there are two distinct currents of feeling passing through the minds of the miners and shipbuilders of the north-east coast. They are disgusted with the government and have forgotten all their patriotic emotions about 'winning the war'. The war was lost by the peace as far as they and their families are concerned. But they are also disillusioned about their leaders, and the bulk of them are reverting to acquiescence in the existing order of society lest worse befall them. The failure of the strike and the increasing suspicion that strikes 'don't pay' and have increased unemployment, a growing doubt in their own and their fellow workers' capacity to govern – all this, reinforced by the famine following on Bolshevik government in Russia, has tended to set up in their minds a counter-revolutionary current. Whether these mixed emotions will lead the workmen to vote massively Labour at the general election, or whether it will be general apathy and a casting of votes according to some local or personal circumstance, it is impossible to say. I am inclined to think that on balance it makes for the Labour Party, but for a very unrevolutionary Labour Party. It will lead the Seaham miners to vote for Sidney: it is very doubtful whether they would have voted for one of their own officials. . . .

The treaty establishing the Irish Free State was signed at 2.30 a.m. on 6 December. The Washington conference (11 November 1921–6 February 1922) achieved some measure of disarmament and guarantees of the *status quo* in the Pacific. It was considered a great success for Arthur Balfour, who led the British delegation. In an effort to revive the Soviet economy Lenin had introduced some measure of private enterprise under the New Economic Policy.

7 December. [41 Grosvenor Road]
The Irish Treaty is the big event since the great war and its warlike peace. The amazing skill with which Lloyd George has carried through the negotiations with his own Cabinet and with Sinn Fein has revolutionized the political situation. Whether or not it be true, few enlightened persons, even among Liberals and Labour men, believe that any other man could have got this peace by understanding; no other leader could have whipped the Tories to heel and compelled them to recognize the inevitability of Irish independence. Moreover, the peace puts us right with the world, at any rate until Indian troubles bring up the same question of racial self-determination in a far larger and more complicated way. The other great event (at any rate in appearance), again redounding to the credit of the present government and the present governing class in Great Britain and U.S.A., is the Washington conference. The virtual

repudiation of Communism by Lenin — the readiness of the Bolshevik government to come to terms with capitalist governments — is another blow to international socialism and to the revolutionary movements in all countries. On the other hand, the economic disasters brought about by the peace have discredited capitalism, more perhaps the motives which lie at the base of capitalism than its actual administration of industry. The British working class is worse off now than before the war and whole sections are sinking into chronic poverty made worse by compulsory idleness. . . .

Harold Laski (1893–1950), who had returned from Harvard in 1920 to teach political science at the L.S.E., became a prominent Labour theorist and politician. With Leonard Woolf, R.H. Tawney and other Fabian intellectuals he provided a very different stimulus to Labour policy and propaganda from that of the Guild Socialists.

Christmas Eve. [41 Grosvenor Road]
. . . For us the year has been marked by three distinct strands of vivid consciousness: vigorous and enjoyable work, practical and intellectual; family sorrow; and above and around all our personal concerns, excitement about public affairs.

Sidney has been in fine health and spirits, keenly enjoying the daily task, on the best of terms with his colleagues at the Labour Party, and I think, on the whole, looking forward to his probable parliamentary career. 'No doubt I am old,' he constantly says, 'but I don't feel it either in body or mind.' And I doubt whether at any time of his life he has been more efficient in character and intellect. . . . We have had also a successful year in our joint work: *The Consumers' Co-operative Movement* finished and published; the prison book about to go to press, and a larger cheque from Longman's than we have yet received — £1,700 on the year. And though we have spent what we have received from Longman's for the cheap edition, on printing new books and new editions (altogether about £6,000 during one year), we feel easy about our income being sufficient to enable us to go through with our work with a comfortable consciousness of financial margin. . . .

There has been one change for the worse in our social surroundings: the breach, I fear the final break, with the young people of the Research Department. . . . To take your livelihood from the

391

Russian government, when millions of Russians are starving, for services which are obviously unreal or, at any rate, irrelevant to famine, is rather a poor business. But it was not the thing itself which disgusted us: it was the surreptitious way in which it was done. . . . What troubles me is that I don't want to have anything more to do with them; but I don't like turning my back on them when I know that they are going to be isolated. I feel that especially about the Coles. Cole has been very ill and it looks as if he and his wife were going to have a bad time of it. . . .

The Communists meanwhile have been crumpled up by events in Russia, which oddly enough are now setting the stage for the arrival of a new group of intellectuals. This group, rising up not on our left, but on our right, to which Laski is playing the part of Cole, is made up of young civil servants and is attracting some of the able and sane Oxford and Cambridge undergraduates. Its social philosophy is psychological and its method is strictly scientific: a controlled and modified capitalism is to be the 'next step' in its practical programme. In fact, the young men are turning back to the point we were at in 1899–1910; only they add to the policy of the National Minimum a policy of super-control of the productive forces of the community through the control of banking, money and credit. The acquisitive impulse is not to be suppressed and it is hopeless to supersede it on a great scale until there is a really well-educated democracy. Meanwhile, we must learn to control it in the interests of the nation and encourage the entrepreneur to regard himself more and more as a public servant. And as Lenin has come to the same conclusion after the dismal failure of Russian Communism, the British Communists are in a tight corner. Some of them talk of leading a rebellion against Lenin's influence in the Third International.

⟨ 1922 ⟩

There was much talk in the press of an early general election. A Unionist clique was now particularly anxious to break up the Coalition; but Lloyd George had strong support for its continuance from other Conservatives and Liberals. Their long-standing differences were nothing compared with their common fear of Bolshevism abroad and dislike of the Labour Party at home.

4 January. [41 Grosvenor Road]
We are apparently on the eve of a general election, the P.M. having decided that now is the time to get back into power with a secure majority of personal followers. Henderson and Clynes (with whom we dined on New Year's Eve) are quietly confident that the Labour Party will come back twice, if not three times as strong, and they do not desire any more dramatic turnover. . . .

The issue is: can the party, *as at present constituted* on its trade union basis, become the channel for first-rate character and intelligence? If it cannot do this in the next five or ten years, it will have to give way to some other grouping of democratic forces. Meanwhile, it will have educated the trade unionists, and, to some extent, changed the public opinion of the manual working class.

Poor Chiozza Money lunched here the other day, and we thought he was on the brink of lunacy. He was raging at the Labour Party and quite incoherent in his abuse. 'I have sacrificed my political future in vain,' he shouted at us. 'I might have been a Privy Councillor, a Cabinet Minister, a *leading* Cabinet Minister, if I had not come over to the Labour Party to be insulted and ignored by a lot of boozy and illiterate men.' And then followed such a torrent of miscellaneous instances of insult and neglect that I glanced at Sidney to check him in his retorts, as I thought the poor man might go mad on the spot. . . . It was a clear case of the personal vanity and ambition complex. We were relieved to gather that he had definitely given up standing for the Labour Party. Whether he will end up in a lunatic asylum or in the Liberal Party or even among the Coalition Liberals I don't feel certain. But he is definitely out and down as a Labour politician. Altogether, barring Sidney, Greenwood and the gentle Noel Buxton (and, be it added, the self-complacent C.P. Trevelyan), the intellectuals of the Labour Party are not in a happy frame of mind. Their unpleasant position is partly the inevitable result of the trade union basis but partly also owing to the airs they give themselves without having rendered service. . . .

A conference at Cannes (6–14 January) between Lloyd George and Aristide Briand (1862–1932) the French Premier, discussed German reparations and an Anglo-French security pact. Briand was a leading advocate of post-war conciliation, but his standing was so undermined at this meeting that he was forced to resign. The failure of the meeting also seriously damaged Lloyd George's position. Northern Ireland had contracted out of the Free State on 7 December and representatives of the two governments were now in London to settle differences about the boundary.

7 *February*. [41 Grosvenor Road]
It was a false alarm, and the P.M. – with the failure of Cannes, the revolt of the Tories against a February election and the need for immediate legislation about Ireland – withdrew the threat. So we have got back to our own literary jobs, though Sidney spends much time on Labour Party business. I am working steadily at the last chapter of our final volume on the English local institutions from 1689–1835, a task that I enjoy, seeing that it means an analysis of the old and the new principles of local government during that period. . . .

A question of conscience has been agitating my mind these many days. I read those gruesome accounts of the Russian famine and wonder whether we are not brutes in failing to give all one's available income, over and above the bare requirements for our own work, to the Russian Famine Fund? It is futile to salve one's conscience by giving a few guineas: *if it be right to give anything at all it would be right to make a big sacrifice.* Hitherto Sidney and I have refused to be moved; and for good or for evil I think we shall stand by this heartless decision. If we are to depart from our settled policy of expenditure I would rather do so to save the family of a German professor or Austrian official from semi-starvation. Russia to me is not much better than China – and whoever suggested, outside the official British-China trading and financial firms, subscribing to save a Chinaman from death by famine? The always present doubt whether by saving a Chinese or Russian child from dying this year, you will prevent it from dying the next year, together with the larger question of whether those races are desirable inhabitants, compared to other races, paralyses the charitable impulse. Have we not English children dying from lack of milk? Obviously one would not spend one's available income in saving a Central African Negro from starving or dying from disease; I am not certain that I would deny myself to save a Frenchman! If I decided to consider our personal expenditure I should reconsider it in order to provide more scientific research for the world.

Meanwhile, we go on with our customary standard of life. I am comforted by the thought that our critics always abuse us as penurious and over-economical in our personal expenditure and our clothes – and in our *way* of entertaining our friends. We keep open house, but the food and appointments are of the simplest. Where I am extravagant is in resolutely refusing to use my scanty brains in *thinking out economies*. I either refuse to have the service or commodity, or I afford it without wasting temper and thought on how to get it in the cheapest way. I might of course personally give up the daily stint of tobacco, the tea and coffee and the occasional whisky at the evening meal. I suppose I ought to do so if I really followed the inner call of a scrupulous conscience.

Bertrand Russell returned to England in August 1921 after a long visit to China, where he was seriously ill with double pneumonia. He married Dora Black (b. 1894), a graduate of Girton College, Cambridge, on 27 September 1921, a week after his divorce from Alys Russell was finalized. A son, John Conrad, was born on 16 November. After a series of affairs on both sides the Russells were divorced in 1935. E.M. Lloyd was a Fabian professor of economics at Sheffield. Barbara Wootton (b. 1897) was then an economist and research worker for the T.U.C. and the Labour Party Research Department. Eileen Power (1889–1940) was a distinguished professor of economic history at the London School of Economics. Dr W.H. Rivers (?1862–1922) was a psychologist and anthropologist who had successfully treated shell-shocked soldiers, such as Siegfried Sassoon, during the war. He was a friend of Harold Laski. Kingsley Martin (1897–1969), a writer and journalist then teaching at the L.S.E., became editor of the *New Statesman* in 1930.

16 February. [41 Grosvenor Road]
Our old friend Bertrand Russell, with a new wife and a son and heir (who just managed to scramble into existence 'in wedlock'), has come back into the outer circle of our friends and acquaintances. For some years he has been travelling and living with a young woman – a secretary, she was styled – a Girton girl, the daughter of an Admiralty official. She went with him to Russia two years ago and has spent the last year with him in China and nursed him through a dangerous illness. Last year, at his own request, Alys divorced him, and on his arrival last December in London he married Dora Black, within a fortnight of the birth of John Conrad Russell, the future Earl. I had to decide whether I would recognize the marriage and be friends with them, or run the risk of being thrown in their company without recognition, and I decided to call and ask them here. We spent the last week-end with them among a large party of young Labour economists at Dunford, a party

arranged by Laski for the discussion of the new volume of essays to be published next winter by the Fabian Society.

Bertrand Russell, now nearing fifty, is physically aged with an impaired vitality, but more brilliantly intellectual than he has ever been. He is cynical and witty. His paradoxes are more impatiently perverse than those of GBS. He never seems serious, and his economic and political views follow on his temperamental likes and dislikes. His last book (*An Analysis of Mind*) is amazingly well written, intensely sceptical. He throws about his hypotheses and comes down lightly on one or the other, as provisional conclusions, but as conclusions which he will toss on the scrap-heap of rejected opinions whenever he finds something more to his taste. This is markedly so with his political and economic views. He thinks he believes, with an almost fervent faith, in libertarian pacifism. But I doubt it. If, for instance, there arose a creed war, he would be on the side of a secularist rebellion. Religious faith with puritan morality is to him '*l'infamie*'. He has no interest in the scientific method; he would even object to applying science to society, seeing that it might mean constraint on the will of some who desired to do anything they pleased without considering like liberty in others. He is too indolent or impatient to work out the problems of maximizing freedom by deliberate social action. . . .

I should be sorry to bet on the permanence of the present marital tie. . . . Possibly the boy may keep them together, for Bertie seems inclined to dote on this son and heir. His bad health may also be a restraining factor preserving his domesticity. But there is a strange excited look in his eye (does he take opium?), and he is not at peace either with himself or the world. His present role of a fallen angel with Mephistophelian wit, and his brilliantly analytic and scoffing intellect makes him stimulating company. All the same, I look back on this vision of an old friend with sadness. He may be successful as a *littérateur*; I doubt whether he will be of value as a thinker, and I am pretty well certain he will not attain happiness of love given and taken and the peacefulness of constructive work. When one remembers the Bertrand Russell of twenty years ago, with his intense concentration on abstract thought, his virile body and chivalrous ways, his comradeship and pleasant kindly humour, the perfect personal dignity with a touch of puritanism, it is melancholy to look on this rather frowsy, unhealthy and cynical personage, prematurely old. . . .

For the rest, the Laskis were there; the Hugh Daltons, Ted Lloyd, and three distinguished women economic writers – Barbara Wootton, Barbara Drake, Eileen Power – and two or three clever young university men, with Professor Rivers, the psychologist, to keep us company in our relative old age. We had a clever paper by Martin on the control of the press, a discussion on a National Assembly on an occupational basis, opened by Barbara Drake and disputed by Sidney, and Bertrand Russell's amusing talk about the Far East. Laski and Russell picked each other out to talk over the fire, whilst Sidney and I took long walks over the Downs with Lloyd, the Daltons, Rivers and one or two of the women. Altogether a pleasant healthful and stimulating week-end. . . .

20 February. [41 Grosvenor Road]
Clifford Sharp, who lunched here today, and Lord [Noel] Buxton, who lunched here on Sunday, are both of them confident of great victories for the Free Liberals at the next election. Four hundred candidates, they each of them stated, are going to run. They were quite incredulous when we told them that the Labour Party had four hundred-odd candidates already fixed up and guaranteed. . . . Clifford Sharp, alas, looks as if the rumour that he is a heavy drinker was correct: he has the unmistakable lines about the mouth which one recognizes as the result of alcoholic self-indulgence. At present he is tumbling downhill, physically and mentally, at a great rate. Will any obstacle or shock stop him before he becomes a hopeless case? The strength of his constitution is in itself a danger, as it enables him to go on with his work. The Asquith set has deteriorated him in a way I could not have believed possible. But while there is youth there is hope; some event may yet turn the current of his life. What little influence Sidney and I have on him is gone – we cannot help: all we can do for him and poor little Rosamund is to be silent. . . .

Mary Meinertzhagen (1889–1943) was the ninth child of Beatrice's older sister, Georgina.

2 May. Dunford
. . . I have been anxious about dear old Kate – who has been suffering for a couple of months from persistent headache, which may or may not be the beginning of more serious trouble. It was a

shock to find myself as her nearest and most responsible relation, practically her only sister: neither Rosy nor Mary count, Rosy because she is herself a care and anxiety to her sisters, and Mary because of her own infirmities and complete loss of memory. There are nieces, however, and I have left one of them, Mary Meinertzhagen, in charge whilst I take a rest which I badly need. Dear old Kate: if she had complete and unquestioning faith in rejoining her dear man – she keeps his photograph facing her at the bottom of her bed – she would go gladly. But she doubts the reality of a future life; she has a natural fear of death and she enjoys her existence, with all her keen interest and affectionate friends. Much beloved she undoubtedly is by many men and women. She and I have never been intimate; there is no point of contact between our intellects, and though living in much the same circumstances and among the same sort of persons, in no single instance have we both been keen on the same public ends. Indeed, what the Courtneys have worked for, the Webbs have thought unimportant, and vice versa. But throughout our lives there has never been the remotest approach to ill feeling between us; we have always met in affectionate and kindly intercourse. . . .

Herman Finer (1898–1969) was a lecturer in public administration at the L.S.E.; K.B. Smellie (b. 1897) a lecturer in political science. Jessie Mair (1876–1959), who had worked with Beveridge during the war, was the new secretary of the School. Her relationship to Beveridge was a source of difficulty and embarrassment throughout his term of office. They were married in 1942 after the death of Mrs Mair's husband, Beveridge's cousin, David Beveridge Mair (1868–1942). Sir Gregory Foster (1866–1931) was provost of University College, London and became vice-chancellor of London University in 1928. In 1911, when Laski was still a student at Oxford, he married Frida Kerry (1885–1977), a lecturer on eugenics and medical gymnast. As she was a gentile the marriage caused a long-lasting rift with his orthodox Jewish family.

14 May. Dunford
The eve of our departure. The two last week-ends the house has been filled with congenial guests who have timed their visit to be with us. Last week-end the Laskis brought down Finer and Smellie (the two youngest lecturers, with Labour and socialist sympathies) and we had the Tawneys to meet them. This week-end the Director and Mrs Mair, her husband and daughter and the Gregory Fosters (University College) joined us. From all these separate persons we

heard a good deal about the School and its internal life. Laski is the most brilliant of the lecturers and his little wife is as restless and critical as he. He attracts me by his lively talk, witty epigrammatic gossip, not distinguished for accuracy, and his extraordinary range of intellectual interests and book knowledge. He knows, or says he knows, everyone of importance; his sympathies and likings are volatile; he scoffs at the Labour leaders, dismisses the Asquith-Grey combination with scorn and hates Lloyd George. . . . He is anti-Guild Socialist, dislikes the Cole set intensely, an antagonism which perhaps makes him sympathetic to our standpoint. He has a strong Jewish racial feeling and his scoffing little sceptic of a wife has become a Jewess to bridge over the displeasure of the family at his marriage to a gentile. . . .

What interested and perturbed us was the hatred of Mrs Mair, the secretary of the School. Mrs Mair is a tall, fine-looking Scottish woman, very much a Scot in manner and speech and in her ambitious and domineering temperament. To us she is as sweet as can be. She is reported to be all-powerful with Beveridge, who brought her as his secretary into the School administration. She is married to Beveridge's cousin, a distinguished and good looking civil servant who is quite clearly suffering mentally from the intimate companionship of his wife and his cousin – a companionship which involves perpetual association, an official relationship combined with more than sufficient sympathy and cousinly affection. How near the relationship borders on a domestic tragedy I do not know: Sidney pooh-poohs my concern. But Mrs Tawney, Beveridge's sister, burst out with expressions of hot dislike, and the dislike is shared by Tawney, by the Laskis and by Lloyd, by Wallas and apparently by the great majority of the staff. 'Ruining Beveridge's influence', 'comes between the Director and his staff', 'the talk of the place', are the expressions which were hurled at me. 'Could you possibly stop it or get her transferred to another sphere?', one or two of them asked anxiously. I suggested that every institution has a devil and Mrs Mair is perhaps as harmless a one as they will get. 'It is better than hating your Director,' I remark soothingly. 'Beveridge had great qualities and obviously he has the defects of his qualities. Accept Mrs Mair as one of the defects.' This morning, Mrs Mair complained of Tawney's outrageous manners and of Mrs Tawney's lack of tact. And there you are!

I neither like nor dislike her. Beveridge himself has never

399

attracted me: he is too mechanical-minded. One never comes into contact either with his intellect or his emotions. But to us he has been most considerate and generous, and at the School he has done wonders in the way of organization. Sidney has the utmost confidence in him and is always congratulating himself at having got him as Director. It would be horribly annoying if there was an upset over his stalwart and handsome colleague and cousin. . . .

25 May. Llandrindod
Again in London I found dear old Kate better, but longing to get out of town: no one to go with her, so Sidney and I decided that I had to take her here until her companion friend could join her.

After an interval of five months I am back again at my little book, with the summer before me to be broken by one visit to Seaham and Edinburgh with incidental lectures, my secretary's absence on her honeymoon, all of which stops any continuous concentrated work. . . . For the purpose of the book I have been reading through my diaries and dictating extracts so as to base the autobiographical element in it not on memories but on contemporary evidence – exactly as if it were about somebody else. It is amazing how one forgets what one thought and felt in the past, and even what one did and with whom one was intimate. Reading of all our intrigues over the Education Bill was a shock to me: not so much the intrigues themselves as our evident pleasure in them! How far is intrigue permissible?

Richard Meinertzhagen (1878–1967) was Georgina's third child. Wells published *The Secret Places of the Heart* in 1922. He had been on intimate terms with the writer Rebecca West since 1912, but the relationship was now beginning to break up. *Washington and the Hope of Peace* was based on articles commissioned by the *Daily Mail* but Northcliffe disapproved of the criticisms Wells made of the French at the conference and rejected his despatches. Beaverbrook then bought Wells for the *Sunday Express*. Laski had persuaded Dr Rivers to stand as Labour candidate for London University but he died suddenly that summer.

10 July. [41 Grosvenor Road]
We hear that the Harben *ménage* has come to grief: Harben and wife have separated, the fine mansion and estate are up for sale. Harben has departed in charge of a company of tourists, the elder daughter has gone on to the stage, the eldest son left for South

Africa. This wreck of a home is the direct result of increased wealth combined with the philosophy of following anarchic impulse. . . . The particular group of young intellectuals among whom we worked in the early days of the *New Statesman* and Fabian Research Department have not worn well, with the one exception of C.M. Lloyd. He is gloomy and disgruntled, but he is a success as journalist and lecturer and an exemplary husband and father. The war wrecked many things, upset the government of races and the self-control of individuals. As for divorces, they are as common as flies in a hot summer. . . . The most conservative and conventional of my nephews, Dick Meinertzhagen, a distinguished army officer who acted as political officer in Palestine after the war and is now at the Colonial Office for Palestinian purposes – the most exemplary person – recently got a collusive divorce from a silly flirtatious wife, (now remarried,) and promptly married a Scottish lady of property. No one apparently thinks any the worse of any of the parties concerned! He and his new wife came to see us and treated us as revolutionaries!

For the richer classes, there is practically free divorce without scandal, so long as the man is ready to go through rather unpleasant and expensive preliminaries so as to dodge the written law. This reputable divorce by consent is by far the most significant change in manners and morals that has taken place in my lifetime, and it has taken place without any change in the law, and without being the subject matter of any public controversy. But over and above these divorces by arrangement, with respectable re-marriages on both sides, there is now an amazing tolerance, on the part of the respectable bourgeoisie, of what would have been thought the last word of wickedness. The various Freudian 'complexes' are joked about, and the character of the emotions of young girls for the father, or of mothers for their sons, and vice versa, is openly discussed without any apparent reprehension. 'Never talk about your dreams in mixed company,' is *Punch*'s typical joke. . . . The consequence is that old people like ourselves, who have never thought out social morals, find ourselves more and more troubled as to what line to take in the public interest . . . one sits in judgement with increasing bewilderment.

Such a problem is H.G. Wells, now Labour Party candidate for London University. Rivers dead, H.G. Wells was approached because he had signified his wish to stand, and to refuse such an obviously eligible candidate, except for his scandalous exploits (none of which, however, have come into the courts), seemed an unjustifiable insult. So Sidney and I acquiesced and he accepted the candidature. Whereupon R.H. Tawney resigns from the chairmanship of the University Labour Party, but before doing so, proposes as the alternative Bertrand Russell! He declares that Bertrand Russell is a gentleman and H.G. a cad, which is hardly relevant if it is sexual morality which is to be the test.

Once a Labour candidate, it seemed desirable to bring Wells under Henderson's and Clynes's influence. So that with some hesitation I ask him and his wife to lunch to meet the leaders and their wives and Normal Angell, which invitation the Wells's promptly accept.

When he sat by me I could not help feeling that in some ways he. is an unclean beast, not so much on account of his various paramours but because he is perpetually making 'copy' out of his love affairs – his last book being a bad example, with its quite obvious portrait of Rebecca West. He is no longer agreeable company. He is deteriorating intellectually: he orates to any company he is in, never tries to discuss as he used to do, and never listens seriously to anything that is said. I suppose this tendency to orate comes from his enormous earnings. If the world will pay you £2,500 a week for writing about an international conference – the sum he was paid at Washington – obviously, if you are willing to talk for nothing, all present should be eager to listen to your gold-priced words. How ridiculous for other mortals whose words are priced low or not at all, to talk in his presence! . . . The impression left on my mind is that I now like Mrs Wells much better than H.G. himself. She has regained self-respect and is much softened by her trials.

9 August. Bryan's Ground
About a fortnight ago we started from London, taking in Longfords on our way, with a great kit-bag of work which we proposed to do down here during our six weeks' stay. We find ourselves in the hands of the local doctor: Sidney for severe nervous breakdown and I for equally severe colitis, living the life of invalids, anxious about each other and unpleasantly doubtful about the future of 'the Webbs'. Sidney's breakdown is the most disconcerting. Right through the last year, up to and over the Labour Party conference, he seemed in the best of health, working easily and steadily. One

little episode made me anxious. When we were at Hastings in the winter he and I went out immediately after lunch and walked quickly up a steep hill, the sun hot and he with a heavy overcoat. Quite suddenly his face became purple and he became faint, with cold perspiration, and I had to put him on the ground for two or three minutes before he recovered full consciousness. But he was quite well the next day and walked some nine miles in a bitter wind to Winchelsea. The present breakdown started off suddenly with an attack of vertigo in the night, followed by occasional dizziness. When we got here, having to call in the local medical man for my own complaint, I asked him to examine Sidney. Every organ was found to be healthy – no blood pressure and arteries very young for his age – the only apparent cause of the vertigo and dizziness being a pad of wax in the ear, which was removed.

But the dizziness and weakness and uncertainty in walking continued and even got worse, and the doctor became seriously concerned. 'Must stop work for three or four months,' was the verdict. Meanwhile, I was feeling horribly unwell with bowel and backache and losing weight. I am now undergoing treatment and slowly, I think, improving. What troubles me is not my own health. I don't believe my life is a good one and I don't much want to drift into a long senility. But what would Sidney do without me if he became an invalid? I have always contemplated leaving him still vigorous, with Parliament as a new career to interest and absorb him. There is no one to look after him and he is so absurdly dependent on me. However, the Lord will provide! We have had a good life together; we leave finished work, and the one who is left behind for a few years' more life will have, as consolation, the memory of a perfect marriage. What more can a human being expect or demand?

4 September. Southport. Trades Union Congress
Our six weeks at Bryan's Ground sees both of us fairly normal. Except for occasional giddiness when he gets up in the morning or suddenly bends down, Sidney is as vigorous as ever, whilst I have got rid of colitis and gained weight (7 stone 5 oz) and I can walk eight or nine miles without being too exhausted. But we both feel that we are definitely old people; Sidney for the first time. And everyone tells us that we must slack off, and Sidney certainly *looks* older than he did a year ago. . . .

By September political events were moving towards a crisis. There was strong pressure in the Conservative Party for an end to the Coalition, although the leadership – Chamberlain, Birkenhead and Balfour – continued to support Lloyd George. At a dramatic meeting of Conservative M.P.s at the Carlton Club on 19 October, Bonar Law advised the party to leave the Coalition to preserve its own unity and he was backed up with a vote of 187 to 87. Chamberlain and the other Ministers then resigned their position in the government and Lloyd George tendered his resignation. The King sent for Bonar Law, who called for a dissolution of Parliament; the election took place on 15 November. The Diehards were the anti-Coalition Conservatives. At a by-election at Newport a Tory named R.G. Clarry pushed a Coalition Liberal to the bottom of the poll and beat Labour by 3,000. *The Decay of Capitalist Civilization* by the Webbs was published in 1923.

17 October. [41 Grosvenor Road]
The political world is tumultuous, but we hear little of its tumult, though it may whirl us among a multitude of other folk into the rapids of a general election.

When we returned to London six weeks ago we found our MS on the capitalist system, written some three years ago, approved by Laski, Pease and Galton for publication by the Fabian Society and we had to set to, to prepare it for the printer. This took me the better part of the month or six weeks and occupied Sidney's time spared from more pressing business. Now the first proof is in GBS's hands being pointed and perfected. He has been incredibly generous over this little book, giving up days to going through it. . . . Meanwhile I have been brooding over my own little book, deciding to recast the first chapter in a more autobiographical form. . . . I prefer giving my own experience – it interests me more – than summarizing and analysing the net result of experience plus reading. So when once I am free again I shall describe my apprenticeship to social investigation instead of the more imper-sonal – 'how to approach the science of society'.

Absorbed in our own work, we have only heard the echoes of the battles of Downing Street and the Carlton Club and the fall of Lloyd George brought about by the Newport victory of the Diehard. 'Except that one does not like to lose a single election,' said Henderson yesterday, 'the Newport defeat is a fine piece of luck for us.' All the same, the omen is unpleasant; Eccleston Square was quite confident of victory at Newport.

Sidney and I are becoming every day more philosophical. We do not want a Labour government before the labour movement has found its soul. At present the mass is dully apathetic, thinking only of the next meal, the next drink, the next smoke, or the next 'odds' – whilst the advance guard lives on hot air. The state of society which is demanded by the enthusiastic cannot happen. What could happen if we were all united in policy, though it would make a far better life for the whole body of the people, would be repulsive to all the rebels. We shall get this better life or western civilization will go under, but not for many a long day, and then only by a slow process of education and discipline. . . .

24 October. [41 Grosvenor Road]
. . . Sidney goes to Seaham on Friday and I follow the next week with Mrs Bolton. Sidney believes he will win, though less confidently, because of the general depression, than six weeks ago. . . . Meanwhile, we have applied for permission to build a cottage at Dunford, with right of exclusive possession during our lifetime but to fall in to the School with its equipment and a £1,000 endowment to rates and taxes at our death. We felt that we must make some provision for retirement and relaxation and that it was now or never! If Sidney gets into Parliament we can't go on working through every week-end; if Sidney is rejected, continued residence in London in the spring and summer is a futile waste of diminishing strength. . . . I spend this week-end before going to Seaham at Dunford, consulting with the Director [Beveridge] and Mrs Mair about a site.

28 October. [41 Grosvenor Road]
I did not go to Dunford, fearing the cold just before my journey northward. Depressed at the prospect of the larger life of Sidney in Parliament. I shall hate him to be beaten: I shall thoroughly enjoy a rattling big majority on the day of the count and a few days after, but if he were beaten, through no fault of our own, there would be a subconscious sigh of relief when I had got over the first shock. . . . The life of learned leisure is what we both best enjoy: at work every morning, and walking and browsing over books and seeing a few intimates in the afternoon and evening. And especially now that I have this little book of my own, which is a big book in its high endeavour really to explain my craft and my creed. I long for leisure and a quiet mind. . . .

9 November. [Seaham]
Sidney is thoroughly enjoying himself in this election: six meetings he is taking today, morning, afternoon and four 'appearances' in the evening. He is remarkably fit – all his giddiness has ceased; he sleeps well and eats sufficiently. . . . His enjoyment is partly due to the nature of the constituency. The thirteen miners' lodges stand solidly behind him, acting as committee rooms and placing their 'halls' at his disposal. These simple-minded miners listen to his words, as the words not of a politician but of a teacher. . . . His return seems certain, but whether he is a majority or a minority member remains doubtful. Meanwhile I have broken down to the extent of giving up three out of the nine meetings arranged for me. It was not worth making myself really ill to get a few extra votes. And whenever I get overstrained, especially if I get also chilled through in the bitterly cold miners' hall, my old trouble of ulcerated colon begins to vex me. . . .

15 November. Polling Day. Seaham Harbour
Spent this morning touring the miners' villages: received every-where by a little band of enthusiasts. In the pit villages Webb is strong – those who oppose him are lying low, and seem about equally divided between Bradford and Hayward. In Seaham Harbour itself the Bradford cars, scores of them, are whizzing around conveying women to the poll. If we lose, it will be the women who will have done it. Sidney keeps cool: he feels he is doing what he had to do, even at considerable cost in money and effort. I have been living in an unpleasant dream, feeling ill and old and not suited to the talk of a candidate's wife, hating the thought that he should be beaten and yet disliking the prospect of a change in our daily life. I do not like the speaking involved in an election: one has to think too much of pleasing one's audience and too little of expressing the faith that is in one. . . .

The result was: Webb (Labour) 20,203; T.A. Bradford (Conservative) 8,315; E. Hayward (Liberal incumbent) 5,247.

17 November. [Seaham Harbour]
The long day at the count – from ten o'clock to six – was an exciting, tiring but triumphant experience. We knew we were winning after the first box had been opened, and after the first two

hours it became apparent that Sidney would have a great vote and a great majority. There was a little patch of Bradfords in Seaham Harbour and a thinner patch of Haywards in the remoter pit villages. But the larger collieries were solid for Webb; the ballot papers were counted in lots of five and twenties, looking almost as if they had been marked by a machine with here and there a fault in the working of it.

Sidney continued his almost boyish pleasure in the adventure to the very end. I really believe he is going to enjoy Parliament. He is amazingly young for his age. The miners from the first treated him as their 'property': the serious ones regarded him as their local preacher and the younger ones as their 'professional' football-player whom they had acquired at a high price and had to look after. I gather the Seaham miners had betted heavily on him in Sunderland. . . .

The election, nationally, resulted in a Conservative majority of 88 over all other parties. The result was 347 Conservatives, 60 Asquithian Liberals; 57 National Liberals following Lloyd George; 142 Labour and 2 Communists. Despite the Conservative gains, the big jump in the Labour vote was the most significant fact of the election. Arthur Henderson failed to win his seat but was returned in a by-election in January. MacDonald was now back in the House as M.P. for Aberavon, and in November he was elected by 61 votes to 56 leader of the Parliamentary Party.

23 November. 41 Grosvenor Road

To enter Parliament for the first time at sixty-three years of age is a risky adventure from the standpoint alike of health and reputation. It would be a foolhardy risk if the need within the Parliamentary Labour Party for steady-going intellectuals were not so great and Sidney's training in government departments, L.C.C. administration and sociological research did not fit him in a peculiar way for the task. Also his very age, the fact that he can hardly look forward to being in any Labour government or even to becoming an outstanding popular leader in the country, makes his presence as a detached and disinterested counsellor of special value to the party. Even more than the older parties, the Labour Party is broken up into circles within circles of slightly different economic creeds and of clashing temperaments and of separately organized occupations.

The story of the Parliamentary Party of 1922 opened yesterday with what might have been a discreditable struggle for leadership.

It was generally assumed that Clynes would be re-elected chairman for the first year and MacDonald deputy chairman. But the I.L.P. members, reinforced by the Scottish group of extremists, had determined to give that pride of place straight away to their chief man. Whilst more than twenty trade union members failed to attend the party meeting, the I.L.P. and Scottish groups had already met and decided to carry MacDonald by bringing up their full contingent and out-voting the right wing. Clynes behaved with admirable manners; he accepted the position of deputy chairman without demur and appealed for unity under MacDonald. . . . And looked at impartially and without considering the way it was done, MacDonald's chairmanship has much to recommend it. He is abler than Clynes; he is free to devote his whole energy to being parliamentary leader; he has a greater hold over the Scottish contingent and his chairmanship prevents him from depreciating the Parliamentary Party in the country which he would have done if he had been passed over. If he is not the best man for the post, he is at any rate, the worst and most dangerous man out of it! He has now the opportunity of his life, and it remains to be seen whether he is a big enough man to rise superior to his personal hatreds and personal vanities and sectarian prejudices and do what is wisest for the cause in its largest aspects.

We are rapidly settling down to the new life. So far as I can foresee, I shall have a quiet time of it. Except for little dinners and lunches of Labour M.P.s during the session and the monthly gatherings of the Half Circle Club, I shall avoid all social functions, excusing myself on grounds of age and health and pressure of work. There will be some preoccupation with Seaham – I feel that now we are in we must do something to rouse the miners and their wives to be interested in public affairs. So I am planning a monthly letter to the Women's Sections and I shall have to lecture there twice a year and do odds and ends of letter-writing in the intervals between our regular visits in the spring and autumn. I am haunted by the vision of those pit villages and those strained faces of the miners, their wives listening to our words. Can we get into an intimate and sincere relation to them, so that we may understand their lives? . . .

10 December. [41 Grosvenor Road]
Our relations with Clifford Sharp and the *New Statesman* practically

though not ostensibly severed. For some time Sidney has felt his position as chairman of the *New Statesman* company untenable: in the notes and editorials there were too frequent depreciations of the Labour Party and all its works. So he took the excuse of 'pressure of parliamentary duties' to resign from the chairmanship and this fact is published by arrangement with the editor in this week's issue. The parting was quite amicable. Sidney asked Clifford Sharp to lunch here, I going out so that they should be free to talk. There were no complaints on either side, merely an acceptance of the position and a friendly discussion as to who should succeed as chairman. . . .

The breach was inevitable and was foretold by GBS before the war. Clifford Sharp had a natural affinity for the Asquiths and their set, and when the door was opened wide to this delectable social abode, and Margot with her wit, flattery and caressing familiarities beckoned to him, he was doomed to enter in and to have the door sharply closed behind him. The liking was spontaneous on his side. Sharp has the same political temperament as Asquith; the same coarse-grained character and strong commonplace intelligence; the same conventionality of culture and outlook; the same contempt for enthusiasm and idealism; the same liking for heavy drinking, smoking and card-playing, the same taste for ornamental and parasitic women. And brought up in ugly undistinguished sub-urban society, the glamour of the past power and the present social prestige and luxurious living of the Asquith set were irresistible. . . . The measure of his partisanship for the Liberal as against the Labour Party is his willingness, if not eagerness, to welcome back into the Liberal fold Lloyd George and Winston Churchill, both statesmen that he has virulently criticized and condemned, because he thinks their inclusion will strengthen the Liberal against the Labour Party. Whether he will remain editor of the *New Statesman* or gravitate into more lucrative journalistic enterprise depends on how far he can control the amount of alcohol he consumes. . . . A melancholy ending to our one journalistic adventure. Poor poverty-stricken Labour! The Webbs lost control of the *New Statesman* because they could not contribute the money necessary to its upkeep.

The Liberal weekly, the *Nation*, was controlled by the Rowntree family. Walter Layton (1884–1966) was editor of the *Economist* 1922–38. Ramsay

Muir (1872–1941) was professor of modern history at Manchester. J.M. Keynes had made his name as an economist with his controversial view of the peace treaty in *The Economic Consequences of the Peace* in 1919. He resigned from the Treasury in 1919 and returned to Cambridge to teach economics. The *Nation* was absorbed by the *New Statesman* in 1931. Germany had for some time been in difficulties over reparation payments. On 9 January the Reparations Commission declared Germany in default on coal deliveries and two days later the French and Belgians began the occupation of the Ruhr. This marked the end of the Anglo-French Entente. Britain's policy of reconciliation clashed with France's anxiety about security and the need to balance her own finances. Although the British condemned the occupation, coal exports improved with the Ruhr mines at a standstill. A treaty with Turkey agreed at a conference at Lausanne that winter restored Britain's friendship with Turkey and re-established British leadership in Europe. Mussolini had come to power in Italy on 30 October 1922.

∽ 1923 ∾

11 January. [41 Grosvenor Road]
Oddly enough, I have left space for another entry in my diary about the *New Statesman* which gives the obvious sequel to the last entry – and yet belies its conclusion! Ten days ago Clifford Sharp told Sidney that the Manchester group of Liberals – E.D. Simon, Layton, Ramsay Muir etc., and supported by Keynes – had been offered the option of controlling the *Nation*, the Rowntrees and Massingham having quarrelled over the policy of the paper, the brilliant editor wishing to 'go Labour'. It immediately occurred to their group that the *New Statesman*, with Clifford Sharp as editor, represented their views; that both papers were losing money, that the two together had a combined circulation of near 20,000, and that even if some of this double circulation were lost, on amalgamation there would be sufficient left to make the amalgamated paper a handsome commercial proposition. Sharp was anxious to close with the offer if Sidney had no objection and if he could secure for himself as editor virtual security of tenure and complete freedom of control and the political independence of the paper. . . .

After the first shock to our *amour propre* Sidney saw some advantages in clearing out completely! With Sharp's Liberal leanings, the *New Statesman* had ceased to be of use to us. And Sidney's position had changed. In 1913 he was a freelance, not individually

410

and organically attached to the Labour Party; permeation of other parties, notably of the Liberal Party, was still a conceivable policy. . . . Today the lines were drawn; the Labour Party was His Majesty's Opposition, and any accession of strength to the Liberals by their adoption of a left policy was detrimental to the Labour Party. . . . He was therefore prepared to be bought out if the other collectivist shareholders were given the same terms and took the same view. It turned out, however, that Edward Whitley and Glynne Williams objected to the amalgamation and they were prepared to finance the paper. Meanwhile, the Liberal group had submitted and it was clear they intended to make the now amalgamated organ *definitely Liberal in substance and form* and expressly intended to exclude 'collectivist dogma'. Even Sharp was disillusioned. We met last night at dinner with E.D. Simon at the Berkeley Hotel. Sidney stated the case for amalgamation sympathetically. But when Glynne Williams and E. Whitley objected to the proposal and announced their willingness to underwrite the loss, Arnold Bennett remarked, 'That settles it,' and the proposal was turned down. . . . What will happen now to the *Nation?*

How absurdly trivial all this reads contrasted with the catastrophic events in Europe: the march of the French into German territory, the re-establishment of the Ottoman Empire in Europe, the economic and political decadence of Germany and Austria and of large parts of Poland, the tragi-comic-creed autocracies of Russia and Italy, the dissolution of social order in Ireland, Egypt and India, and the two million unemployed in Great Britain – the whole civilized world turned into 'devastated areas', devastated not so much by the Great War as by the infamous peace. And the U.S.A. looking on angry and contemptuous and not too happy about the worthwhileness and security of her own civilization. The publication of our little book on *The Decay of Capitalist Civilization* certainly ought to be timely. Sidney, of course, retains his optimism – human affairs can't be so bad as they look, he says, human beings are fundamentally sane. I become every day *more* pessimistic, more fearful that present generations of men are agents of destruction, not construction. . . .

Patrick Hastings (1880–1952) was a lawyer who became a Labour M.P. in 1922 and Attorney-General in 1924. Henderson won Newcastle North-East by a majority of 4,384. Some of Beatrice's reports to the Seaham women are included in the Webb *Letters*, Volume III.

9 February. Lyme Regis

We came here a week ago for a spell of rest and walking. Sidney has returned to London today and I follow on Sunday evening. A happy time, wandering together six or seven miles over the cliffs and hills every morning, reading and talking over our bedroom fire in the afternoon and evening, with another little stroll for me on the Cobb while Sidney stuck to the twenty books we accumulated here for this week's reading, even too many for him to get through! He starts next Tuesday on his parliamentary work in good spirits: J.R. MacDonald has repeated his invitation to sit on the Front Bench, given also to Snowden and Patrick Hastings, and treats him in all ways as a principal colleague. The party has had two electoral successes during the recess – Newcastle and Whitechapel – and the Liberals have had two heavy defeats, which is even better in view of their stampede back into extreme individualism. . . .

My life will now be divided into quite unconnected strands. My first duty is co-operating with Sidney's parliamentary work, the monthly letter to the Seaham women, the spell of meetings in Easter week, entertaining Labour men and running the Half Circle Club. . . . The other strand is getting on with my little book. . . . There is a certain morbid tendency in writing this book – it is practically an autobiography with the love affairs left out – the constantly recurring decision of what degree of self-revelation is permissible and desirable. The ideal conduct would be to treat the diaries exactly as I should treat them if they were someone else's. . . . But it is almost impracticable to get into that frame of mind – one's self-esteem is too deeply concerned, also Sidney's feelings have to be considered. . . . But how short is the time before Sidney and I will be nothing more than names on the title-pages of some thirty books! I suppose all old persons are haunted by the nearness of death. . . . We sometimes agree that the ideal ending would be for both of us to be simultaneously shot dead by an anarchist on the day of our golden wedding, 23 July 1942.

VOLUME 37

13 February. [41 Grosvenor Road]
Sidney is like a boy going for his first term to a public school! This light-heartedness, odd for a man of sixty-three, is due to the youthfulness of the party, as individuals and as an organization, and to being elected on the Executive committee of the Parliamentary Party and also to being asked by J.R. MacDonald to sit on the Front Bench. How long this phase of youthful keenness will continue, when exactly it will give way to physical fatigue and mental nausea, it is difficult to foresee. He used to be intolerant of the public sittings of the L.C.C., and his enjoyment of the work was limited to administration by committees over which he presided. To be happy in Parliament he has got to be successful as a debater. In debate he excelled on the L.C.C. − he has still to make his maiden speech at Westminster. . . .

6 March. 41 Grosvenor Road
My old friend Alice Green staying here for a week's respite from a Senator's life in Dublin, with an armed guard always on her house, the armed guard being almost as dangerous as the I.R.A.! She is now an old woman of seventy-six who has been living an heroic existence doing her little best − and alas! it is little she can do to save Ireland, her romantically loved country. She is desperately pessimistic. 'All the idealism is dead; the people have become thoroughly demoralized; they no longer care about Ireland; all they care about is living to indulge fanatical passions or mere lawless crime and to avoid the results to themselves of fanatical passion and lawless crime in other people. Every man's hand is against his neighbour either in offence or defence. Religion is dead; Irish tradition is dead; co-operation is dead; decent methods of trading and agriculture are dead; there are a few heroes and many martyrs, but the bulk of the people have no notion of being citizens.' She is querulous, poor dear, with old age and loneliness, but she has kept her wits and has developed her wisdom. And she is only too grateful for affection. She thinks she sees in her old friends the Webbs an amazingly fortunate couple living an ideal existence of

successful citizenship. And it is true that Sidney is enjoying himself in Parliament. He likes being on the Front Opposition Bench. His first speech, in the dinner-hour, on pensions was a success. But his more prepared speech, when he was appointed by the party to wind up the debate on Unemployment Insurance, was half and half — first part success and last part failure. He was nervous, and the jeers of the Tory Back Benches . . . threw him off his subject; he repeated himself and failed to make all his points, and sat down without making his last words intelligible for the reporters of Hansard. . . .

Sidney is well in health, which is an immense comfort to me. I suffer from a chronic bowel trouble and I find my life distracted, distressingly distracted. . . . Looking in to my consciousness I think I see the source of my *malaise* in the steadily worsening condition of Europe. . . . And on the economic plane within each country class hatred is being intensified. Never before have I been so aware of belonging to an army of persons who will either be oppressed by, or will oppress, their fellow countrymen. As I looked down on the House of Commons last night I seemed to see a system of government in process of dissolution, a dissolution of which our last book is a tiny echo. Has the British race the good conduct or the intellect to pull through this dissolution to a new and better order for themselves and the world? That is the all-absorbing question. The fundamental good nature of the English is their great asset; their lack of intellect, or rather in intellectual endeavour, is their great defect.

9 March. *Longfords*

Came down here to be with dear old Mary during the first days of her widowhood. Ten days ago I hurried her away, at ten minutes' notice, from Grosvenor Road, where she had spent a week with me, on an urgent telephone message that her old man was dying. He lingered on for another three days and sank peacefully into unconsciousness. In their declining years, he and she became equally fragile in intelligence and frail in body; they were constant companions in the large family sitting-room and during short walks in the woods and on the common. In some ways they had never been so much to each other; her superiority in energy and capacity ceased with age and the loss of her memory. She has taken his death with gentle but haunting sorrow; she *would* sit in the room where lay his body with its peaceful smile, and this morning she and I walked up together to the church to see the casket with the ashes. The devoted and capable Bice begged me to come and be with her these four intervening days and I was only too glad to do so. . . .

Lady Warwick (1861–1938) was a celebrated Society beauty and intimate of Edward VII: she was converted to socialism and used her money for social and charitable purposes. Easton Lodge was her country estate in Essex and H.G. Wells was her neighbour. C.G. Ammon (1873–1960) was a Labour M.P. and trade unionist.

11 April. [41 Grosvenor Road]
An odd and not altogether pleasing episode in the social life of the Labour Party. Early in the year the notorious Countess of Warwick, who has been a member of the Labour Party for nearly twenty years, made an attractive and discreetly worded and generous offer to the Executive of the Labour Party. She put at their disposal Easton Lodge as a week-end resort for small conferences and intimate consultations. There would be little more to pay than the railway tickets. The number of guests were to be notified to the housekeeper, it being left uncertain whether or not she herself would be present. The offer was so unexceptional that the Executive decided to accept it; and a small party consisting of Henderson, MacDonald, Egerton Wake, the Frank Hodges, Ammons and Mrs Clynes and ourselves were deputed to go over and prospect. Unfortunately, Lady Warwick unwittingly published the fact, and from the beginning to the end of the episode we were pestered with photographers and film producers. As our hostess obviously desired these attentions, the rest of the party had to submit, and we appeared in groups not only in the newspapers but also on the movies. . . . 'Can the party touch the pitch of luxurious living without being defiled?', many of the left ask. And personally, though I agreed to the acceptance of the offer, I am in two minds as to the wisdom of this acquiescence. In principle there is nothing wrong in it. Lady Warwick cannot help being a Countess, and the best use she can make of her trust property is to lend it for co-operative entertainments. The Labour Party does not preach or practise a fanatical carrying out of the 'simple life'. The middle-class members of it have always lived according to the simpler

canons of expenditure current in their own class, and that is exactly what Lady Warwick is doing. . . .

Lady Warwick herself, whom I had not seen for twelve years, ever since I stayed at Warwick Castle for a Minority Report meeting, has become an old woman like myself, a benign and hard-working old woman who has gained the respect of her neighbours by a sterling public spirit, supporting a secondary school, by turning a medieval barn into a fine hall for plays and meetings, by promoting the local Labour Party and by opening her park to all sorts of festivals and jaunts for the common people. Of course, H.G. Wells says she is a spoilt child and that she is moved by a desire for notoriety, but I am convinced that there is also an element of genuine conviction and sincere reforming zeal – otherwise she would not have persisted in her good intention. . . .

The Wellses were much in evidence with their two boys. Of the two I liked the wife best – she has mellowed with age, he has coarsened. The two sons are devoted to the mother but somewhat critical, I think, of the father and his ways. Probably they resent the atmosphere of scandal that surrounds the establishment. The eldest son, particularly, looks as if he were quite capable of giving his father a bit of his mind. . . .

The Tories were bitter towards middle-class members of the Labour Party whom they considered traitors. Patrick Hastings was jeered when he condemned the government for deporting to Ireland Irishmen suspected of plotting against the Free State. David Kirkwood (1872–1955), leader of the Clyde shop stewards during the war, had become a fiery M.P. for Dunbarton Burghs.

11 May. [41 Grosvenor Road]
Now that I have this autobiographical book on hand I have not the energy to write up current events. And yet Sidney's life in the Parliamentary Labour Party is full of interest. The Parliamentary Labour Party is unlike either of the other political parties as I knew them through my brothers-in-law and friendly M.P.s. It is a closely-knit organization with a vivid internal life of its own. The leaders do not dominate, and in so far as they lead, they lead by perpetual consultation with the rank-and-file members. . . . The Tories are of course very hostile to Sidney, as they are to Hastings K.C. – they resent these two newcomers being on the Front Opposition Bench; they want to run them down as leaders. . . .

When Sidney wound up the debate on the Housing Bill (I was in the Ladies' Gallery) the Tories kept up a continuous hum broken by interjections, and when he rose to correct a statement by the Minister who referred to him, a young 'gentleman of England' shouted 'Sit down, Nannie.' Whereupon Kirkwood protested furiously and the row ended in the Minister not being able to complete his speech. . . .

This week all my energy has been taken up with political work. On Monday I travelled up to York to the conference of Women's Sections, spent the whole day in conference, entertained the four Seaham delegates to lunch, and left York 6.20 arriving in London 10.30. Yesterday I had an M.P.'s dinner – with Lord Acton thrown in as a possible Labour Peer. Today a lunch of twelve Labour M.P.s to meet Shaw and Henderson. Tomorrow I must draft the monthly letter to the Seaham women; in the evening I have 130 Fabians coming here for a reception. On Saturday I shall have to finish the monthly letter and I have a Half Circle entertainment all the afternoon. Not a stroke of work done at the book! . . . Fortunately I have ideal servants and no friction: if it had not been for the admirable running of my housekeeping it could not have been done.

30 May. [41 Grosvenor Road]
We have just spent ten days with the British delegation at Hamburg attending the International Socialist Congress. . . . The countryside through which we passed to and from Hamburg looked the picture of prosperity. . . . But Hamburg struck me as strangely empty of traffic. . . . What was painful to see was the pallor and the apathy of the faces, the lack of joy and laughter, the 'oldness' of the quite young children; above all, the suppressed anger in some faces as they stared silently at us. Our French and Belgian comrades were frequently insulted in the streets; the British and Americans were treated with effusive politeness, especially by officials, everything being done for our comfort. For the rest, the population was dignified, but there was silence – dark, brooding silence. . . .

During the last week or so, Sidney has much improved his position as a Front Bencher by a brilliant speech on the Labour Party amendment for the rejection of the Rent Restriction Bill on second reading: the first really successful speech he has made. . . . Now I think he has caught the right tone. . . .

Sir Oswald Mosley (1896–1980) had been a Tory M.P. since 1918 but he had become an independent in November 1920. He joined the Labour Party in March 1924 but, critical of the party's failure to deal effectively with un-employment, he broke away to form the New Party in February 1931. When the New Party failed to make headway in the general election in October it fell apart, and Mosley launched the British Union of Fascists in October 1932. His wife Cynthia (1898–1933) was the daughter of Lord Curzon, the Tory Foreign Secretary, and herself a Labour M.P. 1929–31. Thomas Johnston (1881–1965) was a journalist and politician, one of the Clydeside group of M.P.s. He founded and edited *Forward* for twenty-seven years.

8 June. [41 Grosvenor Road]
We have made the acquaintance of the most brilliant man in the House of Commons – Oswald Mosley. 'Here is the perfect politician who is also a perfect gentleman,' said I to myself as he entered the room (Sidney having asked him to come back to dinner from the House). If there were a word for the direct opposite of a caricature, for something which is almost absurdly a *perfect type*, I should apply it to him. Tall and slim, his features not too handsome to be strikingly peculiar to himself, modest yet dignified in manner, with a pleasant voice and unegotistical conversation, this young person would make his way in the world without his adventitious advantages, which are many – birth, wealth and a beautiful aristocratic wife. He is also an accomplished orator in the old grand style, and an assiduous worker in the modern manner – keeps two secretaries at work supplying him with information but realizes that he himself has to do the thinking! So much perfection argues rottenness somewhere. I shall not easily forget my desolating experience with the fascinating Betty Balfour. Oswald Mosley reminds me of her in this respect – he seems to combine great personal charm with solid qualities of character, aristocratic refine-ment with democratic opinions. Is there in him, as there was in the charming Betty, some weak spot which will be revealed in a time of stress, exactly at the very time when you need support, by letting you or your cause down or sweeping it out of the way? And what about his wife, the daughter of Lord Curzon?

This question is a pertinent one, as it seems likely that he will, either now or in the near future, join the Parliamentary Labour Party. J.R. MacDonald is much taken with him, and he with MacDonald. Even the Clyde contingent have been fascinated by his personal charm and the wit and wisdom of his speeches. It is, by the way, interesting to note that the Scottish Covenanters are prejudiced in favour of anyone who is particularly hated by the other side. 'There are three men in the House who are detested and reviled by the Tories,' says Johnston, the editor of *Forward*, who is himself in the House: 'Sidney Webb, Patrick Hastings and Oswald Mosley' – a remark that accounts for the growing popularity among the extremists of the two very 'bourgeois' figures and the one super-aristocrat. 'Why are they so hated?' asks Johnston. 'Because they are traitors to their class,' he answers triumphantly, as if he were canonizing them!

Sidney is completely absorbed in his parliamentary work and it is clear there will be no time for the writing of books. . . . For four days he is at the House from 2.30 to 11 or 12 o'clock at night, coming home for 1½ or 2 hours' dinner-hour. On Friday he is there from 11 in the morning till 4 in the afternoon. . . . Now he is on the Standing Committee on the Rent Restriction Bill which will meet in the morning. . . . Parliament in fact is not a half-time job as the L.C.C. was: it is a full-time job. . . . I watch his career in Parliament with a sort of motherly interest. He is singularly simple about it; just does what the party tells him to do, to the best of his ability, enjoying the life and interested not only in all questions which come up but also in the ups and downs of party organization. . . . He has lost his will to power, even to hidden and unrecognized power. Here again the disinterestedness of old age comes in. 'I am no longer quite so certain that I am right,' he says; 'in any case, it will be younger men who will settle the matter'. . . .

It was at this conference that Sidney, in his chairman's address, used the phrase 'the inevitability of gradualness' by which he is most remembered. It was not intended to be an approving gloss on the Fabian tactic of step-by-step social change. He was arguing that the steady increase in labour representation was bringing the party inexorably to a parliamentary majority and the formation of a Labour government.

28 June. [41 Grosvenor Road]
About this time of year I am always utterly exhausted if I have spent the preceding months in London. . . . It is clear that if I am to finish my book I must provide for a country residence after Whitsuntide each year, as we used to do when we were writing *Industrial Democracy* and the early volumes of *Local Government*. I

cannot stand the noise of the perpetual motor traffic in front of the house and the constant seeing and talking to people. We had looked forward to the cottage at Dunford. That is now impracticable. Then we had hoped for six weeks at the Russell-Holt cottage; that has to be given up owing to the breakdown in Betty's health and their inability to get servants. . . .

Sidney is presiding over the Labour Party conference for five days this week and doing it very successfully. His opening address, 'Labour on the Threshold', has been well received and considerably reported. But even he is no longer fit for day and night work and I persuaded him to 'shut off' Parliament for these five days. . . .

Sir Charles Eliot (1862–1931) was a diplomat and distinguished orientalist. Sir Edward Grey became Viscount Grey of Fallodon in July 1916 before resigning as Foreign Secretary in December 1916. He married Pamela Glenconner (1871–1928), the widow of Asquith's brother-in-law, Edward Tennant (Lord Glenconner) (1859–1920) in June 1922. Bonar Law's health had been failing for some time and he resigned as Prime Minister on 20 May. It was Balfour who advised the King to invite Stanley Baldwin to be the new Premier rather than Lord Curzon, whose membership of the House of Lords made him unsuitable in a period when the Labour Party had become the official Opposition and had recruited only a handful of peers. The *Punch* cartoon showed Sidney walking down the road waving a red flag in front of a steamroller.

7 July. [41 Grosvenor Road]
After an interval of a dozen years, like an echo of past relationships – or is it an echo of present prominence? – came Lady Wemyss to see me this afternoon. She had communicated her desire to resume relations through our common friend Sir Charles Eliot, who was dining with us yesterday. Much older, somewhat wizened in appearance, but with the pleasant friendly manner she used to have before she began to dislike us (a change of feeling we never understood), she tried in an apologetic tone and in confused words to explain exactly why we had not met for all those years. I helped her out gallantly by suggesting common absorption in the war, and our own retirement, through old age, from general society. Obviously relieved by my unconcern and ease of manner she chattered on, telling me all about her two sons who were killed in the war, her sister's marriage to Lord Grey, and Margot's abominable stories about her sister's neglect of her first husband (Margot's

420

brother). Then about A.J. Balfour's splendid career during the war, and the King's summons to him during the recent crisis brought about by Bonar Law's resignation, to tender advice to His Majesty as to who should be sent for, and how Balfour had decided that Baldwin, and not Curzon, ought to be P.M., much to 'George's' disgust, she added. She asked a few vague questions about the Labour Party – 'I know nothing about movements' – and we parted, after an hour's talk, on the most friendly terms but neither of us suggesting any future meetings. Cynically I reflected that if Sidney had not been returned to Parliament by a triumphant majority and seated on the Front Opposition Bench – not to mention the cartoon in *Punch* – I should not have been 'resumed' by the former Lady Elcho. It is amusing but unpleasing to note that among the complimentary letters to Sidney on his election was one to me from Miss Wedgwood, Lady Wemyss's companion and friend, and dated Stanway, and another to Sidney from the charming Betty Balfour, ending with 'May I send my love to Mrs Webb.' My 'lost friend' got a cordial reply from Sidney about his election but no message from me. 'She cannot send what she has not got,' I said to Sidney. 'You had better leave me out of the picture.'

For Lady Wemyss I have the most friendly feeling; she never pretended to be more than an acquaintance, and was a very pleasant and useful one, we returning the compliment in kind. But I am still sore about the strange behaviour of the fascinating Betty, who had enticed me into a warm and intimate friendship and then dismissed me from her circle in a manner that was bordering on insolence.

It is an odd coincidence that this afternoon H.G. Wells drives us down to stay with him and Mrs Wells for a week-end during the Half Circle Club visit to Easton Lodge. Lady Wemyss remained friendly with the Wellses after she had ceased to ask us, and I am inclined to think that it was H.G.W. who had something to do with her marked change of feeling with regard to the Webbs. Curiosity tempts me to ask him whether he is still friendly with that group, but such a question might raise uncomfortable memories. Let the sleeping cur lie!

26 July. [41 Grosvenor Road]
Our visit to H.G. Wells during the Easton Lodge Half Circle Club week-end was most pleasant and friendly. Sidney had a slight attack of faintness at breakfast on the first morning, which fright-

ened me and led to a great display of considerate concern from H.G.W. and a certain amount of intimacy with both the Wellses. In fact, we are very nearly on the old footing now, our relations being still slightly tainted by mutual suspicion. Mrs Wells shines as a hostess; she is alike more dignified and more natural than she used to be. She has won through a terrible ordeal and come out the mistress of her circumstances. He is the same brilliant talker and pleasant companion, except that he orates more than he used to do and listens less intelligently to other people. He is far too conscious of literary success, measured in great prices for articles and books. He has become a sort of 'little god' demanding payment in flattery, as well as in gold, for his very marketable goods, and he has grown contemptuous of his customers. Moreover, he has another and even more damaging consciousness – he feels himself to be a chartered libertine. Everyone knows he is a polygamist and everyone puts up with it. He is aware of this acquiescence in his sins – an acquiescence accompanied with contempt. And this contemptuous acquiescence on the part of friends and acquaintances results in Wells having a contempt for all of us, because we disapprove, and yet associate with him. In short, he feels that he has *imposed himself, sins and all, on the world by the sheer force of acknowledged and marketable genius.* . . .

The Webbs advertised for a retirement home in the *New Statesman* – 'it must be relatively high, with pretty view; and above all completely isolated from houses harbouring cocks or dogs.' Professor E.S. Beesly (1831–1915) was professor of history at University College, London. Sir John Fischer Williams (1870–1947) was a British legal adviser on the Reparations Commission.

11 August. Longfords
The fortnight here, looking after Mary while the faithful Bice takes her holiday, has passed happily enough, with Sidney down for a week of the time and the old school-room for our sanctum. I have actually written, or rather 'put together' out of my diary some dozen or more pages of the second chapter of my little work, Sidney meanwhile lazing at my side, finishing up parliamentary correspondence, writing an article for the *Labour Magazine* and discussing with me the offers of cottages and sites arriving by every post – owing to the gratuitous repetition of our *New Statesman* advertisement in a dozen papers, some of them with leaderettes on

our dislike of dogs and cocks. Such are the pecuniary benefits arising out of a little fame.

Without a private sitting-room it would have been impossible for me to have stood the nervous strain of taking Bice's place. To be with the dear old Mary all day long, without the rest of hours of undisturbed work, would have meant a nervous breakdown in a week's time. She is as sweet-tempered and beneficent as ever. . . . But owing to her absent-mindedness, in the literal as well as the metaphorical sense, she has become in everyday life a mental automaton, repeating questions or statements according to particular stimuli in her environment, so that one waits to hear one of the old tags as if one was pressing the button of a speaking doll. But what is even more distracting is her physical restlessness. She must walk many miles a day out of doors; but when she is not walking she is jumping up and down from one momentary occupation to another – knitting, smoking, pianola, playing patience, or glancing at a stray book or newspaper, rarely spending more than five minutes, if so much, doing one thing. . . . All the same, she never tires of expressing her gratitude for a happy life, her love for her old man, her appreciation of Bice and her joy in visits from Kate and myself. . . .

At this point the other of the three old wives, Kate Courtney, arrives – aged seventy-six. She jumps out of the pony-cart like a girl of fifteen and greets me with rapid remarks on foreign affairs, the wickedness of the French and the dull apathy of the English government, promising to show me letters from Professor Beesly and Fischer Williams. Well in health and alert in mind . . . this eldest of the remaining sisters is a model of what an old woman ought to be and do. But in spite of continuous kindness, she bores me – she has always bored me – but that may well be my fault, not hers. I think it is the combination of acute sentimentality with political dogmatism reminiscent of Leonard, together with her incapacity to listen to, or read, the other side of the case, that makes it difficult for me to take her thought and emotion seriously. . . .

Blood relationship is a strange tie – so much affection and helpfulness, so little sympathy and understanding. There is the barrier of a long common past which has been imperfectly shared and has given rise to endless little misunderstandings and small grudges. . . . There is perhaps even a subtler and subconscious jealousy – jealousy which disappears when misfortune or pain bears

423

down on the beloved sister but which rises to the surface in calm weather when everyone speaks well of her, when the world insists, as the others think, on over-rating her. Certainly Georgie Meinertzhagen and some of my other sisters had that feeling about me, and Maggie had it about Kate. But for this slight distemper, the relations between the Potter sisters have been almost ideal — no quarrels and loyal helpfulness in all the obvious troubles of life. . . .

Kate Courtney's manuscript diary is with the Passfield Papers at the British Library of Political and Economic Science.

12 August. [Longfords]
Just had a long morning's walk and talk with dear old Kate about her diary, which is full of interesting matter and which she is leaving to me. . . . She gave me some volumes of her diary to read afterwards — mostly reporting the facts of her life and Leonard's career, speeches, sayings, etc. — essentially the diary of a devoted wife of a 'great man' and the friend of distinguished people whose conversation is carefully noted — all useful matter for future historians, giving the impressions of an excellent and charming married woman with great intelligence but no intellect.

31 August. [41 Grosvenor Road]
After Longfords we went for four days to the Radnorshire Arms at Presteigne to see Betty Russell, who is threatened with Graves's disease, and to arrange for her seeing a London consultant. Then back to London and from thence in search of our proposed country home. This was a tiresome but, thank heaven! a quickly successful venture, lasting only four days in all. After seeing two or three other impossible places we plunged on 8½ acres with a habitable cottage two miles from Liphook and four miles from Hindhead, costing £1,750 for the freehold, a sum well within our means. With the addition of a third sitting-room for our sanctum and three more bedrooms it will be a home we can retire to in case either of us breaks down, and it can meanwhile be used as a holiday residence. Enclosed in the estate of a wealthy bachelor, it seems free of 'barking dogs and crowing cocks'. It is a sufficiently pretty view and includes a delightful corner of woodland with big forest trees and some acres of hayfield. I mean to plant the garden with heather,

424

broom and gorse and bushes of lavender, sweeping away all the ugly patches of cabbage and potatoes and silly little beds of formal flowers, so as to dispense with a gardener. Happy hours Sidney and I spend in discussing alterations and possible extensions, and if we keep our health and strength we can hope for a happy old age under our own oak tree, with intervals of creative work and friendly intercourse. . . .

22 September. Longfords
Watching over the dear old sister dying of cancer of the lung. . . . Again one asks as one watches the painful process of dying – is it necessary that men and women should pass through this long-drawn-out weariness, discomfort and pain, when there can be only one end to it? Would Mary prefer to be told the truth – that she had to die in a few weeks, probably a few days, and would get gradually or rapidly more weary and miserable?

25 September. [Longfords]
Bill [Playne] came last night and is staying in the house. All is well for the last days of my dear old sister. . . . As Mary does not know she is dying and as apparently she wants to get well and believes she will get up again, what could be better than Bill's cheery ways, with the added touch of reverent affection which he will now give her. . . . The dear soul may depart this life in a halo of love. I go back today to my old man.

12 October. [41 Grosvenor Road]
After I left her end came quickly, accelerated by morphia. The dear old sister passed into the unknown peacefully sleeping. . . . I went down from London with Barbara Drake, Seddon Cripps and Henry Hobhouse for the funeral, all of us returning on the same day. The Bill Playnes marched together out of the church to the grave – Mannie with an odious smirk on her face – Bice and I following arm in arm, a dreary procession around the churchyard in the pouring rain, the little group of relatives, unconnected one with the other, gathering together as the casket of ashes was lowered into the grave. . . . Kate and I are left alone in the world; the dear old lady clings to me and is as loving and open-handed as ever; whilst poor neurotic Rosy and her neurotic children are a burden on us both. So dwindles out of sight the 'R.P. family'!

The economic situation had grown worse during the autumn, with more than 11 per cent unemployed. At the Imperial Economic conference in October there was talk of a protective tariff to help the British worker and manufacturer. Baldwin made Protection his rallying cry at the National Unionist conference at Plymouth on 25 October, thus reuniting the Tory party after the tensions of the Lloyd George Coalition. Parliament was dissolved on 16 November and the election held on 6 December.

27 October. 41 Grosvenor Road

Ten days with Sidney at Seaham Harbour in our comfortable lodgings with the peaceful view of the dale and, at night, the twinkling lights of the collieries on the horizon of the hills surrounding us. . . . I return here exhausted but satisfied with our position at Seaham. There is something very touching in these few hundred miners' wives, with here and there a professional woman, gathering round me with a sort of hero worship. . . . The monthly letter I started last spring has been a great success. This time I have begun another experiment – a free circulating library of some 150 or 200 books distributed in dozens among the eleven Women's Sections, each local secretary having a complete descriptive card catalogue of all the books. Whether the books will get read, except by the select few, remains to be seen. . . .

Two big events happened while we were at Seaham: General Smuts's speech on the European situation, which was broadcast as he spoke it, asides and interruptions included, and Baldwin's declaration in favour of Protection with its intimation of a general election to secure a national mandate for protection as a cure for unemployment. . . . Apparently a full-blooded Protectionist policy is to be put before the country in the near future and a verdict taken. But it is not merely Protectionist. It is openly said that two other reforms are to be carried if the Conservative government gets this blank cheque from the constituencies: the re-establishment of the veto of the House of Lords and its extension to finance, and the cutting-off of the political activities of the trade unions. In short, the destruction of the present Labour Party, based as it is on trade union funds. This is reaction with a vengeance! So we are in for a hot fight and the expenditure of some six hundred pounds on Seaham. We shall hold our seat – perhaps with a big majority – but it is a poor prospect for the Labour Party as a whole. . . . With no press, no money for literature or motor cars in the constituencies we contest, and unable to contest more than 350 seats, the outlook is not promising. . . .

Meanwhile, I have to set about furnishing the cottage so that we can occupy it in December and decide on the extensions to be made early in the year. The book has again to be put on one side while more pressing jobs are done. Then, in all probability, an election and three weeks of exhausting turmoil at Seaham, with a new Parliamentary Party to cater for during the session. Damn it! How I long for a country home and time and strength to finish the work of art(?) I have begun. . . .

5 November. [41 Grosvenor Road]
Went yesterday to the luncheon of J.R. MacDonald: some hundred Labour M.P.s and candidates and the General Council of the T.U.C. The Leader was looking fit and well, courteous and conciliatory in his manner to everyone, and especially civil and friendly to me. He delivered a clever and, in places, eloquent speech — not the oration of a *great* leader of men, but certainly of an accomplished leader of the Labour Party. There were few mistakes, sufficient and not too much definiteness, some very clever hits at Baldwin and his sudden adoption of Protection as a cure for unemployment, but the speech lacked intellectual and emotional grip and utter sincerity. J.R.M. is certainly more than a passable leader. He is an extremely *accomplished* leader, nothing ragged or obviously defective in him, but he is not more than that except perhaps in the tenacity of his purpose, and it is certainly marvellous how the achievement of his ambition has improved his manners and swept away his rancours. . . .

19 November. [41 Grosvenor Road]
Sidney off this morning for Seaham in first-rate form with no anxiety about his own seat, merely a question of whether the majority is less or more than last year. . . . Hence, our whole concern this time is: what will happen in the country? One result is practically certain. On the referendum demanded by Baldwin, Protection will be beaten, probably conclusively beaten. The unfortunate Premier has, by his method of approach, foredoomed Protection. He tells the country that he cannot introduce Protective tariffs as a fiscal principle to cure unemployment and raise revenue unless he has a clear mandate from the country. This is taken to

mean a majority vote for Protection of the total voting electorate. Now as the government at present is a minority government (5½ million out of 11 million voters), that eventuality is ruled out, for it is inconceivable that the government candidates will do better than last year. Indeed the Conservatives themselves admit that they will lose seats on balance, though not enough they say to put them out of office. . . . The real and significant issue before the country is Liberalism v. Labour – there is no other issue of any importance. That issue *is* of importance. If Liberalism were to secure the first place as His Majesty's Opposition, Labour would be set back for a decade or more.

The Liberals, reunited under the ostensible leadership of Asquith, but really under the leadership of Lloyd George and Winston (Simon having faded into the background), supplied with both oratory and money by the Lloyd George faction, seems to be in a first-rate position to win in the fight with Labour. . . . To read the capitalist press, whether Tory or Liberal, the Labour Party barely exists as a political party. . . . With the exception of an occasional paragraph about J.R.M. (never more than a paragraph), they report no speeches – the last few days Henderson and Clynes have been boycotted. Lloyd George and Winston, and less usually Asquith, are given verbatim reports; they are treated as His Majesty's Opposition. As for the Liberals themselves, we are told they are already making up their Cabinet – or rather, Lloyd George and Winston are, whilst the Asquith group try to look sly and say 'wait and see'. . . .

At Eccleston Square all is buzzing: candidates plentiful, money slowly but surely trickling in, sufficient to enable candidates to take the field, and constituencies are being fitted with candidates every hour of the day. There will be 400 by nomination day, it is thought. But the wisest heads say the least. . . . Whether it is old age I do not know, but I am singularly indifferent. With Germany slowly drowning and those damned French knocking her on the head whenever she tries to save herself, what does it matter who wins this election! . . .

I am moving today into the cottage, having arranged this before the election. This day week I go to Seaham for ten days' speaking and the excitement of the election day, and journey down the day after. It is fortunate that I am not otherwise than well for a woman of my age; I still suffer from intestinal trouble and wonder whether

I ought to live more ascetically — give up tea, coffee, tobacco, and the whisky at my evening meal, but I don't do it because I am not convinced that it makes any difference, and no medical man will tell me that it will. . . .

Jessie was a domestic servant who worked at Grosvenor Road for many years.

22 November. Passfield Corner
Entered with furniture and Jessie yesterday according to plans made before the general election. . . . Impression of our new home not altogether favourable in this dank weather. Silence absolute — no crowing cocks or barking dogs, not even the hoot of the motor. Cottage comfortable with distinct charm; country beautiful for walking and dry under foot on commons. But dankly cold after sundown owing to prevalence of water — near to river, and series of ponds. Also cottage arrangements about water, relying on pump which is tedious to work and troublesome after the modern conveniences. Not a possible all-round-the-year place because of the ground mist. But is this not true of all country places that are below the highest hill in the neighbourhood?. . . We shall come here for a fortnight at Xmas and then see whether we like it sufficiently to plunge into extensive building and expensive upkeep. . . . We might decide to keep it as a week-end and summer cottage and not retire here for old age or illness. . . . Certainly the silence is weirdly attractive. . . .

In the election Sidney increased his vote by 1,000 on a lower poll. Webb: 21,281, Ross (Unionist): 8,546.

3 December. [Seaham Harbour]
The Sunday before an election is always a day of rest in your *own* constituency, as it is bad form for the candidates not to seem to go to church or chapel, or at any rate refrain from speaking to his own electors. . . . So far as we are concerned, we are on velvet in this ideal constituency. There is far more enthusiasm than a year ago, far more voluntary work. The miners have become genuinely attached to their member. They are proud of him, they trust him and they feel that he is 'their man' — that they have put him into Parliament, that he sits on the Front Opposition Bench, that he has proved himself to be, even in the eyes of many Conservatives, the

best member Seaham has ever had for local purposes. And the miners' wives are fond of me. I have raised their status with their husbands and neighbours. They regard me as *their* representative and they are delighted with the monthly letter giving them special news from London. There is a certain charm in the packed little meetings at the pit villages and the atmosphere of intimate comradeship within the Labour Party – all of us on terms of social equality. There is not the relationship of angling for votes in order to win the seat as at Deptford L.C.C. election, far more the relationship of teacher and student, quick question and answer, the answer taking the form of exposition, quite frank exposition of difficult and intricate subjects. . . . The miners like the pedagogue! And what surprises me is the number of quite young men who come and listen intently in silence, leaving it to a few older men to ask questions. Also this time there is always a group of women, sometimes sixty or seventy, at the meetings. Last year, if there were two or three women one was agreeably surprised. . . .

The election result was a decisive rejection of Protection, although the Conservatives remained the largest party, with 258 members. Against expectations the Labour Party increased from 142 to 191 seats and the nominally reunited Liberals could only win 158 constituencies. This indecisive result meant either a new Coalition or a minority government by one party with the tacit support of another. Oscar and Altiora Bailey were the names Wells gave to his caricatures of the Webbs in *The New Machiavelli*.

12 December. [41 Grosvenor Road]
These are the hectic days of victory tempered by the cold feet of the leaders at the consequences of victory! On the Saturday, the day of our return, Massingham appeared in the evening to implore us *not* to allow the Labour Party to enter into any relations with the Liberal Party, even with regard to conditional support of a Labour government by the Liberals or vice versa (we did not remind him that it is barely a year ago that he was denouncing Sidney in the *Nation* for being the main obstacle to such an understanding!). On Sunday Henderson lunched here; and after lunch, talking alone with Sidney, he pressed for taking office at once if J.R.M. was sent for by the King, as seemed likely then; bringing in a moderate programme and continuing in office, with support of Liberals. Sidney agreed to taking office but demurred to 'moderateness' if it was moderateness in order to get Liberal support, and not a

moderateness synonymous with administrative practicability. He was definitely against governing with consent of Liberals to a specific policy. Far better be defeated early in the day, perhaps on the King's speech. At first I was against taking office, instinctively fearing the 'John Burns' attitude on the part of the Labour leaders when once they are face to face with officials. . . .

On Monday we had a dinner here of leaders – J.R.M., Henderson, Clynes, Thomas and Snowden – to discuss taking office and what exactly they would do if they did. Sidney reports that they have all, except Henderson, 'cold feet' at the thought of office, though all of them believe that J.R.M. ought not to refuse. Henderson wants to take office, to concentrate on unemployment, to set up committees to enquire how the capital levy and nationalization can best be carried out. Sidney sticks to a bold declaration of policy with the probability of being beaten on the Budget or before. What came out was that Snowden, who thinks he has a right to be Chancellor of the Exchequer, is chicken-hearted and will try to cut down expenditure. He even demurred to a programme of public works for the unemployed. Where was the money to come from? he asked, with a Treasury clerk's intonation. . . . The leading propagandist socialists like Snowden and even J.R.M. are Utopians who start back from every step towards their Utopia. If Sidney and I were not philosophers we should be disheartened. But what happens to the first Labour Cabinet, acting merely as a stopgap government, is not really of much importance. If they can get over their teething troubles before they have a majority in the House of Commons, J.R.M. may consider himself uncommonly fortunate. And these few weeks or months of office, if it comes off, is like a scouting expedition in the world of administration, a testing of men and measure before they are actually called to assume majority power. . . .

The reception, on the Wednesday after the poll, to the Half Circle Club and the 'victors and non-victors in the battle for Labour' was a great success and certainly justifies the starting of the Club three years ago. . . . It was a funny thought – this first gathering of the victorious Labour Party, at the house of Altiora and Oscar Bailey. H.G. Wells ought to have been here to describe it! Funniest of all is the cordial relationship between J.R.M. and ourselves, all the more cordial because there is no pretence of personal intimacy or friendship. We have learnt not only to accept

431

each other but to respect and value our respective qualities. J.R.M. is apparently not capable of personal intimacy. He never had 'loves' among his colleagues. What has happened to him in the blaze of success is that he has lost his hatreds. All men and women are to him just circumstances – an attitude in a leader which I can readily understand and do not altogether disapprove! It is not unlikely that J.R.M. and Sidney will end in a sort of intimacy based on the common task of discovering the greatest measure of administrative and political efficiency. It will be interesting to watch the development of this relationship of mutual confidence and helpfulness without personal friendship.

My general conclusion about the present political situation is this: that while I agree that the Labour Party *must accept* rather than refuse office, it seems absurd, from a mere commonsense community standpoint, that they should govern without having a majority in Parliament or in the country. The honest way out of the *impasse*, the course which would be approved by the majority of the British people, would be a Liberal–Conservative Coalition – Asquith, Baldwin, Chamberlain, Lloyd George Cabinet, Free Trade and anti-socialist in home affairs and pacific in foreign policy. It is only the struggle for power between the leaders and parties that prevents this carrying out of the clearly expressed will of the people. It is the realization that this Coalition would be the right course that causes a stop in my mind when I look forward to a Labour government, trying to govern in spite of having no mandate for carrying out its distinctive policy. We shall accept because we dare not let it be said that we were not a practicable alternative government. . . .

Henderson, who lost his Newcastle seat, came back at a by-election in March at Burnley, and served as Home Secretary in the new government.

18 December. [41 Grosvenor Road]
I had a talk with Henderson this afternoon. Considering that he has lost his seat and has no immediate prospect of getting back again in time to be included in the Cabinet he is amazingly cheerful, good-tempered, and determined to do his level best in organizing for the next general election. The more I see of that man the more I respect his sterling character. But when it comes to policy I distrust his judgement: right down in his consciousness is the old Liberal who does not himself want any considerable change in social structure

and is contented with a very moderate measure of social reform within that present system. He is a 'socialist of circumstances': a socialist because that political party of which he is a loyal member has adopted the socialist creed. This innate tendency to mere liberalism is reflected in his desire that the Labour Party should remain the government indefinitely and govern according to the will of the present House of Commons, that it should be a mildly Liberal administration doing little things passably well. His policy would be such that it would be difficult if not impossible for the Liberal members to turn out the Labour government and it would go lingering on in legislative impotence until the summer of 1925! That, in our opinion, would be intolerable and would make the political organ of the labour movement an absurdity, an absurdity because a Liberal bourgeois government would be more efficient for this purpose than a Cabinet of Labour men. I think the rank and file of the party will make that course impracticable. But when one recollects the record of the Parliamentary Labour Party 1910—14 one begins to doubt the leadership of J.R.M. However, you cannot get better bread than there is wheat, and the next three months will prove the quality of the grain grown in the field of trade unionism. All may depend on the intellectual and moral stamina of MacDonald. The trade union officials will follow where he leads. I doubt their independent initiative.

꿈 1924 ꙮ

Labour took office with Liberal support, and MacDonald wrote to Sidney offering him the post of Minister of Labour, with special responsibility for 'shouldering the unemployment difficulties'. In the course of Cabinet-making this offer was amended, and Sidney became president of the Board of Trade — the post Joseph Chamberlain had held at the time of Beatrice's infatuation for him in the 1880s.

3 January. [Passfield Corner]
This time last year Sidney was on the threshold of his Parliamentary career; today he is on the threshold of the Cabinet! So far as I know, no member of the Labour Party, certainly not any Front Bench man, foresaw the possibility of a Labour government arising out of the election. We all imagined that if the Conservatives were

defeated, it would be by a narrow majority and that there would emerge a Conservative-Liberal or Liberal-Conservative government. And I still think that would have been the logical result of the election and would in fact have best represented the opinions of the majority of the electorate. The British Constitution, however, has a certain strange wisdom in it. From the standpoint of eventual stability, the constitutional custom that H.M.O. is the only alternative to H.M.G. has the advantage that it gives to a young party, presumably representing a new movement of thought or emotion, a chance to go in and learn the business of government. . . .

For Labour to accept the responsibilities of government is a big risk: it may lead to immediate disaster. But its leaders will become educated in the realities of *political* life and in the work of administration; and even their future behaviour as H.M.O. will become more responsible – more intelligently courteous and bold.

Meanwhile Sidney and I have had a peaceful Xmas in our dear little cottage though, in his case, there has been considerable suppressed excitement owing to his immediate destiny. He has felt certain of Cabinet office – but which office? . . . On New Year's Eve came the letter from J.R.M. offering him the Ministry of Labour. 'He has learnt the manner,' says Sidney in a contemplative tone. 'He tells me that it is the post of greatest difficulty! Anyway, it just suits me – it is an unpretentious office with a low salary and no social duties'. . . .

'What a joke – what an unexpected and slightly ludicrous adventure,' said he to me as we smoked the after-lunch cigarette, 'for a man of sixty-four to become, first, a Member of Parliament, and within a year, a Cabinet Minister; and that with colleagues none of whom have held Cabinet office before; whilst only three of them have been in the government – and these three do not include the Premier! If anyone had prophesied ten years ago that J.R.M. would be Prime Minister and would invite me to be in his Cabinet, I should have thought the first extraordinarily unlikely, but the two combined a sheer impossibility.'

And what about my own life this coming year? We are agreed that it would be undesirable for me to take any active part in his administration. If I had been ten years younger I might have thrown my energies into helping him with his plans – more especially if there had seemed to be a long spell of administration in front of him. But I am no longer so energetic or so capable of mastering a new technique. A wife intervening would, in any case, upset official decorum, and there will probably not be time for the officials to get used to it. The most I can do for him is to undertake that part of his ordinary correspondence and interviewing – now likely to be increased – with strangers, acquaintances and friends, who want, for one reason or another, to see and talk to him. . . . I shall pursue my intimacy with the women of Seaham. I shall take part in the social life of the Labour Party and be an active hostess to the Parliamentary Labour Party, to his departmental officials and others connected with the Ministry of Labour. But beyond that I shall not go. I intend to refuse all invitations to dinner, to keep out of London Society and Court functions, on the plea of age and delicate health. One might as well make the fullest use of the disability of 'old age' in avoiding useless dissipation of time and energy. Also I want to give a lead against participation in London Society, as a desirable part of the routine of a Cabinet Minister and his family. My lead will not be followed by those with social ambition but it will strengthen those whose instinct is against it. For the rest, I shall go on, as steadily as I can, with my book – alas! poor book, you will not be finished this coming year – and I shall make our country home fit to retire to, if one or both of us breaks down. . . .

Haldane did not join the Labour Party, though he held office. Beatrice's brother-in-law, Lord Parmoor, was a deeply religious pacifist who had drifted away from his Tory connections during the war years. C.B. Thomson (1875–1930) was a military man who joined the Labour Party in 1919 and was created Secretary of State for Air in 1924. He was killed in the crash of the airship R101 at Beauvais. Stephen Walsh, a former miner who became trade union leader, had been a Labour M.P. since 1906. He became Secretary of State for War in 1924. Josiah Wedgwood (1872–1943) became a Liberal M.P. in 1906 and went over to the Labour Party in 1919. He became Chancellor of the Duchy of Lancaster in 1924.

15 January. [41 Grosvenor Road]
'The blank page between the Old and the New Testament,' Sidney calls this last week before the opening of Parliament today. To me it has been distracting – seeing one person after another, mainly on the personnel of the Labour government. This 'inner circle' of possible Cabinet Ministers has been a monument of discretion and apparent disinterestedness – not a single word having been said at

the various party meetings about men and offices. . . . The only light on MacDonald's intentions has come, characteristically, through the two outsiders who are joining the government – Haldane and Parmoor. On Saturday we dined with the former – one of those little confabs we have had now for over thirty years with this fellow conspirator. J.R.M. had consulted him about appointments and had persuaded him to become Lord Chancellor and Leader of the House of Lords. We talked to him freely about all the possible persons for all the possible posts; and he was to pass these suggestions on as his own to J.R.M. before MacDonald's dinner on Monday night at Haldane's house to the Front Bench of the Labour Party. . . . Then on Monday morning, Parmoor came in to tell us that he had consented to be Lord President of the Council and act as J.R.M.'s deputy on foreign affairs in the House of Lords. So there will be two 'R.P.' husbands in the Labour government – the Tory and the Socialist! He did so, he said, because he had faith in J.R.M. and had worked with him through the war and since.

To end the tale: there was the secret dinner at Haldane's last night, to which Sidney and others had been invited by J.R.M. to discuss the King's speech and procedure. Sidney sat between Ben Spoor and Snowden. 'I'm Labour,' said Sidney, hoping that confidence would bring out confidence. 'I have not the remotest notion what I am going to be,' said Snowden in evident bewilderment. 'Mac tells me not to expect to be more than "Chief Whip",' said Ben Spoor disconsolately. 'Thomson is to be Colonies,' said Henderson to Sidney, 'and he is quite pleased with himself.' As Sidney walked away with General Thomas they exchanged confidences. Thomson is to be Air Force and in the Lords. So there will be three peers at any rate in the Cabinet. There were seventeen present at the dinner: J.R.M., Haldane, Parmoor, Henderson, Thomas, Clynes, Hastings, Spoor, Greenwood, Trevelyan, Buxton, Webb, General Thomson, Snowden, Adamson, Walsh, Wedgwood. J.R.M. was careful to explain that it was not a meeting of the future Cabinet, but only of the Front Bench, to discuss the King's speech. The dinner seems to have been a model of good humour, joint discussion and dignified self-restraint – 'the best Cabinet meeting I have ever attended', said Haldane to Sidney, which was of course mere 'preliminary compliments' on the part of our old diplomatist.

The main business which I have been doing has concerned the social life of the Labour Party. We started our weekly lunch last Wednesday — ten of the new members to meet J.R.M. and Henderson; tomorrow we have eleven new members to meet GBS and Henderson. Last week we had a gathering of 700 H.C.C. and Parliamentary Labour Party at the University of London; on the following Friday there was a fancy-dress dance which I did not attend. The women are delighted with the H.C.C. and the Press is beginning to say that 'the Labour Party, with its usual foresight, has organized its own London Society'! It is precious lucky we have done so, as it is clear we shall need all our sense of solidarity and puritanism to keep some of the frailer vessels upstanding against the onslaughts of duchesses and millionaires against their integrity. 'Are Labour Privy Councillors to appear at Court in uniform?' is one of the questions. 'Are Cabinet Ministers' wives to attend evening Courts?' is another. And then there is that mark of servility — the curtsy! It is all very ludicrous; though not altogether un-important. Altering the form may easily transform the substance!

John Wheatley (1869–1930) was the owner of a prosperous printing business and one of the group of M.P.s from the Clydeside. He was an uncompromising socialist and had been a Labour M.P. since 1922. He now became Minister of Health. F.J. Thesiger (1868–1933), who succeeded his father as Lord Chelmsford in 1905, was appointed First Lord of the Admiralty.

18 January. [41 Grosvenor Road]
J.R.M. sent for Sidney on Thursday and Friday to consult him alike about his own post and also about others. Apparently some of the inner circle had objected to Sidney being relegated to so small a post as the Ministry of Labour, and J.R.M. said that he had not realized that the Ministry of Labour was so much the 'Cinderella of the government offices', and pressed Sidney to take the Board of Trade. Sidney replied that the lowly status of the Ministry of Labour did not concern him: he would prefer to remain there, especially as Wedgwood, he understood, wanted the Board of Trade and would not be content with Labour. 'If they were all as considerate as you have been,' remarked J.R.M., 'there would not be any difficulty in making a Cabinet.' And then he explained how Lansbury had insisted on Cabinet rank which he, J.R.M., would not give him: how this man or that had held out for a superior office, and so on. And he said that he would consider it but that he

437

wanted Sidney to be chairman of the group of Ministers dealing with unemployment, and that would hardly be possible if he were head of the least important and most recently created Department. Sidney left it in his hands, and they discussed other affairs. Sidney came away feeling that the Cabinet would err on the side of *respectability* – too many outsiders and too many peers. J.R.M., oddly enough, does not like the plebeian element and chooses as his more intimate associates not the workman but the lawyer or big administrator, with the manner and attitude of the ruling and 'thoroughly comfortable' class. If Sidney had had the making of the Cabinet it would have been far more working class and more to the 'left' of the Labour Party. For instance, he would have taken Lansbury, and if possible Wheatley, into the Cabinet, and would not have had so many peers, nor would have asked Chelmsford to come in. A good fellow but a timid Conservative. Henderson, we are glad to find, is to be Home Secretary – a post which is sufficiently impressive. . . .

'And what do *you* feel about the change in *your* life?' asked Kate, somewhat perturbed at my detached and unexcited attitude. 'Personally I prefer a quiet student's life, but of course I am glad for Sidney's sake,' I replied. 'I believe you long to settle down to write at Passfield,' she remonstrated. 'Well, yes; personally, I should prefer it, but Sidney as Cabinet Minister is one job like another. I shall chime in with it,' I concluded.

Here ends the Old Testament.

Chronology

1905

November Beatrice appointed to the Royal Commission on the Poor Law

December Arthur Balfour resigns. Campbell-Bannerman becomes Prime Minister

1906

January Great Liberal victory in general election
February H.G. Wells makes a bid to take over the Fabian Society
May Death of Lawrencina Holt
November Beatrice withdraws her opposition to women's suffrage
December Defeat of Wells over Fabian reform

1907

March Sidney Webb again returned for Deptford in L.C.C. election
June Webbs in Scotland
July Webbs staying at Ayot St Lawrence
September Mary Playne has operation for cancer

1908

January Charles Booth resigns from Poor Law Commission
February Beatrice at Hadleigh Farm colony, then in Lancashire and Yorkshire
April Death of Campbell-Bannerman. Asquith becomes Prime Minister. Beatrice in Ireland
May W. Pember Reeves appointed Director of the L.S.E.
July Webbs stay at Wernher's house at Luton Hoo
August Webbs at Fabian summer school near Harlech

1909

January End of Royal Commission

February Publication of Majority and Minority Reports
March Webbs on holiday in Italy
April Introduction of the 'People's Budget' by Lloyd George
May Webbs start campaign for the break-up of the Poor Law
June The suffragettes step up militancy with hunger strikes and violent reactions to forced feeding
July Beatrice receives honorary degree from Manchester University
August Affair of Wells and Amber Reeves becomes public
November Finance Bill passed but rejected by House of Lords
December Publication of *Ann Veronica*. Osborne Judgment upheld in House of Lords

1910
January Liberal victory in general election
February Galsworthy's *Justice* opens, and Shaw's *Misalliance*
March Sidney Webb resigns from the L.C.C. *Madras House* opens
April Budget passed House of Lords
May Death of Edward VII
June Webbs in Switzerland
July Railway strike
September Strike in Lancashire cotton industry
November Publication of *The New Machiavelli*. Strike and riots in South Wales coalfields at Tonypandy. Parliament dissolved
December General election gives renewed mandate to Liberals

1911
February Parliament Bill introduced
June Webbs leave for tour of Japan, China and India. Coronation of George V. Seamen's strike
July Agadir crisis
August Parliament Act passed. Dock and railway strikes. Rioting in Liverpool. Troops called out
October Rebellion in China and Republic proclaimed
November Balfour resigns. Bonar Law replaces him as leader of the Tories. National Insurance Bill passed. Renewed suffragette protests. King and Queen visit India

1912
February Coalminers strike for a national minimum wage. Defeat of Suffrage Bill

April Introduction of third Home Rule Bill. First issue of *Daily Herald*

May Webbs return from Asian tour. Strike of dockers and transport workers

June R.B. Haldane becomes Lord Chancellor

July Insurance Act comes into force. Intensification of suffragette militancy led by Christabel Pankhurst

September Threats of rebellion from Ulster Irish against Home Rule Bill

October Beatrice founds Fabian Research Department

1913

April First issue of the *New Statesman*. Introduction of the 'cat and mouse' Act to deal with militant suffragettes on hunger strike

September Webbs at Fabian summer school in Lake District

1914

January The Triple Alliance formed between miners, railway and transport workers for co-ordinating disputes. The Webbs on holiday in Cornwall with Shaw

March Curragh mutiny in protest against government policy in Ulster

July Death of Joseph Chamberlain

August Outbreak of war. MacDonald resigns as leader of the Parliamentary Labour Party

September Formation of Union of Democratic Control

October First Battle of Ypres. Turkey enters war against the allies

November Georgina Meinertzhagen dies

December First Zeppelin raids over Britain

1915

April British troops attack Gallipoli. Air bombardment of London. Second Battle of Ypres. First use of poison gas by the Germans

May Asquith forms a Coalition government. Arthur Henderson represents Labour. Sinking of the *Lusitania*

November Haig replaced French as commander-in-chief

December Gallipoli evacuated

1916

January Military Services Act imposes compulsory recruitment for unmarried men aged eighteen to forty-one with allowance for conscientious objectors

February Battle of Verdun begins
April Surrender of British at Kut. Rebellion in Dublin
May Battle of Jutland. Military Service Act for married and unmarried up to forty-one
June Kitchener drowned. Lloyd George becomes Secretary for War
July Battle of the Somme. Webbs at Wyndham Croft, Sussex
October Shaw resigns from *New Statesman*
December Lloyd George replaces Asquith as Prime Minister and reorganizes the Coalition

1917
February Beatrice joins Reconstruction Committee
March Revolution in Russia
April America declares war. Battle of Arras
May Henderson visits Russia as representative of War Cabinet
June Convention at Leeds of United Socialist Council against War
July Third Battle of Ypres
August Henderson resigns from government
November Bolsheviks seize power and make armistice with Germany. First tank battle on Western Front

1918
February Introduction of food rationing
March Germany makes a new offensive on the Somme
May Death of Leonard Courtney
June Representation of the People Act (women's vote) becomes law
October Germany appeals to President Wilson for an armistice
November End of war with Germany
December Victory for Lloyd George in 'coupon' election

1919
February Triple Alliance resumed
March Miners' strike. Sidney Webb appointed to Sankey Coal Commission
June Treaty of Versailles signed. Sankey Commission reports
September Railway strike
October Woodrow Wilson has a stroke. William Beveridge becomes Director of L.S.E.

1920
February George Lansbury goes to Russia
July Sidney Webb nominated as Labour candidate for Seaham.

Formation of Communist Party
August Second International meets at Geneva
October Miners' strike

1921

March Death of Margaret Hobhouse
April Miners' strike and 'Black Friday'. Massacre at Amritsar in India. Beatrice starts the Half Circle Club. Unemployment passes two million
June Truce in Ireland
October Conference on Ireland
November Washington Conference on naval affairs and Far East
December Treaty with Ireland marks the end of Irish unity

1922

February Government committee on public expenditure under Sir Eric Geddes
May Beatrice in Wales with her sister Kate Courtney
August Webbs spend summer at Presteigne
October Tories meet at Carlton Club and bring the Coalition government to an end
November Tories victory in general election. Sidney Webb returned as Labour M.P.

1923

March Death of Arthur Playne
April Lady Warwick offers Easton Lodge to the Labour Party
May Bonar Law resigns and is replaced by Stanley Baldwin
August The Webbs buy cottage at Liphook, Hampshire
October Deaths of Bonar Law and Mary Playne
November Webbs move into Passfield Corner
December General election results in first Labour government

A Short Bibliography

Biographies

R. Adam and K. Muggeridge, *Beatrice Webb* (London, 1967).

Robert Blake, *The Unknown Prime Minister* [Bonar Law] (London, 1955).

L.P. Carpenter, *G.D.H. Cole. An Intellectual Portrait* (Cambridge, 1972).

Margaret Cole, *The Life of G.D.H. Cole* (London, 1971).
The Webbs and their Work (London, 1969).

Max Egremont, *Balfour* (London, 1980).

Martin Gilbert, *Winston Churchill* Vols. 3–5 (London, 1971–76).

John Grigg, *The Young Lloyd George* (London, 1973).

José Harris, *William Beveridge* (London, 1977).

Michael Holroyd (ed.), *The Genius of Shaw* (London, 1979).

Stephen Koss, *Asquith* (New York, 1976).
Lord Haldane (New York, 1969).

Norman and Jeanne MacKenzie, *The Time Traveller; The Biography of H.G. Wells* (London, 1973).

David Marquand, *Ramsay MacDonald* (London, 1977).

Kenneth O. Morgan, *Lloyd George* (London, 1974).

Hesketh Pearson, *GBS* (London, 1961).

Raymond Postgate, *George Lansbury* (London, 1959).

D. Rowland, *Lloyd George* (London, 1975).

R. Skidelsky, *John Maynard Keynes* (London, 1983).

John Wilson, *CB: The Life of Campbell-Bannerman* (London, 1973).

Leonard Woolf, *Autobiography* (London, 4 vols., 1961–69).

Kenneth Young, *Arthur James Balfour* (London, 1963).
Stanley Baldwin (London, 1976).

Labour Politics

R.P. Arnot, *The Miners: Years of Struggle* (London, 1953).

Asa Briggs & John Saville (eds.), *Essays in Labour History* (Oxford, 1972).

G.D.H. Cole, *The Second International (Part 1)* (London, 1956). *The History of the Labour Party since 1914* (London, 1948).

H.A. Clegg, Alan Fox and A.F. Thompson, *A History of British Trade Unions since 1889* (Oxford, 1964).

Maurice Cowling, *The Impact of Labour 1920–1924* (London, 1971).

R.E. Dowse, *Left in the Centre: The Independent Labour Party 1893–1940* (London, 1966).

S.R. Graubard, *British Labour and the Russian Revolution* (London, 1956).

B. Holton, *British Syndicalism 1900–14* (London, 1976).

Wallis Kendall, *The Revolutionary Movement in Great Britain 1900–21* (London, 1969).

Ross McKibbin, *The Evolution of the Labour Party 1910–24* (London, 1974).

Keith Middlemas, *The Clydesiders* (London, 1965).

S. Pierson, *British Socialists* (London, 1979).

The War

Raymond Challinor, *The Origin of British Bolshevism* (London, 1977).

C. Hazlehurst, *Politicians at War* (London, 1971).

James Hinton, *The First Shop Stewards' Movement* (London, 1973).

A.J.A. Morris, *Radicalism Against War 1906–1914* (London, 1972).

John Rae, *Conscience and Politics* (London, 1970).

P. Stansky, *The Left and the War* (Oxford, 1969).

Marvin Swartz, *The U.D.C. and British Politics* (Oxford, 1971).

J.M. Winter, *Socialism and the Challenge of the War* (London, 1974).

Fabianism

Ian Britain, *Fabianism and Culture* (Cambridge, 1982).
M. Cole, *The Story of Fabian Socialism* (London, 1961).
Edward Hyams, *The New Statesman* (London, 1963).

Norman and Jeanne MacKenzie, *The First Fabians* (London, 1977).

A.M. McBriar, *Fabian Socialism and English Politics* (Cambridge, 1962).

Social Problems

M. Bruce, *The Rise of the Welfare State* (London, 1973).

M.A. Crowther, *The Workhouse System, 1834–1929* (London, 1983).

D. Fraser, *The Evolution of the British Welfare State* (London, 1973).

R.M. Hartwell, *The Long Debate on Poverty* (London, 1972).

C.L. Mowat, *The Charity Organisation Society* (London, 1961).

James H. Treble, *Urban Poverty in Britain, 1830–1914* (London, 1983).

G. Williams, *The Origins of the Welfare State* (London, 1967).

Liberalism

Peter Clarke, *Liberals and Social Democrats* (Cambridge, 1978).

J.R. Hay, *The Origins of the Liberal Welfare Reforms 1906–14* (London, 1975).

Roy Jenkins, *Mr. Balfour's Poodle* (London, 1966).

Stephen Koss, *Nonconformity in Modern British Politics* (London, 1973).

A.J.A. Morris, *Edwardian Radicalism 1900–1914* (London, 1972).

Peter Rowland, *The Last Liberal Government: The Promised Land 1905–1910* (London, 1968).

A.K. Russell, *Liberal Landslide: the General Election of 1906* (Newton Abbot, 1973).

Trevor Wilson, *The Downfall of the Liberal Party 1914–1935* (London, 1966).

The Suffrage Movement

R.J. Evans, *The Feminists* (London, 1977).

David Morgan, *Suffragists and Liberals* (London, 1975).

Andrew Rose, *Rise up Women!* (London, 1974).

Ray Strachey, *The Cause* (London, 1928, rep. London, 1978).

Miscellaneous

N. Blewett, *The Peers, the Parties and the People* (London, 1972).

Hugh Dalton, *Call Back Yesterday* (London, 1953).

A. Dent (ed.), *Bernard Shaw and Mrs. P. Campbell: Correspondence* (London, 1952).

S. Hynes, *The Edwardian Frame of Mind* (London, 1968). *Edwardian Occasions* (London, 1972).

M. Kirby, *The British Coalmining Industry 1870–1946* (London, 1977).

Dan Laurence (ed.), *The Collected Letters of GBS* (London, 1965 and 1972).

Norman MacKenzie (ed.), *The Letters of Sidney & Beatrice Webb* (Cambridge, 1978).

N. Mansergh, *The Irish Question 1840–1921* (London, 1965).

Arthur Marwick, *The Deluge: British Society and the First World War* (London, 1968).

C.L. Mowat, *Britain Between the Wars* (London, 1955).

Simon Nowell-Smith (ed.), *Edwardian England 1900–1914* (London, 1964).

John Ramsden, *The Age of Balfour and Baldwin 1902–1940* (London, 1978).

A.T. Stewart, *The Ulster Crisis* (London, 1967).

A.J.P. Taylor, *English History 1914–1945* (Oxford, 1965).

Index

The italic numeral *I* or *II* indicates that previous references may be found in these volumes of the diary.

449

INDEX